# CCNP Support Exam Certification Guide

**Amir S. Ranjbar, MSc.**

Cisco Press
201 W 103rd Street
Indianapolis, IN 46290 USA

# CCNP Support Exam Certification Guide

Amir S. Ranjbar, MSc.

Copyright© 2001 Cisco Systems, Inc.

Cisco Press logo is a trademark of Cisco Systems, Inc.

Published by:
Cisco Press
201 West 103rd Street
Indianapolis, IN 46290 USA

Printed in the United States of America 1 2 3 4 5 6 7 8 9 0

First printing October 2000

Library of Congress Cataloging-in-Publication Number: 00-105174

ISBN: 0-7357-0995-5

## Warning and Disclaimer

This book is designed to provide information about building scalable Cisco networks. Every effort has been made to make this book as complete and as accurate as possible, but no warranty or fitness is implied.

The information is provided on an "as is" basis. The authors, Cisco Press, and Cisco Systems, Inc., shall have neither liability nor responsibility to any person or entity with respect to any loss or damages arising from the information contained in this book or from the use of the discs or programs that may accompany it.

The opinions expressed in this book belong to the authors and are not necessarily those of Cisco Systems, Inc.

## Trademark Acknowledgments

All terms mentioned in this book that are known to be trademarks or service marks have been appropriately capitalized. Cisco Press or Cisco Systems, Inc., cannot attest to the accuracy of this information. Use of a term in this book should not be regarded as affecting the validity of any trademark or service mark.

## Feedback Information

At Cisco Press, our goal is to create in-depth technical books of the highest quality and value. Each book is crafted with care and precision, undergoing rigorous development that involves the unique expertise of members from the professional technical community.

Readers' feedback is a natural continuation of this process. If you have any comments regarding how we could improve the quality of this book or otherwise alter it to better suit your needs, you can contact us through e-mail at ciscopress@mcp.com. Please make sure to include the book title and ISBN in your message.

We greatly appreciate your assistance.

| | |
|---|---|
| Publisher | John Wait |
| Editor-in-Chief | John Kane |
| Executive Editor | Brett Bartow |
| Cisco Systems Program Manager | Bob Anstey |
| Managing Editor | Patrick Kanouse |
| Development Editors | Andrew Cupp |
| | Howard Jones |
| Technical Editors | Elan Beer |
| | Steve Kalman |
| Book Designer | Gina Rexrode |
| Cover Designer | Louisa Klucznik |
| Editorial and Production Team | Argosy |
| Indexer | Tim Wright |

CISCO SYSTEMS

CISCO PRESS

**Corporate Headquarters**
Cisco Systems, Inc.
170 West Tasman Drive
San Jose, CA 95134-1706
USA
http://www.cisco.com
Tel: 408 526-4000
 800 553-NETS (6387)
Fax: 408 526-4100

**European Headquarters**
Cisco Systems Europe s.a.r.l.
Parc Evolic, Batiment L1/L2
16 Avenue du Quebec
Villebon, BP 706
91961 Courtaboeuf Cedex
France
http://www-europe.cisco.com
Tel: 33 1 69 18 61 00
Fax: 33 1 69 28 83 26

**American
Headquarters**
Cisco Systems, Inc.
170 West Tasman Drive
San Jose, CA 95134-1706
USA
http://www.cisco.com
Tel: 408 526-7660
Fax: 408 527-0883

**Asia Headquarters**
Nihon Cisco Systems K.K.
Fuji Building, 9th Floor
3-2-3 Marunouchi
Chiyoda-ku, Tokyo 100
Japan
http://www.cisco.com
Tel: 81 3 5219 6250
Fax: 81 3 5219 6001

**Cisco Systems has more than 200 offices in the following countries. Addresses, phone numbers, and fax numbers are listed on
the Cisco Connection Online Web site at http://www.cisco.com/offices.**

Argentina • Australia • Austria • Belgium • Brazil • Canada • Chile • China • Colombia • Costa Rica • Croatia • Czech Republic
• Denmark • Dubai, UAE Finland • France • Germany • Greece • Hong Kong • Hungary • India • Indonesia • Ireland • Israel
• Italy • Japan • Korea • Luxembourg • Malaysia • Mexico • The Netherlands • New Zealand • Norway • Peru • Philippines •
Poland • Portugal • Puerto Rico • Romania • Russia • Saudi Arabia • Singapore • Slovakia • Slovenia • South Africa • Spain •
Sweden • Switzerland • Taiwan • Thailand • Turkey • Ukraine • United Kingdom • United States • Venezuela

# About the Author

**Amir S. Ranjbar** (CCNP) is an instructor and senior network architect for Global Knowledge, Cisco's largest training partner. He is a Certified Cisco Systems Instructor (CCSI) who teaches the Cisco Internetwork Troubleshooting course on a regular basis. Born in Tehran, Iran, Amir moved to Canada in 1983 and obtained his Bachelors degree in Computing and Information Science (1988) and Master of Science degree in Knowledge Based Systems (1991) from the University of Guelph (Guelph, Ontario). After graduation, Amir developed software applications in the areas of statistical analysis and systems simulation for a number of institutes such as Statistics Canada, University of Waterloo, and University of Ottawa. Amir started his training career by joining Digital Equipment Corporation's Learning Services in 1995, and after a few years of working exclusively as a Microsoft Certified Trainer (MCSE, MCT), he decided to shift his focus to Cisco Systems' internetworking products. In 1998, Amir joined Geotrain Corporation, which was acquired by Global Knowledge in 1999. Currently, Amir, already a CCNP, is preparing for the CCIE examinations and is a full-time instructor for Global Knowledge. Among the courses Amir teaches are Interconnecting Cisco Network Devices (ICND), Building Scalable Cisco Networks (BSCN), Building Cisco Remote Access Networks (BCRAN), Cisco Internetwork Troubleshooting (CIT), OSPF, and BGP. You can contact Amir by email at amir.ranjbar@globalknowledge.com.

## About the Technical Reviewers

**Elan Beer**, CCIE #1837, is president and founder of Synaptic Solutions, Inc. For the past 14 years, Elan has held several key positions within the telecommunications industry, including Senior Telecommunication Consultant, Project Manager, and Telecommunications Instructor, as well as Canadian Training Manager with GeoTrain Corporation, a multinational training and consulting organization. Through his global consulting and training engagements, Elan is recognized internationally as a telecommunications industry expert. Elan's strong technical skills have enabled him to attain several top-level industry certifications, including Cisco System's top-level certification, the Cisco Certified Internetwork Expert (CCIE). As one of the first product-based public Certified Cisco Instructors in the world, Elan has utilized his expertise in multiprotocol internetworking, LAN, WAN, and MAN technology, network management, and software engineering to provide training and consulting services to many of Canada's top companies. As a senior trainer and course developer, Elan has designed and presented intensive public and implementation-specific technical courses for clients in North America, Europe, Australia, Africa, Asia, and Scandinavia.

**Steve Kalman** is a data communications trainer. He is the author or technical editor of 12 CBT titles and has been the author, technical editor, or trainer for eight instructor-led courses. Steve is also beginning a new distance-learning project as both author and presenter. In addition to those responsibilities, he runs a consulting company, Esquire Micro Consultants, that specializes in data network design.

# Dedication

I would like to dedicate my first book to all those who strive freedom of thought, applaud creative thinking, and respect others' opinions. Among those are my parents, my wife Elke, and other good family members and friends of mine, who are my treasures. I wish that my children, Thalia, Ariana, and Armando, grow up to be independent, creative, and respectful individuals, and hence, become treasures of tomorrow.

# Acknowledgments

I did not have the pleasure of getting to know or communicating with all of the individuals that have put their valuable time and effort into this book, but I would like to use this opportunity to sincerely thank each and every one of them.

Among those who I did directly work with was Brett Bartow, whose patience, professionalism, and understanding I will never forget. Brett played a key role in the development of this book from the very beginning. Thanks to Andrew Cupp for his sharp eyes and valuable corrections and suggestions. Also, thanks to Howard Jones and Patrick Kanouse. I feel very lucky that Elan Beer and Steve Kalman joined this team as the technical reviewers.

# Contents at a Glance

# Table of Contents

# Introduction

This book is one of the members of the Cisco Press family of publications that has been developed to help you prepare yourself for the Cisco Certification examinations. This book's specific target is the Support exam (formerly the Cisco Internetwork Troubleshooting [CIT] Exam). I am a Certified Cisco Systems Instructor, and CIT is one of the courses that I teach. I started teaching this course in the first quarter of 1999. I have passed both the old CIT 4.0 and the new Support exams, and I am fully familiar with the structure, content, and objectives of each of those exams. My students often ask me how I think the Support exam is different from the old CIT 4.0 exam. My answer is that I did not notice much change; therefore, any training material that can enhance your knowledge of the subjects covered in Cisco's instructor-based CIT course is still very much valid and useful.

The Support (640-506) exam is one of the four exams you will need to pass to achieve Cisco Certified Network Professional (CCNP) certification in the Routing and Switching career track. The other three exams are the Routing (640-503), Switching (640-504), and Remote Access (640-505) exams. Optionally, you can take one exam that combines these three exams, Foundation 2.0 (640-509), but you will still need to pass the Support exam separately to attain CCNP status. Also note that Cisco Certified Network Associate (CCNA) status is a prerequisite to becoming CCNP certified.

Cisco strongly recommends that you attend its CCNP training courses before taking the CCNP exams. Table I-1 shows these courses and how they roughly map to the various exams. Cisco Press publishes coursebooks and Exam Certification Guides like this one to support your preparation for these exams.

**Table I-1**  *Cisco Courses and Exams for CCNP Routing and Switching Certification*

| Course | Exam |
| --- | --- |
| Building Scalable Cisco Networks (BSCN) | Routing (640-503) |
| Building Cisco Multilayer Switched Networks (BCMSN) | Switching (640-504) |
| Building Cisco Remote Access Networks (BCRAN) | Remote Access (640-505) |
| Cisco Internetwork Troubleshooting (CIT) | Support (640-506) |

## Objectives

During the time that I was preparing this book, I kept my focus on only one goal: preparing the readers for the CCNP Support exam. It was difficult at times to keep from adding more and more extraneous material. My goal is not to teach you, from scratch, the technologies of Cisco internetworking. Instead, I do assume a CCNA or better level of understanding of these technologies. From there, I will show you the methodology of support, what tools you have available, and how to apply them to specific networks. Throughout the book, I present what I think is absolutely essential for you to know before you attempt the CCNP Support exam.

This book makes a strong companion to the CIT course and the *Cisco Internetwork Troubleshooting* coursebook that is published by Cisco Press. While this book presents some information that is very similar to the course and coursebook, I discuss the material in a tone and fashion that my experience has shown me an audience responds well to. My presentation is short, to the point, and very much oriented to exam preparation. Those topics that I elaborate on are those that I believe, based on my teaching experience with many CIT students, need rewording or a different angle for best understanding. Of course, this book also contains additional features designed specifically for test preparation, such as quick-reference Foundation Summary sections and a testing engine on the CD-ROM.

## Target Audience

This book's target audience is primarily those who want a condensed, exam-oriented book to prepare them for the CCNP Support exam. On the other hand, very often a great portion of my students who have thoroughly enjoyed the CIT course they have taken express their desire to have my discussions and presentation in a written and organized format. This book provides that, too. Indeed, the material adds explanations, output, configuration examples, and exercises to those you might have seen in CIT training, to help you better understand the topics being discussed.

I would like to share the following thought with the readers of this book. This book is not a magic tool that somebody without the proper background can pick up, read, and use to pass the Support exam. My assumption of the target audience's background is a more-than-basic familiarity with internetworking, routing, switching, and wide-area networking. You should have at least a CCNA's knowledge of these subjects. With reference to Cisco's training curriculum, this book's prerequisite, if you will, is similar to the CIT course's prerequisite. In other words, I assume that the reader has a good grasp of the material presented in the ICND (or CRLS/ICRC), BSCN (or ACRC), and BCMSN (or CLSC) Cisco official training curriculum courses.

## Support Exam Preparation Method

My personal opinion about preparing for any of the examinations is an orthodox one. I believe that once somebody meets the prerequisites of a course, he or she should then take the official training curriculum course. Next, he/she should practice the material learned in the course through hands-on experimentation and/or using other reference material, such as this book. This method is solid and effective and has been proven effective repeatedly. Indeed, that is how I prepare myself for the exams that I attempt.

However, we are not all the same, and we do not all have the same budget, time, or learning behaviors. What I can tell you with all honesty is that the material presented in this book more than prepares you for the Support exam. I can't and won't, in good conscience, tell you that this book is all you need to have in order to pass the Support exam, even though it is very tempting to say so. At the very minimum, make sure you meet the course prerequisite, familiarize yourself with the CIT course materials, and then use all of the tools presented in this book.

## The Organization and Features of This Book

Since the Support examination (and also the old CIT exam) closely reflects the material presented in Cisco's official CIT training material, I made a point of making sure the flow of this book matches that of the CIT's official training curriculum. Even though those of you who have read the CIT book will find quite a bit of overlap and many similarities between that book and this one, you should not be surprised. I wanted to make sure that all the material you need will be presented here, and that I present it to you in my words and in my training-oriented tone. Something new you will find in this book and its CD is a concentrated effort to present the materials specifically in exam-preparation format—review summaries, examples, quiz questions, and so on. I have packed this book with questions and answers, quizzes, examples, and tables to make sure that you not only understand the material but also get fully prepared for the Support examination.

After this brief introductory material, there are 11 chapters (and one answers appendix) in this book, each of which targets its counterpart chapter in the CIT course. Each chapter starts with a "Do I Know This Already?" quiz that allows you to decide how much time you need to devote to studying the subject at hand. Next, the Foundation Topics (the core material of the chapter) are presented. This section is the bulk of each chapter. Near the end of each chapter you will find a Foundation Summary section that is a collection of tables and quick-reference material that can be used as the last-minute review notes. Finally, each chapter ends with many review questions taken directly out of that chapter's contents. Each chapter's review questions highlight the points that I want you to retain and to consider very important.

This book is also accompanied by a CD-ROM that offers multiple-choice questions out of the entire book's content. Each question in the CD-ROM refers you to the chapter and section it is drawn from. Being a quick and accurate reader, and having the knowledge and skill to recognize the correct answer—or at least eliminate the incorrect answers—are the skills that those who want to score well in multiple-choice exams must acquire.

## Command Syntax Conventions

The conventions used to present command syntax in this book are the same conventions used in the *Cisco IOS Command Reference*, as follows:

- **Boldface** indicates commands and keywords that are entered literally as shown. In examples (not syntax), boldface indicates user input (for example, a **show** command).

- *Italics* indicates arguments for which you supply values.

- Square brackets [ ] indicate optional elements.

- Braces { } contain a choice of required keywords.

- Vertical bars (|) separate alternative, mutually exclusive elements.

- Braces and vertical bars within square brackets—for example, [x {y | z}]—indicate a required choice within an optional element. You do not need to enter what is in the brackets, but if you do, you have some required choices in the braces.

# Book Layout

This final section of the introduction covers briefly the contents of each chapter in the book.

## Chapter 1

Chapter 1 covers three main topics. First, it lists and introduces you to a number of troubleshooting tools that are adequate for testing different aspects or components of an internetworking model. You must learn when and why each tool is used, and what information may be obtained from each. Next, Cisco Connection Online is introduced. You should know who can access CCO and how. Familiarity with the content and structure of CCO is required for the Support examination. Finally, Chapter 1 discusses the methodology and the information required to escalate trouble scenarios to Cisco Service and Support.

## Chapter 2

Chapter 2 discusses what systematic troubleshooting is and why it is absolutely essential for every organization to have a formal methodology in place for this purpose. A generally accepted troubleshooting methodology that is appropriate for internetwork support is discussed element by element.

## Chapter 3

Chapter 3 covers identifying troubleshooting targets, and most of its attention is given to the data-link layer. This chapter gives you a lot of information about the **show** interface command's output. In addition, the connection sequence in TCP/IP, IPX, and AppleTalk environments are discussed.

## Chapter 4

Chapter 4 has many topics and I consider it the core of CIT's course material. Proper handling of troubleshooting tools such as debug and logging, understanding router internal operations (routing, switching, buffering), reachability testing, and troubleshooting commands appropriate for performance degradation and crash cases are presented at reasonable length.

## Chapters 5, 6, and 7

These chapters are very brief, due to the assumption that you have a good understanding of TCP/IP, IPX/SPX, and AppleTalk protocol suites and their associated routing protocols. The purpose of these chapters is to present many troubleshooting commands and explain when and where you would use them.

## Chapters 8 and 9

Chapter 8 provides a condensed coverage of troubleshooting-related topics on Catalyst 5000 switches. Catalyst LEDs, cabling, power-up self-test, trunking, VTP, and Catalyst **show** commands are the type of topics discussed in this chapter. Chapter 9 adds to Chapter 8; the topic is troubleshooting routers in inter-VLAN routing environments.

## Chapter 10

Chapter 10 is about troubleshooting Frame Relay connections. You are provided with a troubleshooting checklist and a set of **show** and **debug** commands that are discussed in reasonable depth. The commands presented in this chapter need extra attention as they are given a special weight in the Support exam.

## Chapter 11

Troubleshooting ISDN BRI is the topic of this final chapter. The Support exam has developed a reputation for being quite heavy on the ISDN topic. For that reason, in this chapter I gave my utmost effort to both teach the topics and prepare the audience for a successful exam result.

## Appendix A

This appendix repeats all of the "Do I Know This Already" and "Q&A" questions from throughout the book and provides the answers.

This chapter covers the following topics that you will need to master to pass the CCNP Support exam:

| Objective | Description |
|-----------|-------------|
| 1 | List the tools and resources available for problem prevention, troubleshooting, and support. |
| 2 | Understand what each tool and resource offers and which layer it tests. |
| 3 | Describe network media test equipment and their applications. |
| 4 | Explain network monitors, protocol analyzers, network management systems, and network design/simulation tools. |
| 5 | Provide an overview of CiscoWorks and its components. |
| 6 | Describe CCO's organization and the services, tools, and resources it offers. |
| 7 | List the escalation steps to Cisco service and support. |

# CHAPTER 1

# Support Resources for Troubleshooting

Today's internetworks are large and complex. Furthermore, many businesses rely heavily on steady and correct operation of their network infrastructure. Today's networks are mission critical resources, meaning that many companies stand to lose thousands, sometimes millions, of dollars in a relatively short period, should their computing and communications devices lose their local and remote connectivity. All of this makes the network support task very essential. Should a component break down or be misconfigured, the support group must be able to diagnose and fix the problem in a timely manner while they allow for connectivity to be reinstated through alternate devices and paths during their troubleshooting efforts. As a result, a wide variety of tools has been created to help network support engineers. Hardware testing and troubleshooting devices, software applications for traffic capturing and analysis, enterprise network management tools, and so on, can all be of tremendous help at appropriate times. In addition, knowledge bases, troubleshooting engines, online support, technical assistance centers, and other similar resources can be of crucial value. The purpose of this chapter is to provide a survey of the wide spectrum of troubleshooting resources that can assist in supporting internetworks so that the right tool can be quickly chosen and correctly used in order to minimize downtime.

## "Do I Know This Already?" Quiz

If you wish to evaluate your knowledge of the contents of this chapter before you get started, answer the following questions. The answers are provided in Appendix A, "Answers to Quiz Questions." If you are having difficulty providing correct answers, you should thoroughly review the entire chapter. If all or most of your answers are correct, you might want to skim this chapter for only those subjects you need to review. You can also use the "Foundation Summary" section to quickly review topics. Once you have completed the chapter, you should reevaluate yourself with the questions in the "Q&A" section at the end. Finally, use the companion CD-ROM to evaluate your knowledge of the topics and see if you need a review.

1 Name three classes of network media test equipment.

_____

_____

_____

**2**  What are the tasks network monitors can perform?

_____

_____

_____

**3**  Name the tool that does multilayer analysis of network traffic.

_____

_____

_____

**4**  What are the five functional areas of network management?

_____

_____

_____

**5**  What is Cisco Systems' flagship network management software called?

_____

_____

_____

**6**  List at least three members of the CWSI Campus Application.

_____

_____

_____

**7**  Name Cisco's network simulation and modeling tool.

_____

_____

_____

**8**  What does the acronym CCO stand for, and what is the URL address for CCO?

_____

_____

_____

**9** Name at least two tools or resources from CCO available for problem prevention.

_____

_____

_____

**10** Name at least three tools or resources that CCO provides for problem correction and troubleshooting.

_____

_____

_____

## Foundation Topics

# Network Media Test Equipment

There are three classes of equipment for testing the physical layer medium:

- **Volt/Ohm meters and digital multimeters**—The parameters tested by this equipment are voltage, current, resistance, and capacitance. In fact, the purpose of using these products is to check for cable connectivity and continuity. These devices are usually very affordable, but one who uses them must be familiar with the specifications of the medium being tested. For example, if you use a Volt/Ohm meter to test a 10Base2 segment, and observe resistance of 50 Ohms, you must be able to interpret this resistance value as normal or unacceptable for this medium type.

- **Cable testers**—Also called scanners, these tools, which also test for connectivity, are more sophisticated than Volt/Ohm meters. Different models of cable testers are available for different cable types (for example, 10BaseT, UTP, and fiber-optic). However, scanners also report on cable conditions such as attenuation, near-end crosstalk (NEXT), and noise. One advantage of these tools is that they can provide the measurement of a cable's impedance, while Volt/Ohm meters do not offer this capability.

- **TDRs and OTDRs**—At the top end of cable testing equipment are those devices that provide time domain reflectometer (TDR), wire-map, and traffic monitoring functionality. The more expensive equipment of this kind surpasses the physical layer and reports on Media Access Control (MAC) layer information such as frame, error, and utilization statistics. Some can actually perform a Layer 3 (network) test, such as ping. A TDR made for fiber-optic cable testing is called an optical TDR (OTDR). TDRs act as cable sonar and can locate opens, shorts, kinks, sharp bends, crimps, and impedance mismatches.

Obviously, the products available in the market evolve and improve rapidly and usually provide features that might make it difficult to fit them clearly into one of the categories above.

As an example, Figure 1-1 shows a cable tester on the left side and two fiber-optic cable testers on the middle and right sides.

**Figure 1-1**    *Cable Testers*

# Network Monitors

Network monitors were first built to capture, display, and save traffic going through a network cable. Since frames are captured, and the information gathered and displayed is pertaining to the data link layer, this tool is considered a Layer 2 tool. Of course, many vendors created different brands and models of this tool with different capabilities. The most common feature of network monitors is their ability to take the raw data and provide some summarization and statistics for the user. Information such as frame sizes, number of erroneous frames, MAC addresses observed, and number of broadcasts are a few examples of the statistics displayed by network monitors. Figure 1-2 shows three sample network monitor outputs displaying alarm information, frame summary, and global statistics.

Network monitors are considered valuable tools to perform the following tasks:

- **Establishing network baseline**—Making a recording of regular network activity over a period of time.

- **Observing consistent patterns of changing network utilization**—Hence, planning to deal with future needs (this is called network capacity planning).

- **Discovering traffic overloads and bottlenecks**—Therefore, identifying the solutions more clearly.

**Figure 1-2**   *Sample Information Provided by Network Monitors*

```
ALARM LOG      Oct 30 17:55:09
Priority       Time       Sourse          Type/Description
1  Critical    17:52:10   Intrln03C801    Unknown station
2  Critical    17:52:31   Intrln07EB9A    Unknown station
3  Critical    17:52:40   KIRK            Idle 1 minute
4  Critical    17:53:58   Terry           Rel usage exceeded 5%
5  Minor       17:53:00   Christine's Mac Rel usage exceeded 5%
6  Critical    17:54:18   Broadcast       5 or more broadcasts
7  Critical    17:55:15   Global Network  1 or more frame error
8  Warning     17:55:33   Anita           No response 5 seconds
9  Critical    17:55:54   SERVER          Idle 4 minutes
```

```
FRAME SIZES  Oct 30 17:59:05
Frame Bytes Percent
Under 17     0.00
17           0.01
10-32        9.52
33-54        43.63
55-120       30.23
129-256      1.87
257-512      1.45
1025-2048    4.51
2049-4096    0.30
4097-4608    0.14
Over 4608    0.00
```

```
GLOBAL STATISTICS          Nov 30 17:53:42
                  Traffic Counts
Total Stations   37          Active Stations   4
Average Usage    6.46        Current Usage     7.18
Total Frames     138,954     Current Frames    513
Total Bytes      28,152,842  Current Bytes     87,448
Avg Frame Size   202         Avg Frame Size    170
```

There are other features that make network monitors even more useful. The option for setting up filters (based on source and/or destination frame address, protocol type, and so on) makes a network monitor a good troubleshooting or educational tool. Should certain conditions, such as the number of broadcasts exceeding a set threshold, arise, visible or audible alarms are great for informing the appropriate personnel. Moreover, the ability to generate and release frames to the wire is quite useful for benchmarking and stress testing. Lastly, some network monitors implement Simple Network Management Protocol (SNMP) and Remote Monitoring (RMON) Management Information Bases (MIBs) for central management systems.

# Protocol Analyzers

Protocol analyzers capture (record), display (interpret), analyze (decode), and save network traffic. The difference between protocol analyzers and network monitors is that in addition to displaying and interpreting the frame (data link layer) information, protocol analyzers are capable of interpreting and displaying the packet, segment, and other (higher) protocol data units (PDUs) as well. This functionality is usually provided for many different protocol stacks. Figure 1-3 shows a number of packets captured using the LANWatch32 software. Note that the detail of the highlighted packet is displayed on the bottom of the shown screen.

---

**NOTE**     Sometimes the terms *network monitor* and *protocol analyzer* are used synonymously and that can cause some confusion. For instance, the Network Monitor application that Microsoft provides for Windows NT Server 4.0, despite its name, fits in the category of protocol analyzers.

---

**Figure 1-3**     *Sample LANWatch32 Output*

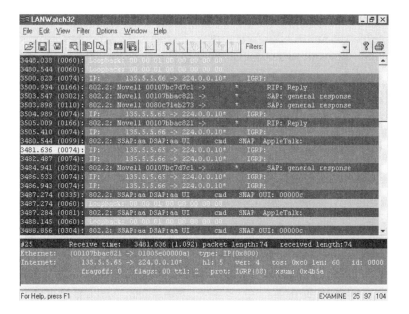

Displaying the content of the captured traffic in a structured and easy-to-understand format is only the most basic functionality of protocol analyzers. Time-stamping each frame, providing filtering options for the displayed data, allowing flags to trigger the program to start and stop capturing the traffic, and permitting the user to generate a frame(s) are other capabilities you may find in protocol analyzers.

The application areas for protocol analyzers are diverse. You may use a protocol analyzer to study the format or behavior of a certain protocol. Another usage would be to check time delays between a certain request and response, using the time-stamp differences. The option to generate and transmit frames with desired content allows the user to do effective diagnostics and/or stress testing. Hence, protocol analyzers make valuable educational, testing (troubleshooting), and capacity-planning tools. The Cisco Internetwork Troubleshooting (CIT) instructor-led course provides students with the LANWatch32 software as an example of a commercial protocol analyzer. Students are encouraged to observe captured traffic of different network activities to help them better appreciate the intricacies of network protocols.

# Network Management Systems

Computer networks have become complex for several reasons. There are many different makes and models of devices. Most networks deploy a variety of protocols and applications. Several local-area, wide-area, and remote access technologies and techniques have been invented. Making all of these components work together reliably with maximum availability is not a trivial task. Network management systems are tools to help understand, monitor, troubleshoot, modify, scale, and secure networks.

The five key functional areas of network management, as per the International Organization for Standardization (ISO) definition, are

- Fault management
- Accounting management
- Configuration/name management
- Performance management
- Security management

Fault management, a major troubleshooting topic, is about discovering abnormal behavior before or shortly after it happens. Once a problem is detected, take the following sequence of actions:

1 Determine the problem area.

2 Isolate the problem area and take advantage of alternate paths (complex networks usually have fault-tolerance and/or redundancy built in).

3 Attempt to minimize the impact of the failure(s).

4 Discover the specific device(s) causing the fault(s).

5 Identify the component/subsystem that is malfunctioning and needs to be replaced or reconfigured.

6 Implement the solution and pave the way for restoring the normal network operation.

---

**NOTE**     The systematic troubleshooting methodology that guides you from problem definition
through discovery of the problem and implementing the solution is discussed in Chapter 2,
"Understanding Troubleshooting Methods."

---

The remainder of this section covers the following:

- CiscoWorks
- TrafficDirector remote monitoring software
- CiscoWorks for Switched Internetworks (CWSI)

## CiscoWorks

CiscoWorks is Cisco Systems' network management software. This software is based on
Simple Network Management Protocol and it is for managing networks with one integrated
platform. CiscoWorks provides services that have both operations and management value.
Network managers can monitor routers (down to port activity), observe traffic patterns,
modify configurations, observe and report inventory, capture data (for accounting
purposes), and observe security settings all from their one central station. Some of the main
components of CiscoWorks (classic—that is, prior to CiscoWorks 2000) are

- Configuration file management
- Path tool
- Health monitor
- Environmental monitor
- Device monitor (using Device Management Database)
- Security features

There are other software applications, such as CiscoView, bundled with CiscoWorks.
CiscoView is also available as a standalone product and can be integrated with other
network management platforms such as SunNet Manager, HP OpenView, and IBM
NetView. CiscoView is a GUI software that provides real-time device level monitoring
(providing status and statistics information), fault management, and troubleshooting.

Another valuable network management tool is Cisco Resource Manager (CRM). CRM is
web-based and among its components there are four essential applications: Inventory
Manager, Availability Manager, Syslog Analyzer, and Software Image Manager. CRM
complements CiscoView and other parts of CiscoWorks network management software.

## CiscoWorks for Switched Internetworks Software

CWSI Campus is a suite of network management applications that together provide remote monitoring, configuration, and management of switched internetworks. The following are included in the CWSI Campus package:

- TrafficDirector
- VlanDirector
- AtmDirector
- CiscoView
- UserTracking

For a description of these components, refer to www.cisco.com/univercd/cc/td/doc/product/rtrmgmt/sw_ntman/cwsimain/cwsi2/cwsiug2/gsg/gsin.htm at the Cisco Documentation site. CWSI can be integrated with other SNMP-based network management systems, such as SunNet Manager, HP OpenView, and IBM NetView. Protocols such as SNMP, Cisco Discovery Protocol (CDP), VLAN Trunking Protocol (VTP), and RMON form the foundation of the CWSI application suite. One of the valuable features of CWSI Campus is Network Map. This application provides a map of the physical devices and links in your network, which it automatically discovers, provided that there is a Cisco seed device present. You can then locate specific devices in the network and view how they are linked together. Network Map can also display the network virtual topology (virtual LAN configuration) in relation to the physical topology.

## TrafficDirector Remote Monitoring Software

The TrafficDirector software is an application in the CWSI Campus suite of network management applications. This software allows you to monitor traffic (on network segments) leading to the diagnosis of any abnormalities. TrafficDirector obtains traffic information from embedded RMON agents (of Catalyst switches) and standalone Cisco SwitchProbe products. With this information, TrafficDirector can inform you of collisions, errors, utilization, and broadcast rates on a port (or port group) basis. You can also set up TrafficDirector to receive threshold-based traps from Catalyst switches. Hence, TrafficDirector is considered an excellent fault and performance management tool. Furthermore, since you can capture remote packets and profile network traffic on a multilayer basis, TrafficDirector is also considered a remote monitoring and traffic analysis tool.

# Simulation and Modeling Tools

As the name implies, simulation and modeling tools are meant to allow you to put a network together (using the software) and see how it performs. You can use these tools to design a brand new network or to see how an existing network will perform if you modify it, expand it, or put traffic stress on it. Simulation tools allow you to select networking devices and interconnect them with a variety of serial, LAN media, dialup, and WAN services. You can configure the selected devices line by line or assign preexisting real configuration files to them, and analyze the simulated network's operation. If you have a network analyzer that can export captured data into a format that you can feed to your simulation software, you can then see how the simulated network behaves or reacts to the real traffic.

A useful function of simulation tools is reporting on throughput, utilization, response time, error rate, dropped packets, and other performance-related data during the simulation period. This capability is valuable for evaluating small or significant proposed changes before committing to them and, hence, can prevent financial and operational disasters. Additionally, the impact of failed segments and/or devices can be analyzed and used to evaluate options such as implementing fault tolerant devices, redundant links, or high capacity/reliable technologies. Cisco Netsys is a product that offers such services. The demonstration version of Netsys (installable on Windows NT platforms, for example) provides a video presentation about the capabilities of this software; furthermore, it provides you with a subset of the full version's capabilities for your evaluation.

# Cisco Connection Online (CCO)

CCO provides a suite of interactive web-based services that offer open access to Cisco's information, systems, resources, and personnel—24 hours a day, 7 days a week, from anywhere in the world. Figure 1-4 displays CCO's home page (www.cisco.com).

The online/interactive services offered by Cisco over the Internet have evolved and grown over time. Today you have access to a wealth of technical knowledge, tips, bug information, support services, and other valuable resources all from one place. CCO is not only about obtaining information; you may, for example, access the online price list on Cisco products, place orders, download Cisco Internetwork Operating System (IOS) software images, or receive technical assistance and many other services. There are two levels of access available: guest access and registered access. Table 1-1 shows the benefits of each and how they relate to troubleshooting.

**Figure 1-4**   *CCO Home Page*

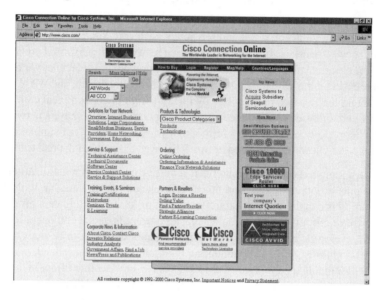

**Table 1-1**   *Troubleshooting Benefits of Guest and Registered Access to CCO*

| Benefits of Guest User Access to CCO | Benefits of Registered User Access to CCO |
| --- | --- |
| Immediate access to basic information about Cisco and its networking solutions, services, and programs | Access to all the benefits, information, tools, and services available to CCO guest users |
| Ability to download and test selected software packages | Access to a variety of online support services (such as Bug Toolkit, Stack Decoder) |
| Access to technical documentation and information about online support services | If registered users have software service contracts, access to the Software Center |
| Access to Cisco event calendars, which provide information on conferences, training programs, and trade shows in which Cisco participates | If registered users have appropriate service or contract agreements, ability to order Cisco networking hardware/software products, parts and services (through Cisco MarketPlace) |

The remaining topics of this chapter demonstrate the different services and tools offered through CCO that are of special value to internetwork troubleshooting personnel. The material is presented under two classifications:

- Using CCO to prevent problems
- Using CCO to correct problems

# Using CCO to Prevent Problems

This section presents the Cisco Documentation CD-ROM (also available online at CCO), CCO MarketPlace, and CCO Software Center. You can use the Cisco Documentation CD-ROM to help you design, troubleshoot, and enhance your network. Cisco MarketPlace is the page on CCO where you can check the price list and also order Cisco software, devices, and spare parts (to order online, you need an e-commerce agreement with Cisco Systems). Through CCO Software Center you may download IOS images, software patches, and maintenance releases (this is also based on your service or contract agreement with Cisco Systems).

## Cisco Documentation CD-ROM

Cisco Documentation is an interactive library of technical information provided on CCO. Figure 1-5 shows the Cisco Documentation home page on CCO.

**Figure 1-5**   *Cisco Documentation on CCO*

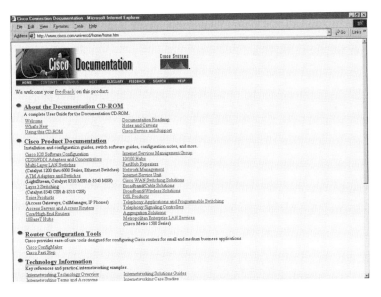

You can also purchase Cisco's subscription service to receive monthly, quarterly, or semiannual Documentation CD-ROM updates.

The CD-ROM package includes two discs that contain the following documentation (as per CCO) in HTML format:

- Cisco IOS release notes, configuration guides, command references, and command summaries

- Debug command reference and system error messages

- Cisco Management Information Base (MIB) User Quick Reference and Access Services Quick Configuration Guide

- Cisco product catalog

- Router and hub installation and configuration guides

- Switch installation and configuration guides, switch command reference guides, and switch MIB reference guides

- Client/server software installation guides

- Configuration notes for memory upgrades, network interface cards, rack-mount kits, and other field upgrade products

Navigating through the Documentation CD-ROM is facilitated by the online help, a table of contents, hypertext links, a search engine, book marking, and the history window.

---

**NOTE**    On disc one of the Documentation CD-ROM there is a mini web server that is installed on your PC. This allows the second disc to work properly. Otherwise, you can read individual files (they're HTML) but you cannot navigate properly.

---

## Cisco MarketPlace

The Cisco MarketPlace is the page on CCO through which you can order Cisco networking products, promotional merchandise, and training materials (see Figure 1-6). Since they save time and money, shorten lead times, and improve efficiency, Internet commerce applications are now very popular. To order direct from Cisco using the Internet commerce applications, you need to perform the following:

1 Obtain a valid Cisco purchase order or sales order number for your company, as well as your company billing information.

2 Complete the online registration form to become a CCO user.

3 Complete and send a hard copy of an Internet Commerce Agreement (ICA) to the appropriate Cisco Systems personnel.

**Figure 1-6**    *Cisco MarketPlace*

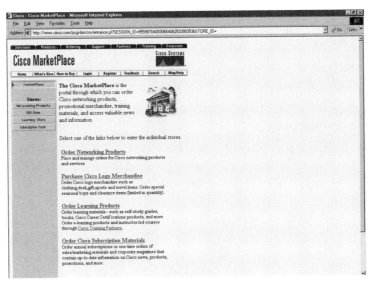

Cisco MarketPlace has four stores:

- Networking products (formerly known as Internetworking Products Center or IPC)

- Gift store

- Learning store

- Subscription store

Using the Networking Products MarketPlace, you can improve your productivity by ordering products and service online (at any time), find out where your order is in the manufacturing and shipment process and how soon to expect delivery, and obtain the latest product quotes by accessing the most current price lists.

## CCO Software Library

Cisco describes the Software Library as a full-service one-stop-shopping location for all phases of Cisco software product lifecycles. You can obtain upgrades and learn more about Cisco's software products, including Cisco IOS software (for routers, switches, or gateway platforms), network management and security applications for workstation servers, and internetworking protocol sites for host systems all from one place.

In addition to offering major upgrades and maintenance releases of Cisco software products, the Software Center provides:

- Selected demo and beta distributions for latest products, downloadable to try before you buy.

- Software upgrade planners, which present product literature, release information, documentation and release notes, plus known defect information.

- Software checklists, which provide current availability and compatibility of Cisco software products.

- Custom-file-access postings of various software. These are software such as critical and customized defect fixes that are not generally or publicly available on CCO. (You need a Cisco service representative to grant you access.)

# Using CCO to Correct Problems

In this section the troubleshooting tools and resources of CCO are introduced. The Bug Toolkit, Troubleshooting Engine, Stack Decoder, and Open Forum, all of which aid diagnosis and corrective activities, are discussed in sequence. Finally, the method for escalating trouble cases to Cisco service and support and using the CCO Case Management Toolkit is discussed. You might use all or some of these tools and the associated methodologies during the course of a project. Even if you do not use all of these tools and the associated methodologies, as a troubleshooting expert you are expected to be thoroughly familiar with all of the tools at your disposal and how to use them effectively.

## CCO Bug Toolkit

The Bug Toolkit is a set of tools including the Bug Navigator II, Bug Watcher, and watcher agents, all of which are made available to registered users on CCO from one place: www.cisco.com/support/bugtools/ (see Figure 1-7). If you experience abnormal behavior in your network, or are thinking of upgrading your IOS, you can search for reported defects based on IOS version/release number or keywords related to the symptoms you have observed or the technology you are concerned with. Next, you can see the status on the defect and find out if there is a solution, workaround, or software patch that can solve your problem. Furthermore, you can arrange to continually receive information regarding a specific bug (using the Watcher Bin) or receive alerts (from an alert agent) based on your network profile. The settings for all the aforementioned arrangements are editable, so you may tune them differently, add new ones, or simply delete those you don't need, at any time.

**Figure 1-7**  *CCO Service and Support—The Bug Toolkit*

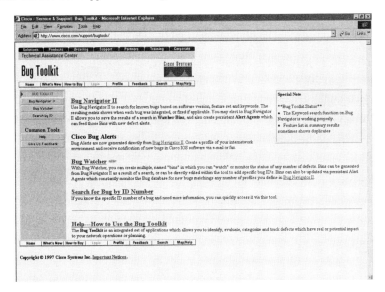

The Bug Navigator II has two applications:

- **Symptom diagnostics**—To perform symptom diagnostics, select the major release version and the maintenance revision of your IOS, enter the observed symptoms in the Keyword field, and press the Search button to see the detailed listing on the results page that provides the most likely causes of the problem in rank order.

- **Upgrade planning**—The Bug Description button gives you the detailed release note information (should there be any) for that defect. If you are planning to upgrade your IOS, you should go through the same set of steps but enter the feature of interest (for example, DDR using ISDN) in the Keyword field, instead of the bug symptoms.

After the Bug Navigator II generates a list of defects based on the information you entered, you can then select some of the items and assign them to a Watcher Bin (to an existing one or to a new one you create). Watcher Bins, when created, are placed on the Bug Watcher page and are used to monitor the status of the selected defects. For example, if the fix for a defect is integrated into a new software release, you will be able to view the status of that defect in real time. The bins that you create and that appear on the Bug Watcher page can be edited at any time by adding new bug IDs. You can also configure for receiving alert messages by e-mail or fax. In other words, when creating a Watcher Bin, you can simply have a bug watcher agent continuously update your Watcher Bin with new defect information that matches the specific profile you have entered. However, you also have the option to enter your e-mail address and/or fax number to receive bug alert notifications when new information is available or the state of a bug is changed.

## CCO Troubleshooting Engine

The Troubleshooting Engine link on the Cisco Technical Assistance Center (TAC) page takes you to the Troubleshooting Engine page. The Troubleshooting Engine helps you solve common problems involving hardware, configuration, and performance. However, to deal with complex issues such as incompatibilities or software defects, you must go to the Open Forum page (discussed later in this chapter).

The Troubleshooting Engine presents you with a list of various topics (such as IP routing protocols). Next, you are expected to click on the Step-by-Step Help or Advanced Search links from within the box related to the topic of interest. Then a sequence of questions is presented to you, one at a time, and eventually solutions are suggested in order of their likelihood (a score of 100 is the highest). If the Troubleshooting Engine can't come up with a solution or suggestion, it will encourage you to take the matter to the Open Forum or use the Bug Toolkit to see if your trouble is possibly due to product defects.

## CCO Stack Decoder

Stack Decoder (see Figure 1-8) is another troubleshooting tool available at CCO (www.cisco.com/stack).

This tool is used when a router crashes: it decodes the stack trace generated by Cisco routers and switches. If you execute the privileged command **show stack** from the exec prompt of the router, the stack trace appears. Next, you can paste the results in the input field of the Stack Decoder page.

Stack Decoder decodes the stack trace and creates a symbol file. The symbol file (perhaps along with other information in the trace) usually gives enough information to isolate the cause of any problems you are experiencing. In the past, this tool was not available to the public; you had to send your stack trace to Cisco TAC, and they would in turn decode the trace, analyze it, and come up with a solution or suggestion. Now you can do this yourself directly online.

## CCO Open Forum

The CCO Open Forum (www.cisco.com/openf/), as the name implies, is an online Q&A facility that Cisco Systems has provided for its customers. If you have a technical question that relates to Cisco Systems products (hardware or software), you can use the Open Forum (see Figure 1-9) to look for your answer in two ways:

* By searching the existing Q&A database

* By submitting your question to the Open Forum (if you could not find your answer in the current database)

**Figure 1-8**  *CCO Stack Decoder*

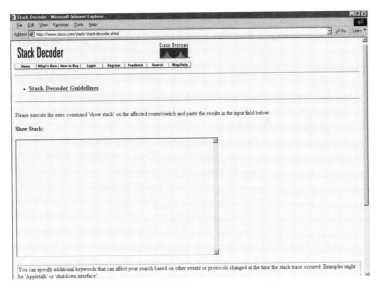

**Figure 1-9**  *CCO Open Forum*

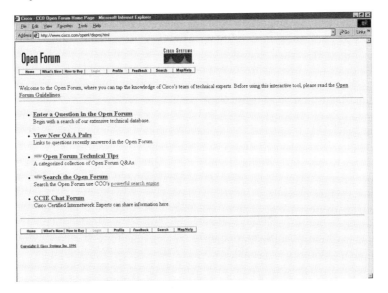

As is indicated in the Open Forum Guidelines, the Open Forum Q&A database on CCO contains thousands of questions and answers that were submitted to the Forum by customers, then answered and reviewed by Cisco Certified Internetwork Experts (CCIEs).The Open Forum Guidelines indicate that the Open Forum consists of CCIEs who may or may not work for Cisco, so the answers provided do not necessarily represent the views of Cisco.

## Escalation to Cisco Service and Support

Cisco Systems customer engineers that are members of the Cisco TAC are yet another resource available to you worldwide. There may be a time when the effort to solve your internetwork problems using the variety of tools and resources surveyed in this chapter does not lead you to a solution. This assistance may be obtained based on your warranty or contract or on a billable basis. You may contact Cisco TAC via telephone, facsimile, e-mail, or online from the Case Open page on CCO.

To open a case with Cisco TAC effectively, you are generally required to provide the following information:

- The maintenance contract number for the product that needs service, as well as the product's serial number.

- A brief description of the problem.

- The relevant facts surrounding your network and your case, sometimes including your network diagram, configuration files, the output of several **show** and **debug** commands, and data captured using network monitors or protocol analyzers. Note that the command **show tech-support**, available as of version 11.0 of the Cisco IOS software, generates output equivalent to several of the **show** commands that you would otherwise have to enter one at a time

- The priority level of the problem. The Cisco TAC Case Open Help Guide on CCO describes the priority levels as follows:

    — Priority 1—Production network is down, causing critical impact to business operations if service is not restored quickly.

    — Priority 2—Production network is severely degraded, impacting significant aspects of your business operations.

    — Priority 3—Network performance is degraded. Network functionality is noticeably impaired, but most business operations continue.

    — Priority 4—Customer requires information or assistance on Cisco product capabilities, installation, or configuration.

After you submit your request to open the case, the TAC Customer Service Engineer (CSE) assigns a number to your case. You will need this number to refer to your case from this point on. The following section describes how you can use the CCO Case Management Toolkit to open a brand new case or to interact with your existing case.

## CCO Case Management Toolkit

The CCO Case Management Toolkit is a web tool for customers with appropriate service arrangements to open, query, and update cases with Cisco TAC. Figure 1-10 displays the Case Open Help Guide (accessed from the TAC home page).

**Figure 1-10**  *The Case Open Help Guide*

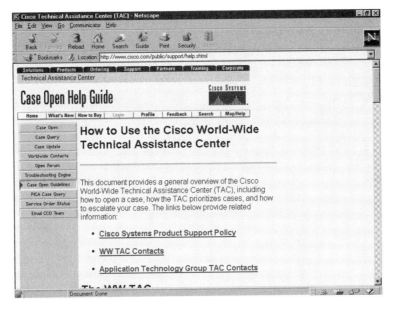

There are several buttons available on the left side of the Case Open Help Guide page, including Case Open, Case Query, Case Update, Open Forum, Troubleshooting Engine, Service Order Status, and Email CCO Team.

# Foundation Summary

The Foundation Summary is a collection of quick reference information that provides a convenient review of many key concepts in this chapter. For those of you who already feel comfortable with the topics in this chapter, this summary helps you recall a few details. For those of you who just read this chapter, this review should help solidify some key facts. For any of you doing your final prep before the exam, these tables and figures are a convenient way to review the day before the exam.

**Table 1-2**    *Network Media Test Equipment*

| Tool | Tests, Measures, or Detects |
|---|---|
| Volt/Ohm meter | Voltage, current, resistance, and capacitance. |
| Cable tester (scanner) | Impedance, attenuation, near-end crosstalk (NEXT), and noise. |
| TDR/OTDR | Opens, shorts, kinks, sharp bends, crimps, and impedance mismatches. |

**Table 1-3**    *Upper Layer Monitoring, Testing, and Analysis Tools*

| Tool | Application/Usage |
|---|---|
| Network monitors | Network baselining, capacity planning, problem detection. |
| Multi-protocol analyzers | Studying network traffic, testing, troubleshooting. |
| Network management systems | Fault management, accounting management, configuration/name management, performance management, security management. |
| Simulation/planning tools | Network design, performance analysis, stress testing. |

**Table 1-4**    *Cisco's Network Management Software*

| Application | Description |
|---|---|
| CiscoWorks | Allows network managers to monitor routers (down to port activity), observe traffic patterns, modify configurations, observe and report inventory, capture data (for accounting purposes), and observe security settings, all from their one central station. |

**Table 1-4**    *Cisco's Network Management Software (Continued)*

| Application | Description |
| --- | --- |
| CiscoView | Provides real-time device level monitoring (providing status and statistics information), fault management, and troubleshooting, with a Graphic User Interface. |
| Cisco Resource Manager (CRM) | Offers four essential applications: Inventory Manager, Availability Manager, Syslog Analyzer, and Software Image Manager. |
| CWSI Campus | This suite of network management applications provides remote monitoring, configuration, and management of switched internetworks. The following are included in the CWSI Campus package: TrafficDirector, VlanDirector, AtmDirector, CiscoView, UserTracking. |
| TrafficDirector | TrafficDirector obtains traffic information from embedded RMON agents (of Catalyst switches) and standalone Cisco SwitchProbe products. With this information about different segments, TrafficDirector can inform you of collision, error, utilization, and broadcast rates on a port (or port group) basis. |

**Table 1-5**    *CCO Summary*

| CCO Problem Prevention Components | CCO Problem Correction Components |
| --- | --- |
| Cisco Documentation CD-ROM | Cisco Bug Toolkit |
| Cisco MarketPlace | Cisco Troubleshooting Engine (Its new name is Troubleshooting Assistant.) |
| Cisco Software Library | Cisco Stack Decoder |
| | Cisco Open Forum |
| | Cisco Case Management Toolkit |

# Q&A

The answers to the following questions can be found in Appendix A. Some of the questions in this section are repeated from the "Do I Know This Already" Quiz so that you can gauge the advancement of your knowledge of this subject matter.

1  What parameters do Volt/Ohm meters test?

_____

_____

_____

2  Give two examples of the cable conditions reported by Scanners.

_____

_____

_____

3  Which cable-testing function is offered only by the high-end equipment?

_____

_____

_____

4  Name the tasks testing equipment with TDR functionality can perform.

_____

_____

_____

5  Which OSI Reference Model layer does the information gathered by network monitors correspond to?

_____

_____

_____

6  What is one of the major applications of network monitors?

_____

_____

_____

**7** Which application that can be bundled with CiscoWorks provides real-time device monitoring?

_____

_____

_____

**8** What does the acronym CRM stand for?

_____

_____

_____

**9** Name the components of CRM.

_____

_____

_____

**10** What does the TrafficDirector work with in order to obtain traffic information about different segments?

_____

_____

_____

**11** Which tasks are generally facilitated by network simulation and modeling tools? (Name at least two.)

_____

_____

_____

**12** Which Cisco component, also available online, provides the IOS command reference, product reference, and other valuable information?

_____

_____

_____

**13** Which tasks do you need to complete before ordering direct from Cisco using the Internet Commerce Apps?

_____

_____

_____

**14** What does CCO MarketPlace allow you to do?

_____

_____

_____

**15** Name at least one major service that the CCO Software Library makes available.

_____

_____

_____

**16** What are the member components of Cisco Bug Toolkit?

_____

_____

_____

**17** Who can submit questions to the CCO Open Forum, and who provides answers to questions on CCO Open Forum?

_____

_____

_____

**18** What are the four general pieces of information that the customer must provide to TAC when opening a case?

_____

_____

_____

**19**  How many priority levels are available to be assigned to a new case to be opened with TAC?

_____

_____

_____

**20**  What are the tasks that the Case Management Toolkit allows you to do?

_____

_____

_____

**21**  Name three classes of network media test equipment.

_____

_____

_____

**22**  What are the tasks network monitors can perform?

_____

_____

_____

**23**  Name the tool that does multilayer analysis of network traffic?

_____

_____

_____

**24**  What are the five functional areas of network management?

_____

_____

_____

**25**  What is Cisco Systems' flagship network management software called?

_____

_____

_____

**26**  List at least three members of the CWSI Campus Application.

_____

_____

_____

**27**  Name Cisco's network simulation and modeling tool.

_____

_____

_____

**28**  What does the acronym CCO stand for, and what is the URL address for CCO?

_____

_____

_____

**29**  Name at least two tools or resources from CCO available for problem prevention.

_____

_____

_____

**30**  Name at least three tools or resources that CCO provides for problem correction and troubleshooting.

_____

_____

_____

This chapter covers the following topics that you will need to master to pass the CCNP Support exam:

| Objective | Description |
|-----------|-------------|
| 1 | Define systematic troubleshooting |
| 2 | Explain the benefits of using systematic troubleshooting |
| 3 | Provide a systematic troubleshooting model |
| 4 | Discuss each step of the systematic troubleshooting model |
| 5 | Outline the documentation required for internetwork maintenance |

# Understanding Troubleshooting Methods

The internetworks of today are very complex and experience change constantly. One of the important tasks within organizations is supporting these complex networks. Because many jobs and essential business functions rely on availability of network services, there is a lot of pressure on those who maintain and troubleshoot networks. This group of personnel must understand their network and also possess a troubleshooting methodology that can help them to effectively and efficiently discover causes of malfunctions and fix them. This chapter discusses the importance of using a systematic troubleshooting method and provides an elementary presentation of it.

## "Do I Know This Already?" Quiz

If you wish to evaluate your knowledge of the contents of this chapter before you get started, answer the following questions. The answers are provided in Appendix A, "Answers to Quiz Questions." If you are having difficulty providing correct answers, you should thoroughly review the entire chapter. If all or most of your answers are correct, you might want to skim this chapter for only those subjects you need to review. You can also use the "Foundation Summary" section to quickly review topics. Once you have completed the chapter, you should reevaluate yourself with the questions in the "Q&A" section at the end. Finally, use the companion CD-ROM to evaluate your knowledge of the topics and see if you need a review.

1 Explain the importance of using a systematic troubleshooting method.

_____

_____

_____

2 Draw a flow diagram of a systematic troubleshooting model.

_____

_____

_____

**3** What are the general tasks performed during the problem definition step?

_____

_____

_____

**4** What tools/resources can assist you during the fact gathering step?

_____

_____

_____

**5** Based on what information do you eliminate possibilities (those you considered during the problem definition step) and consider new possibilities?

_____

_____

_____

**6** What do you do if you hypothesize many possibilities for the network problem?

_____

_____

_____

**7** Name a common technique that is deployed when you plan actions.

_____

_____

_____

**8** What kind of mistakes can happen during the action implementation step?

_____

_____

_____

**9** What do you do if none of the possibilities you hypothesized ends up being the cause of your network problem?

_____

_____

_____

**10**  What are some of the benefits of documenting a solved problem?

_____

_____

_____

## Foundation Topics

# The Importance of Using a Systematic Troubleshooting Method

In order to appreciate the importance of using a systematic troubleshooting method, you must understand the steps and scope of systematic troubleshooting. Many people describe systematic troubleshooting as *step-by-step*, *ordered*, *organized*, *thoughtful*, *methodological*, and so on. I agree with all of those terms. I also tell my students that I believe a troubleshooting method is systematic if it guarantees progress. In other words, a method that can possibly get into circles and can cause you to get more confused than when you started would not be a systematic method.

Simply put, you cannot afford not to use a systematic troubleshooting method. In today's internetworks, downtime can mean large amounts of dollars lost. Downtime may even lead to a company's bankruptcy in some instances. In any case, network support people are usually under tremendous pressure to discover and fix problems very quickly. If you know the cause of a failure and can fix it, you should do it without hesitation. Most of the time, however, that will not be the case. Therefore, you must deploy a technique that can eliminate different possibilities and will move you step-by-step toward the real causes of your problem. Such a technique ensures that you are always making progress and will not get into loops and confusion. Ultimately, you either will recognize what has broken, failed, or been misconfigured or can make a report of everything you have done and discovered and hand the case over to somebody else, who can then use that information in further troubleshooting efforts. Most importantly, you will not be wasting your time and other people's time, and your effort will have results regardless of whether you have fixed the problem or not.

# A Problem-Solving Model

A generally accepted troubleshooting model is presented in Figure 2-1. This model presents a process flow that can effectively guide you during your troubleshooting tasks.

Most organizations have a standard method like this one in place. One important benefit of this model is that as you solve your problems, you are also adding to your knowledge and skill set. Furthermore, each time a troubleshooting task is completed, all the gathered data and actions taken are recorded for future reference. This section covers the following topics, which are the elements of this model, in sequence:

- Define the Problem
- Gather the Facts

**Figure 2-1**    *General Problem-Solving Model*

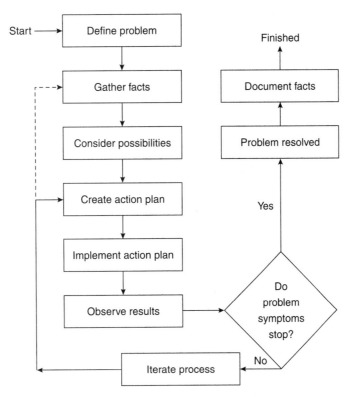

- Consider the Possibilities
- Create an Action Plan
- Implement Your Action Plan
- Observe the Results
- Iterate the Process
- Resolution

## Define the Problem

Defining the problem is a very straightforward task. Problem definition is a clear statement (with few, preferably no ambiguous terms) of the problem in terms of the associated symptoms and possible causes. It is often useful to make a reference (or comparison) to the normal and expected behavior. If you have your network baseline information, refer to it in your problem statement. Along with identifying the observed symptoms, the problem definition should also mention what faults and/or misconfigurations could be the possible causes of these symptoms.

The problem definition step flows smoothly into the fact gathering step. As you learn of the problem and go about defining it, you are inevitably gathering preliminary facts. Take what is reported by the user(s) and see if it needs rewording, broadening, and so on. It is beneficial to see the problem for yourself. The following are some common questions that you would ask the user(s) during the initial interview/conversation:

- Are you authorized to perform this action?

- When was the last time you performed this action?

- When did you first notice the problem?

- Are you aware of any recent change?

- Is the problem persistent or intermittent?

- Do you know if somebody else is experiencing the same problem(s)?

The preceding questions are not part of the fact gathering stage. During the fact gathering step you gather more in-depth data and make more technical observations. In fact, to many people's surprise, you must even think of possible causes (for the symptoms that you have discovered and documented) during the problem definition step. Remember that in your problem statements, you must also make reference to the network baseline.

## Gather the Facts

You gather facts from different sources. You have to talk to network administrators, other support engineers, managers, and anybody else that can provide relevant key information. In many cases, a change that is believed to have no effect on other traffic/activities is not reported (even when you explicitly ask); you may end up finding such changes for yourself in this step. The fact gathering step may involve some basic testing tools (such as **ping**, **trace**, and so on) or some more involved ones such as debugging, network monitors, protocol analyzers, and network management systems. You may have to verify for yourself whether any changes have taken place. This will involve comparing the current configurations of your routers, switches, servers, and other devices to their backed-up counterparts (before and recent changes). The most important outcome of this step is that many possibilities or hypotheses (that you have thought of or have documented) are usually eliminated based on the gathered facts. You end up with a few possibilities surrounding a subset of your full network.

## Consider the Possibilities

The main focus here is to use your knowledge of the network, devices, and software releases along with the gathered facts to formally eliminate improbable possibilities and set a boundary for the problem area. It is quite usual to end up with a few hypotheses surrounding a small portion of the network. Hence, you will have a better focus (on a few devices as opposed to the whole network), and a narrowed set of possibilities. One last step you are supposed to take is to order the remaining possibilities based on their likelihood. The possibilities should be tested and corrected according to the order of their likelihood, in the following steps.

## Create an Action Plan

For each possibility (among those that are remaining), you must come up with one or more actions that will need to be implemented in order to solve the problem(s). It is crucial that discrete actions do not get mixed—they should remain separate. Often people change too many things at once. If they fix the problem, they will not be able to tell what the real problem was and, hence, which action corrected it. Furthermore, it is possible that a change will be implemented that is not necessary—indeed, that may have a negative effect on other traffic and/or operations. On the other hand, if the problems remain, even after many changes are made, the situation can get out of hand.

When you have a set of possibilities that you believe might be the cause of your network problems, you must first order them based on their likelihood. Then you must plan one or more actions for each possibility (hypothesis). It is a good practice to partition the problem area into discrete sections and plan on repairing one section at a time. It is not always the case that only one section or one device is misconfigured or broken, but your initial assumption must be that. Once you focus on a section, prepare some tests (such as **ping**, **show ip route**, and so on) to determine precisely what works and what doesn't. These tests will either confirm the validity of your action plan or make you revisit your action plan. This technique is often called *divide and conquer* or *using a partitioning effect*. It is evident that how one forms hypotheses, action plans, and test plans and goes about partitioning the network is a reflection of one's knowledge, experience, and the facts gathered.

## Implement Your Action Plan

At this point you take the most promising hypothesis and implement the corresponding action plan that you believe will correct the problem(s). This plan may be composed of only one or more than one action. If the latter case is true, it is important to make sure that every one of the (individual) actions *is required to be implemented at once*. Otherwise, you should, without a doubt, separate the actions and implement them one at the time. For example, your plan might be to start an OSPF process on a particular interface of a router and redistribute RIP into it. In this case, if you do not expect much result from merely starting OSPF and not implementing the redistribution, then you may do both at once. But if implementing redistribution serves a second purpose, you should first start OSPF and observe the results, and save the redistribution task until after you have confirmed correct operation of OSPF.

During the period that you implement an action plan, you must keep the preceding guidelines in mind. Every action and change must be documented. You have to be able to reverse your actions quickly. Pay attention to the security and performance implications of your actions (even for a short period of time) and make sure that they are acceptable. Try to stay away from invasive actions, such as router reload, if possible.

## Observe the Results

After implementing each atomic action, the results must be observed. You not only look to see if your problems/symptoms have been eliminated, but you also have to make sure that other normal operations are not disrupted or otherwise affected. If the symptoms have disappeared and you are confident that the problem has been solved (without creating new ones), you proceed to the next step: Report the problem as solved and document the results. If you still have unresolved issues, however, you have to go through another iteration of implementing actions and observing results.

As discussed earlier, for each hypothesis an action plan is created. If you did not get the desired results from your actions, before you go after your next hypothesis, you must make an important decision. Do you think you should keep the actions that you just implemented, or do you think you should reverse them? Depending on the situation, either decision might be justifiable, regardless of whether you have fixed the problem. The reason for this claim is that your problem might be a complex one and it may indeed need multiple corrections and/or changes. On the other hand, if your actions falsify your hypothesis, then you definitely want to reverse your actions. You might even want to try your next action step with the previous changes in place and then try it without the changes.

## Iterate the Process

Assuming that even after implementing your previous action plans the problems still persist, you need to consider the next hypothesis and go about implementing its corresponding actions. If you have not spelled out the actions of the next hypothesis, of course, you now have to do that. Inevitably, there will be times that you remain with no possibility or hypothesis in hand while your network problems still exist. What do you do then? The answer is that you have to think of more possibilities. If you cannot think of more possibilities, the reason is merely that you do not have all of the facts. You might have overlooked certain configurations. You may not know some of the details about certain protocols or devices. And, lastly, you may not be aware of an IOS bug that has been reported for your IOS version/release number. Therefore, you must either gather more facts or seek help. Talk to other support engineers and consultants, use CCO's troubleshooting engine, take advantage of CCO's Open Forum or Bug Toolkit, or simply open a case with Cisco's Technical Assistance Center (TAC).

## Resolution

In most cases, when the reported or observed symptoms disappear, chances are that the problem is solved. Naturally, you want to make sure that that is indeed the case and that you did not make more changes in your network than necessary. Most of the concerns just mentioned can be addressed by reporting to others about the status of your work and asking them if they have noticed any abnormalities.

The last step you have to take is to document your work. This will save you and others a lot of time and effort in the future. You and your colleagues will want to understand what you have changed and why you did it. You may also want to document any recommendations and tips and lessons learned that you think might be useful to those parties involved. Please remember that, at least for a while, you may want to save the old configuration files (the "before" picture) of the devices you have modified. Accurate documentation of the date and time that you made changes and your name and the names of those who were involved with this project would also be valuable information to add to your documentation. Optionally, a table or index of the devices, protocols, interfaces, and so on that were somehow affected by the experienced problem and its solutions can be a useful addition to your documentation.

# A Baseline Model of the Network

In order to be able to effectively support, troubleshoot, or modify an internetwork, you have to gather and maintain a certain amount of information about it. The following list includes some of the essential information recommended for inclusion in your ongoing (consistently updated) network documentation:

- The physical and logical map of your network
- Active protocols
- The addressing scheme (protocol specific)
- Network's baseline traffic and performance statistics and measurements about your internetwork and its devices that you have periodically collected during periods of normal operation
- The devices, configurations, operating systems, and software in the network
- Past troubleshooting cases
- An historical profile of how and why the network arrived at its current state

# Foundation Summary

The Foundation Summary is a collection of quick reference information that provides a convenient review of many key concepts in this chapter. For those of you who already feel comfortable with the topics in this chapter, this summary will help you recall a few details. For those of you who just read this chapter, this review should help solidify some key facts. For any of you doing your final prep before the exam, these tables and figures will be a convenient way to review the day before the exam.

**Table 2-1**  *Systematic Troubleshooting Summary*

| Step | Actions Taken |
| --- | --- |
| Define the problem | State the problem clearly in terms of the associated symptoms and possible causes. It is often useful to make a reference to the normal or expected behavior and the network baseline information. Ask the following questions from the user and/or other involved personnel: |
| | Are you authorized to perform this action? |
| | When was the last time you did this? |
| | When did you first notice or experience this problem? |
| | Is the problem persistent or intermittent? |
| | Are you aware of any recent changes? |
| | Do you know if someone else is experiencing similar difficulties? |
| Gather facts | Gather facts from all possible sources. You may have to talk to network administrators, other support engineers, managers, and anybody else that can provide relevant key information. |
| | Use the available testing tools and the Cisco IOS troubleshooting commands to gather more technical and in-depth data. |
| | The most important outcome of this step is that based on its results, many possibilities or hypotheses are usually eliminated. You end up with a few possibilities surrounding a subset of your full network. |
| Consider possibilities | Use your knowledge of the network, devices, software releases, and gathered facts to formally eliminate improbable possibilities and set a boundary for the problem area. |
| | Order the remaining possibilities based on their likelihood. The possibilities should be tested and corrected according to the order of their likelihood, in the following steps. |

**Table 2-1**    *Systematic Troubleshooting Summary (Continued)*

| Step | Actions Taken |
| --- | --- |
| Create action plan | For each remaining possibility (arranged in order of likelihood), you must come up with one or more actions or solutions to be implemented. It is crucial that discrete actions do not get mixed. |
| | Partition the problem area into discrete sections and plan on repairing one section at a time (the divide and conquer method). |
| | Technical tests must be planned at this stage. |
| Implement action plan | Implement the most promising action plan. If this plan is composed of more than one action, it is important to make sure that every one of the (individual) actions *is required to be implemented at once*. Otherwise, you must separate the actions and implement them one at a time. |
| | Every action and change must be documented. If necessary, you must be able to reverse your actions quickly. Pay attention to the security and performance implications of your actions and make sure that they are acceptable. Try to stay away from invasive actions, if possible. |
| Observe results | See if your problems/symptoms have been eliminated, but also investigate how your actions may have affected other operations. |
| | If the symptoms have disappeared and you are confident that the problem has been solved (without creating new ones), you proceed to the next step: report the problem as solved and document the results. If you still have unresolved issues, however, you have to go through another iteration of implementing actions and observing results. |
| | Before moving to the next hypothesis, you must make an important decision. Do you think you should keep the actions that you just implemented, or do you think you should reverse them? Depending on the situation, either decision might be justifiable, regardless of whether you have fixed the problem. |

*continues*

**Table 2-1**    *Systematic Troubleshooting Summary (Continued)*

| Step | Actions Taken |
|---|---|
| Iterate process | Proceed to the next hypothesis and go about implementing its corresponding actions. |
| | Inevitably, there will be times that you remain with no possibility or hypothesis in hand while your network problems still exist. If you cannot think of more possibilities, the reason is merely that you do not have all the facts. You might have overlooked certain configurations. You may not know some of the details about certain protocols or devices. And lastly, you may not be aware of an IOS bug that has been reported for your IOS version/release number. Therefore, you must either gather more facts or seek help. Talk to other support engineers or consultants, use CCO's troubleshooting engine, take advantage of CCO's Open Forum or Bug Toolkit, or simply open a case with Cisco's Technical Assistance Center (TAC). |
| Problem solved, document facts | When the symptoms are eliminated, document your work. This will save you and others a lot of time and effort in the future. You may also want to document any recommendations, tips, and lessons learned that you think might be useful to those parties involved. Accurate documentation of the date and time that you made changes and your name and the names of those who were involved with this project would also be valuable information to add to your documentation. Optionally, a table or index of the devices, protocols, interfaces, and so on that were somehow affected by the experienced problem and its solution can be a useful addition to your documentation. |

# Q&A

The answers to the following questions can be found in Appendix A. Some of the questions in this section are repeated from the "Do I Know This Already" Quiz so that you can gauge the advancement of your knowledge of this subject matter.

1   Write the title of each of the systematic troubleshooting method's steps in the appropriate box on the diagram below:

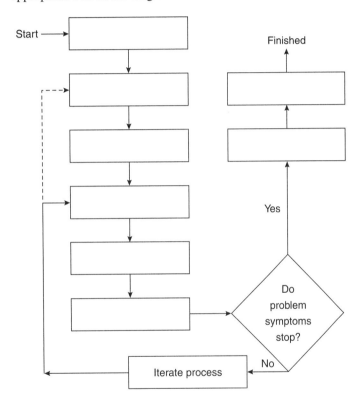

2   Explain the importance of using a systematic troubleshooting method.

**3** What are the general tasks performed during the problem definition step?

_____

_____

_____

**4** What tools/resources can assist you during the fact gathering step?

_____

_____

_____

**5** Based on what information do you eliminate possibilities (those you considered during the problem definition step) and consider new possibilities?

_____

_____

_____

**6** What do you do if you hypothesize many possibilities for the network problem?

_____

_____

_____

**7** Name a common technique that is deployed when you plan actions.

_____

_____

_____

**8** What kind of mistakes can happen during the action implementation step?

_____

_____

_____

**9** What do you do if none of the possibilities you hypothesized ends up being the cause of your network problem?

_____

_____

_____

**10** What are some of the benefits of documenting a solved problem?

_____

_____

_____

This chapter covers the following topics that you will need to master to pass the CCNP Support exam:

| Objective | Description |
|---|---|
| 1 | Discuss data link troubleshooting targets using Cisco innate **show interface**, **show controller**, and **show cdp** commands. |
| 2 | Identify common protocol characteristics and connection sequences. |
| 3 | Understand TCP connection sequence and discuss the IP ARP protocol. |
| 4 | Understand Novell connection sequence and the **show novell traffic** command's output. |
| 5 | Understand AppleTalk connection sequence and the **show appletalk traffic** command's output. |

# CHAPTER 3

# Identifying Troubleshooting Targets

During systematic internetwork troubleshooting, based on the gathered facts—and also, of course, on your expertise and knowledge of the network baseline—you consider possibilities. It is natural to desire to become more and more effective in identifying the troubleshooting targets. Your success in troubleshooting is often measured by how fast you can correctly identify the trouble causes, fix the faults, and communicate the results. You are familiar with the layered network model (OSI) and understand the dependency of each layer on the correct operation of the layers below it. If user applications have problems connecting over the network, you must first ensure that the underlying protocols (routing, transport, and routed protocols) are working correctly. If the lower layer protocols also have problems, before you start troubleshooting those you must ensure that all data link layer protocols are functioning properly. And likewise, you should not start troubleshooting the data link layer unless you are confident that the physical layer is in good working condition.

## "Do I Know This Already?" Quiz

If you wish to evaluate your knowledge of the contents of this chapter before you get started, answer the following questions. The answers are provided in Appendix A, "Answers to Quiz Questions." If you are having difficulty providing correct answers, you should thoroughly review the entire chapter. If all or most of your answers are correct, you might want to skim this chapter for only those subjects you need to review. You can also use the "Foundation Summary" section to quickly review topics. Once you have completed the chapter, you should reevaluate yourself with the questions in the "Q&A" section at the end. Finally, use the companion CD-ROM to evaluate your knowledge of the topics and see if you need a review.

1   What is a key point in identifying troubleshooting targets, with respect to internetwork component dependencies?

_____

_____

_____

**2**  Before starting to troubleshoot the data link layer, what must you assure yourself of?

_____

_____

_____

**3**  Name two of the router components that are often examined when troubleshooting the data link layer.

_____

_____

_____

**4**  What information does the output of the **show interfaces** command provide?

_____

_____

_____

**5**  List at least two types of information displayed by the **show controllers** command.

_____

_____

_____

**6**  How is the MAC address of an interface card formed? How can you see it? Where is it stored? Is it always identical to the bia?

_____

_____

_____

**7**  Why would an Ethernet interface be reported as up and the line protocol be reported as down?

_____

_____

_____

**8**  List at least two types of errors that are common in Token Ring networks.

_____

_____

_____

**9**  What information does a CDP device send out about itself?

_____

_____

_____

**10**  What are the two general classes of networking protocols? (Briefly explain each one.)

_____

_____

_____

## Foundation Topics

# Understanding Data Link Troubleshooting Targets

All networking layers, except the physical layer, rely on the correct operation of the data link (control). If there are faults at this layer, problems such as application fails, cannot make connection, network is slow, data is distorted, and so on will be reported. The data link layer connects devices, which are subsequently called *adjacent devices*. For adjacent devices to communicate, they must send and receive error-free data with a reasonable delay (latency). When troubleshooting the data link layer (with Cisco Routers in place), the interface and in some cases the controller is examined.

# Troubleshooting Physical and Data Link Protocol Characteristics

Troubleshooting of the data link layer should not begin before you are confident that the physical layer is functioning properly. Here are some basic methods of checking the physical layer:

- Look at the first line of the **show interfaces** command and make sure that the interface is up and line protocol is up.

- Look at the link LED of the appropriate interface.

- Manually check and observe for yourself the condition and type of cables, jacks, and connectors (look for damage, standards violation, compatibility, and appropriateness).

- Use physical media test equipment.

By default, a device considers its interface to have a good *link* if the interface is in a good physical state (has initialized properly and the main system can internally communicate with it) and it can send and receive frames to and from the connected medium. The method used to check the latter condition will vary depending on the type of interface.

For example, an Ethernet interface sends (transmits) keepalives every 10 seconds (by default) and listens to traffic (and keepalives) on the segment it is connected to, in order to report on the state of its link. That is why many people say that a connection has hardware and software components.

# Clearing Interface Counters

If you suspect interface problems, the output of the **show interfaces** command gives you a great amount of information about the state of the interface (physical and logical) and also some statistics about the data sent and received, errors encountered, and so on. Consider Example 3-1 for this discussion.

**Example 3-1**  *Interface Counters*

```
A_StubR#show interfaces serial 1
Serial1 is up, line protocol is up
  Hardware is HD64570
  MTU 1500 bytes, BW 1544 Kbit, DLY 20000 usec, rely 255/255, load 1/255
  Encapsulation FRAME-RELAY, loopback not set, keepalive set (10 sec)
  LMI enq sent 22, LMI stat recvd 22, LMI upd recvd 0, DTE LMI up
  LMI enq recvd 0, LMI stat sent 0, LMI upd sent 0
  LMI DLCI 0  LMI type is ANSI Annex D  frame relay DTE
  FR SVC disabled, LAPF state down
  Broadcast queue 0/64, broadcasts sent/dropped 0/0, interface broadcasts 0
  Last input 0:00:06, output 0:00:06, output hang never
  Last clearing of "show interface" counters 00:03:45
  Input queue 0/75/0 (size/max/drops); Total output drops: 0
  Queueing strategy: weighted fair
  Output queue: 0/1000/64/0 (size/max total/threshold/drops)
     Conversations 0/1/256 (allocated/max active/max total)
     Reserved Conversations 0/0 (allocated/max allocated)
  Five minute input rate 0 bits/sec, 0 packets/sec
  Five minute output rate 0 bits/sec, 0 packets/sec
     22 packets input, 368 bytes, 0 no buffer
     Received 0 broadcasts, 0 runts, 0 giants, 0 throttles
     0 input errors, 0 CRC, 0 frame, 0 overrun, 0 ignored, 0 abort
     22 packets output, 308 bytes, 0 underruns
     0 output errors, 0 collisions, 2 interface resets
     0 output buffer failures, 0 output buffers swapped out
     0 carrier transitions
--More--
```

On the bottom section of the output in Example 3-1, you can see that different input, output, and error statistics are shown. In a real troubleshooting scenario, how would the value of those counters be interpreted? The answer to this question is that a set of numbers might be delivering good news in one case and bad news in another case. How you would interpret those numbers depends on two other essential pieces of information:

- When those counters were cleared last

- Knowing the time period through which those counters have accumulated, how those statistics compare to your baseline

Near the middle section of Example 3-1, the output tells you how long ago the "show interface" counters were cleared (3 minutes and 45 seconds ago in this case). If this number grows beyond 24 hours, then it is displayed as the number of days and weeks. The syntax for clearing "show interface" counters is displayed in Example 3-2.

**Example 3-2** *Syntax for Clearing* **show interface** *Counters*

```
A_StubR#clear counters ?
  Ethernet   IEEE 802.3
  Null       Null interface
  Serial     Serial
  TokenRing  IEEE 802.5
  <cr>
A_StubR#clear counters serial ?
  <0-1>  Serial interface number
A_StubR#clear counters serial 1
Clear "show interface" counters on this interface [confirm]
```

# The show interfaces Command

The **show interfaces** command displays the status and statistics information about all of your router's interfaces.

- You cannot display a subset of interfaces based on their type. On the Cisco 7000 series, if you type **show interfaces ethernet**, the **ethernet** keyword is ignored and your command is interpreted as **show interfaces**. On the other hand, if you type **show interfaces ethernet** on a Cisco 2502 router running IOS version 11.2(13), you get the "% Incomplete command" response:

```
A_StubR#show interfaces ethernet
% Incomplete command.
A_StubR#
```

Hence, you have a choice to see all the interfaces by typing **show interfaces**, or you can look at one interface at a time by typing the interface type and slot/port number as well.

- Those interfaces that have been removed continue to be displayed until the time that the router reloads. However, on the output you will see the "Hardware has been removed" message. On the other hand, removed software interfaces (for example, a sub-interface) will continue to be displayed (until reload), but will be reported as deleted:

```
Serial0.1 is deleted, line protocol is down
  Hardware is HD64570
  MTU 1500 bytes, BW 1544 Kbit, DLY 20000 usec, rely 255/255, load 1/255
  Encapsulation HDLC
```

- Those interfaces that you shut down are displayed as administratively down:

```
A_StubR#show interfaces serial 0
Serial0 is administratively down, line protocol is down
  Hardware is HD64570
  MTU 1500 bytes, BW 1544 Kbit, DLY 20000 usec, rely 255/255, load 1/255
  Encapsulation HDLC, loopback not set, keepalive set (10 sec)
```

# The show interfaces ethernet *n* Command

The **show interfaces ethernet** *n* command allows you to examine the status of an Ethernet interface (*n* specifies which one) and to get some fairly in-depth information on that interface's performance. Example 3-3 shows a sample output of the **show interfaces ethernet0** command.

**Example 3-3**   *The show interfaces ethernet 0 Command Output*

```
A_BackR# show interfaces ethernet 0

Ethernet 0 is up, Line protocol is up
  Hardware is Lance, address is 0010.7b2c.5b18 (bia 0010.7b2c.5b18)
  Description: To Switch
  Internet address is 131.1.18.1/22
  MTU 1500 bytes, BW 10000 Kbit, DLY 1000 usec, rely 255/255, load 1/255
  Encapsulation ARPA, loopback not set, keepalive set (10 sec)
  ARP type: ARPA, ARP Timeout 04:00:00
  Last input 00:00:01, output 00:00:06, output hang never
  Last clearing of "show interface" counters never
  Queueing strategy: fifo
  Output queue 0/40, 0 drops; input queue 0/75, 0 drops
  5 minute input rate 0 bits/sec, 0 packets/sec
  5 minute output rate 0 bits/sec, 0 packets/sec
     21605 packets input, 1876439 bytes, 0 no buffer
     Received 16892 broadcasts, 0 runts, 0 giants, 0 throttles
     0 input errors, 0 CRC, 0 frame, 0 overrun, 0 ignored, 0 abort
     0 input packets with dribble condition detected
     27823 packets output, 2994125 bytes, 0 underruns
     1 output errors, 0 collisions, 5 interface resets
```

The Cisco Documentation CD provides the descriptions for the fields of the **show interfaces ethernet** *n* command (see Table 3-1).

**Table 3-1**   *show interfaces ethernet Field Descriptions (from the Cisco Documentation CD)*

| Field | Description |
|---|---|
| Ethernet n is {up l down l administratively down} | Indicates whether the interface hardware is currently active and if it has been taken down by an administrator. "Disabled" indicates that the router has received over 5000 errors in a keepalive interval, which is 10 seconds by default. |
| Line protocol is {up l down} | Indicates whether the software processes that handle the line protocol believe that the interface is usable (that is, whether keepalives are successful). |
| Hardware | Hardware type (for example, MCI Ethernet, SCI, cBus Ethernet) and address. |

*continues*

**Table 3-1** *show interfaces ethernet Field Descriptions (from the Cisco Documentation CD) (Continued)*

| Field | Description |
|-------|-------------|
| Internet address | Internet address followed by subnet mask. |
| MTU | Maximum Transmission Unit of the interface. |
| BW | Bandwidth of the interface in kilobits per second. |
| DLY | Delay of the interface in microseconds. |
| Rely | Reliability of the interface as a fraction of 255 (255/255 is 100% reliability), calculated as an exponential average over 5 minutes. |
| Load | Load on the interface as a fraction of 255 (255/255 is completely saturated), calculated as an exponential average over 5 minutes. |
| Encapsulation | Encapsulation method assigned to interface. |
| ARP type | Type of Address Resolution Protocol assigned. |
| Loopback | Indicates whether loopback is set or not. |
| Keepalive | Indicates whether keepalives are set or not. |
| Last input | Number of hours, minutes, and seconds since the last packet was successfully received by an interface. Useful for knowing when a dead interface failed. |
| Last output | Number of hours, minutes, and seconds since the last packet was successfully transmitted by the interface. Useful for knowing when a dead interface failed. |
| Output hang | Number of hours, minutes, and seconds (or never) since the interface was last reset because of a transmission that took too long. When the number of hours in any of the "last" fields exceeds 24 hours, the number of days and hours is printed. If that field overflows, asterisks are printed. |

**Table 3-1**    *show interfaces ethernet* Field Descriptions (from the Cisco Documentation CD) (Continued)

| Field | Description |
| --- | --- |
| Last clearing | Time at which the counters that measure cumulative statistics (such as number of bytes transmitted and received) shown in this report were last reset to zero. Note that variables that might affect routing (for example, load and reliability) are not cleared when the counters are cleared. |
| | Asterisks indicate the elapsed time is too large to be displayed. |
| | 0:00:00 indicates the counters were cleared more than 231ms (and less than 232ms) ago. |
| Output queue, input queue, drops | Number of packets in output and input queues. Each number is followed by a slash, the maximum size of the queue, and the number of packets dropped due to a full queue. |
| 5 minute input rate<br><br>5 minute output rate | Average number of bits and packets transmitted per second in the last 5 minutes. If the interface is not in promiscuous mode, it senses network traffic it sends and receives (rather than all network traffic). |
| | The 5-minute input and output rates should be used only as an approximation of traffic per second during a given 5-minute period. These rates are exponentially weighted averages with a time constant of 5 minutes. A period of four time constants must pass before the average will be within two percent of the instantaneous rate of a uniform stream of traffic over that period. |
| Packets input | Total number of error-free packets received by the system. |
| No buffers | Number of received packets discarded because there was no buffer space in the main system. Compare with ignored count. Broadcast storms on Ethernets and bursts of noise on serial lines are often responsible for no input buffer events. |
| Received *n* broadcasts by the interface | Total number of broadcast or multicast packets received. |

*continues*

**Table 3-1** *show interfaces ethernet Field Descriptions (from the Cisco Documentation CD) (Continued)*

| Field | Description |
| --- | --- |
| Total runts | Number of packets that are discarded because they are smaller than the medium's minimum packet size. For instance, any Ethernet packet that is less than 64 bytes is considered a runt. |
| Total giants | Number of packets that are discarded because they exceed the medium's maximum packet size. For example, any Ethernet packet that is greater than 1518 bytes is considered a giant.<br><br>(There is an exception to this rule. When 802.1q trunking is implemented, if the frame is larger than 1518 bytes, it is registered as a giant, but it is not discarded.) |
| Input error | Includes runts, giants, no buffer, CRC, frame, overrun, and ignored counts. Other input-related errors can also cause the input errors count to be increased, and some datagrams may have more than one error; therefore, this sum may not balance with the sum of enumerated input error counts. |
| CRC | Cyclic redundancy checksum generated by the originating LAN station or far-end device does not match the checksum calculated from the data received. On a LAN, this usually indicates noise or transmission problems on the LAN interface or the LAN bus itself. A high number of CRCs is usually the result of collisions or a station transmitting bad data. |
| Frame | Number of packets received incorrectly having a CRC error and a noninteger number of octets. On a LAN, this is usually the result of collisions or a malfunctioning Ethernet device. |
| Overrun | Number of times the receiver hardware was unable to hand received data to a hardware buffer because the input rate exceeded the receiver's ability to handle the data. |

**Table 3-1**     *show interfaces ethernet Field Descriptions (from the Cisco Documentation CD) (Continued)*

| Field | Description |
|---|---|
| Ignored | Number of received packets ignored by the interface because the interface hardware ran low on internal buffers. These buffers are different than the system buffers that reside in the shared memory. Broadcast storms and bursts of noise can cause the ignored count to be increased. |
| Dribble condition detected | Dribble bit condition indicates that carrier sense did not go inactive on a receive data byte boundary. |
| Packets output | Total number of messages transmitted by the system. |
| Bytes | Total number of bytes, including data and MAC encapsulation, transmitted by the system. |
| Underruns | Number of times that the transmitter has been running faster than the router can handle. This may never be reported on some interfaces. |
| Output errors | Sum of all errors that prevented the final transmission of datagrams out of the interface being examined. Note that this may not balance with the sum of the enumerated output errors, as some datagrams may have more than one error, and others may have errors that do not fall into any of the specifically tabulated categories. |
| Collisions | Number of messages retransmitted due to an Ethernet collision. Collisions are considered normal in Ethernet environment (CSMA/CD). However, excessive collisions are not acceptable and they are usually due to a malfunctioning card somewhere on the Ethernet. The rule of thumb is that a segment has too many collisions if the number of collisions is higher than about 0.1% of the total number of the output packets. A packet that collides is counted only once in output packets. |
| Late collisions | This is usually the result of an overextended LAN (Ethernet or transceiver cable too long, more than two repeaters between stations, or too many cascaded multiport transceivers). |

*continues*

**Table 3-1** *show interfaces ethernet Field Descriptions (from the Cisco Documentation CD) (Continued)*

| Field | Description |
|-------|-------------|
| Interface resets | Number of times an interface has been completely reset. This can happen if packets queued for transmission were not sent within several seconds. On a serial line, this can be caused by a malfunctioning modem that is not supplying the transmit clock signal, or by a cable problem. If the system notices that the carrier detect line of a serial interface is up, but the line protocol is down, it periodically resets the interface in an effort to restart it. Interface resets can also occur when an interface is looped back or shut down. |
| Restarts | Number of times a Type 2 Ethernet controller was restarted because of errors. |

In the **show interfaces ethernet 0** output in Example 3-3, you can see the following line:

```
Ethernet0 is up, Line Protocol is up
```

If the interface experiences more than 5000 errors during the keepalive interval (10 seconds by default), it will be reported as disabled. If the interface is configured with the **shutdown** command, it will be reported as administratively down. If the interface is not up, the line protocol will not be up either. Now consider cases where the interface is up, but still there are problems on the interface:

- **Case 1, Ethernet0 is Up, Line Protocol is Down**—In this case, the interface keepalive is failing. One reason might be that the interface is not (or is improperly) connected to the media. In certain types of interfaces where connectors—for example, an AUI and an RJ-45—are both provided, the AUI is usually the default medium. Hence, another reason for this condition could be that the media type is not auto-sensed and the administrator failed to specify the correct media type (this is an interface configuration task). To check the current media-type setting, use the **show controllers ethernet** *n* command (*n* identifies the Ethernet interface to be examined).

- **Case 2, Ethernet0 is Up, Line Protocol is Up**—If you experience problems with an interface that is up and shows the line protocol as up too, it is possible that the interface card needs to be reseated. This, of course, applies to modular routers such as the 4000 series. It is also possible that the cable is not connected to the interface card. You might say that in this case the line protocol must be down. However, if you disable the keepalive on an interface (the **no keepalive** command is an interface configuration task), even though the interface is not connected to the medium, the line protocol will be reported as being up. (I sometimes do this in the Cisco Internetwork Troubleshooting course trouble-ticket labs.)

On the second line of the **show interfaces ethernet 0** output in Example 3-3, the MAC (Media Access Control) address and bia (burned-in address) of the interface are shown. The bia is composed of OUI (Organizational Unique Identifier, the 6 leftmost hex digits/24 bits) and serial number (the 6 rightmost hex digits/24 bits). The bia is stored in the ROM (Read-Only Memory) of the interface hardware. Each manufacturer has at least one unique OUI registered. The bia of an interface card is theoretically unique universally (due to the 24-bit limitation, manufacturers may reuse very old serial numbers). The MAC address of the interface is stored in the RAM (Random Access Memory is read/write). The MAC address of the interface is copied from its ROM/bia during the initialization of the interface card. Hence, the bia and the MAC address are usually identical. However, in the following cases the bia and MAC address may not be the same:

- The administrator of the router hard-codes the MAC address (the ability to do this is IOS/version dependent).

- An upper-layer protocol modifies the MAC address (e.g. DECNET does that).

For example, assume that the **show interfaces ethernet 0** command displays the following as the second line of the output:

```
Hardware is MCI ethernet, address is aa00.0400.0134 (bia 0000.0c00.4369)
```

The bia and the MAC address are different in this case. The OUI component of the MAC address is aa0004. The number aa0004 is registered as the local logical address for systems running DECNET. Now we know the reason for the bia and the MAC address not being identical.

You might wonder, however, where the rest of the digits of the MAC address come from. The 16-bit addressing mechanism of DECNET embeds the logical address (Layer 3) of a node in its MAC address in a unique way. The DECNET address of an interface is a dotted decimal number (area.node). The area is a decimal number between 1 and 63 (6 bits) and the node is a decimal number between 1 and 1023 (10 bits). In this example, the Ethernet interface is configured with the address 13.1 (area.node).

In case you are wondering how I know that, I calculated this address backward from the MAC address. You will be able to do that too, but first concentrate on how DECNET converts an area.node dotted decimal notation to a DECNET MAC address. DECNET multiplies the area number by 1024 and adds it to the node number. The result, in this example, is 13313 ($1024 \times 13 + 1$) in decimal format. The decimal number 13313 translates to 3401 in hexadecimal (base 16) format. Next, the place of two leftmost hex digits and the two rightmost hex digits are interchanged (this is DECNET's famous byte-swapping), resulting in 0134. Finally, this number is added to aa00.0400, resulting in aa00.0400.0134, as shown on the sample line before this paragraph.

# The show interfaces tokenring *n* Command

The **show interfaces tokenring** *n* command allows you to examine the status of a Token Ring interface (*n* specifies which one) and the state of source-route bridging, and to get some fairly in-depth information on that interface's performance. Example 3-4 shows a sample output of the **show interfaces tokenring** command. The Cisco Documentation CD provides the descriptions for the fields of the **show interfaces tokenring** *n* command. Table 3-2 presents some of the field descriptions (from the Cisco Documentation CD). Since this section focuses on Token Ring–specific topics, those fields that are already presented in Table 3-1 (for Ethernet interface) are not repeated in Table 3-2.

**Example 3-4**   *The show interfaces tokenring 0 Command Output*

```
A_StubR#show interfaces tokenring 0
TokenRing0 is up, line protocol is up
  Hardware is TMS380, address is 5500.2000.dc27 (bia 0008.deec.9d1a)
  description: Stub Token Ring
  Internet address is 131.1.15.100/22
  MTU 4464 bytes, BW 16000 kbit, DLY 630 usec, rely 255/255, load 1/255
  Encapsulation SNAP, loopback not set, keepalive set (10 sec)
  ARP type: SNAP, ARP timeout 04:00:00
  Ring speed: 16 Mbps
  Single ring node, Source Route Transparent Bridge capable
  Group Address: 0x00000000, Functional Address: 0x48808000
  Last input 0:00:01, output 0:00:01, output hang never
  Output queue 0/40, 0 drops; input queue 0/75, 0 drops
  Five minute input rate 0 bits/sec, 0 packets/sec
  Five minute output rate 0 bits/sec, 0 packets/sec
     16339 packets input, 1496515 bytes, 0 no buffer
     Received 9895 broadcasts, 0 runts, 0 giants
     0 input errors, 0 CRC, 0 frame, 0 overrun, 0 ignored, 0 abort
     32648 packets output, 9738303 bytes, 0 underruns
     0 output errors, 0 collisions, 2 interface resets, 0 restarts
     5 transitions
```

**Table 3-2**   *show interfaces tokenring 0 Command Output Field Descriptions*

| Field | Description |
| --- | --- |
| Token Ring is {up | down} | Interface is either currently active and inserted into ring (up) or inactive and not inserted (down). |
| | The Cisco 7000, for example, gives the interface processor type, slot number, and port number. |
| | "Disabled" indicates the router has received over 5000 errors in a keepalive interval, which is 10 seconds by default. |
| Token Ring is reset | Hardware error has occurred. |

**Table 3-2**    *show interfaces tokenring 0 Command Output Field Descriptions (Continued)*

| Field | Description |
|---|---|
| Token Ring is initializing | Hardware is up, in the process of inserting the ring. |
| Token Ring is administratively down | Hardware has been taken down by an administrator. |
| Line protocol is {up \| down \| administratively down} | Indicates whether the software processes that handle the line protocol believe the interface is usable (that is, whether keepalives are successful). |
| Hardware | Hardware type. "Hardware is Token Ring" indicates that the board is a CSC-R board. "Hardware is 16/4 Token Ring" indicates that the board is a CSC-R16 board. Also shows the address of the interface. |
| Ring speed | Speed of Token Ring—4 or 16 Mbps. |
| {Single ring/multiring node} | Indicates whether a node is enabled to collect and use source routing information (RIF), for Source Route Bridging purposes, for instance. |
| Group address | Interface's group address, if any. The group address is a multicast address; any number of interfaces on the ring may share the same group address. Each interface may have at most one group address. |
| Functional address | A severely restricted form of multicast addressing implemented on Token Ring interfaces. There are only 31 Functional Addresses available. |
| Collisions | Since a Token Ring cannot have collisions, this statistic is nonzero only if an unusual event occurred when frames were being queued or dequeued by the system software. |

In contrast to the Ethernet case, if you disconnect the cable from the Token Ring interface, the first line of the **show interface tokenring** *n* output will not report the interface being up and the line protocol as down. What you will see is: "Interface is Initializing." The reason is that the Token Ring firmware insists on an operational ring and seeing itself properly inserted into the ring. That is why Token Ring is often referred to as a reliable/self-administered technology. The interface goes into down state after a series of unsuccessful initialization attempts. The cycle continues, until the problem is fixed.

On the second line of the output in Example 3-4, the bia is reported as 0008.deec.9d1a, and the MAC address is reported as 5500.2000.dc27. If you recall, the MAC address might be configured by an administrator or by an upper-layer protocol. How do you find out? You must see if the 6 leftmost hex digits match any OUIs. But here, since this is a Token Ring interface address, you must first reverse the bit ordering of each byte.

If you reverse the bits of each byte in 550020 (this is a hex number), the result will be aa0004 in hexadecimal. As you may recall from the previous section, systems running DECNET have the aa0004 as their MAC's OUI.

# The show controllers Command

The **show controllers** command displays information on all of the router's controllers. However, you can specify the type of controller so that only the information on that particular controller is displayed. Depending on the router you work with, it may have BRI, CBus, E1, Ethernet, FastEthernet, FDDI, Lex, MCI, PCBus, serial, T1, T3, Token, or VG-Anylan controllers. This command displays a variety of data such as firmware versions, memory management, and error counters for each controller's interface card(s). The displayed output may seem overwhelming; the reason is that a large portion of the displayed output comprises proprietary (and in some cases obsolete and irrelevant) information. However, in each set of output there are pieces of information that can be extremely useful for troubleshooting. For instance, the output of the **show controllers ethernet** command displays the media type each Ethernet interface is configured for. This section (in accordance with the CIT student book) will examine certain components of the **show controllers token** output (see Example 3-5 for a sample of this command's output) that can be useful for troubleshooting purposes.

**Example 3-5**  *The **show controllers token** Command Output*

```
A_StubR# show controllers token
TR Unit 0 is board 0 - ring 0
 state 3, dev blk: 0x1D2EBC, mailbox: 0x2100010, sca: 0x2010000
   current address: 0000.3080.6f40, burned in address: 0000.3080.6f40
   current TX ptr: 0xBA8, current RX ptr: 0x800
   Last Ring Status: none
 Stats: soft:0/0, hard:0/0, sig loss:0/0
        tx beacon: 0/0, wire fault 0/0, recovery: 0/0
        only station: 0/0, remote removal: 0/0
   Bridge: local 3330, bnum 1, target 3583
     max_hops 7, target idb: 0x0, not local
   Interface failures: 0  -- Bkgnd Ints: 0
   TX shorts 0, TX giants 0
   Monitor state: (active)
     flags 0xC0, state 0x0, test 0x0, code 0x0, reason 0x0
 f/w ver: 1.0, chip f/w: '000000.ME31100', [bridge capable]
     SMT versions: 1.01 kernel, 4.02 fastmac
     ring mode: F00, internal enables:  SRB REM RPS CRS/NetMgr
     internal functional: 0000011A (0000011A), group: 00000000 (00000000)
```

**Example 3-5**  *The **show controllers token** Command Output (Continued)*

```
        if_state: 1, ints: 0/0, ghosts: 0/0, bad_states: 0/0
        t2m fifo purges: 0/0
        t2m fifo current: 0, t2m fifo max: 0/0, proto_errs: 0/0
        ring: 3330, bridge num: 1, target: 3583, max hops: 7
Packet counts:
        receive total:  298/6197, small: 298/6197, large 0/0
                runts: 0/0, giants: 0/0
                local: 298/6197, bridged: 0/0, promis: 0/0
            bad rif: 0/0, multiframe: 0/0
        ring num mismatch 0/0, spanning violations 0
        transmit total: 1/25, small: 1/25, large 0/0
                runts: 0/0, giants: 0/0, errors 0/0
bad fs: 0/0, bad ac: 0
congested: 0/0, not present: 0/0
        Unexpected interrupts: 0/0,  last unexp. int: 0
        Internal controller counts:
            line errors: 0/0,  internal errors: 0/0
            burst errors: 0/0,  ari/fci errors: 0/0
            abort errors: 0/0, lost frame: 0/0
            copy errors: 0/0, rcvr congestion: 0/0
            token errors: 0/0, frequency errors: 0/0
            dma bus errors: -/-, dma parity errors: -/-
        Internal controller smt state:
            Adapter MAC:      0000.3080.6f40, Physical drop:      00000000
            NAUN Address:     0000.a6e0.11a6, NAUN drop:         00000000
            Last source:      0000.a6e0.11a6, Last poll:         0000.3080.6f40
            Last MVID:        0006,           Last attn code:    0006
            Txmit priority:   0006,           Auth Class:        7FFF
            Monitor Error:    0000,           Interface Errors:  FFFF
            Correlator:       0000,           Soft Error Timer:  00C8
            Local Ring:       0000,           Ring Status:       0000
            Beacon rcv type:  0000,           Beacon txmit type: 0000
            Beacon type:      0000,           Beacon NAUN:       0000.a6e0.11a6
```

As you can see, the **show controller token** command also displays the MAC address and bia of the Token Ring interface(s). Now let us examine some selected pieces of the output from Example 3-5, one at a time.

# The show controller token Command Section 1

```
        Stats: soft:0/0, hard:0/0, sig loss:0/0
               tx beacon: 0/0, wire fault 0/0, recovery: 0/0
               only station: 0/0, remote removal: 0/0
        Bridge: local 3330, bnum 1, target 3583
          max_hops 7, target idb: 0x0, not local
        Interface failures: 0  -- Bkgnd Ints: 0
        TX shorts 0, TX giants 0
        Monitor state: (active)
```

In the preceding lines, you can see that certain parameters such as soft, hard, and sig loss are displayed with a number/number. The number before the slash—for example soft (errors)—counts the number of errors since the last time the show controllers token was executed. The number after the slash counts the total number of errors (since the counter was cleared) minus the number before the slash. On the following two lines, the number of transmitted beacons, wire faults, recoveries, the only station (on the ring) conditions, and the number of times this node was remotely removed from the ring by a management application are also displayed. The following line informs you that the Token Ring interface is configured as being connected to the local ring number 3330 and is connected to the target ring number 3583 via bridge number 1 (which this router is configured to act as). Next, the number of interface failures and background initializations, transmitted shorts (runts) and giants, and the monitor state are displayed.

As a review point, it is worthwhile mentioning that stations on a Token Ring transmit beacon frames as a Token Ring fault detection/repair mechanism whenever they experience network problems such as wire fault and signal loss.

## The show controller token Command Section 2

```
Packet counts:
      receive total:  298/6197, small: 298/6197, large 0/0
             runts: 0/0, giants: 0/0
             local: 298/6197, bridged: 0/0, promis: 0/0
          bad rif: 0/0, multiframe: 0/0
      ring num mismatch 0/0, spanning violations 0
      transmit total: 1/25, small: 1/25, large 0/0
             runts: 0/0, giants: 0/0, errors 0/0
```

In the preceding lines you can see that several different packet counts are displayed. Notice that the ring number mismatch and spanning tree violations counters could be significant for troubleshooting purposes. For instance, if the value for the ring num mismatch is nonzero, you have evidence that this device and other devices refer to the same ring with different ring numbers. As a part of your action, you must discover which devices disagree about the ring number and fix the misconfigured device(s).

## The show controller token Command Section 3

```
Internal controller counts:
      line errors: 0/0,  internal errors: 0/0
      burst errors: 0/0,  ari/fci errors: 0/0
      abort errors: 0/0, lost frame: 0/0
      copy errors: 0/0, rcvr congestion: 0/0
      token errors: 0/0, frequency errors: 0/0
      dma bus errors: -/-, dma parity errors: -/-
Internal controller smt state:
      Adapter MAC:      0000.3080.6f40, Physical drop:      00000000
      NAUN Address:     0000.a6e0.11a6, NAUN drop:          00000000
      Last source:      0000.a6e0.11a6, Last poll:          0000.3080.6f40
      Last MVID:        0006,           Last attn code:     0006
      Txmit priority:   0006,           Auth Class:         7FFF
```

```
Monitor Error:    0000,        Interface Errors:  FFFF
Correlator:       0000,        Soft Error Timer:  00C8
Local Ring:       0000,        Ring Status:       0000
Beacon rcv type:  0000,        Beacon txmit type: 0000
Beacon type:      0000,        Beacon NAUN:       0000.a6e0.11a6
```

The preceding information is provided by the controller chipset. The top portion of this section reports the soft errors this station has experienced. The line errors, burst errors, and receive-congested errors are among the most common errors in tokenring networks. The line error counter increments as CRC check failures occur. The burst error counters report on signaling errors seen (these are usually due to noise and/or crosstalk). The receive-congested error counter tells you if the station has had difficulty keeping up with processing of the received traffic. In cases where these counters are nonzero and require investigation, use a network monitor or protocol analyzer to capture traffic and investigate which stations are acting up or to find out if you need to test the media or tokenring hardware and cabling.

## Token Ring Soft Errors

The Token Ring soft errors are divided into two classes: isolating soft errors and non-isolating soft errors. Isolating soft errors are those that are caused by the local station, its NAUN (Nearest Active Upstream Neighbor), or devices/medium in between the two. Notice that the lower part from "The **show controller token** Command Section 3" output informs you of the local station's and NAUN's MAC addresses. The non-isolating soft errors are not necessarily caused by the local station or its NAUN; these errors can be caused by device(s) anywhere in the ring. Tables 3-3 and 3-4 list the group of soft errors belonging to each class with a short description of each error.

**Table 3-3**    *Token Ring Isolating Soft Errors*

| | |
|---|---|
| Line error | CRC errors |
| Internal error | The number of recoverable internal station errors (station is in a marginal state). |
| Burst error | Incorrect incoming signal (usually due to cross-talk or noise). |
| ARI/FCI error | More than one "active monitor present" or "standby monitor present" frame was received, where the address was recognized and the frame copied bits equal zero. Indicates a problem with the neighbor notification (ring poll). This is usually caused by NAUN. |
| Abort error | Errors during frame transmission. |

**Table 3-4**    *Token Ring Non-Isolating Soft Errors*

| | |
|---|---|
| Lost frame | Sent frame never returned to the sender. |
| Copy error | Frame destined for the station was received with the address-recognized bit set. This is due to duplicate MAC addresses. |
| Receive congested | The station has been unable to copy all the data sent to it. The station could be congested because another station sends it too much data. |
| Token error | Generated by Active Monitor and is a valid action, unless it happens too often. |
| Frequency error | Error in the frequency of the incoming signal. The Active Monitor is responsible for compensating for this. You may want to replace the Active Monitor by temporarily removing it from the ring. |

# The show interfaces fddi Command

The **show interfaces fddi** command, similarly to other **show interface** commands, displays information about the state of your FDDI interface(s). Understanding the output of the **show interfaces fddi** command requires at least a basic level of knowledge of how different devices (SAS, DAS, DAC) connect to the FDDI ring, and of the initialization sequences of the FDDI management components (PCM, CMT, CFM, RMT, ECM, and SMT). Detailed coverage of FDDI technology, FDDI Finite State Machine, and FDDI component initialization processes are beyond the scope of this material. Hence, in this section only sample output of the **show interfaces fddi** command is displayed in Example 3-6. Immediately following Example 3-6, Table 3-5 provides a brief description of the FDDI-specific fields of the **show interfaces fddi** command for your reference.

**Example 3-6**    *The show interfaces fddi Command Output*

```
Test> show interfaces fddi 3/0
Fddi3/0 is up, line protocol is up
  Hardware is cxBus Fddi, address is 0000.0c02.adf1 (bia 0000.0c02.adf1)
  Internet address is 192.168.33.14, subnet mask is 255.255.255.0
  MTU 4470 bytes, BW 100000 Kbit, DLY 100 usec, rely 255/255, load 1/255
  Encapsulation SNAP, loopback not set, keepalive not set
  ARP type: SNAP, ARP Timeout 4:00:00
  Phy-A state is  active, neighbor is B, cmt signal bits 008/20C, status ILS
  Phy-B state is  active, neighbor is A, cmt signal bits 20C/008, status ILS
  ECM is in, CFM is thru, RMT is ring_op
  Token rotation 5000 usec, ring operational 21:32:34
  Upstream neighbor 0000.0c02.ba83, downstream neighbor 0000.0c02.ba83
  Last input 0:00:05, output 0:00:00, output hang never
  Last clearing of "show interface" counters 0:59:10
```

**Example 3-6**   *The show interfaces fddi Command Output (Continued)*

```
Output queue 0/40, 0 drops; input queue 0/75, 0 drops
Five minute input rate 69000 bits/sec, 44 packets/sec
Five minute output rate 0 bits/sec, 1 packets/sec
    113157 packets input, 21622582 bytes, 0 no buffer
    Received 276 broadcasts, 0 runts, 0 giants
    0 input errors, 0 CRC, 0 frame, 0 overrun, 0 ignored, 0 abort
    4740 packets output, 487346 bytes, 0 underruns
    0 output errors, 0 collisions, 0 interface resets, 0 restarts
    0 transitions, 2 traces, 3 claims, 2 beacons
```

**Table 3-5**   *show interfaces fddi Field Descriptions (from the Cisco Documentation CD)*

| Field | Description |
|---|---|
| Phy-{A ǀ B} | Lists the state the Physical A or Physical B connection is in: off, break, trace, connect, next, signal, join, verify, or active: |
| | **Off**—Indicates that the CMT is not running on the Physical Sublayer. The state will be off if the interface has been shut down or if the **cmt disconnect** command has been issued for Physical A or Physical B. |
| | **Brk**—Break State is the entry point in the start of a PCM connection. |
| | **Tra**—Trace State localizes a stuck beacon condition. |
| | **Con**—Connect State synchronizes the ends of the connection for the signaling sequence. |
| | **Nxt**—Next State separates the signaling performed in the Signal State and transmits Protocol Data Units (PDUs) while MAC Local Loop is performed. |
| | **Sig**—Signal State is entered from the Next State when a bit is ready to be transmitted. |
| | **Join**—Join State is the first of three states in a unique sequence of transmitted symbol streams received as line states—the Halt Line State, Master Line State, and Idle Line State, or HLS-MLS-ILS—that lead to an active connection. |
| | **Vfy**—Verify State is the second state in the path to the Active State and will not be reached by a connection that is not synchronized. |
| | **Act**—Active State indicates that the CMT process has established communications with its physical neighbor. |
| | The transition states are defined in the X3T9.5 specification. You are referred to the specification for details about these states. |

*continues*

**Table 3-5**   *show interfaces fddi Field Descriptions (from the Cisco Documentation CD) (Continued)*

| Field | Description |
| --- | --- |
| Neighbor | State of the neighbor: |
| | **A**—Indicates that the CMT process has established a connection with its neighbor. The bits received during the CMT signaling process indicate that the neighbor is a Physical A type dual-attachment station or concentrator that attaches to the primary ring IN and the secondary ring OUT when attaching to the dual ring. |
| | **S**—Indicates that the CMT process has established a connection with its neighbor and that the bits received during the CMT signaling process indicate that the neighbor is one Physical type in a single-attached station (SAS). |
| | **B**—Indicates that the CMT process has established a connection with its neighbor and that the bits received during the CMT signaling process indicate that the neighbor is a Physical B dual-attached station or concentrator that attaches to the secondary ring IN and the primary ring OUT when attaching to the dual ring. |
| | **M**—Indicates that the CMT process has established a connection with its neighbor and that the bits received during the CMT signaling process indicate that the router's neighbor is a Physical M-type concentrator that serves as a Master to a connected station or concentrator. |
| | **unk**—Indicates that the network server has not completed the CMT process and, as a result, does not know about its neighbor. |
| Cmt signal bits | Shows the transmitted/received CMT bits. The transmitted bits are 0x008 for a Physical A type and 0x20C for Physical B type. The number after the slash (/) is the received signal bits. If the connection is not active, the received bits are zero (0); see the line beginning "Phy-{A \| B}" earlier in this table. |

**Table 3-5**    *show interfaces fddi* Field Descriptions (from the Cisco Documentation CD) (Continued)

| Field | Description |
|---|---|
| Status | Status value displayed is the actual status on the fiber. The FDDI standard defines the following values: |
| | **LSU**—Line State Unknown. Indicates that the criteria for entering or remaining in any other line state have not been met. |
| | **NLS**—Noise Line State. Entered upon the occurrence of 16 potential noise events without satisfying the criteria for entry into another line state. |
| | **MLS**—Master Line State. Entered upon the reception of eight or nine consecutive HQ or QH symbol pairs. |
| | **ILS**—Idle Line State. Entered upon the receipt of four or five idle symbols. |
| | **HLS**—Halt Line State. Entered upon the receipt of 16 or 17 consecutive H symbols. |
| | **QLS**—Quiet Line State. Entered upon the receipt of 16 or 17 consecutive Q symbols or when carrier detect goes low. |
| | **ALS**—Active Line State. Entered upon receipt of a JK symbol pair when carrier detect is high. |
| | **OVUF**—Elasticity buffer Overflow/Underflow. The normal states for a connected Physical type are ILS or ALS. If the report displays the QLS status, this indicates that the fiber is disconnected from Physical B, or that it is not connected to another Physical type, or that the other station is not running. |
| ECM is . . . | ECM is the SMT state entity coordination management, which overlooks the operation of CFM and PCM. The ECM state can be one of the following: |
| | **out**—The router is isolated from the network. |
| | **in**—The router is actively inserted in the network. This is the normal state for a connected router. |
| | **trace**—The router is trying to localize a stuck beacon condition. |
| | **leave**—The router is allowing time for all the connections to break before leaving the network. |
| | **path_test**—The router is testing its internal paths. |
| | **insert**—The router is allowing time for the optical bypass to insert. |
| | **check**—The router is making sure optical bypasses switched correctly. |
| | **deinsert**—The router is allowing time for the optical bypass to deinsert. |

*continues*

**Table 3-5**   *show interfaces fddi* Field Descriptions (from the Cisco Documentation CD) (Continued)

| Field | Description |
|---|---|
| CFM is . . . | Contains information about the current state of the MAC connection. The Configuration Management(CFM) state can be one of the following: |
| | **Isolated**—The MAC is not attached to any Physical type. |
| | **Wrap A**—The MAC is attached to Physical A. Data is received on Physical A and transmitted on Physical A. |
| | **Wrap B**—The MAC is attached to Physical B. Data is received on Physical B and transmitted on Physical B. |
| | **Thru A**—The MAC is attached to Physical A and B. Data is received on Physical A and transmitted on Physical B. This is the normal mode for a dual attachment station (DAS) with one MAC. |
| RMT is . . . | RMT (Ring Management) is the SMT MAC-related state machine. The RMT state can be one of the following: |
| | **Isolated**—The MAC is not trying to participate in the ring. This is the initial state. |
| | **non_op**—The MAC is participating in ring recovery and ring is not operational. |
| | **ring_op**—The MAC is participating in an operational ring. This is the normal state while the MAC is connected to the ring. |
| | **detect**—The ring has been nonoperational for longer than normal. Duplicate address conditions are being checked. |
| | **non_op_dup**—Indications have been received that the address of the MAC is a duplicate of another MAC on the ring. Ring is not operational. |
| | **ring_op_dup**—Indications have been received that the address of the MAC is a duplicate of another MAC on the ring. Ring is operational in this state. |
| | **directed**—The MAC is sending beacon frames notifying the ring of the stuck condition. |
| | **trace**—Trace has been initiated by this MAC, and the RMT state machine is waiting for its completion before starting an internal path test. |
| Token rotation | Token rotation value is the default or configured rotation value as determined by the **fddi token rotation-time** command. This value is used by all stations on the ring. The default is 5000 microseconds. |

**Table 3-5**    *show interfaces fddi* Field Descriptions (from the Cisco Documentation CD) (Continued)

| Field | Description |
|---|---|
| Ring operational | When the ring is operational, the displayed value will be the negotiated token rotation time of all stations on the ring. Operational times are displayed by the number of hours:minutes:seconds the ring has been up. If the ring is not operational, the message "ring not operational" is displayed. |
| Upstream \| downstream neighbor | Displays the canonical MAC address of outgoing upstream and downstream neighbors. If the interface is not up, these values will be zero (0). |

# The show interfaces atm Command

As you can see from the sample output of the **show interfaces atm** command in Example 3-7, there are some fields displayed similar to those displayed when you issue other **show interface** commands. For example, the first line of the output of this command displays the state of the physical ATM interface along with the state of its link integrity, as explained in Table 3-6.

**Example 3-7**    *The show interfaces atm Command Output*

```
Test> show int atm 1/0
ATM1/0 is up, line protocol is up
  Hardware is cxBus ATM
  Internet address is 172.16.4.1/24
  MTU 4470 bytes, sub MTU 4470, BW 156250 Kbit, DLY 80 usec, rely 255/255, load 1/255
  NSAP address: 47.0091810000000000605C720201.112233445566.77
  Encapsulation ATM, loopback not set, keepalive not supported
  Encapsulation(s): AAL5, PVC mode
  256 TX buffers, 256 RX buffers,
  2048 maximum active VCs, 1024 VCs per VP, 9 current VCCs
  VC idle disconnect time: 3600 seconds
  Signalling vc = 2, vpi = 0, vci = 5
  UNI Version = 3.0, Link Side = user
  Last input 00:00:00, output 00:00:00, output hang never
  Last clearing of "show interface" counters never
  Queueing strategy: fifo
  Output queue 0/40, 0 drops; input queue 0/75, 0 drops
  5 minute input rate 0 bits/sec, 0 packets/sec
  5 minute output rate 0 bits/sec, 0 packets/sec
     5785 packets input, 308097 bytes, 0 no buffer
     Received 0 broadcasts, 0 runts, 0 giants, 0 throttles
     0 input errors, 0 CRC, 0 frame, 0 overrun, 0 ignored, 0 abort
     6129 packets output, 343264 bytes, 0 underruns
     0 output errors, 0 collisions, 2 interface resets
     0 output buffer failures, 0 output buffers swapped out
```

**Table 3-6**   *Explanation on the First Line of the **show interfaces atm** Command Output*

| Field | Description |
|---|---|
| ATM *x* is {up | down | administratively down} | Indicates if the interface hardware is active, is down, or has been shut down. |
| Line protocol is {up | down} | Indicates if the software processes handling the line protocol consider the link as usable or not. |

On the other hand, there are some fields displayed in the output of the **show interfaces atm** command that are unique to ATM interfaces. Refer to Table 3-7 for a brief description of those fields.

**Table 3-7**   ***show interfaces atm** Field Descriptions (from the Cisco Documentation CD)*

| Field | Description |
|---|---|
| NSAP address | The ATM address (20 byte) based on the structure of the OSI network service access point (NSAP) addresses. |
| Encapsulation(s) | ATM adaptation layer (AAL) and encapsulation type (AAL5, PVC, or SVC mode). |
| TX buffers | The maximum number of transmit buffers for simultaneous packet fragmentation, set using the **atm txbuff** interface configuration command. |
| RX buffers | The maximum number of receive buffers for simultaneous packet reassembly, set using the **atm rxbuff** interface configuration command. |
| Maximum active VCs | Maximum number of supported virtual circuits, set using the **atm maxvc** interface configuration command. Valid values are 256, 512, 1024, or 2048. Default is 2048. |
| VCs per VP | The maximum number of VCIs to support per VPI, set using the **atm vc-per-vp** interface configuration command. |
| Current VCCs | Number of Current Virtual Circuits. |
| VC idle disconnect time | Number of seconds the VC can be inactive before disconnecting. |

**Table 3-7**   *show interfaces atm Field Descriptions (from the Cisco Documentation CD) (Continued)*

| Field | Description |
|---|---|
| Signaling vc = *x*, vpi = *x*, vci = *x* | The signaling Virtual Circuit number, along with its associated vpi/vci pair. |
| | vpi: ATM network virtual path identifier (of PVC) |
| | vci: ATM network virtual channel identifier (of PVC) |
| | The VPI is an 8-bit field in the header of the ATM cell. The VPI value must match that of the switch. |
| | The VCI is a 16-bit field in the header of the ATM cell. The arguments **vpi** and **vci** cannot both be set to 0; if one is 0, the other cannot be 0. |
| UNI version = | The User-Network Interface (UNI) version (3.0, 3.1, or 4.0) determined through ILMI link autodetermination or using the **atm uni-version** interface configuration command. |

# Cisco Discovery Protocol

Cisco Discovery Protocol (CDP) is a Cisco proprietary layer 2 (data link layer) protocol that is bundled in Cisco IOS release 10.3 and later versions. This protocol can run on all Cisco manufactured devices including: routers, switches, hubs, bridges, and communication servers. CDP uses SNAP (layer 2 frame type) and it is multicast based, utilizing the Cisco multicast address 0100.0ccc.cccc as the destination address on the frame header.

Because a Cisco device running CDP periodically sends (multicasts) information about itself on all its links (every 60 seconds by default), neighbor devices (those directly connected) add this device and its corresponding information to their dynamic CDP tables. Neighbors hold the CDP-learned entries/information in their CDP tables and refresh them upon receiving the periodic updates. If a particular device's update is not received by its neighbors, those neighbors hold the entry/information corresponding to that device for up to a period specified by the CDP hold-time value, which is equal to 180 seconds by default. The information supplied by CDP makes it a valuable tool for administrators who can then display information about a Cisco device's directly connected neighbors (Cisco devices as well). A device sends (multicasts) the following information about itself in its CDP updates:

- Device name
- Device capabilities

- Hardware platform

- The port type and number through which CDP information is being sent out

- One address per upper layer protocol

The CDP example of a device is displayed using the **show cdp neighbors** [**detail**] command (see Example 3-8).

**Example 3-8** *Example of the **show cdp neighbors** [**detail**] Command*

```
Test#show cdp neighbors
Capability Codes: R - Router, T - Trans Bridge,
                  B - Source Route Bridge,
                  S - Switch, H - Host, I - IGMP


Device ID     Local Intrfce  Holdtme  Capability Platform  Port ID
sneezy          Eth 0          145       R T        AGS       Eth 0
sleepy          Ser 0          165       R T        AGS       Ser 3


Test#show cdp neighbors detail
-------------------------
Device ID: sneezy
Entry address(es):
  IP address: 192.168.68.18
  CLNS address: 490001.1111.1111.1111.00
  Appletalk address: 69.1
Platform: AGS,  Capabilities: Router Trans-Bridge
Interface: Ethernet0,  Port ID (outgoing port): Ethernet0
Holdtime : 141 sec
```

CDP can be disabled on a router at the global configuration level ([**no**] **cdp run**), which will then disable sending CDP updates out of all interfaces, or it can be disabled on a particular interface only ([**no**] **cdp enable**). The CDP timer and holddown values are only controlled at the global level (using **cdp timer** *x* and **cdp holddown** *y* commands) and cannot be configured on a per-interface basis. The CDP timers should be consistent among neighboring devices. For instance, if router A multicasts its CDP information every 30 seconds (i.e., its CDP timer is set to 30 seconds), but its neighbor, router B, has a holdtime of 20 seconds, router B will delete router A from its CDP table before router A's next multicast. This means that during the next 10 seconds, until router A multicasts its information and is reinserted in router B's table, router B's table is inaccurate.

# Common Protocol Characteristics

Network protocols are divided into two classes based on their characteristics:

- Connection-oriented protocols

- Connectionless protocols

Connection-oriented protocols are those that establish an end-to-end connection before submitting data. The sequence of steps performed by a connection-oriented protocol is as follows:

**Step 1**    Establish a connection.

**Step 2**    Send (and perhaps receive) data.

**Step 3**    Terminate (tear down) the connection.

Most of the connection-oriented protocols are also reliable; in other words, they also guarantee delivery of the data through usage of sequence numbers, acknowledgements, error control mechanisms (such as retransmission), and flow control mechanisms (such as windowing). The TCP transport layer member of the TCP/IP protocol suite and the SPX transport layer member of the IPX/SPX protocol suite are two popular transport layer protocols that are connection oriented and reliable. When troubleshooting these types of protocols, you must watch for connection sequence failure and multiple retransmissions. Some common reasons for connection establishment failures are routing problems, access control configurations, and security policies. Multiple retransmissions could be due to intermittent/marginal/bad links and paths, congestion, or busy devices.

Connectionless protocols, on the other hand, do not establish a connection prior to sending data. In other words, a device using a connectionless protocol sends or receives data to or from its counterpart(s), hoping that the other device is reachable, active, and ready to receive or send data.

An example of this behavior can be observed when using the TFTP (Trivial File Transfer Protocol) application layer member of the TCP/IP protocol suite. TFTP can be used to upload or download files to or from a TFTP server. The syntax of this application layer protocol requires you to enter the address of the TFTP server and the name of the file you wish to download or upload to or from the TFTP server. Upon entering the correct TFTP command and appropriate parameters (for example, for uploading), the data is sent to the requested destination. If the destination is unreachable, or it is merely not available, the data delivery fails and the action has to be repeated. The TFTP application relies on the UDP protocol member of the TCP/IP suite, which is a connectionless/best effort (unreliable) transport layer protocol. You might ask, why would anybody use a connectionless/ unreliable protocol? The answer to this question is that since connectionless protocols have less overhead, they are faster, and also less demanding of network resources. When troubleshooting connectionless protocols, look for failing transactions (such as file transfer failing); these could be due to bad routes, access control configurations, congestion, or other conditions making the path between end devices faulty.

# Understanding Protocol Connection Troubleshooting Targets

In order for a connection between two hosts to be successfully established, all the lower layer protocols must be in working order. For example, a transport layer protocol cannot establish a connection unless the physical layer, data link layer, and network layer are configured and performing properly. You must also keep in mind that in a lot of cases the trouble experienced may not be due to a single cause. This situation is more likely in a large (multi-hop), multi-protocol, and multi-vendor environment. In the following sections, connection sequences of TCP/IP, IPX/SPX, and AppleTalk are presented, in order to help you understand troubleshooting targets in cases where users (client devices) are having trouble making connections to a server.

# TCP Connection Sequence

In this section the sequence of steps involved for a host (host A) to make a TCP connection to a remote host (host B) is presented, based on Figure 3.1.

**Figure 3-1**   *TCP Connection Sequence*

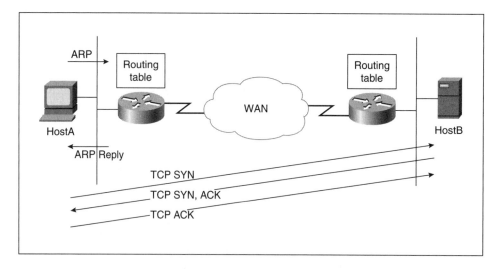

If the remote host (host B) must be accessed using its name, host A needs to have a working name resolution method. For example, PCs running Microsoft Windows software can use a DNS, Wins, LMHOSTS file, HOSTS file, or NetBIOS broadcast to resolve a name to an IP address. Routers can use a DNS or an IP host table for name-to-IP-address resolution.

Once host B's IP address is discovered by host A, host A must gather a MAC address for the frame (i.e., device) via which it shall send the first IP packet (encapsulating the TCP SYN segment) to host B. If the IP address of host B falls within the subnet that host A is connected to, host A simply performs a local ARP to obtain host B's MAC address. However, since host A and host B are on remote networks in this example, host A will either ARP for the local router's IP address (if host A has the local router's interface IP address as its default gateway), or it will ARP for host B's address, hoping that a local router will reply. A local router will reply to the ARP request for host B's IP address if all of the following apply:

- The local router's interface is configured with IP proxy-ARP enabled.

- The router can route (forward) the IP address of host B.

- The local router has not learned about host B's network via the interface on which it is hearing the ARP request.

Host A submits the first TCP segment (SYN) to host B via the local router, which in turn might forward the packet to the next router, and so on, all the way to host B. Please note that the term "segment" in this context refers to the transport layer protocol data unit (PDU)—i.e., do not confuse TCP's segment with a network or subnetwork.

If host B is configured to respond favorably to the TCP segment (SYN) received from host A, it will perform similar functions in order to send the TCP reply segment (SYN, ACK) back to host A. It is worthwhile mentioning that in many cases a packet may correctly get forwarded to a remote device, but the remote device is not able to send the response back (the return path is not working).

Host A will send the third TCP segment (ACK) to host B, and once host B receives that segment, the TCP connection between host A and B is established.

Host A and B can now send data to each other, back and forth.

After data transmissions complete, the connection between host A and host B is terminated.

# The show ip arp Command

Address Resolution Protocol (ARP) is a network layer member of the TCP/IP protocol suite. After an outbound interface is selected by IP routing process, a frame with an encapsulation appropriate for that interface must be formed. An important and necessary field of the frame is its destination MAC address. If the outbound interface is a LAN interface (such as Ethernet), ARP discovers a MAC address to be used for the outgoing frame through a broadcast-based request. The request includes the IP address for which the ARP process is attempting to find a MAC address. If no reply is received, frame delivery (and naturally the intended IP packet delivery) fails and an appropriate ICMP message is generated. If a reply is received with a MAC address, the MAC address will be used and also stored in the ARP table (cache) for a predetermined period of time. The purpose of the ARP cache is to prevent sending ARP requests repeatedly for the following frames that are part of the same conversation as the first (for which the original ARP request was performed). To display the Address Resolution Protocol (ARP) cache, use the **show ip arp** EXEC command:

```
show ip arp [ip-address] [hostname] [mac-address] [type number]
```

The following explains the syntax of the command:

- *ip-address*—(Optional) ARP entries matching this IP address are displayed.

- *hostname*—(Optional) ARP entries matching this hostname are displayed.

- *mac-address*—(Optional) ARP entries matching this 48-bit MAC address are displayed.

- *type number*—(Optional) ARP entries learned via this interface type and number are displayed.

Viewing the IP ARP table allows you to determine which device replied to the ARP request sent out for a particular IP address and whether that is a desirable behavior. Furthermore, you can check accuracy of any static ARP entries currently in the table. Remember that an interface that has IP proxy-ARP enabled on it responds to ARP requests that do not necessarily contain the replying interface's IP address. Hence, it is possible that an ARP table may contain multiple entries (with different IP addresses), all of which have the same MAC address in front of them.

# Novell Connection Sequence

Assume that a Novell client intends to make a connection to a Novell server that offers a particular service such as file services (type 4). The client sends a GNS (get nearest server) broadcast request out of its LAN interface card. If a Novell server offering this particular type of service (file service = type 4) is present on the local LAN, it will reply to the client's request and the local router(s) remain silent. Otherwise, the router searches in its IPX servers table (sometimes referred to as SAP [Service Advertisement Protocol] table) to see if an entry that matches the client's request is present.

Routers build and maintain IPX server tables by accepting SAP broadcasts that are generated by other neighbor devices. If more than one entry is present, the closest one (hop count) is furnished, and in case of a tie, the most recent entry is chosen. A reply is not sent if there is a GNS-reply filter configured on the corresponding interface of the router. The router's reply contains the selected server's internal IPX address. When the client receives the router's reply (containing a remote IPX address), it will generate a RIP (broadcast) request for the received (server's internal) network address. Once again, the router has to do a search, this time in its IPX route table to see if there is an entry that matches the client's request. If the router finds a match, it sends a RIP reply to the client. Finally, the client sends an NCP (Novell Core Protocol) request to the remote Novell server to establish a connection (log in). Once a connection is built between the Novell client and server, the file sharing mechanism begins.

# The show novell traffic Command

The **show novell traffic** command is a useful troubleshooting command that displays traffic statistics regarding the number of IPX packets sent and received, input and output errors encountered, and the broadcast and SAPs generated and received. Example 3-9 displays part of a sample output from this command. Table 3-8 provides short descriptions for various fields of the **show novell traffic** command's output.

**Example 3-9**    *The show novell traffic Command Output*

```
Test> show novell traffic

Rcvd:      68112 total, 0 format errors, 0 checksum errors, 1 bad hop count,
           68102 local destination, 0 multicast
Bcast:     68102 received, 43745 sent
Sent:      43745 generated, 0 forwarded
           0 encapsulation failed, 10 no route
SAP:       18 SAP requests, 18 SAP replies
           7 SAP advertisements received, 0 sent
```

**Table 3-8**    *show novell traffic Field Descriptions*

| Field | Description |
|---|---|
| Format errors | The number of bad packets received (such as those with corrupted headers). A high number of format errors can be a sign of encapsulation mismatch on the local network. |
| Checksum errors | Checksum errors should not be reported, because IPX does not use a checksum. |
| Bad hop count | Bad hop count increments when a packet's hop count exceeds 16. |
| Encapsulation failed | Encapsulation failed is registered when the router is unable to encapsulate a packet. |

# AppleTalk Connection Sequence

In order to troubleshoot AppleTalk connection problems, you must understand the AppleTalk connection sequence. The connection sequence often begins when an Apple Macintosh client opens the Chooser applet from Apple's pull-down menu. This action triggers the Macintosh device to send a GetZoneList request on its connected network. The Router(s) on the local segment respond using GetZoneList reply, based on their Apple Zone table and any GetZoneList filters that may be applied to their appropriate interface(s). Upon receiving the list of zones, the chooser zone field is populated. The user of the Apple Macintosh selects a zone and a service (on the chooser) and this action in turn causes the Apple device to generate an NBP (Name Binding Protocol) request. The NBP request is forwarded by the connected routers towards the selected zone. On those segments that are part of the destination zone, all devices that offer the selected service will reply to the Apple device (unicast). The Apple device populates the appropriate box in the chooser with the name of all those servers that sent a reply back. Next, the user selects one of the servers. This action triggers an ATP (AppleTalk Transaction Protocol) connection sequence between the client and the server. After this transport layer connection successfully completes, AFP (Apple Filing Protocol) is used for accessing shared files on the server.

# The show appletalk traffic Command

The **show appletalk traffic** command displays AppleTalk traffic information, as shown in Example 3-10. The output displays information such as the number of packets sent and received, various errors encountered, and a classified set of statistics on various AppleTalk protocols and services. Table 3-9 provides short descriptions for some of the fields included in this command's output.

**Example 3-10** *The show appletalk traffic Command Output*

```
Test> Show Appletalk Traffic

AppleTalk statistics:
 Rcvd: 719 total, 0 checksum errors, 0 bad hop count
    0 local destination, 0 access denied
    2 port disabled
 Bcast: 640 received, 164 access denied
 Sent: 164 generated, 0 forwarded
      1736 encapsulation failed, 0 no route
 DDP: 719 long, 0 short, 0 wrong size
 NBP: 5 received, 0 sent, 0 forwarded, 0 lookups
 RTMP: 709 received, 240 sent, 0 requests
 ATP: 0 received
 AMP: 0 received, 0 sent
 ZIP: 3 received, 1659 sent
 Echo: 0 received, 0 illegal
 ARP: 1476 requests, 0 replies, 9 probes
```

**Example 3-10** *The **show appletalk traffic** Command Output (Continued)*

```
Lost: 0 no buffers
Unknown: 0 packets
Discarded: 1577 wrong encapsulation, 0 bad SNAP discriminator
```

**Table 3-9**    *show appletalk traffic Field Descriptions*

| Field | Description |
|---|---|
| Checksum errors | Number of packets dropped since their DDP checksum was bad. |
| Bad hop count | Number of packets dropped since the number of hops they traveled was larger than 15. |
| Access denied | Number of packets dropped since access list didn't permit them. |
| Port disabled | Number of packets dropped since routing was disabled for port (extended AppleTalk only). This happens due to config error or if a packet is received while in verification/discovery mode. |
| Encapsulation failed | Number of times packets were received for a connected network, but the node was not found (such as when AppleTalk ARP address resolution failed). |
| No buffers | Number of times attempted packet buffer allocation failed. |
| Unknown | Number of times Unknown AppleTalk packet types were seen. |
| Wrong encapsulation | Nonextended AppleTalk packet on extended AppleTalk port (or vice versa) |

# Foundation Summary

The Foundation Summary is a collection of quick reference information that provides a convenient review of many key concepts in this chapter. For those of you who already feel comfortable with the topics in this chapter, this summary helps you recall a few details. For those of you who just read this chapter, this review should help solidify some key facts. For any of you doing your final prep before the exam, these tables and figures are a convenient way to review the day before the exam.

Identifying troubleshooting targets is an important part of the troubleshooting task as a whole. One effective approach to identifying troubleshooting targets is taking advantage of the layered model of internetworking. Since different components of a networking model have direct and indirect dependencies on each other, you can work your way from the lowest layer that is in good working order up to the layer where trouble starts. Troubleshooting the layers above the faulty layer must be done after, as it is not beneficial at this stage. If your network's physical layer is intact, the data link layer will be the most important layer for you to check before you proceed to test the other layers.

Router interfaces and controllers are two primary targets to be examined in order to evaluate the health of your data link layer. Cisco's CDP is a simple yet powerful data link layer protocol that not only allows you to test the functioning of the data link layer but also allows you to get information about the neighbors (adjacent Cisco devices) by using simple **show cdp** commands. Once your examination and correction of the data link layer completes, you can proceed to upper layer protocol troubleshooting. Understanding upper layer protocols' characteristics and behavior helps you incorporate the layered (modular and step-by-step) approach in troubleshooting those layers as well. Cisco IOS has relevant and focused commands for diagnosing each specific upper layer protocol. It is imperative that you understand those commands' usage and be able to interpret their output thoroughly.

**Basic methods for checking the status of the physical layer:**

- Look at the first line of the **show interface** command and make sure that the interface is up and line protocol is up.

- Look at the link LED of the appropriate interface.

- Manually check and observe for yourself the condition and type of cables, jacks, connectors (look for damage, standards violation, compatibility, and appropriateness).

- Use physical media test equipment.

**Three important points about the show interfaces command:**

- You cannot display a subset of interfaces based on their type.

- Those interfaces that have been removed continue to be displayed until the time that the router reloads. However, on the output you will see the "Hardware has been removed" message. On the other hand, removed software interfaces (for example, a subinterface) will continue to be displayed (until reload), but will be reported as deleted.

- Those interfaces that you shut down are displayed as administratively down.

**Table 3-10** *Summary of the show interface Command's Output Fields*

| Field | Description |
|-------|-------------|
| Ethernet n is {up | down | administratively down} | Indicates whether the interface hardware is currently active and if it has been taken down by an administrator. "Disabled" indicates the router has received over 5000 errors in a keepalive interval, which is 10 seconds by default. |
| Line protocol is {up | down | administratively down} | Indicates whether the software processes that handle the line protocol believe the interface is usable (that is, whether keepalives are successful) or if it has been taken down by an administrator. |
| Hardware | Hardware type (for example, MCI Ethernet, SCI, cBus Ethernet) and address. |
| Internet address | Internet address followed by subnet mask. |
| MTU | Maximum Transmission Unit of the interface. |
| BW | Bandwidth of the interface in kilobits per second. |
| DLY | Delay of the interface in microseconds. |
| Rely | Reliability of the interface as a fraction of 255. |
| Load | Load on the interface as a fraction of 255. |
| Encapsulation | Encapsulation method assigned to interface. |
| ARP type | Type of Address Resolution Protocol assigned. |
| Loopback | Indicates whether loopback is set or not. |
| Keepalive | Indicates whether keepalives are set or not. |

*continues*

**Table 3-10**    *Summary of the show interface Command's Output Fields (Continued)*

| Field | Description |
| --- | --- |
| Last input | Amount of time since the last packet was successfully received by an interface. Useful for knowing when a dead interface failed. |
| Last output | Amount of time since the last packet was successfully transmitted by the interface. Useful for knowing when a dead interface failed. |
| Output hang | Amount of time since the interface was last reset because of a transmission that took too long. |
| Last clearing | Time at which the counters that measure cumulative statistics (such as number of bytes transmitted and received) shown in this report were last reset to zero. |
| | Asterisks indicate the elapsed time is too large to be displayed. |
| Output queue, input queue, drops | Number of packets in output and input queues. Each number is followed by a slash, the maximum size of the queue, and the number of packets dropped due to a full queue. |
| 5 minute input rate<br>5 minute output rate | Average number of bits and packets received and transmitted per second in the last 5 minutes. |
| Packets input | Total number of error-free packets received by the system. |
| No buffers | Number of received packets discarded because there was no buffer space in the main system. |
| Received *n* broadcasts by the interface | Total number of broadcast or multicast packets received. |
| Total runts | Number of packets that are discarded because they are smaller than the medium's minimum packet size. |
| Total giants | Number of packets that are discarded because they exceed the medium's maximum packet size. |

**Table 3-10**    *Summary of the show interface Command's Output Fields (Continued)*

| Field | Description |
| --- | --- |
| Input error | Includes runts, giants, no buffer, CRC, frame, overrun, and ignored counts. Other input-related errors can also cause the input errors count to be increased, and some datagrams may have more than one error. |
| CRC | Cyclic redundancy checksum generated by the originating LAN station or far-end device does not match the checksum calculated from the data received. |
| Frame | Number of packets received incorrectly having a CRC error and a noninteger number of octets. |
| Overrun | Number of times the receiver hardware was unable to hand received data to a hardware buffer because the input rate exceeded the receiver's ability to handle the data. |
| Ignored | Number of received packets ignored by the interface because the interface hardware ran low on internal buffers. |
| Dribble condition detected | Dribble bit condition indicates that carrier sense did not go inactive on a receive data byte boundary. |
| Packets output | Total number of messages transmitted by the system. |
| Bytes | Total number of bytes, including data and MAC encapsulation, transmitted by the system. |
| Underruns | Number of times that the transmitter has been running faster than the router can handle. This may never be reported on some interfaces. |
| Output errors | Sum of all errors that prevented the final transmission of datagrams out of the interface being examined. |
| Late collisions | This is usually the result of an overextended LAN. |
| Interface resets | Number of times an interface has been completely reset. |
| Restarts | Restarts are usually due to too many errors during a fixed time period. |

**Possible reasons for a different bia and MAC address being reported for the same interface by the show interfaces command:**

- The administrator of the router hard-codes the MAC address (the ability to do this is IOS/version dependent).

- An upper-layer protocol modifies the MAC address (DECNET does that).

**Notes on Token Ring Soft Errors:**

- The line errors, burst errors, and the receive-congested errors are among the most common errors in tokenring networks:

  — The line error counter increments as CRC check failures occur.

  — The burst error counters report on signaling errors seen (these are usually due to noise and/or crosstalk).

  — The receive-congested error counter tells you if the station has had difficulty keeping up with processing of the received traffic.

  — In cases where these counters are nonzero and require investigation, use a network monitor or protocol analyzer to capture traffic and investigate which stations are acting up or to find out if you need to test the media or tokenring hardware and cabling.

- The Token Ring soft errors are divided into two classes:

  — Isolating soft errors: Caused by the local station, its NAUN, or devices/ medium in between the two.

  — Non-isolating soft errors: Not necessarily caused by the local station or its NAUN; these errors can be caused by device(s) anywhere in the ring.

**Table 3-11**   *Notes on Connection-Oriented and Connectionless Protocols*

| Protocol | Note |
|---|---|
| Connection-Oriented Protocols | Connection-oriented protocols are those that establish an end-to-end connection before submitting data. |
| | The sequence of steps performed by a connection-oriented protocol is as follows: |
| | Step 1. Establish a connection. |
| | Step 2. Send (and perhaps receive) data. |
| | Step 3. Terminate (tear down) the connection. |
| | Examples: |
| | TCP, FTP |

**Table 3-11**  *Notes on Connection-Oriented and Connectionless Protocols (Continued)*

| Protocol | Note |
|---|---|
| Connectionless Protocols | Connectionless protocols do not establish a connection prior to sending data. In other words, a device using a connectionless protocol sends (or receives) data to and from its counterpart without pre-establishing a connection or session.<br><br>Examples:<br><br>UDP, TFTP |

# Q&A

The answers to the following questions can be found in Appendix A. Some of the questions in this section are repeated from the "Do I Know This Already" Quiz so that you can gauge the advancement of your knowledge of this subject matter.

**1** Why is the correct function of the data link layer so significant, and if this layer is faulty, what kinds of symptoms will you experience?

_____

_____

_____

**2** List a few methods that can be used to test proper functioning of the physical layer.

_____

_____

_____

**3** What is the term used to refer to devices that are on a common data link?

_____

_____

_____

**4** How does a router check the state of its link on an Ethernet interface?

_____

_____

_____

**5** The interpretation of the performance (I/O) and error statistics displayed by the **show interfaces** command depends on what other pieces of information?

_____

_____

_____

**6**  What is a router's IOS response to the **show interfaces ethernet** command?

_____

_____

_____

**7**  If you enter the **show interfaces** command for an interface that has been removed, what will the command output show?

_____

_____

_____

**8**  Why would the first line of the **show interfaces ethernet 0** output display Ethernet0 to be disabled?

_____

_____

_____

**9**  Which command must you enter to specify which one of the available physical connectors of a router's interface should be used?

_____

_____

_____

**10**  How do you check current settings of the **media-type** command on an Ethernet 0 interface?

_____

_____

_____

**11**  What is the bia of an interface? How can you see it? Where is it stored? And what is it composed of?

_____

_____

_____

**12**  How is the MAC address of an interface card formed? How can you see it? Where is it stored? And is it always identical to the bia?

_____

_____

_____

**13**  What is the format that the output of the **show interfaces ethernet 0** uses for displaying the reliability and load parameters? Over what time interval are these parameters measured?

_____

_____

_____

**14**  Provide a reason for a **show interfaces** command output showing a nonzero value for the No Buffer counter.

_____

_____

_____

**15**  What do the Total Runts and the Total Giants counters inform you about?

_____

_____

_____

**16**  The Total Errors counter includes the number of occurrences of which error conditions?

_____

_____

_____

**17**  What does a high number of reported CRC errors on an interface usually indicate?

_____

_____

_____

**18**  What is a generally acceptable rate of collisions on an Ethernet? What are late collisions?

_____

_____

_____

**19**  Explain the reason(s) why a router interface would report resets.

_____

_____

_____

**20**  What will the first line of the **show interfaces tokenring** *n* output report about the state of the Token Ring interface if the cable is not plugged into the interface card?

_____

_____

_____

**21**  What does the Single ring/multiring node field on the output of the **show interfaces tokenring** *n* indicate?

_____

_____

_____

**22**  On the output of the **show interfaces tokenring** *n* command, what does the field Group Address indicate?

_____

_____

_____

**23**  Provide a short description for the line errors, burst errors, and receive-congested errors of Token Ring networks. Suggest a troubleshooting action to be taken in case these counters are reported with nonzero values.

_____

_____

_____

**24** Specify the two classes of soft errors in Token Ring and briefly describe each.

_____

_____

_____

**25** On the output of the **show interfaces fddi** command, what are the key fields and their expected values for a dual attached device that is in good working condition and reports no errors?

_____

_____

_____

**26** List two of ATM interface encapsulation types.

_____

_____

_____

**27** What do the TX Buffers and RX Buffers fields of the **show interfaces atm** command output report on?

_____

_____

_____

**28** How is the value of the Maximum active VCs field from the **show interfaces atm** command output interpreted?

_____

_____

_____

**29** How is the value of the VCs per VP field from the **show interfaces atm** command output interpreted?

_____

_____

_____

**30**  How can you display the content of a device's CDP table?

_____

_____

_____

**31**  List the general actions of a connection-oriented protocol.

_____

_____

_____

**32**  What is the IP ARP table? How can you display it?

_____

_____

_____

**33**  What would a high number of format errors on the output of the **show novell traffic** indicate?

_____

_____

_____

**34**  What is the normal value for the Checksum Errors field on the output of the **show novell traffic** command?

_____

_____

_____

**35**  Explain the meaning of the Encapsulation failed field on the output of the **show appletalk traffic** command.

_____

_____

_____

**36** What is the most common reason for routers to report Wrong encapsulation on the output of the **show appletalk traffic** command?

_____

_____

_____

**37** Based on the captured traffic displayed as follows, specify the frame type and explain its purpose.

```
DLC: -----DLC Header -----
DLC:
DLC: Frame 2 arrived at 14:53:37.6592; frame size is 60 (003C hex) bytes.
DLC: Destination = FF FF FF FF FF FF
DLC: Source = Station cisco 01 56 A8
DLC: Ethertype = 0806 (ARP)
DLC:
DLC: ----- ARP/RARP frame -----
DLC:
DLC: Hardware type = 1 (10 MB ETHERNET)
DLC: Protocol type = 0800 (IP)
DLC: Length of hardware address = 6 bytes
DLC: Length of protocol address = 4 bytes
DLC: Opcode 1 (ARP Request)
DLC: Sender's hardware address = cisco 0156A8
DLC: Sender's protocol address = [144.251.100.204]
DLC: Target hardware address = 00 00 00 00 00 00
DLC: Target protocol address = [144.251.100.100]
```

_____

_____

_____

**38** Based on the captured traffic displayed as follows, specify the frame type and explain its purpose.

```
DLC: ----- DLC Header -----
DLC:
DLC: Frame 3 arrived at 15:06:34.789; frame size is 141 (008D hex) bytes..
DLC: Destination = 09 00 07 FF FF FF
DLC: Source = cisco 059AC2
DLC: Length = 127

LLC: ----- LLC Header -----
LLC:
LLC: DSAP = AA, SSAP = AA, Command, Unnumbered frame: UI
LLC:

SNAP: --- SNAP Header ----
SNAP:
SNAP: OUI = 080007 (Apple)
SNAP: Type = 809B (AppleTalk)
SNAP:
DDP:----- DDP Header -----
DDP:
DDP:  Hop Count = 0
```

```
DDP:  Length = 119
DDP:  Checksum = 396A (correct)
DDP: Destination network number = 0
DDP: Destination node = 255
DDP: Destination socket = 1 (RTMP)
DDP: Source network number = 1140
DDP: Source node = 100
DDP: Source socket = 1 (RTMP)
DDP: DDP protocol type = 1 (RTMP data)
DDP:
RTMP: ----- RTMP Data -----
RTMP:
RTMP: Extended packet, Version 2
RTMP: Net = 1140
RTMP: Node ID Length = 8 Bits
RTMP: Node ID = 100
RTMP: Tuple 1 (Extended): Cable range = 1140 TO 1140, Distance = 0
RTMP: Tuple 2 (Extended): Range = 47 TO 47, Distance = 2
RTMP: Tuple 3 (Extended): Range = 1000 TO 1005, Distance = 1
RTMP: Tuple 4 (Extended): Range = 1010 TO 1010, Distance = 2
...
```

_____

_____

_____

**39** Based on the captured traffic displayed as follows, specify the frame type and explain its purpose.

```
DLC: ----- DLC Header -----
DLC:
DLC: Frame 4 arrived at 15:07:13.281; frame size is 238 (00EE hex) bytes.
DLC: Destination = Broadcast
DLC: Source = 3Com C25C79
DLC: 802.3 length = 224

IPX: ----- IPX Header -----
IPX:
IPX: Checksum = FFFF
IPX: Length = 224
IPX: Transport control = 00
IPX:     0000 .... = Reserved
IPX:     .... 0000 = Hop Count
IPX: Packet type = 0 (Novell)
IPX:
IPX: Dest Network.Node = 1000.FFFFFFFFFFFF Socket=1106(SAP)
IPX: Source Network.Node = 1000.02 60 8C C2 5C 79 Socket=1106(SAP)
```

_____

_____

_____

**40** Based on the captured traffic displayed as follows, specify the frame type and explain its purpose.

```
DLC: ----- DLC Header -----
DLC:
DLC: Frame 1 arrived at 15:05:33.389; frame size is 62 (003E hex) bytes.
DLC: AC: Frame priority 0, Reservation priority 0, Monitor count 0
DLC: FC: LLC frame, PCF attention code: None
DLC: FS: Addr recognized indicators: 00, Frame copied indicators: 00
DLC: Destination = Station cisco A05903
DLC: Source      = Station IBM 0AE591
DLC:
LLC: ----- LLC Header -----
LLC:
LLC: DSAP = AA, SSAP = AA, Command, Unnumbered frame: UI
LLC:
SNAP: ----- SNAP Header -----
SNAP:
SNAP: Type = 0800 (IP)
SNAP:
```

_____

_____

_____

This chapter covers the following topics that you will need to master to pass the CCNP Support exam:

| Objective | Description |
|---|---|
| 1 | Understand how to handle the impact of Cisco IOS troubleshooting tools. |
| 2 | Define the concepts of routing and switching, and identify the components that are involved in performing these tasks. |
| 3 | Identify the route caching methods available in different Cisco routers. Explain how they are enabled/disabled. |
| 4 | Define the Cisco IOS Debug tool, specify its impact on a router's performance, and suggest how it can be used effectively. |
| 5 | Explain how and why you alter the message logging levels and destinations. |
| 6 | Explain the usage of Ping and Trace troubleshooting tools, and which protocols can they be used for. |
| 7 | Be familiar with the type of information that is provided by the technical support staff, and which commands produce part of that information. |
| 8 | Explain system buffers, how they are managed, and how and why their behavior can be monitored and altered. |
| 9 | Understand how the CPU and memory utilization of a router are monitored |
| 10 | List and describe the tools used when troubleshooting router crash scenarios. |

# CHAPTER 4

# Applying Cisco Troubleshooting Tools

This chapter introduces some powerful troubleshooting tools that are built into the Cisco IOS. As with other tools, it is important that you identify when to use them and what information they reveal. Because some of these tools have an impact on the way routers operate and may impede the routers' utmost performance, it is essential to use them with care. To better understand the output of these commands, and to recognize what router internal operations they affect, this chapter discusses router internal components and operations. As each tool/command is introduced, its usefulness is described and tips are given on how to use it effectively.

The Cisco IOS troubleshooting commands help you gather valuable information about the state of the network and its devices. The gathered facts help eliminate some of the possibilities, at the same time strengthening the likelihood of the hypotheses that you may have formed. Again, due to the impact that certain troubleshooting commands (debug, for example) have on some of the router's internal operations—and ultimately on the router's performance—these commands have to be used selectively, properly, and temporarily.

## "Do I Know This Already?" Quiz

If you wish to evaluate your knowledge of the contents of this chapter before you get started, answer the following questions. The answers are provided in Appendix A, "Answers to Quiz Questions." If you are having difficulty providing correct answers, you should thoroughly review the entire chapter. If all or most of your answers are correct, you might want to skim this chapter for only those subjects you need to review. You can also use the "Foundation Summary" section to quickly review topics. Once you have completed the chapter, you should reevaluate yourself with the questions in the "Q&A" section at the end. Finally, use the companion CD-ROM to evaluate your knowledge of the topics and see if you need a review.

1 Briefly explain why Cisco IOS troubleshooting commands/tools need proper handling.

_____

_____

_____

**2** What does proper handling of troubleshooting tools entail?

_____

_____

_____

**3** Provide a generic explanation for route caching (or fast switching) and the motivation behind it.

_____

_____

_____

**4** Which of the route caching methods are not enabled by default? And from which configuration mode (prompt level) can they be enabled?

_____

_____

_____

**5** With regard to speed and switching optimization, how did Cisco Systems improve the Cisco 7500 routers (in comparison to the 7000 series)?

_____

_____

_____

**6** Briefly describe the advantages of Netflow switching. Also specify whether there should be any precautions with respect to enabling Netflow switching.

_____

_____

_____

**7** Provide at least three examples of operations or packet types that are process switched.

_____

_____

_____

**8**  Before you activate Debug, what are some of its characteristics that you should
consider?

_____

_____

_____

**9**  Before you enable debugging on a router, you are encouraged to check the router's
CPU utilization. What is the command that allows you to do that? If the utilization is
above 50%, are you encouraged to debug packets or to debug events?

_____

_____

_____

**10**  What is the default setting (for example, enabled/disabled, default destination) for
message logging?

_____

_____

_____

**11**  What information does the output of the **show logging** Cisco IOS exec command
display?

_____

_____

_____

**12**  The outputs of the **show memory** and the **show processes [cpu]** commands will most
likely be asked for in which situation (loss of functionality, crash, or performance
degradation)?

_____

_____

_____

**13** If the output of **show buffer** command displays a large number of misses, increasing the value of which one of the buffer management parameters (Permanent, Min-Free, Max-Free, Initial) will most likely remedy the situation?

_____

_____

_____

**14** The **show processes** command's output provides two numbers separated by a slash (for example, 4%/4%) for the CPU utilization over the last five seconds. How are those numbers interpreted?

_____

_____

_____

**15** Which command causes the router to attempt to produce a core dump when it crashes?

_____

_____

_____

# Foundation Topics

## System Impact of Cisco Troubleshooting Tools

After completing the problem definition step, your next step (following the systematic troubleshooting process) is to start gathering detailed facts about the behavior of the devices and protocols of the production network. This task usually entails using several IOS troubleshooting tools and commands. Despite their importance in terms of the valuable information they provide, these tools inevitably utilize some processing cycles and memory of the router. Furthermore, they may disable or at least have a negative effect on some of router's internal (optimized) operations (for example, fast switching).

If you are responsible for fixing a production network's problems, you need to be familiar with troubleshooting tools. In other words, you have to know which tools you need, how to interpret each tool's output, and, very importantly, how to use each tool properly. Proper usage of a tool means that you should use it with appropriate focus and selectiveness, yet to an extent that you will gather the desired information. You must stop using these tools immediately after you attain your objective, thus you should limit the period of time during which these tools are used.

Several of the Cisco IOS **show** commands display information about the status of the router, its interfaces, and the rate of utilization of router resources. **debug** is a powerful command for finding out which packets are generated, received, and forwarded by a router. Several parameters of the **debug** command help focus the output on what you are interested in seeing, and hence give you a great insight on the current events and how the router handles them. But **debug** lowers a router's performance substantially, and that is why you need to give this command special attention.

## Cisco Routers' Routing Processes and Switching Processes

Routing and switching processes are two of the most essential tasks performed by routers. Some people in the internetworking field have a little difficulty with the idea that routers perform switching, but of course everybody is comfortable with the fact that routers perform routing. Nonetheless, as you will see, the distinctions between these operations will be quite useful in optimizing the router's performance. In the following paragraphs the concepts of routing and switching are defined. A discussion then follows about the benefit of distinguishing among these tasks while troubleshooting and about methods for examining the distinct processes and components of the routing and switching process.

Switching is commonly defined as the process that takes charge of moving data units (frames or packets) through the anatomy of internetworking devices. From the time data units arrive at an interface until they leave the router, several issues need to be constantly addressed. Where is the data unit stored? What type of information should accompany the data unit? Where does the data unit go next? How is the next destination determined? And which statistics need to be collected about this data unit? As you can imagine, the mere task of moving a data unit (a packet, in the context of routers) from one place to the next is one of the simplest and least resource-consuming internetworking tasks.

Routing can be simply defined as the operation that attempts to select an output interface and perhaps a next hop for a packet based on the packet's destination address. Different routing processes perform the task of routing different protocols' packets. For example, the IP routing process, which is enabled by default, handles routing of IP packets. The routing process makes its routing decision by consulting its routing table, which it builds and maintains dynamically. The sources of information of a routing process for building its routing table are

1   The network segments that the router is actively connected to.

2   The usable static routes available in the router configuration.

3   The dynamic routing entries that the routing protocols offer.

4   The routing policies or restrictions that are imposed.

5   The usable default routes available.

Imagine that a router (call it R1) is receiving a bunch of packets from its ethernet 0 interface and all of these packets have the same destination address. When the router receives the first layer 3 packet (call it P1), the data link header (layer 2 frame) is discarded and the packet stored in the E0 interface's buffer. Next, the packet will be moved through R1's internal bus into main memory, then stored in a packet buffer where it will wait its turn to be examined by the routing process. It is important to note that the packet is accompanied by additional information such as the interface the packet entered the router from. When it is P1's turn, the routing process uses the destination address of the packet and the routing table to select an interface for the packet to leave the router from. Finally, a frame appropriate to that interface must be created. This entails building a frame header, usually composed of layer 2 addressing and perhaps other information such as protocol type.

Notice that during this process the packet is moved by the switching process from one place to another (from the interface internal buffer to the main memory, for instance) several times. Hence, the first packet (P1) must be handled by both the routing and the switching processes. Performing both routing and switching tasks on a packet is called process switching. Now think about the second packet (call it P2) that has the same destination as P1. Does P2 have to be routed and switched (i.e., process switched) as well? The answer is usually negative.

To enhance efficiency and speed, the experience gained from the effort spent (through the routing task) on the first packet (P1, in our example) can be reused. P1's destination address and the outgoing interface (selected by the routing process) can be stored in a place referred to as a switching cache, and can be reused for quick processing of the subsequent packets (P2, P3, and so on, which have the same destination address as P1). Inside the switching cache, the router needs to store the first packet's destination address along with the output interface number. The information stored in the switching cache is used to quickly discover the output interface for the following packets (destined for the same network as P1), without having to perform the time-consuming task of routing on each of them.

You must remember that the router also caches information such as MAC addresses (in the ARP cache) so that it does not have to generate an ARP request for every packet. Hence, when dealing with a number of packets (with identical destination addresses) arriving at the router one after the other, the router must perform both the routing and the switching task on the first packet.

To process the following packets, using the information kept in the switching cache, the router can skip the routing task. This is commonly referred to as route caching (and loosely speaking, also called fast switching). Please keep in mind that there are more operations and tasks involved in the processing of each packet, most of which have to be performed for each packet individually. For example, security tasks (checking access lists) and accounting/queuing tasks still need to be performed for each packet (except in case of Netflow switching, which is presented later in this chapter).

Since the routing task is more resource consuming, is more complex, and introduces a longer latency, skipping this operation on all the packets except the first (all with the same destination address) is very advantageous and efficient. When a packet (such as P2) is not process switched (not subjected to routing), the packet is said to be fast switched. The switch cache, where the network layer destination address and the corresponding selected output interface (based on processing of the first packet) are stored, can be on one or more of the router's components. Where that information is stored depends on the type of router and its components, and based on that, the cache is referred to by a special term.

# Switching in 7000, 7500, 4000, 3000, and 2500 Series Routers

This section discusses the switching options and their initialization on different router models. As you will notice, most of the methods are performing the same task, but some are faster than others due to highly specialized internal techniques and microchips.

It is important to know that all the switching features, except fast switching, need to be turned on manually. Enabling a specific type of switching is an interface configuration task and must be done for each protocol individually. Of course the type of switching that is available is dependent upon the router.

## Switching in 7000 Series Routers

The 7000 series routers, similar to other Cisco routers, have a fast switching option that is enabled by default. Fast switching is performed using a Fast Switch Cache in the Route Processor. Two major components that participate in the routing and switching operations are RP (Route Processor) and SSP (Silicon Switch Processor). The early models of the 7000 series had RP and SP (Switch Processor). The SP (in the earlier models) only had an Autonomous Switch Cache. The SSP was introduced later and is equipped with both an Autonomous Switch Cache and a Silicon Switch Cache (see Figure 4-1). Autonomous and silicon switching are not enabled by default. The administrator of a router may enable either or both of these switching options on a per-protocol basis at each interface. The commands for enabling and disabling fast switching, autonomous switching, and silicon switching are:

Fast switching:

```
Router(config-if)# [no] [protocol] route-cache
```

Autonomous switching:

```
Router(config-if)# [no] [protocol] route-cache cbus
```

Silicon switching:

```
Router(config-if)# [no] [protocol] route-cache sse
```

---

**NOTE**     You must specify a protocol name, such as **ip** or **ipx**.

---

Assume that fast switching, autonomous switching, and silicon switching are all enabled on all of the interfaces of a router (call it R1) for all protocols, including IP. Now, for the sake of the example, take a look at the sequence of tasks and operations executed by R1 to process some packets (call them P1, P2, and so on) entering into the router via its ethernet 0 interface. When the frame carrying P1 is accepted by the ethernet 0 interface (E0 of R1), the header (layer 2 frame) is discarded and the encapsulated packet (P1) is kept in the interface buffer.

The E0 interface must wait its turn to get a chance to send P1 through the router's bus (CxBus in the case of 7000 series routers operating at 533Mbps) to the SSP. When P1 arrives at the SSP, it is stored in a buffer, and then its destination address is first checked against the entries in the Silicon Switch Cache (to find a match).

Since P1 is the first packet from the sequence of packets with the same destination (P1, P2, and so on), there won't be a match in the SSP's Silicon Switch Cache for P1. There will be no entries matching P1's destination address in the Autonomous Switch Cache, either.

**Figure 4-1**    *Routing and Switching in 7000 Routers*

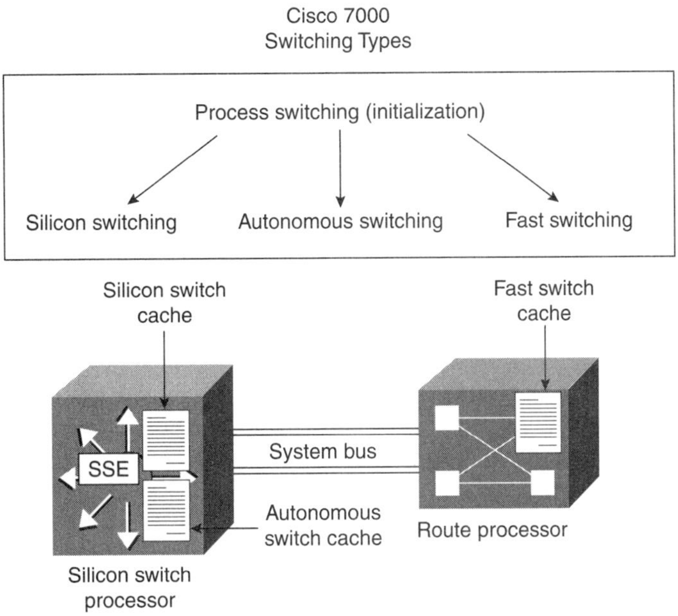

Next, P1's header is moved through a system bus (operating at only 153 Mbps) to the Route Processor for a quick search and match against the entries in the Fast Switch Cache (residing in the RP). Again, there won't be a match. Now the entire packet (*not* only the packet header) must be moved from the SSP to the RP, stored in a buffer, and in turn be looked after by the routing process. Hence, the entire P1 packet waits its turn in a buffer (within RP's memory) until the routing process gets a chance to administer it.

The routing process uses the destination address of P1 and the content of its routing table to select the best (if any) interface to send P1 out from. Say TokenRing 0 is selected. Of course an appropriate frame must be created for P1 to be encapsulated into, before it is sent to the TokenRing 0 interface (To0) and ultimately out to the wire. Once these tasks (perhaps including ARP) are completed, the router sends the P1 packet (encapsulated in a Token Ring frame) from the RP to the SSP and then to the T0 interface.

The knowledge gained from processing the P1 packet is saved in the router's switching caches, to be used for processing P2, P3, and so on. Assuming that all switching options are enabled, P1's destination address—the network component of it, to be accurate—along with the destination interface (number), are stored in the Fast Switch Cache (in RP) and the Autonomous and Silicon Switch Caches (in SSP). When P2 arrives from an interface into the SSP and the Silicon Switch Cache is checked, a match is found. The matching entry from the Silicon Switch Cache quickly identifies which interface P2 must exit from (To0 in this case). Recall that the router keeps information such as the recently used MAC addresses in its ARP cache, as well. As you can imagine, processing of P2 (and P3 and so on) will be much faster than the processing of P1. These packets are not process-switched: they don't interrupt the RP, they don't have to travel through the slow system bus (153 Mbps) to go to the RP, and they don't have to wait in a buffer in RP for their turn to be looked after by the routing process.

In our example, if silicon switching was not enabled on To0, but autonomous switching was, then the match would be found in the Autonomous Switch Cache. If both silicon and autonomous switching were disabled for To0 (notice that it is the output interface that matters), then the match would be found only in the Fast Switch Cache in the RP. Recall that if a match is not found in either of SSP's caches, the header of the packet is moved from the SSP (through the slow system bus) to the RP to do a quick check on the Fast Switch Cache. In a Cisco 7000 router, silicon switching is considered to be roughly 35% faster than autonomous switching, and autonomous switching is roughly 6.6 times faster than fast switching. Finally, fast switching in a Cisco 7000 router is about 12 times faster than process switching. All of the mentioned estimations are based on tests performed using packets of 64 byte in size.

## Switching in 7500 Series Routers

To enhance the performance and efficiency of its high-end routers, Cisco Systems made some major improvements in the 7500 series routers:

- The internal bus of the 7500 series router (CyBus) operates at1 Gbps, which is about twice as fast as the 7000 router's CxBus.

- Instead of having two separate components for routing and switching (SSP and RP) as in 7000 routers, the 7500 router is equipped with one component called the Route/ Switch Processor (which eliminates the slow 153 Mbps system bus previously needed to connect the RP and SSP).

- The switch cache of the 7500 series router, called Optimum Switch Cache, is faster than the Silicon Switch Cache of the 7000 router (see Figure 4-2).

As with the 7000 router and other routers, fast switching in the 7500 router is enabled by default and it is accomplished using the Fast Switch Cache (located in the Route Switch Processor [RSP]). However, the second type of switching performed by the 7500 router, called optimum switching, is the winning card for the 7500 router, as it is even faster than the 7000 router's Silicon Switch Cache. The Optimum Switch Cache is also located on the RSP. Optimum switching must be manually enabled on each interface for each protocol, except for IP. In other words, this feature is enabled by default for IP on all supported interfaces (Ethernet, FDDI, and Serial with HDLC encapsulation). Use the following interface configuration command to enable/disable optimum switching for a protocol on an interface:

```
Router(config-if)# [no] [protocol] route-cache optimum
```

**Figure 4-2**    *Routing and Switching in 7500 Routers*

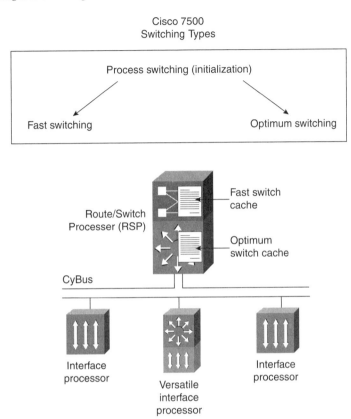

After a packet is extracted from its frame by the ingress interface, it is stored in the interface buffer and waits its turn to be sent through the CyBus to the RSP. In the RSP, the packet is stored in a buffer, and then its destination address is compared to the entries in the Optimum Switch Cache. If a match is found, the output interface is known, and an appropriate frame is swiftly created (using the information stored in the ARP cache, for example) and the packet is sent to the output interface through the CyBus. On the other hand, if a match is not found in the Optimum Switch Cache, the Fast Switch Cache is checked. If no match is found in the Fast Switch Cache either, the packet must wait in the buffer for its turn to be looked after by the appropriate routing process. The destination address (destination network, to be accurate) of this packet along with the output interface that the routing process selects for it are stored in the Fast Switch Cache and the Optimum Switch Cache (if enabled). This information shall be used for swift forwarding of the packets destined for the same network as the first packet.

The 7500 routers also feature Versatile Interface Processors (VIPs) that have a RISC processor and memory locally (on the blade). The 7500 routers can be configured to distribute routing information to be stored on the VIP. The VIP can then use the cached information to switch the packets on its own without having to send packets over to the RSP. This method of switching is called distributed switching. Distributed switching can make the processing of packets more than three times faster than silicon switching. Use the following interface configuration command to enable/disable distributed switching for a protocol on a VIP card:

```
Router(config-if)# [no] [protocol] route-cache distributed
```

## Netflow Switching

Netflow switching was introduced with Cisco IOS version 11.1(2) for the Cisco 7000, 7200, and 7500 routers with an RSP (Cisco offers the RSP7000 card for the 7000 routers). Netflow identifies a flow based on the source and destination IP address, source and destination port, protocol type (number), type of service (TOS), and input interface. The other switching types keep network layer destination address and output interface pairs in the cache. If a packet's destination address matches an entry in the cache, it is sent out of the destination interface specified by the cache, regardless of which interface the packet has entered the router from and what conversation it belongs to.

With other switching methods, even though the routing process is not performed for those packets with destination addresses matching the cache entry, other tasks (security and accounting, for example) are still performed on each packet. Netflow switching, on the other hand, caches security information and accounting information as well as routing information for each flow. As a result, once a network flow is identified and the first packet (of this flow) is processed, access list checks for subsequent packets belonging to the flow are bypassed and packet switching and statistics capture are performed in tandem.

Netflow also allows for exporting captured data to management utilities. Netflow switching, especially with the export option, can be quite resource consuming, so caution must be exercised when enabling this feature in production network routers. On 7000 and 7500 routers with RSP, Netflow switching can also be performed on a distributed basis on individual VIPs. Netflow switching can be disabled/enabled on a supported interface with the following interface configuration command:

```
router(config-if)# [no] [protocol] route-cache flow
```

## Switching in 4000, 3000, and 2500 Series Routers

On the 4000, 3000, and 2500 series routers, unlike the high-end routers discussed previously, the options are process switching and fast switching only (see Figure 4-3). Fast switching, a term often used when referring to route caching in shared memory, is enabled by default on all interfaces for all supported protocols.

**Figure 4-3**    *Routing and Switching in 4000, 3000, and 2500 Routers*

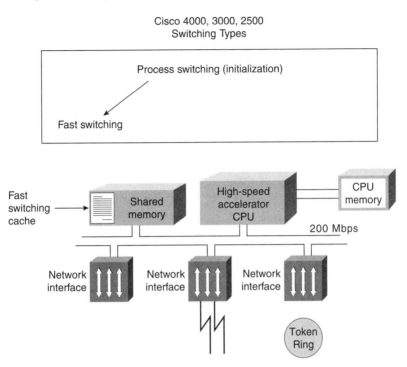

Depending on the operations performed on a particular interface, fast switching might have to be disabled manually or it may get disabled automatically by the IOS while that operation or configuration is in effect (this is IOS dependent). For instance, say you enter the command that applies a priority queue to an interface; depending on the IOS version, fast switching on that interface might be disabled by the IOS automatically, or the IOS might prompt you to disable fast switching before it allows you to apply the priority queue to the interface. You may disable/enable fast switching on an interface for a particular protocol using the following command:

```
router(config-if)# [no] [protocol] route-cache
```

The output of the following command includes information about whether fast switching is enabled/disabled for a particular protocol on a particular interface:

```
router# show [protocol] interface type number
```

Example 4-1 displays a sample output of the **show interface ethernet 0** command. IP fast switching, as the output shows, is enabled on the ethernet 0 interface of the router being examined.

**Example 4-1**   *A Sample Output of the **show interface ethernet 0** Command*

```
A_StubR#show ip interface ethernet 0
Ethernet0 is up, line protocol is up
  Internet address is 131.1.18.14/22
  Broadcast address is 255.255.255.255
  Address determined by setup command
  MTU is 1500 bytes
  Helper address is not set
  Directed broadcast forwarding is enabled
  Outgoing access list is not set
  Inbound  access list is not set
  Proxy ARP is enabled
  Security level is default
  Split horizon is enabled
  ICMP redirects are always sent
  ICMP unreachables are always sent
  ICMP mask replies are never sent
  IP fast switching is enabled
  IP fast switching on the same interface is disabled
  IP multicast fast switching is enabled
  Router Discovery is disabled
  IP output packet accounting is disabled
  IP access violation accounting is disabled
  TCP/IP header compression is disabled
  Probe proxy name replies are disabled
  Gateway Discovery is disabled
  Policy routing is disabled
  Network address translation is disabled
```

To see the statistics on the number of packets that are process switched and fast switched, issue this command:

```
router# show interface stats
```

## Process-Switched Packets

With each new release of the Cisco IOS, more tasks may get added to the list of fast-switched tasks. It is important to notice that when one talks about whether a task is process switched as opposed to fast switched, one is really talking about whether the packets associated with this particular task are fast switched or process switched. To clarify this point, assume that you have enabled IPX packet debugging on a particular router's Ethernet interface. Instead of thinking that IPX debugging is a process-switched task, you must understand that only those packets that are subject to this debug—in other words, all IPX packets that exit the router through this interface—are process-switched. Here is a list of some operations (in other words, packet types) that are process switched:

- Data-link layer broadcasts
- Packets subjected to Debug

- Packets delivering error log messages to syslog

- SNMP packets

- Protocol translations—for example, 1. SR/TLB, 2. DEC and LAT to Telnet

- Tunneling—for example, 1. GRE, 2. X25 remote switching

- Custom and priority queuing

- Link compression

- Keepalives

---

**NOTE**    For an accurate list of tasks (packet types) that are process switched, refer to the Cisco documentation for each device and the IOS version it is running.

---

# Handling the Cisco IOS Debug Troubleshooting Tool

Debug is a troubleshooting command that is available from the privileged exec mode (of Cisco IOS). This command can be used to display information about various router operations and the related traffic generated or received by the router, as well as any error messages. This tool is very useful and informative, but you must be aware of the following facts regarding its use: Debug is treated as a very high priority task. It can consume a significant amount of resources, and the router is forced to process-switch the packets being debugged. Debug must not be used as a monitoring tool—it is meant to be used for a short period of time and as a troubleshooting tool. By using it you discover significant facts about the working and faulty software and/or hardware components. The following is a list of recommendations on proper usage of the **debug** command:

- If you are interested to see a timestamp with each line of the debug output, you must load the timestamp service using this command:

      router(config)#**service timestamps debug** [*datetime* ¦ *uptime*]

- If you plan to see the debug output from within a Telnet session, you need to enter the **terminal monitor** command.

- Usually, the **debug** command is used to diagnose a specific facility, task, or protocol. Sometimes a protocol suite has a specific member (e.g., TCP from among the TCP/IP protocol suite members) that you may want to focus on. When you choose the protocol you want to debug, then you usually have a choice to use the events option or the packets option of the **debug** command for that specific protocol. Event debugging is less resource intensive than packet debugging, but packet debugging produces more information.

- Turning debugging on for everything (using the **debug all** command) is seriously discouraged in production networks. You get a tremendous amount of information, very fast, but it can severely diminish the router's performance or even render it unusable. The **debug all** command is also quite useless since it presents overlapping information that is difficult if not impossible to interpret.

- Before using the **debug** command, see the CPU utilization of your router (using the **show processes cpu** command). If your router's CPU utilization is consistently at 50% or more, you are advised to debug events instead of packets.

- If possible, use the **debug** command during periods when network traffic is not at its peak and fewer critical business applications are active. Cisco routers give the **debug** command higher priority (with respect to CPU cycles) than network traffic.

- Always remember to undo debug as soon as possible. You can use the **no debug** {*argument*} to turn off a specific debugging type. The **no debug all** or **undebug all** commands can be used to turn off all types of debugging that may be on.

- For troubleshooting, also consider using protocol analyzers to capture and display network traffic. These have little or no impact on your network performance, yet they provide valuable information. I also recommend capturing debug info to a file for offline perusal and training.

- Using an access list with your **debug** command helps you focus the debug output on the task you are troubleshooting. See the next section for more information on this technique.

## Using an Access List with Debug

With the **debug ip packet detail** command, you have the option to enter the name or number of an access list. Doing that causes the **debug** command to get focused only on those packets satisfying (permitted by) the access list's statements. Here is an example. Imagine that host A has trouble making a Telnet connection to host B, and you decide to use debug on the router connecting the segments where hosts A and B reside (see Figure 4-4).

Considering the addressing scheme used in Figure 4-4, the access list 100 permits TCP traffic from host A (10.1.1.1) to host B (172.16.2.2) with the Telnet port (23) as the destination. Access list 100 also permits established TCP traffic from host B to host A. Using access list 100 with the **debug ip packet detail** command (as shown in the figure) allows you to see only debug packets that satisfy the access list. This is an effective troubleshooting technique that requires less overhead on your router, while allowing all information on the subject you are troubleshooting to be displayed by the debug facility.

**Figure 4-4**    *Using Access Lists with the **debug** Command*

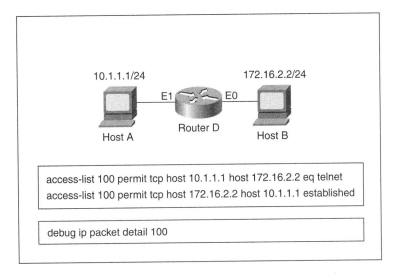

## Error Message Logging and Limiting the Display of Error Messages

Logging messages are important sources of information for network engineers in charge of troubleshooting. This section covers the following topics:

- The options for the logging messages destination

- Which destinations are the default for logging messages

- Which commands enable/disable different destinations

- How usage of different logging destinations compares with regard to the overhead they introduce on the routers

- The eight levels of logging

- Deciphering the logging messages

Message logging is enabled by default and it is directed to the console and the internal buffer. The privileged exec command **logging on** is the default setting, and if you enter **no**

**logging on,** all logging except console logging will be turned off. The options for logging message destinations are:

- Console
- Internal buffer
- Virtual terminal session (Telnet)
- Syslog server (see Figure 4-5)

**Figure 4-5** *Error Message Logging Destinations*

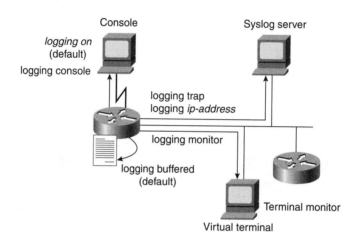

The following relationship demonstrates how different methods of logging compare in terms of the overhead they produce:

Buffered logging < Syslog < Virtual terminal < Console logging

Table 4-1 displays the commands you must use to configure the destination of logging messages and the desired level of logging for each destination.

**Table 4-1** *List of Commands for Logging Message Destinations*

| Command | Usage Explanation |
| --- | --- |
| **logging console** [*level*] | This command turns console logging on and specifies the level of logging to be directed to the console. (The default setting is Enabled.) |
| | The **no logging console** command disables console logging. |

**Table 4-1**   *List of Commands for Logging Message Destinations (Continued)*

| Command | Usage Explanation |
|---|---|
| **logging buffered** [*level*] | Use this command to enable sending logging messages to the internal buffer (use **no logging buffered** to disable it) and specify the level of logging desired to be buffered. This feature is enabled by default. |
| **logging monitor** [*level*] | Use this command to enable sending logging messages to the virtual terminal sessions (use **no logging monitor** to disable it) and specify the level of logging desired to be directed to the virtual terminal lines. |
| | From within a virtual terminal session, typing the command **terminal monitor** enables the display of logging messages. The command **terminal no monitor** turns this feature off. |
| **logging trap** [*level*] | This command allows you to enable sending logging messages to syslog servers and specify the level of these messages. The **no logging trap** command disables this feature. |
| | The default level is Informational. |
| | (Also see the explanation for the **logging** [*ip-address*] command below.) |
| **logging** [*ip-address*] | This command identifies the IP address of the syslog server so that the router can direct its logging messages to this address. Ifyou have a list of syslog servers to which you want to send the logging messages, you may enter this command with each server's appropriate address one by one. Use the **no** form of this command to take a server off the list. |

There are eight levels of logging. If you specify a particular level of logging—for console logging, for example—the messages of that level and of the higher levels (numerically lower) are forwarded to the console. The levels of logging messages are explained in Table 4-2.

**Table 4-2**   *Logging Messages*

| Level | Logging Message |
|---|---|
| 0 | Emergencies |
| 1 | Alerts |
| 2 | Critical |
| 3 | Errors |
| 4 | Warnings |

*continues*

**Table 4-2** *Logging Messages (Continued)*

| Level | Logging Message |
|-------|-----------------|
| 5 | Notifications |
| 6 | Informational |
| 7 | Debugging |

Please note that when you enter one of the commands for specifying the level of logging to be directed to a particular place (console or virtual terminal sessions, for example), you must enter the English phrase for the level of logging and not the numeric value for it. For instance, the command to make virtual terminal lines receive logging messages at the errors level and higher (in other words errors, critical, alerts, emergencies) would be:

```
Router(config)# logging monitor error
```

Now let us discuss the anatomy of the logging messages. Each message is associated with one of the eight levels of logging, which is referred to as the severity of the message. Table 4-3 provides the eight levels of logging messages along with their associated severity levels and short descriptions. Logging messages are composed of a % sign followed by the facility, the severity, the mnemonic, and a text message. For instance, in this message:

```
%TR-3-WIREFAULT:Unit[0],wirefault:check the lobe cable MAU connection
```

the facility is Token Ring, severity is 3 (error), mnemonic is WIREFAULT, and, of course, the text message is reporting a wire fault condition.

**Table 4-3** *Logging Message Levels with Severity*

| Level Name | Severity | Description | Syslog Definition |
|------------|----------|-------------|-------------------|
| Emergencies | 0 | System unusable | LOG_EMERG |
| Alerts | 1 | Immediate action needed | LOG_ALERT |
| Critical | 2 | Critical conditions | LOG_CRIT |
| Errors | 3 | Error conditions | LOG_ERR |
| Warnings | 4 | Warning conditions | LOG_WARNING |
| Notifications | 5 | Normal significant conditions | LOG_NOTICE |
| Informational | 6 | Informational messages only | LOG_INFO |
| Debugging | 7 | Debugging messages | LOG_DEBUG |

## show logging Command

To display the state of syslog error and event logging, including host addresses, which type of logging (destination) is enabled, and other logging statistics, use the **show logging** (privileged EXEC) command. This command also displays the messages that are logged in the buffer.

Example 4-2 displays sample output of the **show logging** command.

**Example 4-2**  *The show logging Command*

```
Router#show logging
Syslog logging: enabled
    Console logging: disabled
    Monitor logging: level debugging, 13 messages logged.
    Trap logging: level informational, 13 messages logged.
    Logging to 171.16.20.20
SNMP logging: enabled, retransmission after 30 seconds
    69 messages logged
    Logging to 10.1.1.30, 0/10
    Logging to 10.2.1.40, 0/10
    Logging to 10.3.2.50, 0/10
```

# Reachability and Step-by-Step Path Tests

Testing reachability of a node from another node in a network is one of the most basic tests to perform during support tasks. Testing the path a packet takes (identifying the nodes it goes through) is another very useful technique for troubleshooting. These tests are often used during fact gathering or when testing for results of an action taken. Ping has traditionally been known as an IP layer testing application. Ping is now available for other protocols, such as IPX. Cisco IOS provides Ping for IP, IPX, AppleTalk, and a few other protocols such as DECNET, XNS, CLNS, and VINES. Trace is an IP-layer path discovery/ testing tool. Prior to IOS 12.0, Cisco IOS furnished **trace** for IP protocol only; as of IOS 12.0, however, **trace** is also available for IPX.

## ping Command (IP) (User and Privileged)

The **ping** command is supported at the user and privileged exec modes.When used at the user mode, a set of default parameters such as five echoes, 100 bytes each with two-second time-outs will be used (in non-verbose form). You may enter an IP address or a name with the **ping** command (if the name can be resolved to an IP address using the local HOSTS table or using a DNS server).

Ping sends ICMP echo (echo request) to the destination, and the destination node replies to the source with an ICMP echo-reply. If you receive five echo-replies to the five echoes (echo requests) submitted, it means that five 100-byte packets could travel to the destination and back, each within a two-second time interval. There is a distinct possibility that the first of the five echoes times out; the cause is usually attributed to the need for ARP, or, in case of a DDR connection, to the need to build a circuit.

Example 4-3 displays sample outputs of the **ping** command. If all of the five packets don't get to the destination and back, or at least not within the two-second time interval, you need to investigate further. In this situation, you should usually choose closer and closer targets; once you find one that you can communicate with, you can define the problem area and focus your troubleshooting efforts. When you encounter timeouts or administratively prohibited cases, you will have to discover (and deal with) the busy or the protected devices accordingly.

**Example 4-3**    *User Mode ping (IP)*

```
RouterA> ping routerB
Type escape sequence to abort.
Sending 5, 100-byte ICMP Echos to 10.3.2.1, timeout is 2 seconds:
!!!!!
Success rate is 100 percent, round-trip min/avg/max = 1/3/4 ms

RouterA> ping 172.16.5.5
Type escape sequence to abort.
Sending 5, 100-byte ICMP Echos to 172.16.5.5, timeout is 2 seconds:
.U.U.
Success rate is 0 percent (0/5)
```

A fundamental point of the ping tool is that it tests the round-trip path to and from a target. I often notice that when ping fails, people focus all of their effort on trying to troubleshoot the local device (source), and they forget that a ping failure is often caused by the destination device not having a path for sending the echo reply back to the source. See Table 4-4 for short descriptions of the test characters used by the ping facility. To abort a ping session, type the escape sequence (Shift, Control, and the 6 key, all at once). Another useful command that you can use when troubleshooting connectivity issues is the **debug ip icmp** command.

**Table 4-4**    *ping (IP) Response Characters*

| Character | Description |
|-----------|-------------|
| ! | Reply received |
| . | Time-out |
| U | Destination unreachable |
| N | Network unreachable |
| P | Protocol unreachable |
| Q | Source quench |
| M | Could not fragment |
| ? | Unknown packet type |

You also have the option of using the extended ping in privileged exec mode. From the privileged mode, if you just enter the **ping** command, you will be prompted for the protocol (default is IP). After selecting IP, you are prompted for the target IP address, repeat count, datagram size, and timeout in seconds; finally, you are asked if you are interested in extended commands. Table 4-5 provides explanations for the parameters you are prompted for if you choose the extended commands option.

**Table 4-5** *ping (IP) Extended Commands*

| Field | Explanation |
|---|---|
| **Source address:** | You may enter one of the router's local IP addresses or one of its interfaces. |
| **Type of service [0]:** | You may turn this bit to 1 to indicate Internet Service Quality selection. |
| **Set DF bit in IP header? [no]:** | If you answer yes, the Don't Fragment option will not allow this packet to be fragmented when it has to go through a segment with a smaller MTU and you will receive an error message from the device that wanted to fragment the packet. |
| **Data Pattern [0xABCD]:** | This prompt allows you to modify the 16-bit data pattern. All ones and all zeroes testing are commonly used to check sensitivity problems at the CSU/DSU or to detect cable problems such as crosstalk. |
| **Loose, Strict, Record, Timestamp, Verbose [none]:** | Even though it looks like this prompt is offering one (or none) of the options listed, if you select one, the prompt shows up again, in case you wanted to select more than one of the available options. If you select any option, Verbose is automatically selected also. Record is a very useful option because it displays the address(es) of the hops (up to nine) the packet goes through. Loose allows you to influence the path by specifying the address(es) of the hop(s) you want the packet to go through, perhaps as well as other hop(s). With the Strict option you specify the hop(s) that you want the packet to go through, but no other hop(s) are allowed to be visited as well. The difference between using the Record option of this command and using the **traceroute** command is quite interesting and worth discussing. The Record option of this command not only informs you of the hops that the echo request (of **ping**) went through to get to the destination, but it also informs you of the hops it visited on the return path. With the **traceroute** command you do not get information about the path that the echo reply takes. |
| **Sweep range of sizes [n]:** | Allows you to vary the size of the packets. |

# ping Command (IPX and AppleTalk)

Cisco IOS makes ping available for a number of protocols including IPX and AppleTalk. Ping for IPX and AppleTalk is available in user and privileged mode. Example 4-4 shows the syntax and the sample outputs for IPX and AppleTalk user mode pings.

**Example 4-4**   *User Mode **ping** (IPX and AppleTalk)*

```
Router> ping ipx 1000.0000.0c02.f3b4
Type escape sequence to abort.
Sending 5, 100-byte Novell Echoes to 1000.0000.0c02.f3b4, timeout is 2 seconds:
.....
Success rate is 0 percent (0/5)


Router>ping appletalk 100.50
Type escape sequence to abort.
Sending 5, 100-byte AppleTalk Echoes to 100.50, timeout is 2 seconds:
!!!!!
Success rate is 100 percent, round-trip min/avg/max = 3/3/7 ms
```

Cisco introduced ping for IPX as of version 8.2 of the IOS. However, since this is a Cisco proprietary tool, non-Cisco devices such as Novell servers do not respond to it. If you want your Cisco router to generate Novell-compliant pings, you can do so using the global configuration command **ipx ping-default novell**. But what if you want to be able to ping (IPX) Cisco devices as well as non-Cisco (Novell-compliant) devices? If this is the case, you should not use the **ipx ping-default novell** command. If you use the privileged mode ping (IPX), one of the questions you will be prompted with is whether you want a Novell standard echo. Hence, with the privileged mode ping (IPX) you can ping Cisco devices and have the choice to generate a Novell standard ping. Table 4-6 lists the test characters displayed in IPX ping responses along with their associated descriptions.

**Table 4-6**   *IPX **ping** Response Characters*

| Character | Description |
| --- | --- |
| ! | Reply received |
| . | Time-out |
| U | Destination unreachable |
| C | Congestion |
| I | Interrupt (user interrupted the test) |
| ? | Unknown |
| & | Packet lifetime exceeded |

Ping for AppleTalk sends AEP (AppleTalk Echo Protocol) packets to the destination (another AppleTalk node) and waits for replies. The response characters of AppleTalk ping along with their associated descriptions are provided in Table 4-7.

**Table 4-7**    *AppleTalk **ping** Response Characters*

| Character | Description |
| --- | --- |
| ! | Reply received |
| . | Time-out |
| B | Bad echo reply received |
| C | Echo with bad DDP checksum received |
| E | Error encountered during sending of the echo packet |
| R | No route available to send the echo packet |

# traceroute Command (IP) (User and Privileged)

Use the **traceroute** command to find the path between IP devices. Trace, introduced with the release 10.0 of Cisco IOS, is currently available only for the IP protocol. The **traceroute** command can be executed from the user and the privileged exec modes, but from the privileged exec mode, you have the ability to use the extended trace, which is more flexible and informative.

**NOTE**    The command **traceroute** is commonly used in its short form, **trace**.

With the release 12.0 of Cisco IOS, **traceroute** is also available for IPX.

The **traceroute** application starts by sending probes (UDP) with TTL value of 1, and keeps on incrementing the TTL value and sending the probes until the destinationis reached. When the TTL value equals 1, the probe goes as far as the first hop (router), which responds with a time-exceeded message (ICMP TTL exceeded). Note that when a packet reaches a router its TTL is reduced by one. Next, the TTL is incremented to 2, and the probe reaches the second hop in the path to the destination, and so on, until the destination is reached. The destination node sends a port-unreachable message (ICMP port unreachable) back to the source because it cannot deliver the packet to an application (the default destination port of the probe is UDP port 33434). Cisco IOS generates three probes for each TTL value, and if a response is not received within a time interval (times out), it prints an asterisk (*) on its output. Trace terminates when the destination is reached, the maximum TTL is exceeded, or the user interrupts it with the escape sequence.

The basic **traceroute** command (available in the user and privileged exec modes) uses the IP address of the egress interface as its source IP address, uses three seconds for its timeout value, sends three probes for each TTL value, and has 30 for its maximum TTL value. On the other hand, the extended trace, available from the privileged exec mode only, allows you to modify its operational parameters. Furthermore, with the extended trace, similarly to extended ping, you can also specify the source address of your probes and, if needed, choose the Loose, Strict, Record, Timestamp, and Verbose options. Example 4-5 displays a screen capture that shows the behavior of the extended **trace** command.

It is worthwhile mentioning that Cisco documentation warns that you might get a lot of timeouts with **traceroute**. The explanation given indicates that some devices do not generate port unreachable messages, and some attempt to use the TTL value of the received probe for the response packet. Both of these cases may cause the originating device to experience a lot of timeouts (asterisks).

**Example 4-5**  *Extended trace*

```
Router> trace
Protocol [IP]:
Target IP address: A_BackR.ciscocit.com
Source address:
Numeric display [n]:
Timeout in seconds [3]:
Probe count [3]:
Minimum Time to Live [1]:
Maximum Time to Live [30]:
Port number[33434]:
Loose, Strict, Record, Timestamp, Verbose[none]:
Type escape sequence to abort.
Tracing the route to A_BackR.ciscocit.com (10.11.100.200)
  1 A_StubR.ciscocit.com (172.16.15.100) 70 msec 70 msec 79 msec
  2 A_BackR.ciscocit.com (10.11.100.200) 80 msec 84 msec 82 msec
```

# Information Needed by Technical Support

In some troubleshooting cases you have to seek assistance from Cisco Technical Support. When customer support engineers (CSE) at Cisco Systems open a case, they need a set of information from a caller. The following paragraphs list and describe different types of information to furnish to the CSEs.

You must identify your company and your service arrangement. Next, you have to provide a statement of your problem, a brief history of the problem, a list of reported symptoms, an indication of how often the symptoms are observed, and any actions you have taken so far. Network diagram(s) and the output of the **show version** and **show running-config** commands are among the most general information you will have to furnish.

If you are dealing with hang or crash scenarios, the output of **show stacks** and core dump (and exception dump) are usually asked for.

If your case has mostly to do with performance degradation, the following commands' outputs will provide a wealth of related facts, and are therefore necessary:

- **show interfaces**
- **show buffers**
- **show memory**
- **show processes [cpu]**

When you face loss of functionality scenarios, for instance, if a protocol or a connection is faulty, the outputs of the following commands are likely to be requested:

- **show protocol**
- **show** [*protocol*] **protocol**
- **show** [*protocol*] **route**
- **show** [*protocol*] **traffic** (e.g., **show ipx traffic**)
- **show** [*protocol*] **interfaces**
- **show** [*protocol*] **access-lists**

Regardless of the nature of your problem, the outputs of **trace**, **debug**, protocol analyzer captures, and so on may also be asked for.

Also, be aware of the command **show tech-support**, which displays output equivalent to entering many troubleshooting **show** commands at once. The **show tech-support** command output comprises the following sections:

- **show version**
- **show running-config** (in privileged exec mode)
- **show controllers**
- **show stack**
- **show interfaces**
- **show processes mem**
- **show processes cpu**
- **show buffers**

# show version Command

This command is one of the most popular fact-gathering commands. Example 4-6 displays a sample of the **show version** command executed at a Cisco 2514 router.

**Example 4-6**  *show version Command Output*

```
A_StubR#show version
Cisco Internetwork Operating System Software
IOS (tm) 2500 Software (C2500-JS-L), Version 11.3(6), RELEASE SOFTWARE (fc1)
Copyright © 1986-1998 by cisco Systems, Inc.
Compiled Tue 06-Oct-98 22:17 by kpma
Image text-base: 0x03048CF4, data-base: 0x00001000

ROM: System Bootstrap, Version 5.2(8a), RELEASE SOFTWARE
BOOTFLASH: 3000 Bootstrap Software (IGS-RXBOOT), Version 10.2(8a),
    RELEASE SOFTWARE (fc1)

A_StubR uptime is 25 minutes
System restarted by power-on
System image file is "flash:c2500-js-l_113-6.bin", booted via flash

cisco 2500 (68030) processor (revision D) with 4096K/2048K bytes of memory.
Processor board ID 04203139, with hardware revision 00000000
Bridging software.
X.25 software, Version 3.0.0.
SuperLAT software copyright 1990 by Meridian Technology Corp).
TN3270 Emulation software.
2 Ethernet/IEEE 802.3 interface(s)
2 Serial network interface(s)
32K bytes of non-volatile configuration memory.
16384K bytes of processor board System flash (Read ONLY)

Configuration register is 0x2102
```

The output of the **show version** command provides a valuable set of information. Depending on your type of router, different hardware configuration and non-standard software options are displayed by the **show version** command. The following paragraph focuses on the general output of this command:

On the first few lines of output, the **show version** command displays the IOS version number and its internal name. The IOS internal name tells you about its capabilities and options. In Example 4-6 the IOS version is 11.3(6) and its name is C2500-JS-L. For a description of the IOS naming convention for different routers, refer to Cisco Connection Online (CCO).

In the second section of the output, the Bootstrap software and the RXBOOT image versions are displayed.

Next, you can see the system uptime, how the system last restarted, and the image filename and where it loaded from (the image filename is modifiable and may not be the name it was originally given by Cisco Systems). Please note that if the router encounters errors (such as software crashes) that force the router to reload, that information (reason for reload) will be displayed here and it can be quite useful to the Cisco TAC engineer.

The section near the bottom provides hardware information (processor type, memory size, existing controllers) and non-standard software options.

The very last line of the **show version** command's output displays the value of the config-register in hex format.

# Buffers and Queues

System buffers are memory allocated from main system memory (also referred to as shared memory) to hold packets while they are process-switched. There are parameters regarding these buffers that can be tuned, but that is not often recommended, and tuning them has no effect on any route caching methods you may have (fast, autonomous, silicon, or optimum switching, for instance). To enhance the (packet) processing power of your router, you are usually encouraged to take advantage of your router's route caching capabilities. Because the buffers that hold packets while they are being process switched are memory borrowed from the main system (RAM) memory, the memory available is not too limited. One can conjecture that this is an advantage of process switching. There are six buffer sizes, each of which is appropriate for a specific range of packet sizes:

> Small Buffers: 104 Bytes
> Middle Buffers: 600 Bytes
> Big Buffers: 1524 Bytes
> Very Big Buffers: 4520 Bytes
> Large Buffers: 5024 Bytes
> Huge Buffers: 18024 Bytes

You must keep in mind that a buffer must be allocated and free at the time a packet arrives, or the packet will be dropped and the number of misses (shown in the output of the **show buffers** command, discussed later) is incremented. Furthermore, the router cannot afford to have too many buffers allocated and free (to avoid potential drops and misses), as that will reduce the available memory (from the shared pool) needed for other purposes. This challenge is addressed by having a minimum number of buffers (for each size) allocated at all times, and dynamically allocated and de-allocated buffers based on the traffic rate (process-switched packets sent and received). The parameters that are used for managing buffers follow and apply to each buffer size:

- **Permanent**—The minimum number of buffers allocated. Buffers are de-allocated (trimmed) at times, but the number of allocated buffers will not go below this.

- **Max-Free**—When the number of buffers that are allocated but not used (free) exceeds this value, a trim (de-allocation) is triggered. The memory is returned to the shared pool, and can be used for other purposes.

- **Min-Free**—As the allocated (free) buffers are used up, the number of free buffers is reduced. When the number of free buffers reduces to be equal to the Min-Free parameter, buffer allocation (create) is triggered. This attempts to always have a minimum number of allocated and unused buffers available for each packet size.

- **Initial**—This parameter indicates how many buffers should be allocated (for a particular packet size) at the router initialization time. This value is usually larger than Permanent.

When faced with performance degradation support scenarios, the **show buffers** command is very useful. If you see a large number of misses reported for a particular buffer size, you may have to adjust the Permanent or Min-Free parameters for that particular buffer size.

The number of failures indicates how many times the allocation of more buffers has been unsuccessful. Please consult your technical support representative before adjusting any buffer parameters. Example 4-7 shows the syntax for adjusting buffer parameters.

**Example 4-7**    *Adjusting Buffer Parameters*

```
A_StubR(config)#buffers ?
  Ethernet  IEEE 802.3
  Serial    Serial
  big       Big buffers
  huge      Huge buffers
  large     Large buffers
  middle    Middle buffers
  small     Small buffers
  verybig   Very Big buffers

A_StubR(config)#buffers big ?
  initial    Temporary buffers allocated at system reload
  max-free   Maximum number of free buffers
  min-free   Minimum number of free buffers
  permanent  Number of permanent buffers

A_StubR(config)#buffers big min-free ?
  <0-20480>  Number of buffers
```

# Buffers and Queues (Cisco 7000/7010)

In the Cisco 7000, routers' packets are held in interface hardware buffers, SP or SSP buffers, and RP buffers. Figure 4-6 displays those Cisco 7000 router components along with the error conditions associated with each of them.

**Figure 4-6**    *Cisco 7000 Buffers and Error Conditions*

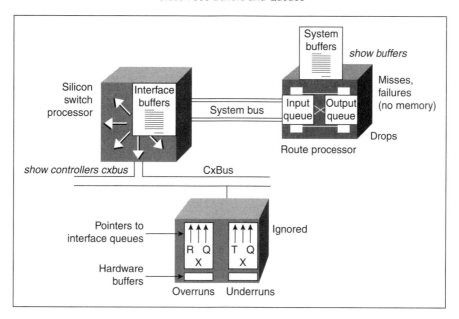

Cisco 7000 Buffers and Queues

Interface input and output queues on the RP are linked lists of processor buffers used for each interface. An interface queue can hence be composed of different-sized buffers. The queue associated with an interface can grow (to a configured limit) and shrink (down to zero). When a packet must be held in the input queue or output queue of an interface (on the RP), a buffer is taken away from the appropriate allocated and free list (based on size). However, if the input or output queue of an interface reaches its maximum size, the queue cannot grow larger. In other words, after a queue reaches its maximum size, it will likely start dropping subsequent packets. When you look at the **show interface** command output, pay attention to the number of drops reported for input and output queues. The default size of the input queue (hold queue) and output queue (hold queue) are 75 (packets) and 40 (packets) correspondingly.

The SP or SSP has 512 KB of memory. This memory is partially used for route caching (autonomous switching) and partially used for buffering the packets copied in from different interface processors. Use the **show controllers cxbus** command to find the allocation of interface buffers on the SP.

There are hardware buffers that are used to hold packets on the interface hardware itself. If an interface buffer gets full, an ignore is registered. In other words, every time an interface cannot accept a frame due to an input buffer being full, the ignore counter is incremented by one. Ignore is the result of either a high-speed interface accepting frames close to wire speed and SP not being able to put the data out of the interface hardware buffer fast enough, or a CxBus that is so busy that the interface hardware does not get enough chances to unload data from its buffers to the SP.

## Buffers and Queues (Cisco 4000/3000/2500)

In Cisco 4000/3000/2500 routers, because there is no SP, SSP, or RSP, buffers reside on the shared memory. Packets enter into an interface (hardware buffer), and they are sent directly to the shared memory.

In shared memory, a packet is kept in the input queue corresponding to the ingress interface. Next, an output interface for the packet is possibly selected (perhaps after the process switching or fast switching task completes). Then the packet is held in the output queue of the egress interface, until it is finally sent to the output interface hardware.

## show buffers Command

The **show buffers** command displays information (statistics) on buffer elements, public buffer pools, and interface buffer pools. Buffer elements are small data structures that are used for internal operating system queues or when a buffer must be associated with more than one queue. The public buffer pools are presented in the second section of the **show buffers** output and each buffer size (small, middle, and so on) is presented with its own statistics. The last section of the **show buffers** command output displays the buffer statistics for each of the router's interfaces. Example 4-8 presents a sample output (partial) from the **show buffers** exec command.

**Example 4-8**   *A Sample Output of the **show buffers** Exec Command*

```
A_StubR#show buffers
Buffer elements:
     500 in free list (500 max allowed)
     3846 hits, 0 misses, 0 created

Public buffer pools:
Small buffers, 104 bytes (total 50, permanent 50):
     49 in free list (20 min, 150 max allowed)
     1440 hits, 0 misses, 0 trims, 0 created
     0 failures (0 no memory)
Middle buffers, 600 bytes (total 25, permanent 25):
     25 in free list (10 min, 150 max allowed)
     703 hits, 0 misses, 0 trims, 0 created
     0 failures (0 no memory)
Big buffers, 1524 bytes (total 50, permanent 50):
```

**Example 4-8**   *A Sample Output of the **show buffers** Exec Command (Continued)*

```
        50 in free list (5 min, 150 max allowed)
        150 hits, 0 misses, 0 trims, 0 created
        0 failures (0 no memory)
VeryBig buffers, 4520 bytes (total 10, permanent 10):
        10 in free list (0 min, 100 max allowed)
        0 hits, 0 misses, 0 trims, 0 created
        0 failures (0 no memory)
Large buffers, 5024 bytes (total 0, permanent 0):
        0 in free list (0 min, 10 max allowed)
        0 hits, 0 misses, 0 trims, 0 created
        0 failures (0 no memory)
Huge buffers, 18024 bytes (total 0, permanent 0):
        0 in free list (0 min, 4 max allowed)
        0 hits, 0 misses, 0 trims, 0 created
        0 failures (0 no memory)

Interface buffer pools:
Ethernet0 buffers, 1524 bytes (total 32, permanent 32):
        8 in free list (0 min, 32 max allowed)
        24 hits, 0 fallbacks
        8 max cache size, 8 in cache
```

# show memory Command

The **show memory** exec command is often used to check the amount of a router's free memory. In troubleshooting cases where router performance is the focus, this is a major command used to see the statistics about the router's memory. Example 4-9 displays a sample output (partial) of this command executed on a Cisco 2514 router.

**Example 4-9**   *A Sample Output of the **show memory** Exec Command*

```
A_BackR#show memory
Head               Total(b)   Used(b)   Free(b)   Lowest(b)   Largest(b)
Processor 90C3C     3597252    983900   2613352    2604696     2611612
I/O       400000    2097152    391980   1705172    1705172     1704752


            Processor memory


Address   Bytes   Prev.   Next   Ref   PrevF   NextF   Alloc PC   What
90C3C     1064    0       91090  1                     1A1630     List Elements
91090     2864    90C3C   91BEC  1                     31A1630    List  Headers
91BEC     2668    91090   92684  1                     3150160    TTY   data
92684     2000    91BEC   92E80  1                     3152534    TTY   Input Buf
92E80     512     92684   930AC  1                     3152564    TTY   Output Buf
930AC     3000    92E80   93C90  1                     31B2252    Interrupt Stack
.
.
.
            I/O memory
```

*continues*

**Example 4-9**  *A Sample Output of the **show memory** Exec Command (Continued)*

```
Address   Bytes   Prev.    Next    Ref   PrevF   NextF   Alloc PC  What
400000    260     0        400130  1                     3183DD8   *Packet Data*
400130    260     400000   400260  1                     3183DD8   *Packet Data*
400260    260     400130   400390  1                     3183DD8   *Packet Data*
400390    260     400260   4004C0  1                     3183DD8   *Packet Data*
.
.
.
```

The **show memory** exec command's output is organized in separate sections. In the first section you can see the summary statistics about processor memory and I/O memory (see Example 4-9). Then you can see the more detailed (block-by-block) display of memory information first for the processor memory, and then for the I/O memory. The output is not uniform across different router platforms. For example, if you execute this command on a Cisco 7000 router, the output will include processor memory and multibus memory statistics. If you execute this command on Cisco 4000 series routers, you will receive information about SRAM and I/O memory as well as processor memory. In all cases, the processor memory statistics are shown. You must pay attention to the total amount of memory, amount used, and the total amount of free memory. The Cisco TAC engineer helping you might ask questions about your router's memory utilization or simply request the output. Ask your technical support representative about the amount of free memory he/ she recommends (on average) to be available.

# show processes Command

The **show processes** exec command displays your router's CPU utilization and a list of active processes along with their corresponding process ID, priority, scheduler test (status), CPU time used, number of times invoked, and so on. This command is also very useful when you are evaluating your router's performance and CPU utilization.

A sample output of the **show processes** command is shown in Example 4-10. As you can see, the first line of the output shows the CPU utilization for the last five seconds, one minute, and five minutes. The output provides 4%/4% in front of the CPU utilization for the last five seconds: the first number is the total utilization and the second number is the utilization due to interrupt routines.

**Example 4-10** *A Sample Output of the **show processes** Exec Command*

```
A_BackR#show processes

CPU utilization for five seconds: 4%/4%; one minute: 6%; fiveminutes: 5%

PID Q Ty PC Runtime(ms) Invoked uSecs Stacks TTY   Process

1   C sp 31B6178  28    353      79    736/1000 0    Load Meter
```

**Example 4-10** *A Sample Output of the **show processes** Exec Command (Continued)*

```
2   M *  0        324   154     2103  2588/4000 0    Exec

3   L st 31A7112 5584  167    33437  1768/2000 0    Check heaps

4   C we 31ACF5A    0    1        0  1732/2000 0    Pool Manager

5   M st 3147E02    4    2     2000  1700/2000 0    Timers

6   M we 30E6690    0    2        0  1700/2000 0    SerialBackgroun

7   L we 31D4BD0    4   52       76  1612/2000 0    ARP Input

8   M we 32D6848    4    2     2000  1624/2000 0    DDR Timers

9   M we 30EA414    0    1        0  1736/2000 0    SERIAL A'detect

10  M we 31F9270  604  398     1517  3024/4000 0    IP Input

11  M we 3264668   84  206      407  1556/2000 0    CDP Protocol
 .
 .
 .
```

When you decide to use the **show processes** command, try to execute it a few times, with a one-minute lapse in between, to get a more reliable idea about which processes are invoked most often and how much CPU time they consumed. You may also execute the **show processes cpu** command to get the five-second, one-minute, and five-minute display of CPU utilization for each process. Table 4-8 shows some of the column headings used in the output of the **show processes** command with a brief description for each of them.

**Table 4-8**    *Some of the Column Headings of the **show processes** Command Output*

| Column Heading | Description |
| --- | --- |
| PID | Process ID |
| Q | Priority (C: Critical, H: High, M: Medium, L: Low) |
| Ty | Scheduler Test (status) |
| | *: currently running |
| | E: waiting |
| | We: waiting for an event |
| | Sa: sleeping until an absolute time |
| | Si: sleeping for a time interval |
| | St: sleeping until a timer expires |
| | Hg: hung |
| | Xx: dead |

*continues*

**Table 4-8**    *Some of the Column Headings of the **show processes** Command Output (Continued)*

| Column Heading | Description |
|---|---|
| PC | Program Counter |
| Runtime | CPU time the process has used (in milliseconds) |
| Invoked | Number of times the process has been invoked |
| uSecs | Number of microseconds of CPU time used at each invoke |

# show controllers cxbus Command

The **show controllers cxbus** exec command is used on the Cisco 7x00 series routers to display information about the SP, the CxBus controller, and the contents and microcode of cards attached to the bus. This command's output for the most part is useful for diagnostic tasks performed by Cisco support engineers only. Example 4-11 is a sample output of the **show controllers cxbus** command executed on a Cisco 7000 router.

**Example 4-11** *A Sample Output of the **show controllers cxbus** Command*

```
Router# show controllers cxbus
Switch Processor 5, hardware version 11.1, microcode version 172.6
  Microcode loaded from system
  512 Kbytes of main memory, 128 Kbytes cache memory
  75 1520 byte buffers, 86 4484 byte buffers
  Restarts: 0 line down, 0 hung output, 0 controller error
CIP 3, hardware version 1.1, microcode version 170.1
  Microcode loaded from system
  CPU utilization 7%, sram 145600/512K, dram 86688/2M
  Interface 24 - Channel 3/0
    43 buffer RX queue threshold, 61 buffer TX queue limit, buffer size 4484
    ift 0007, rql 32, tq 0000 0468, tql 61
    Transmitter delay is 0 microseconds
  Interface 25 - Channel 3/1
    43 buffer RX queue threshold, 61 buffer TX queue limit, buffer size 4484
    ift 0007, rql 34, tq 0000 0000, tql 61
    Transmitter delay is 0 microseconds
  .
  .
  .
```

The top portion of the output displayed by Example 4-11 tells you the SP's hardware and microcode version, main memory and cache memory size, number of different buffer sizes, and the number of restarts due to line down (communication line), hung output, or controller error. The second part of the output displayed by Example 4-11 includes information about the Channel Interface Processor (CIP). In this section, you can see the CIP's hardware and microcode version, CPU utilization, free and total SRAM memory (Static RAM is a high speed memory used for operational code), free and total DRAM memory (Dynamic RAM is normal memory used for packets, data,and so on), and information about each of the CIP interfaces.

# show stacks Command

**show stacks** is an exec command that is commonly used to diagnose system crash situations. The first section of this command's output displays stack utilization of processes and interrupt routines, and the reason for the last system reboot. When a system crash happens, failure type, failure program counter (PC), address (operand address), and a stack trace are saved by the ROM Monitor. The **show stacks** command displays the data saved by the ROM Monitor. The stack trace is displayed in the second section of the **show stacks** command output (if there has been a system failure).

In the past, support engineers would submit the stack trace of their router to Cisco System's technical support representatives, who had access to symbol tables, object files, source code, and the stack decoder software. Today, the stack decoder is available online (from the CCO) and you can cut your router's stack trace from the output of the **show stacks** command and paste it in the input field of the stack decoder software. Stack decoder decodes the stack trace and creates a symbol file. The symbol file (perhaps along with other information in the trace) usually provides enough information to isolate the cause of any problems that were experienced.

Example 4-12 shows an example of the show stacks output from a bus error. The message "System was restarted by bus error" indicates that the processor tried to use a device or a memory location that either did not exist or did not respond properly (this could be due to a software bug or a hardware problem). Operand address, the address the processor was trying to access when the system crashed, is used as the clue to tell if the failure was due to software or hardware. If the operand address (reported on the output of the **show stacks** command) is valid, the problem is probably in the hardware. In other words, the operand address, not the program counter, provides the memory map location of the error, which can be used to infer the general area of the router where the error occurred.

**Example 4-12** *A Sample Output of the **show stacks** Command*

```
Router# show stacks

Minimum process stacks:
Free/Size  Name
 652/1000  Router Init
 726/1000  Init
 744/1000  BGP Open
 686/1200  Virtual Exec
Interrupt Level stacks:
Level  Called  Free/Size  Name
1      0       1000/1000  env-flash
3      738     900/1000   Multiport Communications Interfaces
5      178     970/1000   Console UART
```

*continues*

**Example 4-12** *A Sample Output of the* **show stacks** *Command (Continued)*

```
System was restarted by bus error at PC 0xAD1F4, address 0xD0D0D1A
GS Software (GS3), Version 10.2
Compiled Tue 11-Aug-94 13:27 by jthomas
Stack trace from system failure:
FP: 0x29C158, RA: 0xACFD4
FP: 0x29C184, RA: 0xAD20C
FP: 0x29C1B0, RA: 0xACFD4
FP: 0x29C1DC, RA: 0xAD304
FP: 0x29C1F8, RA: 0xAF774
FP: 0x29C214, RA: 0xAF83E
FP: 0x29C228, RA: 0x3E0CA
FP: 0x29C244, RA: 0x3BD3C
```

Failure types are usually one of the following: bus error, address error, watchdog timeout, parity error, or emulator trap. Table 4-9 displays common failure types with a brief description for each of them.

**Table 4-9**    *Common Failure Types Reported by the* **show stacks** *Command*

| Failure Type | Description |
| --- | --- |
| Bus error | The processor tried to use a device or a memory location that either did not exist or did not respond properly (could be due to software bug or hardware error). |
| Address error (software forced crash) | The software tried to access data on incorrectly aligned boundaries (usually indicates a software bug). |
| Watchdog timeout | Watchdog timer was not reset and caused a trap. Watchdog timers are used by Cisco processors to prevent certain system hangs (indicates a hardware or software bug). |
| Parity error | Internal hardware checks have failed (this is due to hardware problems). |
| Emulator trap | Processor executed an illegal instruction (illegal branching). A hardware problem, such as ROM failure, can also cause an emulator trap error. |

# Core Dumps

The full copy of memory image is called a core dump. This image can be useful for determining the cause of a crash. Core dumps are usually submitted to Cisco support engineers, who are specialized in analyzing the memory image (using source codes, memory maps, etc). The core dump can transfer the binary image file using TFTP, FTP, or RCP protocols (see Figure 4-7). You must remember that performing a core dump disrupts regular network operation.

**Figure 4-7**    *Creating Core Dump*

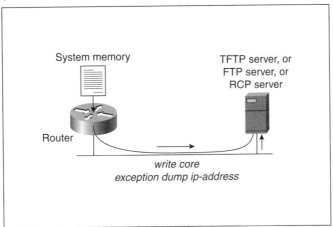

If your router is malfunctioning, but has not crashed, use the **write core** command to generate a core dump without reloading. You must make sure that your server (TFTP, FTP, or RCP server) is reachable and has enough storage space. You must also learn the file-naming convention that the server's operating system supports. Finally, find out whether you need to create an empty file (with the desired name) on the server in advance.

The **exception dump** *ip-address* global configuration command (*ip-address* is the address of your TFTP, FTP, or RCP server) causes the router to attempt to produce a core dump when it crashes. By default, the core dump is written to a file named *hostname*-core on your server (*hostname* is the name of the router). If you want to change the name of the core file, the **exception core-file** *filename* command allows you do that.

Keep in mind that depending on the type of crash, this procedure does not always succeed. Finally, you need to be aware that using TFTP has a limitation. If you use TFTP to dump the core file to a server, the router will only dump the first 16 MB of its memory image (and if the router's memory is larger than 16 MB, part of the image will be missing). Hence, RCP or FTP is recommended to dump the core file for routers with larger than 16 MB of memory.

# Foundation Summary

The Foundation Summary is a collection of quick reference information that provides a convenient review of many key concepts in this chapter. For those of you who already feel comfortable with the topics in this chapter, this summary helps you recall a few details. For those of you who just read this chapter, this review should help solidify some key facts. For any of you doing your final prep before the exam, these tables and figures are a convenient way to review the day before the exam.

## Handling Cisco IOS Troubleshooting Tools

These tools and commands provide a wealth of information that can be very useful for troubleshooting purposes, but due to their impact on router and network performance they need to be handled and used properly. These powerful tools use up a router's CPU cycles and memory, may be given higher priority than network traffic, and may disable some features such as fast switching.

## Routing and Switching Tasks and Route Caching

Routing and switching are two of the important tasks that routers perform. Routing is basically the process of selecting one or more output interfaces for a packet (if possible), whereas switching is basically the process of moving the packet within the anatomy of the router from one location or component of the router to another. Switching is simpler than routing. Routing requires the main processor's attention (it interrupts the main processor) and takes CPU cycles and therefore it is responsible for most of the delay (latency) introduced by a router.

Route caching is a technique that reduces this latency and frees up the main processor from having to handle too many interrupts. Once a packet is processed by the routing process, and an output interface is selected based on the packet's destination (layer 3) address, this address/output-interface pair can be saved in a cache and be used for quick processing of the subsequent packets with the same destination network address. Because both routing and switching tasks were performed on the first packet, it is considered to have been process-switched. The subsequent packets (with the same destination network address) need not be process-switched. Since the routing information built from the processing of the first packet is available in the routing cache, the subsequent packets are fast switched. The place where the route caching information is held varies from router to router, and it also depends on the option enabled.

# Route Caching Methods and Commands

Route caching methods available in different Cisco router series and the commands to enable them are displayed in Table 4-10 (to disable any of these switching modes, use the **no** form of the command):

**Table 4-10**   *Route Caching Methods and Commands*

| Interface Configuration Command (IP is shown as the protocol example) | Route Caching (Switching) Method Enabled | Cisco Router Series Support |
|---|---|---|
| **ip route-cache** | Fast switching | All |
| **ip route-cache cbus** | Fast switching and autonomous switching | 7000 series with SP |
| **ip route-cache sse** | Silicon switching | 7000 series with SSP |
| **ip route-cache optimum** | Optimum switching | 7x00 series with RSP |
| **ip route-cache distributed** | Distributed | 7x00 series with VIP |
| **ip route-cache flow** | Netflow | 7x00 series with RSP |
| **ip route-cache flow** **ip route-cache distributed** | Distributed Netflow | 7x00 series with RSP and VIP |

# Debug Notes

**debug** is a troubleshooting command used to display information about various router operations and the related traffic generated or received by the router, as well as any error messages. This tool lets you discover significant facts about the working and faulty software and/or hardware components.

- **debug** is available from the privileged exec mode (of Cisco IOS).
- **debug** is treated as a very high priority task.
- **debug** can consume a significant amount of resources.
- The router is forced to process-switch the packets being debugged.
- **debug** must not be used as a monitoring tool.
- Use it for a short period of time and as a troubleshooting tool.

If you want to see a timestamp with each line of the **debug** output, you must load the timestamp service using this command:

```
router(config)#service timestamps debug [datetime ¦ uptime]
```

If you plan to see the debug output from within a Telnet session, you need to enter the **terminal monitor** command.

Usually, the **debug** command is used to diagnose a specific facility, task, or protocol. Sometimes the protocol has a specific member that you may want to focus on. Once you decide what you want to debug, then you usually have a choice to use the events option or the packets option of the **debug** command for that specific protocol. Event debugging is less resource intensive than packet debugging, but packet debugging produces more information.

Turning debugging on for everything (using the **debug all** command) is seriously discouraged in production networks. You will get a tremendous amount of information, very fast, but it can severely diminish the router's performance or even render it unusable.

Before starting to use the **debug** command, see the CPU utilization of your router (using the **show processes cpu** command). If your router's CPU utilization is consistently at 50% or more, you are advised to debug events instead of packets.

If possible, use the **debug** command during periods when network traffic is not at its peak and fewer critical business applications are active. Cisco routers give the **debug** command higher priority (with respect to CPU cycles) than network traffic.

Always remember to undo **debug** as soon as possible. You can use the **no debug** {*argument*} to turn off a specific debugging type. The **no debug all** or **undebug all** commands can be used to turn off all types of debugging that may be on.

For troubleshooting, also consider using protocol analyzers to capture and display network traffic. These have little or no impact on your network performance, yet they provide valuable information.

Using an access list with your **debug** command helps you focus the debug output on the task you are troubleshooting. The syntax for using an access list with the **debug** command is:

```
Router# debug ip packet detail access-list-number
```

# Logging Options

Table 4-11 shows logging options and their corresponding commands.

**Table 4-11**   *Logging Options and Their Corresponding Commands*

| Command | Usage Explanation |
| --- | --- |
| **logging console** [*level*] | This command turns console logging on and specifies the level of logging to be directed to the console. (The default setting is Enabled.) |
| | The **no logging console** command disables console logging. |

**Table 4-11**    *Logging Options and Their Corresponding Commands (Continued)*

| Command | Usage Explanation |
| --- | --- |
| **logging buffered** [*level*] | Use this command to enable sending logging messages to the internal buffer (use **no logging buffered** to disable it) and specify the level of logging desired to be buffered. This feature is enabled by default. |
| **logging monitor** [*level*] | Use this command to enable sending logging messages to the virtual terminal sessions (use **no logging monitor** to disable it) and specify the level of logging desired to be directed to the virtual terminal lines. |
| | From within a virtual terminal session, typing the command **terminal monitor** enables displaying of logging messages. The command **terminal no monitor** turns this feature off. |
| **logging trap** [*level*] | This command allows you to enable sending logging messages to syslog servers and specify the level of the these messages. The **no logging trap** command disables this feature. |
| | The default level is Informational. |
| | (See also the explanation for the **logging** [*ip-address*] command below) |
| **logging** [*ip-address*] | This command identifies the IP address of the syslog server so that the router can direct its logging messages to this address. If you have a list of syslog servers to which you want to send the logging messages, you may enter this command one time with each server's appropriate address. Use the **no** form of this command to take a server off the list. |

The following is a comparison of the overhead of different logging methods:

Buffered logging < Syslog < Virtual terminal < Console logging

# Information Needed by Technical Support

## General Information

- Your company's name and service arrangement number
- A statement of the problem
- A brief history of the problem

- A list of reported symptoms, how often the symptoms are observed, and the actions taken so far
- Network diagram(s)
- A list of protocols in use and policies in place
- Outputs of the **show version** and **show running-config** commands

## Crash Situations

- **show stacks**
- Core dump

## Performance Degradation Situations

- **show interfaces**
- **show buffers**
- **show memory**
- **show processes [cpu]**

## Loss of Functionality Situations

- **show protocol**
- **show** [*protocol*] **route**
- **show** [*protocol*] **traffic**
- **show** [*protocol*] **interfaces**
- **show** [*protocol*] **access-lists**

## Output of the show tech-support Command

- **show version**
- **show running-config** (in privileged exec mode)
- **show controllers**
- **show stack**
- **show interfaces**

- **show processes mem**
- **show processes cpu**
- **show buffers**

# Terms and Concepts Related to Buffer and Queues

Buffer Sizes:

- Small buffers: 104 Bytes
- Middle buffers: 600 Bytes
- Big buffers: 1524 Bytes
- Very big buffers: 4520 Bytes
- Large buffers: 5024 Bytes
- Huge buffers: 18024 Bytes

Configuration Parameters:

- **Permanent**—The minimum number of buffers allocated. Buffers are de-allocated (trimmed) at times, but the number of allocated buffers will not go below this.

- **Max-Free**—When the number of buffers that are allocated but not used (free) reaches this value, a trim (de-allocation) is triggered. The memory is returned to the shared pool and can be used for other purposes.

- **Min-Free**—As the allocated (free) buffers are used up, the number of free buffers is reduced. When the number of free buffers reduces to be equal to the Min-Free parameter, buffer allocation (create) is triggered. This attempts to always have a minimum number of allocated and unused buffers available for each packet size.

- **Initial**—This parameter indicates how many buffers should be allocated (for a particular packet size) at the router initialization time. This value is usually larger than Permanent.

# Reported Conditions

- **Ignored**—The number of packets ignored is shown in the output of the **show interfaces** command. If a buffer (on the interface hardware) gets full, an ignore is registered. In other words, every time an interface cannot accept a frame due to the input buffer being full, the ignore counter is incremented by one.

- **Dropped**—The number of dropped packets is shown in the output of the **show interfaces** command. If the input or output queue of an interface reaches its maximum size, the queue cannot grow larger and will start dropping the subsequent packets.

- **Misses**—The number of misses is shown in the output of the **show buffers** command. The number of misses is incremented for each occurrence of a buffer not being allocated and free at the time a packet arrives.

- **Failures (no memory)**—The number of failures is shown in the output of the **show buffers** command, and it indicates how many times the allocation of more buffers has been unsuccessful.

# Q&A

The answers to the following questions can be found in Appendix A. Some of the questions in this section are repeated from the "Do I Know ThisAlready" Quiz so that you can gauge the advancement of your knowledge of this subject matter.

1   Briefly explain why Cisco IOS troubleshooting commands and tools need proper handling.

_____

_____

_____

2   What does proper handling of troubleshooting tools entail?

_____

_____

_____

3   Define switching and specify whether it is considered a complex task.

_____

_____

_____

4   Define routing and compare its complexity to switching.

_____

_____

_____

5   List the sources of information used by a routing process for building its routing table.

_____

_____

_____

6   When a packet is process-switched, what major tasks are performed?

_____

_____

_____

**7**  Provide a short and generic explanation for route caching (or fast switching) and the purpose behind it.

_____

_____

_____

**8**  Which of the route caching methods are not enabled by default? And from which configuration mode (prompt level) can they be enabled?

_____

_____

_____

**9**  On which component of the Cisco 7000 router is the Fast Switch Cache located?

_____

_____

_____

**10**  Name the two major components that participate in the routing and switching tasks within a Cisco 7000 router.

_____

_____

_____

**11**  What is the difference between the Silicon Switch Processor (SSP) and the Switch Processor (SP) with respect to the switching cache options?

_____

_____

_____

**12**  What is the command for enabling IP fast switching on an interface?

_____

_____

_____

**13** What is the command for enabling IP autonomous switching on a Cisco 7000 series router interface?

_____

_____

_____

**14** What is the command for enabling IP silicon switching on a Cisco 7000 series router (with SSP) interface?

_____

_____

_____

**15** With regard to speed and switching optimization, how did Cisco Systems improve the Cisco 7500 routers in comparison to the 7000 series?

_____

_____

_____

**16** What switching method (route caching) can be enabled on the 7000/7500 series routers' VIP cards?

_____

_____

_____

**17** On which Cisco router models is Netflow switching supported? (Specify the IOS version.)

_____

_____

_____

**18** What information does Netflow use as the basis of identifying a flow?

_____

_____

_____

**19** Briefly describe the advantages of Netflow switching. Also specify whether there should be any precautions with respect to enabling Netflow switching.

_____

_____

_____

**20** What is the command for enabling IP Netflow switching on a supported router interface?

_____

_____

_____

**21** What are the only switching (route caching) options on the 4000, 3000, and 2500 series routers?

_____

_____

_____

**22** The output of which command includes information about whether fast switching is enabled/disabled for a particular protocol on a particular interface?

_____

_____

_____

**23** Which command can be used to see the statistics on the number of packets that are process switched and fast switched?

_____

_____

_____

**24** Provide at least three examples of operations or packet types that are process switched.

_____

_____

_____

**25** What are some facts about the **debug** privileged exec mode command that one must keep in mind before using it?

_____

_____

_____

**26** Which service must be loaded if you need to see a timestamp with each of the **debug** output lines? (Also provide the command syntax.)

_____

_____

_____

**27** What command enables you to see the debug output from within a Telnet session?

_____

_____

_____

**28** Compare debugging with the packet option to debugging with the events option.

_____

_____

_____

**29** Which command enables debugging for all protocols and activities? Are there any concerns regarding usage of this command?

_____

_____

_____

**30** Before you enable debugging on a router, you are encouraged to check the router's CPU utilization. What is the command that allows you to do that? If the utilization is above 50%, are you encouraged to debug packets or to debug events?

_____

_____

_____

**31** Specify the command syntax for enabling debugging for those IP packets that satisfy (are permitted by) an access list 100.

_____

_____

_____

**32** What is the default setting (for example, enabled/disabled, default destination) for message logging?

_____

_____

_____

**33** How do the logging message destination options compare in terms of the overhead they introduce to a router?

_____

_____

_____

**34** Which Cisco IOS router command turns console logging on and specifies the level of logging to be directed to the console?

_____

_____

_____

**35** By using which Cisco IOS router command can you enable sending logging messages to the internal buffer and specify the level of logging desired to be buffered?

_____

_____

_____

**36** Specify the Cisco IOS router command that enables sending logging messages to the virtual terminal sessions and specifies the level of logging desired to be directed to the virtual terminal lines.

_____

_____

_____

**37** What Cisco IOS router command would you use to make a router's logging messages be sent to a syslog server at IP address 10.1.2.3?

_____

_____

_____

**38** What Cisco IOS router command would you use to make virtual terminal lines receive logging messages at the errors level and higher (i.e., errors, critical, alerts, emergencies)?

_____

_____

_____

**39** What is the severity of the following logging message?

```
%TR-3-WIREFAULT:Unit[0],wirefault:check the lobe cable MAU connection
```

_____

_____

_____

**40** What information does the output of the **show logging** Cisco IOS exec command display?

_____

_____

_____

**41** What are your choices in order to make your Cisco IOS router generate Novell-compliant (ipx) pings?

_____

_____

_____

**42** In which situation (loss of functionality, crash, or performance degradation) will the output of the **show stack** command most likely be asked for?

_____

_____

_____

**43** The outputs of the **show memory** and the **show processes** [**cpu**] commands will most likely be asked for in which situation (loss of functionality, crash, or performance degradation)?

_____

_____

_____

**44** In which situation (loss of functionality, crash, or performance degradation) will you most likely be asked to produce and provide a core dump for the technical support representative?

_____

_____

_____

**45** Which **show** command conveniently produces output equivalent to the output of **show version**, **show running-config**, **show controllers**, and a few other **show** commands?

_____

_____

_____

**46** Which Cisco IOS router command's output displays the current setting (value) of the config-register?

_____

_____

_____

**47** What is the outcome of not having an allocated and free buffer available for a packet?

_____

_____

_____

**48** Explain the role of the parameter called Permanent in buffer management.

_____

_____

_____

**49**  Explain the role of the parameter called Max-Free in buffer management.

_____

_____

_____

**50**  Explain the role of the parameter called Min-Free in buffer management.

_____

_____

_____

**51**  Explain the role of the parameter called Initial in buffer management.

_____

_____

_____

**52**  If the output of **show buffer** command displays a large number of misses, increasing the value of which one of the buffer management parameters (Permanent, Min-Free, Max-Free, Initial) will most likely remedy the situation?

_____

_____

_____

**53**  What does the number of failures displayed on the output of **show buffer** command indicate?

_____

_____

_____

**54**  Using what command can you find out the allocation of interface buffers on the Switch Processor of the Cisco 7x00 series routers?

_____

_____

_____

**55** What does the **show buffers** command display?

_____

_____

_____

**56** Which Cisco IOS command's output displays statistics about router memory (for example, amount of free processor memory)?

_____

_____

_____

**57** What information does the output of the Cisco IOS **show processes** exec command display?

_____

_____

_____

**58** The **show processes** command's output provides two numbers separated by a slash (for example, 4%/4%) for the CPU utilization over the last five seconds. How are those numbers interpreted?

_____

_____

_____

**59** Specify the command (with appropriate parameters) that displays the five-seconds, one-minute, and five-minute CPU utilization for each of the active processes.

_____

_____

_____

**60** What information can be gathered from the output of the Cisco IOS **show stacks** exec command?

_____

_____

_____

**61** Which command allows you to generate a core dump without reloading?

_____

_____

_____

**62** To ensure that a core dump can be sent to a server and saved successfully, what are some of the preliminary tasks and tests you must perform?

_____

_____

_____

**63** Which command causes the router to attempt to produce a core dump when it crashes?

_____

_____

_____

**64** By default, what is the name of the file that the core dump is written to?

_____

_____

_____

**65** Which command allows you to change the name of the core file?

_____

_____

_____

This chapter covers the following topics that you will need to master to pass the CCNP Support exam:

| Objective | Description |
|-----------|-------------|
| 1 | Using ping and trace for IP troubleshooting. |
| 2 | Cisco IOS **show** commands for IP. |
| 3 | Cisco IOS **debug** commands for IP. |
| 4 | General problem isolation and repair technique of TCP/IP networks. |
| 5 | Browser issues in TCP/IP networks with Microsoft products. |
| 6 | Issues regarding redistribution between IP routing protocols. |

# CHAPTER 5

# Diagnosing and Correcting Campus TCP/IP Problems

This chapter presents some of the important commands and techniques used for diagnosing and identifying problems in TCP/IP networks, and the actions required to fix those problems. A number of **show** and **debug** commands (briefly explained) are presented, the configurations required on the hosts and routers are discussed, and step-by-step diagnostics are shown. This chapter also covers some of the topics related to troubleshooting networks with Windows NT/95 (IP) hosts.

## "Do I Know This Already?" Quiz

If you wish to evaluate your knowledge of the contents of this chapter before you get started, answer the following questions. The answers are provided in Appendix A, "Answers to Quiz Questions." If you are having difficulty providing correct answers, you should thoroughly review the entire chapter. If all or most of your answers are correct, you might want to skim this chapter for only those subjects you need to review. You can also use the "Foundation Summary" section to quickly review topics. Once you have completed the chapter, you should reevaluate yourself with the questions in the "Q&A" section at the end. Finally, use the companion CD-ROM to evaluate your knowledge of the topics and see if you need a review.

1   Name the main TCP/IP tool used for path discovery between IP nodes. Specify the full Cisco IOS command for this tool.

_____

_____

_____

2   What is the IP path discovery command available with Microsoft's Windows 95 and Windows NT TCP/IP stack?

_____

_____

_____

**3** Specify the Cisco IOS command that allows you to see if an IP inbound access list is applied to a router's ethernet 0 interface (note that this is not a command that displays a router's startup or running configuration).

_____

_____

_____

**4** How can you see the content of an IP access list without looking at a router's startup or running configuration?

_____

_____

_____

**5** Which Cisco IOS command allows you to see the IP static routes that are configured on a router (without looking at startup or running configuration)?

_____

_____

_____

**6** Which Cisco IOS command displays the active IP routing protocols and how they are configured to operate (without looking at startup or running configuration)?

_____

_____

_____

**7** Which Cisco IOS command displays the state of each debugging option?

_____

_____

_____

**8** What is the command that allows you to see the IP configuration of a Windows NT machine from the CMD window's prompt?

_____

_____

_____

**9** What is the command that allows you to see the content of the NetBIOS cache of a Windows NT machine from the CMD window's prompt?

_____

_____

_____

**10** When you redistribute routing information from one protocol into another, what is a major source of concern?

_____

_____

_____

## Foundation Topics

# Cisco IOS Troubleshooting Tools and Commands for TCP/IP

This section provides a review of ping and trace tools, and presents a list of **show** and **debug** commands useful for troubleshooting in TCP/IP environments. Knowing about these tools and commands, recognizing when their usage is beneficial, and being able to properly interpret their output is necessary for those who support complex TCP/IP networks.

## Ping and Trace

Ping is a standard application included as a part of the TCP/IP protocol suite. From a particular IP host, you can use ping to test reachability of another IP host. On Cisco routers, a simple **ping** is provided in user mode; but in privileged exec mode, an extended **ping** is also provided, which offers more testing options. For instance, with the extended **ping** you may specify the source address, packet size, repeat count, timeout, and data pattern. Trace is also a testing application that is usually provided as a part of the TCP/IP suite. In Cisco IOS the command is actually called **traceroute**, but usage of the shortened form, **trace**, is more popular. The **traceroute** utility is available from the user mode, but the extended **traceroute** is only available from the privileged exec mode. In Microsoft operating systems the command for the trace utility is called **tracert**. **trace** is used on an IP node to discover the sequence of routers (hops) between the local host and a target IP node. Because **ping** and **trace** are covered in the previous chapter, they are not discussed in further detail here.

## show ip Commands

This section covers various **show** commands and explains their purpose and output. The following commands are covered:

- **show ip interface**
- **show ip access-list**
- **show ip route**
- **show ip arp**
- **show ip traffic**
- **show ip protocols**

## show ip interface

```
show ip interface [type] [number]
```

This command lists a summary of an interface's IP information and status. Example 5-1 displays a sample output of the **show ip interface ethernet 0** command.

**Example 5-1**   *show ip interface ethernet 0 Command Output*

```
00=> A_StubR#show ip interfaces ethernet 0
01=> Ethernet0 is up, line protocol is up
02=>   Internet address is 131.1.18.14/22
03=>   Broadcast address is 255.255.255.255
04=>   Address determined by setup command
05=>   MTU is 1500 bytes
06=>   Helper address is not set
07=>   Directed broadcast forwarding is enabled
08=>   Outgoing access list is not set
09=>   Inbound  access list is not set
10=>   Proxy ARP is enabled
11=>   Security level is default
12=>   Split horizon is enabled
13=>   ICMP redirects are always sent
14=>   ICMP unreachables are always sent
15=>   ICMP mask replies are never sent
16=>   IP fast switching is enabled
17=>   IP fast switching on the same interface is disabled
18=>   IP multicast fast switching is enabled
19=>   Router Discovery is disabled
20=>   IP output packet accounting is disabled
21=>   IP access violation accounting is disabled
22=>   TCP/IP header compression is disabled
23=>   Probe proxy name replies are disabled
24=>   Gateway Discovery is disabled
25=>   Policy routing is disabled
26=>   Network address translation is disabled
```

The line numbers were added on the left side of the example for the purpose of this discussion and are not part of the actual output. Some of the significant information displayed by the **show ip interface** command is as follows:

> **Line 1**—Interface status
> **Line 2**—IP address and subnet mask
> **Line 3**—Broadcast address
> **Line 6**—IP helper-address setting
> **Line 8**—Outgoing access-list setting
> **Line 9**—Incoming access-list setting
> **Line 10**—IP Proxy-ARP setting
> **Line 16**—Status of IP fast-switching
> **Line 19**—Router discovery setting

The settings for these interface IP parameters can cause significant change in a router's behavior. Depending on the context of your troubleshooting, verifying the settings for some or all of these parameters might be necessary. For instance, if the IP devices that are connected to the same segment as a router's ethernet 0 interface rely on this interface to forward their DHCP discovery message to one or more DHCP servers, using the **show ip interfaces ethernet 0** command allows you to find out if this interface is properly configured with an **IP helper-address** command or not. Naturally, without proper configuration of this command on the router under discussion, those DHCP clients will be out of luck.

## show ip access-list

```
show ip access-list [access-list-number ¦ name]
```

This command displays the contents of all current IP access lists. If you specify the access list number or name, only the contents of the specified access list will be displayed. During the course of troubleshooting, if you find out that an access list is applied to an interface, you can use this command to display the content of the access list and investigate whether the access list has anything to do with your problem.

## show ip route

```
show ip route [address [mask]] ¦ [protocol [process-id]]
```

This command displays the current state of the routing table and is shown in Example 5-2. If you specify a protocol name (such as **bgp, igrp, eigrp, rip, ospf, isis**) and AS number or process ID, then only those entries corresponding to the routing protocol specified will be displayed. In case you only want to see the connected or static routes, you may use the keywords **static** or **connected** instead of the routing protocol ID. If no routing table is displayed, it is usually the sign that IP routing is not enabled. If certain entries that you expect to be present are not shown, you have to investigate the configuration and operation of your routing protocols. During the course of a troubleshooting project, this command is used repeatedly, after each configuration change, to verify the results of the change and move towards the solution.

**Example 5-2**   *show ip route Command Output*

```
A_StubR#show ip route ?
  Hostname or A.B.C.D  Network to display information about or hostname
  bgp                  Border Gateway Protocol (BGP)
  connected            Connected
  egp                  Exterior Gateway Protocol (EGP)
  eigrp                Enhanced Interior Gateway Routing Protocol (EIGRP)
  igrp                 Interior Gateway Routing Protocol (IGRP)
  isis                 ISO IS-IS
  odr                  On Demand stub Routes
  ospf                 Open Shortest Path First (OSPF)
  rip                  Routing Information Protocol (RIP)
```

**Example 5-2**  *show ip route Command Output (Continued)*

```
   static              Static routes
   summary             Summary of all routes
   supernets-only      Show supernet entries only
   <cr>

A_StubR#show ip route
Codes: C - connected, S - static, I - IGRP, R - RIP, M - mobile, B - BGP
       D - EIGRP, EX - EIGRP external, O - OSPF, IA - OSPF inter area
       N1 - OSPF NSSA external type 1, N2 - OSPF NSSA external type 2
       E1 - OSPF external type 1, E2 - OSPF external type 2, E - EGP
       i - IS-IS, L1 - IS-IS level-1, L2 - IS-IS level-2,
     * - candidate default, U - per-user static route, o - ODR

Gateway of last resort is not set

I      144.251.0.0/16 [100/1200] via 131.1.18.1, 00:01:13, Ethernet0
       131.1.0.0/22 is subnetted, 2 subnets
C         131.1.12.0 is directly connected, Ethernet1
C         131.1.16.0 is directly connected, Ethernet0
```

## show ip arp

**show ip arp** [*ip-address*] [*hostname*] [*mac-address*] [*type number*]

This command displays the IP Address Resolution Protocol (ARP) cache (see Example 5-3). You can use the optional parameters to see only the ARP entries corresponding to a particular host, or only entries learned via a specific interface. To delete all dynamic entries from the ARP cache, use the **clear arp-cache** EXEC command. On a Windows 95/NT device with Microsoft's TCP/IP stack, the command **arp –g** is used to display the ARP table.

**Example 5-3**  *show ip arp Command Output*

```
A_StubR#show ip arp
Protocol  Address       Age (min)  Hardware Addr   Type   Interface
Internet  131.1.18.1    186        0060.4740.ef9c  ARPA   Ethernet0
Internet  131.1.18.14   -          0060.4740.ebd6  ARPA   Ethernet0
Internet  131.1.15.100  -          0060.4740.ebd7  ARPA   Ethernet1
```

## show ip traffic

**show ip traffic**

This command displays statistics about IP traffic (see Example 5-4). This command allows you to monitor statistics such as the number of packets sent and received, error counts, and broadcasts/multicasts. Also included in the output of this command are statistics corresponding to particular protocols such as ARP, and any routing protocols that are active.

**Example 5-4**    *show ip traffic Command Output*

```
A_StubR#show ip traffic
IP statistics:
  Rcvd:  4793 total, 4793 local destination
         0 format errors, 0 checksum errors, 0 bad hop count
         0 unknown protocol, 0 not a gateway
         0 security failures, 0 bad options, 0 with options
  Opts:  0 end, 0 nop, 0 basic security, 0 loose source route
         0 timestamp, 0 extended security, 0 record route
         0 stream ID, 0 strict source route, 0 alert, 0 cipso
         0 other
  Frags: 0 reassembled, 0 timeouts, 0 couldn't reassemble
         0 fragmented, 0 couldn't fragment
  Bcast: 4488 received, 8764 sent
  Mcast: 0 received, 0 sent
  Sent:  9120 generated, 0 forwarded
         0 encapsulation failed, 0 no route

ICMP statistics:
  Rcvd: 0 format errors, 0 checksum errors, 0 redirects, 0 unreachable
        5 echo, 5 echo reply, 0 mask requests, 0 mask replies, 0 quench
        0 parameter, 0 timestamp, 0 info request, 0 other
        0 irdp solicitations, 0 irdp advertisements
  Sent: 0 redirects, 0 unreachable, 5 echo, 5 echo reply
        0 mask requests, 0 mask replies, 0 quench, 0 timestamp
        0 info reply, 0 time exceeded, 0 parameter problem
        0 irdp solicitations, 0 irdp advertisements
UDP statistics:
  Rcvd: 105 total, 0 checksum errors, 0 no port
  Sent: 12 total, 0 forwarded broadcasts

TCP statistics:
  Rcvd: 295 total, 0 checksum errors, 0 no port
  Sent: 334 total

Probe statistics:
  Rcvd: 0 address requests, 0 address replies
        0 proxy name requests, 0 where-is requests, 0 other
  Sent: 0 address requests, 0 address replies (0 proxy)
        0 proxy name replies, 0 where-is replies

...

IGRP statistics:
  Rcvd: 8766 total, 0 checksum errors
  Sent: 8764 total

OSPF statistics:
  Rcvd: 0 total, 0 checksum errors
        0 hello, 0 database desc, 0 link state req
        0 link state updates, 0 link state acks
  Sent: 0 total
```

**Example 5-4**  *show ip traffic Command Output (Continued)*

```
...

ARP statistics:
  Rcvd: 12 requests, 13 replies, 7 reverse, 0 other
  Sent: 13 requests, 12 replies (0 proxy), 88 reverse
```

## show ip protocols

```
show ip protocols
```

This command displays the parameters and current state of the active routing protocol(s) (see Example 5-5). When troubleshooting IP routing cases, this command is often used to see which routing protocols are active, what their AS-number(s) or process-id(s) are, which networks they are configured for, if they are redistributing any routing information, and if there are any filters active for the routing protocols.

**Example 5-5**  *show ip protocols Command Output*

```
A_StubR#show ip protocols
Routing Protocol is "igrp 100"
  Sending updates every 90 seconds, next due in 4 seconds
  Invalid after 270 seconds, hold down 280, flushed after 630
  Outgoing update filter list for all interfaces is
  Incoming update filter list for all interfaces is
  Default networks flagged in outgoing updates
  Default networks accepted from incoming updates
  IGRP metric weight K1=1, K2=0, K3=1, K4=0, K5=0
  IGRP maximum hopcount 100
  IGRP maximum metric variance 1
  Redistributing: igrp 100
  Routing for Networks:
    131.1.0.0
  Routing Information Sources:
    Gateway         Distance      Last Update
    131.1.18.1           100      00:00:53
  Distance: (default is 100)
```

# debug IP Commands

There are many **debug** IP commands that can be used during the course of a troubleshooting project (see Example 5-6). You must keep in mind that some of the **debug** commands generate a lot of output, and that usage of the **debug** command requires special handling (as discussed in Chapter 4, "Applying Cisco Troubleshooting Tools"). Use the Debug reference manual (also available on Cisco Connection Online [CCO] and the Documentation CD) for the IOS version you work with. To display the state of each debugging option (that is, to find out which types of debugging are enabled for your router), enter the **show debugging** command at the privileged EXEC mode. In this section a few of the **debug** commands are discussed briefly. As you read about each command, refer to

Example 5-7 to see the exact syntax and options for each command. The following commands are covered in this section:

- **debug arp**
- **debug ip packet**
- **debug ip icmp**
- **debug ip rip**
- **debug ip igrp events**
- **debug ip igrp transactions**
- **debug ip eigrp**
- **debug ip ospf**

**Example 5-6** *debug ip ? Command Output*

```
A_StubR#debug ip ?
  bgp       BGP information
  cache     IP cache operations
  cgmp      CGMP protocol activity
  drp       Director response protocol
  dvmrp     DVMRP protocol activity
  egp       EGP information
  eigrp     IP-EIGRP information
  error     IP error debugging
  ftp       FTP dialogue
  http      HTTP connections
  icmp      ICMP transactions
  igmp      IGMP protocol activity
  igrp      IGRP information
  mcache    IP multicast cache operations
  mobile    Mobility protocols
  mpacket   IP multicast packet debugging
  mrouting  IP multicast routing table activity
  nat       NAT events
  ospf      OSPF information
  packet    General IP debugging and IPSO security transactions
  peer      IP peer address activity
  pim       PIM protocol activity
  policy    Policy routing
  rip       RIP protocol transactions
  routing   Routing table events
  rsvp      RSVP protocol activity
  rtp       RTP information
  sd        Session Directory (SD)
  security  IP security options
  tcp       TCP information
  tempacl   IP temporary ACL
  udp       UDP based transactions
```

## debug arp

```
debug arp
```

When **debug arp** is in use, the router displays all the ARP-related traffic (requests and responses) that the router itself or hosts on the local segment(s) generate. You can monitor the ARP replies to see if they are expected or faulty. Routers normally filter ARP replies that they see as meaningless. Use this command to find out which nodes on a TCP/IP network are and which ones are not responding to ARP requests. You can also monitor if your router is sending or receiving ARPs.

**NOTE**    Since an ARP request is a broadcast, when you have, for instance, two logical networks on the same physical network, a device from a different logical network might send an ARP reply to the ARP request it saw on the same physical network. The router that generated the original ARP Request will filter and ignore the reply per its own discretion. This is just one of many possible examples of an ARP reply that is meaningless.

## debug ip packet

```
debug ip packet [detail] [access-list-number]
```

The **debug ip packet** command is useful for analyzing the flow of IP packets traveling between IP hosts. IP debugging information includes packets received, generated, and forwarded. As discussed in Chapter 4, you have the option to specify an access list number or name after the debug IP packet command to limit the scope of **debug** output (see Example 5-7).

**Example 5-7**  *Various **debug** IP Examples*

```
A_StubR#debug ip packet ?
  <1-199>  Access list
  detail   Print more debugging detail
  <cr>

A_StubR#debug ip packet detail ?
  <1-199>  Access list
  <cr>

A_StubR#debug ip rip ?
  events  RIP protocol events
  <cr>

A_StubR#debug ip igrp ?
  events        IGRP protocol events
  transactions  IGRP protocol transactions

A_StubR#debug ip eigrp ?
  <1-65535>      AS number
```

*continues*

**Example 5-7**    *Various **debug** IP Examples (Continued)*

```
  neighbor      IP-EIGRP neighbor debugging
  notifications IP-EIGRP event notifications
  summary       IP-EIGRP summary route processing
  <cr>
A_StubR#debug ip ospf ?
  adj             OSPF adjacency events
  events          OSPF events
  flood           OSPF flooding
  lsa-generation  OSPF lsa generation
  packet          OSPF packets
  retransmission  OSPF retransmission events
  spf             OSPF spf
  tree            OSPF database tree

A_StubR#debug ip icmp ?
  <cr>

A_StubR#debug ip cache ?
  <1-99>  Access list
  <cr>

A_StubR#debug ip cache 50 ?
  <cr>

A_StubR#debug ip udp ?
  <cr>
```

## debug ip icmp

```
     debug ip icmp
```

This command displays information about Internal Control Message Protocol (ICMP)
transactions and allows you to monitor the ICMP messages sent and received by your
router. Each ICMP message has a source, destination, type, and code number. RFC-792
provides complete coverage of the fields in **debug ip icmp** output. Example 5-8 is a **debug
ip icmp** output sample that shows a case with five echo replies received, and a case with
three host unreachable messages received.

**Example 5-8**    *__debug ip icmp__ Command Output*

```
A_StubR#debug ip icmp
ICMP packet debugging is on
A_StubR#ping 131.1.18.1

Type escape sequence to abort.
Sending 5, 100-byte ICMP Echos to 131.1.18.1, timeout is 2 seconds:
!!!!!
Success rate is 100 percent (5/5), round-trip min/avg/max = 4/5/8 ms
A_StubR#
ICMP: echo reply rcvd, src 131.1.18.1, dst 131.1.18.14
ICMP: echo reply rcvd, src 131.1.18.1, dst 131.1.18.14
```

**Example 5-8**  *debug ip icmp* Command Output (Continued)

```
ICMP: echo reply rcvd, src 131.1.18.1, dst 131.1.18.14
ICMP: echo reply rcvd, src 131.1.18.1, dst 131.1.18.14
ICMP: echo reply rcvd, src 131.1.18.1, dst 131.1.18.14

A_StubR#ping 10.1.1.1

Type escape sequence to abort.
Sending 5, 100-byte ICMP Echos to 10.1.1.1, timeout is 2 seconds:
U.U.U
Success rate is 0 percent (0/5)
ICMP: dst (131.1.18.14) host unreachable rcv from 131.1.18.1
ICMP: dst (131.1.18.14) host unreachable rcv from 131.1.18.1
ICMP: dst (131.1.18.14) host unreachable rcv from 131.1.18.1
A_StubR#
```

## debug ip rip

```
debug ip rip [events]
```

This **debug** command displays information about RIP routing transactions. You may specify the **events** optional keyword if you are only interested in seeing RIP protocol events. Example 5-9 shows updates being received (RIP version 1) from a router with source address 131.1.18.14. The router being debugged also sent updates, in both cases to broadcast address 255.255.255.255 as the destination. Note that if an interface's broadcast address is modified, then information such as distance vector routing updates (including RIP) will no longer be sent to the default broadcast address. This could prevent routing updates from reaching the intended router.

| NOTE | Before multicasting became popular and well accepted, some individuals used to change the broadcast address of an IP device (e.g., router's interface) so that even though this device was generating a broadcast, the information (e.g., RIP routing update) was actually sent to a specific unicast address. Hence, it is entirely possible that you'll encounter a router that (intentionally) has a unicast address instead of 255.255.255.255 configured as the broadcast address on one of its interfaces. |
|---|---|

The first few lines of the output in Example 5-9 (sending general request...) appear at startup or when an event occurs such as an interface transitioning or a user manually clearing the routing table (the latter is obviously the case here). This command is clearly a useful one as you troubleshoot RIP routing issues.

**Example 5-9**  *debug ip rip Command Output*

```
A_BackR#debug ip rip
RIP protocol debugging is on
A_BackR#clear ip route *
A_BackR#
1w0d: RIP: sending general request on Ethernet0 to 255.255.255.255
1w0d: RIP: sending general request on Ethernet0 to 224.0.0.9
1w0d: RIP: sending general request on Ethernet1 to 255.255.255.255
1w0d: RIP: sending general request on Ethernet1 to 224.0.0.9
1w0d: RIP: received v1 update from 131.1.18.14 on Ethernet0
1w0d:       131.1.12.0 in 1 hops
1w0d: RIP: received v1 update from 131.1.18.14 on Ethernet0
1w0d:       131.1.12.0 in 1 hops
1w0d: RIP: sending v1 update to 255.255.255.255 via Ethernet0 (131.1.18.1)
1w0d:       network 144.251.0.0, metric 1
1w0d: RIP: sending v1 update to 255.255.255.255 via Ethernet1 (144.251.100.200)
1w0d:       network 131.1.0.0, metric 1
```

## debug ip igrp events

   **debug ip igrp events** [*ip-address*]

This **debug** command displays summary information on sent and received Interior
Gateway Routing Protocol (IGRP) routing messages (see Example 5-10). The source and
destination of each update as well as the number of routes in each update are indicated for
each message. This command does not display the actual IGRP routing entries that are
exchanged. If you specify the IP address (optional) of a neighbor router (which is an IGRP
peer), IGRP event debugging will only be turned on for the address specified, plus any
updates that the router broadcasts toward that neighbor. The **debug ip igrp events**
command is particularly useful when the routing table is large, and hence, IGRP transaction
debugging (discussed in the next section) would produce too much data and possibly render
the router unusable.

**Example 5-10** *debug ip igrp events Command Output*

```
A_BackR#debug ip igrp events
IGRP event debugging is on
A_BackR#clear ip route *
A_BackR#
1w0d: IGRP: broadcasting request on Ethernet0
1w0d: IGRP: broadcasting request on Ethernet1
1w0d: IGRP: received update from 131.1.18.14 on Ethernet0
1w0d: IGRP: Update contains 1 interior, 0 system, and 0 exterior routes.
1w0d: IGRP: Total routes in update: 1
1w0d: IGRP: edition is now 5
1w0d: IGRP: sending update to 255.255.255.255 via Ethernet0 (131.1.18.1)
1w0d: IGRP: Update contains 0 interior, 1 system, and 0 exterior routes.
1w0d: IGRP: Total routes in update: 1
1w0d: IGRP: sending update to 255.255.255.255 via Ethernet1 (144.251.100.200)
```

**Example 5-10** *debug ip igrp events Command Output (Continued)*

```
1w0d: IGRP: Update contains 0 interior, 1 system, and 0 exterior routes.
1w0d: IGRP: Total routes in update: 1
1w0d: IGRP: sending update to 255.255.255.255 via Ethernet0 (131.1.18.1)
1w0d: IGRP: Update contains 0 interior, 1 system, and 0 exterior routes.
1w0d: IGRP: Total routes in update: 1
1w0d: IGRP: sending update to 255.255.255.255 via Ethernet1 (144.251.100.200)
1w0d: IGRP: Update contains 0 interior, 1 system, and 0 exterior routes.
1w0d: IGRP: Total routes in update: 1
1w0d: IGRP: received update from 131.1.18.14 on Ethernet0
1w0d: IGRP: Update contains 1 interior, 0 system, and 0 exterior routes.
1w0d: IGRP: Total routes in update: 1
```

## debug ip igrp transactions

```
debug ip igrp transactions [ip-address]
```

This **debug** command displays information on Interior Gateway Routing Protocol (IGRP) routing transactions. Example 5-11 shows that the router being debugged sent updates to the broadcast address (255.255.255.255) via ethernet 0 and ethernet 1 interfaces, and it has received an update from a router with the IP address 131.1.18.14 on ethernet 0 interface. Notice that with IGRP transaction debugging the content (routing entries exchanged) of the updates that are sent and received are also displayed. For instance, in Example 5-11 you can see that the update received from neighbor 131.1.18.14 contained an entry about subnet 131.1.12.0. If the routing table is too large, IGRP event debugging might be more practical.

**Example 5-11** *debug ip igrp transactions Command Output*

```
A_BackR#debug ip igrp transactions
IGRP protocol debugging is on
A_BackR#clear ip route *
A_BackR#
1w0d: IGRP: broadcasting request on Ethernet0
1w0d: IGRP: broadcasting request on Ethernet1
1w0d: IGRP: received update from 131.1.18.14 on Ethernet0
1w0d:       subnet 131.1.12.0, metric 1200 (neighbor 1100)
1w0d: IGRP: edition is now 6
1w0d: IGRP: sending update to 255.255.255.255 via Ethernet0 (131.1.18.1)
1w0d:       network 144.251.0.0, metric=1100
1w0d: IGRP: sending update to 255.255.255.255 via Ethernet1 (144.251.100.200)
1w0d:       network 131.1.0.0, metric=1100
1w0d: IGRP: sending update to 255.255.255.255 via Ethernet0 (131.1.18.1)
1w0d:       network 144.251.0.0, metric=1100
1w0d: IGRP: sending update to 255.255.255.255 via Ethernet1 (144.251.100.200)
1w0d:       network 131.1.0.0, metric=1100
1w0d: IGRP: received update from 131.1.18.14 on Ethernet0
1w0d:       subnet 131.1.12.0, metric 1200 (neighbor 1100)
```

## debug ip eigrp

```
debug ip eigrp
```

The **debug ip eigrp** command displays the Enhanced IGRP packets sent and received on your router interfaces. This command produces a lot of output, which can be dangerous in a large and busy network. The top portion of Example 5-12 displays the optional parameters you can specify along with this command. The second portion of Example 5-12 displays sample output of the **debug ip eigrp** command. Use this command and the optional parameters to troubleshoot the Enhanced IGRP routing protocol.

**Example 5-12** *debug ip eigrp Command Output*

```
A_StubR#debug ip eigrp ?
  <1-65535>      AS number
  neighbor       IP-EIGRP neighbor debugging
  notifications  IP-EIGRP event notifications
  summary        IP-EIGRP summary route processing
  <cr>

A_StubR#debug ip eigrp
IP-EIGRP Route Events debugging is on
A_StubR#
IP-EIGRP: 131.1.12.0/22 - do advertise out Ethernet0
IP-EIGRP: Int 131.1.12.0/22 metric 281600 - 256000 25600
IP-EIGRP: 131.1.16.0/22 - do advertise out Ethernet0
IP-EIGRP: Processing incoming UPDATE packet
IP-EIGRP: Int 144.251.0.0/16 M 307200 - 256000 51200 SM 281600 - 256000 25600
IP-EIGRP: Int 144.251.0.0/16 metric 307200 - 256000 51200
A_StubR#
```

## debug ip ospf

```
debug ip ospf options
```

The **debug ip ospf** command is used with one of the following options: **adj**, **events**, **flood**, **lsa-generation**, **packet**, **retransmission**, **spf**, or **tree** (see top portion of Example 5-13). The **debug ip ospf** command with the **events** option displays information on OSPF (Open Shortest Path First) events, such as adjacencies, flooding information, designated router and backup designated router election, and shortest path first (SPF) calculation. Sample output of the **debug ip ospf events** is shown in the bottom portion of Example 5-13. When troubleshooting OSPF, make use of the **debug ip ospf** command with the appropriate options. Some routine OSPF verifications that help you iron out simple OSPF misconfigurations are as follows:

- Check the IP address and subnet mask(s) of OSPF router(s)

- Verify network statements (address, inverse-mask, and area ID)

- Make sure routers within same area agree on area type

Refer to Cisco documentation for notes on configuring OSPF over NBMA networks.

**Example 5-13** *debug ip ospf Command Output*

```
A_StubR#debug ip ospf ?
  adj             OSPF adjacency events
  events          OSPF events
  flood           OSPF flooding
  lsa-generation  OSPF lsa generation
  packet          OSPF packets
  retransmission  OSPF retransmission events
  spf             OSPF spf
  tree            OSPF database tree
A_StubR#debug ip ospf events
OSPF events debugging is on
A_StubR#
OSPF: Rcv hello from 144.251.100.200 area 1 from Ethernet0 131.1.18.1
OSPF: 2 Way Communication to 144.251.100.200 on Ethernet0, state 2WAY
OSPF: DR/BDR election on Ethernet0
OSPF: Elect BDR 131.1.15.100
OSPF: Elect DR 144.251.100.200
      DR: 144.251.100.200 (Id)    BDR: 131.1.15.100 (Id)
OSPF: Send DBD to 144.251.100.200 on Ethernet0 seq 0x11CD opt 0x2 flag 0x7 len 32
OSPF: End of hello processing
A_StubR#
OSPF: Rcv DBD from 144.251.100.200 on Ethernet0 seq 0x1371 opt 0x2 flag 0x7
      len 32 state EXSTART
OSPF: NBR Negotiation Done. We are the SLAVE
OSPF: Send DBD to 144.251.100.200 on Ethernet0 seq 0x1371 opt 0x2 flag 0x2
      len 52
OSPF: Rcv DBD from 144.251.100.200 on Ethernet0 seq 0x1372 opt 0x2 flag 0x3
      len92 state EXCHANGE
OSPF: Send DBD to 144.251.100.200 on Ethernet0 seq 0x1372 opt 0x2 flag 0x0
      len 32
OSPF: Database request to 144.251.100.200
OSPF: sent LS REQ packet to 131.1.18.1, length 36
OSPF: Rcv DBD from 144.251.100.200 on Ethernet0 seq 0x1373 opt 0x2 flag 0x1
      len 32 state EXCHANGE
OSPF: Exchange Done with 144.251.100.200 on Ethernet0
OSPF: Send DBD to 144.251.100.200 on Ethernet0 seq 0x1373 opt 0x2 flag 0x0 len 32
OSPF: Synchronized with 144.251.100.200 on Ethernet0, state FULL
A_StubR#
```

# General Problem Isolation Method for TCP/IP Connectivity

In this section, a sample TCP/IP network (with Microsoft hosts) is presented and the general requirements for proper operation of Telnet application in that network are specified. After that, the example is turned into a troubleshooting case. You will be walked through the step-by-step tests and checks you must run to isolate the cause of problems, and what you need to do in order to fix them. The network presented in Figure 5-1 will be used for the example.

**Figure 5-1**   *A Sample TCP/IP Network*

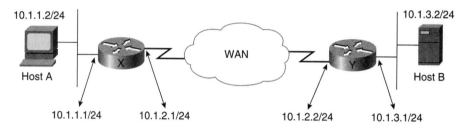

As you can see, hosts A and B (running a Microsoft operating system such as Windows 95 or Windows NT version 4.0) reside on two separate segments, and are hence considered remote from each other. Communication between remote hosts in TCP/IP networks is dependent on proper configuration and operation of the routers between remote hosts (as well as correct configuration and operation of the hosts). Devices such as routers need proper address and routing information in order to forward packets correctly. Furthermore, for certain applications or protocols to successfully operate, some additional configurations might be necessary (for example, special handling of broadcasts).

Assume that host A needs to Telnet into host B. For this operation to be successful, the following must be in place:

- Host A needs an IP address and subnet mask appropriate for the segment it is connected to. This information can be entered statically, or it can be obtained through usage of the DHCP protocol. Correct operation of DHCP requires the presence of at least one DHCP server with an appropriate configuration and proper configuration of the routers.

- For the default gateway, host A can either have 10.1.1.1 (router X's local Ethernet address) or can use its own IP address (this relies on **ip proxy-arp** being enabled on router X's local interface).

- If any NetBIOS application (such as browser service, domain logon, and file and printer sharing) is in use, hosts A and B need unique NetBIOS names.

- If host A needs to communicate with host B using a NetBIOS name or a FQDN (Fully Qualified Domain Name), presence or correct configuration of one or more of the following name-to-IP-address resolution systems is necessary: WINS, DNS, HOSTS file, LMHOSTS file.

- The Telnet application must be properly installed and in good working order on host A (the Telnet client) and host B (the Telnet server).

- Router X and router Y must have correct IP address, subnet mask, and broadcast addresses on their interfaces; their interfaces are in Up and have proper routing information to handle the packets travelling between hosts A and B.

- Router X and router Y cannot have access lists applied to their involved interfaces that prevent entering or exiting of Telnet traffic (sent between hosts A and B).

- All the LANs and WANs (or at least those between hosts A and B) must be in good working order, and routers X and Y must be able to communicate.

Now assume that the user of host A has reported that he or she cannot Telnet into host B. You will need to go through step-by-step diagnosis of this case and correction of any existing problems. Usually, not everything is misconfigured or broken at the same time. However, here you need to consider quite a few conditions. The following is a list of tasks/ tests to be performed along with any corrections that might be necessary:

- On host A (running Windows NT Workstation 4.0), check the IP configuration with the **ipconfig /all** command from the CMD window. (On computers running Windows 95 the corresponding utility program is called **winipcfg**.) If host A is a DHCP client and **ipconfig /renew** fails to obtain an IP address for host A, you can assign a valid IP address to host A temporarily. For example, assign the 10.1.1.2/24 address and mask to host A, use its own address (10.1.1.2) as the default gateway, and configure the correct address for WINS server and DNS server. These tasks are performed from the Network Neighborhood Properties (or the Network applet in the Control Panel), Protocols, TCP/IP Properties on host A.

- Host A should be able to ping all devices on its local segment, including router X's ethernet 0 address 10.1.1.1. If all nodes on the local Ethernet except router X's ethernet 0 interface (10.1.1.1) respond successfully, you must check router X's ethernet 0 interface (use the **show ip interface ethernet 0** exec command).

- On router X, the state of its ethernet 0 interface and the keepalive setting, along with its IP address, subnet mask, broadcast address, IP proxy-arp setting, inbound and outbound access lists, and IP helper-address setting can all be checked using the Cisco IOS **show ip interface ethernet 0** exec command. Also, if router X has multiple connectors on its ethernet 0 interface (in case it is a Cisco 4000 series router), the setting of the media type can be checked using the **show controllers ethernet 0** command. You must get host A to be able to ping the IP address of router X's ethernet 0 (10.1.1.1) successfully.

Next, attempt to ping router X's serial 0 IP address (10.1.2.1). If host A can ping the 10.1.1.1 address, but not the 10.1.2.1 address, the problem is probably due to its default gateway setting. If host A's default gateway is set to 10.1.1.2 (its own IP address), then router X's ethernet 0 is probably configured with the **no ip proxy-arp** command. Also make sure that router X's serial 0 interface is in Up and has the correct IP configurations (address and so on).

Now make sure that host A can successfully ping the IP address of router Y's serial 0 interface (10.1.2.2). If host A can ping router X's serial 0 address (10.1.2.1) but not the IP address of router Y's serial 0 interface (10.1.2.2), the reason is probably either an access list on router Y's serial interface or that router Y does not have a path back to host A's subnet (a routing issue). In this example, assume that routers X and Y can successfully ping each other's serial 0 IP address.

For router Y to be able to communicate with a device (such as host A) in subnet 10.1.1.0, it could learn about that subnet through a dynamic protocol (such as RIP, IGRP, EIGRP, OSPF), through a static route, or by possessing a useful gateway of last resort. To see if router Y has a path to host A's subnet, check router Y's IP routing table using the **show ip route** command. To check router Y's routing protocols and their settings, use the **show ip protocols** command.

Once you get host A to successfully ping router Y's serial 0 interface, pinging the IP address of router Y's ethernet 0 (10.1.3.1) should be straightforward. If that doesn't work, check router Y's ethernet 0 status and configuration using the **show ip interface ethernet 0** exec command.

The next challenge is being able to ping host B. If you can ping router Y's ethernet 0 (10.1.3.1) and not host B's address (10.1.3.2), you must check host B's address, subnet mask, and default gateway. Also, if host B uses its own address as the default gateway, make sure that **ip proxy-arp** is enabled on router Y's ethernet 0 interface.

Now assume that you can ping host B by IP address, but you cannot Telnet into it. If Telnet server is running on host B and at least one other host (such as router Y) can Telnet into it, it is likely that access lists on routers X and Y prevent the Telnet traffic between host A and host B.

Once you can Telnet into host B (from host A) by using host B's IP address, you can start testing whether Telnet using host B's name (either its NetBIOS name or its FQDN) works. Host A can resolve host B's NetBIOS name to IP address using a local LMHOSTS file. On systems running Windows NT 4.0, the LMHOSTS file usually resides in the \winnt\system32\drivers\etc directory. Also, host A can find out host B's IP address by sending an inquiry to the WINS server (provided that the WINS server has such information). If both of host A and host B are clients to the WINS server and can communicate with it successfully, NetBIOS-name-to-IP-address conversion becomes a smooth operation. In addition, host A can resolve host B's FQDN to host B's IP address by using the HOSTS file (which resides in the same location as the LMHOSTS file but is used for FQDN names, which unlike NetBIOS names can be longer than 15 characters and contain one or more embedded dots). Finally, if a DNS server is present, a FQDN can be resolved to an IP address by sending an inquiry to the DNS server as well (assuming that the DNS server itself has no trouble with resolving the FQDN to IP address for this particular host itself). The **nbtstat** command (entered from the CMD/Command window's prompt on Microsoft hosts) is used to display the local NetBIOS names (with the **-n** option), to display the content of the NetBIOS cache (with the **-c** option), and so on. This command is useful when you want to find out if a NetBIOS name is resolved to an incorrect IP address (using any of the above mentioned methods).

Assuming that host A can Telnet into host B by name, most, though not all, of the problems are now fixed. Remember that host A could not obtain an IP address through DHCP. If the DHCP server is up and running and has an available IP address in the appropriate scope for host A, and host A can successfully ping the DHCP server, you have some router work to do. First of all, on router X, make sure that the ethernet 0 interface has the **ip helper-address** command pointing to the correct DHCP server (use the **show ip interface Ethernet 0** command) and that router X can itself ping the DHCP server's IP address. Also, check router X and Y to see if any access lists applied to their interfaces deny DHCP traffic (DHCP runs over UDP and makes use of ports 67 and 68). Finally, look in router X's configuration to see if **ip forward-protocol udp** is disabled using its **no** form (at least for UDP ports 67 and 68). If a router's interface is configured with the **ip helper-address** command, but at the global configuration mode the router is configured with the **no ip forward protocol UPD** command, the **ip helper-address** command will be useless.

---

**TIP**      A trace from client to server used early in the game would reduce the number of steps dramatically.

---

# Browser Issues in Microsoft Products

In networks with hosts running Microsoft Windows NT/95, users often look for servers offering file shares and printer shares through the Network Neighborhood applet. The list of servers offering these services is maintained and distributed through the collective effort of all devices running the Browser service. The Browser service is broadcast-based for the most part and its operation is very smooth in one segment. However, many Windows NT domains span more than one segment, and for the Browser service to have a complete list of servers from all segments some special care is needed.

If the WINS service is in use and all hosts are made sure to be WINS clients, ensure that there is a stable machine on each segment (preferably an NT Domain controller). Having a stable machine (one that does not reload often) on a segment would be beneficial when that machine acts as the Master Browser for that segment. Since the Domain Master Browser is the Primary Domain Controller (PDC) of an NT domain, repeated reloading of that machine is not expected, either.

Devices find the Master Browser of their segment using NetBIOS broadcasts; however, the Master Browser of each segment discovers the Domain Master Browser from the WINS server. Without WINS server(s) you will have to configure the LMHOSTS files of your hosts. Editing the LMHOSTS file of each Master Browser (usually an NT Domain Controller) is the least you must do. You can have a complete LMHOSTS file on each device, or have a central LMHOSTS file that is included in the LMHOSTS files of the other devices using the **#include** statement.

Regardless of whether you use the WINS service or not, the browser list (that is, what the Network Neighborhood displays) is not always up to date. The browser list can take nearly an hour to converge in an internetwork (assuming that machines are not reloading). Also, note that even though the HOSTS file can also be used for storing NetBIOS names, its intention is really to keep a static set of Host(FQDN)/IP address pairs. The DNS server is not meant for NetBIOS name resolution, as the FQDN does not comply with the NetBIOS name specifications.

# Issues Regarding Redistribution between IP Routing Protocols

Two different routing protocols active on the same router do not automatically learn any routing information from each other (in general) and naturally do not advertise the routing entries of the other protocol. When you need the routing information available in one routing protocol to be imported into another routing protocol, you need to configure redistribution.

For instance, if you want a RIP process to take entries from an IGRP 100 process, you need to enter the **redistribute igrp 100** command from within the router configuration mode (for RIP). However, there is a major issue at hand when you perform redistribution. Different routing protocols use different metrics. So when you bring the IGRP 100's entries into RIP's table, you must assign a seed metric to them, and hence you will either enter the command **redistribute igrp 100 metric** *value-in-hops* from within RIP, or merely enter the **default-metric** *value-in-hops* command on a separate line within RIP. In the first case, the metric value specified only applies to the entries taken from IGRP 100. In the second case, the metric value applies every time an entry is imported into RIP's arena and doesn't have a proper metric. When you redistribute into OSPF, be aware that on the **redistribute** statement (within OSPF) you might need the **subnets** keyword. If you do not use the **subnets** keyword, only major networks will be taken into OSPF (and no subnets). The **redistribute** statement can be augmented by a filter (access list) or a route map. For instructions on proper handling of the redistribution statement for each routing protocol, refer to Cisco documentation.

---

**NOTE**    Multiple and mutual redistribution among routing protocols, especially when a network topology contains loops, is a delicate procedure and can be dangerous if not treated with care. In-depth coverage of this topic is not intended in this book.

---

# Foundation Summary

The Foundation Summary is a collection of quick reference information that provides a convenient review of many key concepts in this chapter. For those of you who already feel comfortable with the topics in this chapter, this summary helps you recall a few details. For those of you who just read this chapter, this review should help solidify some key facts. For any of you doing your final prep before the exam, these tables and figures are a convenient way to review the day before the exam.

**Table 5-1**    *Cisco IOS Troubleshooting Tools and Commands for IP*

| Command | Description |
| --- | --- |
| **Ping** | Main tool for reachability tests. Available in user exec mode and privileged exec mode. Extended **ping** is only available in privileged exec mode. |
| **Traceroute** | Main tool for path discovery between IP nodes. Available in user exec mode and privileged exec mode. Extended **trace** is only available in privileged exec mode. |
| **show ip interface** [*type*] [*number*] | Lists a summary of interface(s) IP information and status. |
| **show ip access-list** [***access-list-number*** \| *name*] | Displays the contents of all current IP access lists. If you specify the access list number or name, only the content of the specified access list will be displayed. |
| **show ip route** [*address* [*mask*]] \| [*protocol* [*process-id*]] | Displays the current state of the routing table. If you specify a protocol name (such as **bgp, igrp, eigrp, rip, ospf,** and **isis**) and AS number or process ID, then only those entries corresponding to the routing protocol specified will be displayed. In case you want to see only the connected or static routes, you may use the keywords **static** or **connected** instead of the routing protocol ID. |
| **show ip arp** [*ip-address*] [*hostname*] [*mac-address*] [*type number*] | Displays the IP Address Resolution Protocol (ARP) cache. You can use the optional parameters to see only the ARP entries corresponding to a particular host, or only the entries learned via a specific interface. |
| **show ip traffic** | Displays statistics about IP traffic. |

*continues*

**Table 5-1** *Cisco IOS Troubleshooting Tools and Commands for IP (Continued)*

| Command | Description |
|---|---|
| **show ip protocols** | Displays the parameters and current state of the active routing protocol(s). |
| **debug arp** | Displays information on ARP transactions. |
| **debug ip packet** | Displays general IP debugging information. |
| **debug ip icmp** | Displays information on Internet Control Message Protocol (ICMP) transactions and allows you to monitor the ICMP messages sent and received by your router. |
| **debug ip rip** [events] | Displays information on RIP routing transactions. You may specify the **events** optional keyword if you are only interested in seeing RIP protocol events. |
| **debug ip igrp events** [*ip-address*] | Displays summary information on sent and received Interior Gateway Routing Protocol (IGRP) routing messages. If you specify the IP address (optional) of a neighbor router (IGRP peer), IGRP event debugging will be turned on only for the address specified, plus any updates that the router broadcasts toward that neighbor. |
| **debug ip igrp transactions** [*ip-address*] | Displays information on IGRP routing transactions. |
| **debug ip eigrp** | Displays the Enhanced IGRP packets sent and received on your router interfaces. |
| **debug ip ospf** *options* | Displays the OSPF packets sent and received by your router. The **debug ip ospf** command must be used with one of the following options: **adj, events, flood, lsa-generation, packet, retransmission, spf,** or **tree.** |
| **show debugging** | Displays the types of debugging that are enabled for your router. |

**Table 5-2**    *Important TCP/IP Commands Available from Windows NT (version 4.0) CMD Window Prompt*

| Command | Description |
|---|---|
| **arp** [options] | Displays and modifies the IP-to-physical-address translation tables used by ARP. |
| **Ipconfig** [options] | Displays IP configuration information. Can be used with **/renew** and **/release** switches to renew and release DHCP-assigned parameters. The **/all** switch causes the complete IP information set to be displayed. |
| **Nbtstat** [options] | Displays protocol statistics and current TCP/IP connections using NBT (NetBIOS over TCP/IP). |
| **route** [options] | Manipulates the local host's routing table. |
| **tracert** [options] | Performs a TCP/IP trace operation. |

**Table 5-3**    *Typical TCP/IP Symptoms and Possible Causes*

| Symptom | Possible Cause |
|---|---|
| Host cannot access remote hosts through router(s). | Wrong default gateway or subnet mask configured on host. |
| | Router(s) between hosts are down or misconfigured. |
| Certain remote networks are not reachable from the local host. | Access list(s). |
| | The local router doesn't have routes to those networks (a routing issue). |
| | The remote host(s) or router(s) don't have a route back to the local network/host. |
| | A major network is fragmented (discontinuous) and the protocols in use are not classless (or bad summarizations are performed). |
| Users can access some hosts, but not others. | Access list(s). |
| | Remote host's default gateway misconfigured. |
| Not all remote services are available to local host(s). | Extended access list(s). |
| | The remote service is not available. |
| Routing tables are faulty after redistribution between protocols were configured. | Metric parameter (or default metric) were not used for redistribution. |
| | Routing loops are also possible. |

# Q&A

The answers to the following questions can be found in Appendix A. Some of the questions in this section are repeated from the "Do I Know This Already" Quiz so that you can gauge the advancement of your knowledge of this subject matter.

1 Name the main TCP/IP tool used for reachability testing.

_____

_____

_____

2 Name the main TCP/IP tool used for path discovery between IP nodes. Also specify the full Cisco IOS command for this tool.

_____

_____

_____

3 Can the extended **ping** and **trace** be used from the user exec mode?

_____

_____

_____

4 What is the IP path discovery command available with Microsoft's Windows 95 and Windows NT TCP/IP stack?

_____

_____

_____

5 Name two Cisco IOS commands that allow you to see the IP address and subnet mask configured on a router's ethernet 0 interface (not a command that displays a router's startup or running configuration).

_____

_____

_____

**6** Specify the Cisco IOS command that allows you to see if an IP inbound access list is applied to a router's ethernet 0 interface (not a command that displays a router's startup or running configuration).

_____

_____

_____

**7** Name the Cisco IOS command that allows you to see if IP Proxy-ARP is enabled/ disabled on a router's ethernet 0 interface (not a command that displays a router's startup or running configuration).

_____

_____

_____

**8** If a router's ethernet 0 interface is equipped with both AUI and RJ45 connectors, how can you find out which is the active one?

_____

_____

_____

**9** How can you see the content of an IP access list without looking at a router's startup or running configuration?

_____

_____

_____

**10** Which Cisco IOS command allows you to see the IP static routes that are configured on a router (without looking at startup or running configuration)?

_____

_____

_____

**11** Which Cisco IOS command is used to see the entire IP routing table of a router?

_____

_____

_____

12 Which Cisco IOS command is used to display the IP Address Resolution Protocol cache of a router?

_____

_____

_____

13 Specify the Cisco IOS command that displays IP statistics such as the number of packets sent and received, error counts, and the number of broadcasts/multicasts sent and received.

_____

_____

_____

14 Which Cisco IOS command displays the active IP routing protocols and how they are configured to operate (not a command that displays a router's startup or running configuration)?

_____

_____

_____

15 How can you find out whether a Cisco router has been configured with the **no ip forward-protocol udp** command?

_____

_____

_____

16 How can you check whether the IP helper address is correctly configured on a Cisco router's ethernet 0 interface?

_____

_____

_____

17 What is the command that allows you to see the IP configuration of a Windows NT machine from the CMD window's prompt?

_____

_____

_____

**18** What is the command/utility that allows you to see the IP configuration of a Windows 95 device?

_____

_____

_____

**19** What is the command that allows you to see the contents of the NetBIOS cache of a Windows NT machine from the CMD window's prompt?

_____

_____

_____

**20** When you redistribute routing information from one protocol into another, what is a major source of concern?

_____

_____

_____

This chapter covers the following topics that you will need to master to pass the CCNP Support exam:

| Objective | Description |
|-----------|-------------|
| 1 | Effective usage of IPX ping. |
| 2 | The common IPX **show** commands. |
| 3 | The common IPX **debug** commands. |
| 4 | Basic check points for troubleshooting IPX networks. |
| 5 | Common IPX troubleshooting symptoms, causes, and actions. |

# CHAPTER 6

# Diagnosing and Correcting Novell Networking Problems

To design and configure IPX networks with Novell servers, you need to be familiar with the IPX/SPX protocol stack, understand some or all of the IPX routing protocols, be acquainted with the operation of Novell servers (and SAP), and have knowledge of IPX traffic management. To support IPX networks, you'll need to know all of this plus the necessary troubleshooting tools and commands, and have knowledge of common errors and poor procedures. This chapter lists and briefly explains a set of Cisco IOS tools and commands that are used for monitoring and supporting IPX networks. In addition, a series of common errors and problems and symptoms, along with their associated action plans and solutions, are presented.

## "Do I Know This Already?" Quiz

If you wish to evaluate your knowledge of the contents of this chapter before you get started, answer the following questions. The answers are provided in Appendix A, "Answers to Quiz Question." If you are having difficulty providing correct answers, you should thoroughly review the entire chapter. If all or most of your answers are correct, you might want to skim this chapter for only those subjects you need to review. You can also use the "Foundation Summary" section to quickly review topics. Once you have completed the chapter, you should reevaluate yourself with the questions in the "Q&A" section at the end. Finally, use the companion CD-ROM to evaluate your knowledge of the topics and see if you need a review.

1 Can you use **ping** for IPX reachability testing?

_____

_____

_____

2 Which Cisco IOS global configuration command makes the Cisco routers generate only Novell-compliant pings?

_____

_____

_____

**3** Which IPX **show** command displays the IPX address and encapsulation on a router's interface(s)?

_____

_____

_____

**4** Name the IPX **show** command that displays the contents of the IPX routing table.

_____

_____

_____

**5** Name the IPX **show** command that displays the local router's SAP table.

_____

_____

_____

**6** What is the effect of IPX fast-switching on **debug ipx** output?

_____

_____

_____

**7** What are the Cisco IOS encapsulations available for IPX?

_____

_____

_____

**8** What is the current default value for the **ipx gns-reply-delay** command, and what was its value prior to Cisco IOS release 9.1(13)?

_____

_____

_____

# Foundation Topics

# Cisco IOS Troubleshooting Commands and Tools for IPX

This section focuses on troubleshooting tools and commands for IPX. Specifically, **ping** (ipx), **show** (ipx), and **debug** (ipx) commands will be listed and briefly explained.

## Ping for IPX

Cisco introduced ping for IPX with IOS release 8.2. Ping for IPX has the same usage as ping for IP: they both are great reachability testing tools. Novell Corporation also offered ping for IPX with the NetWare IPX/SPX protocol stack. However, these two ping for IPX implementations are not compatible. In other words, you cannot use the Cisco IOS **ping** command to test network layer reachability to devices running Novell's IPX/SPX stack (a Novell server, for instance). However, in addition to the Cisco proprietary IPX ping, Cisco IOS also allows you to generate a Novell-compliant ping that can be used when the target is a Novell server. If you enter the **ipx ping-default novell** command at the global configuration mode, your Cisco router's ping will be Novell compliant as of that time. However, most of the time, you will want to send ping packets to Cisco routers as well. Hence, when you want to send ping packets to Novell servers, instead of changing the default ping behavior, it is recommended that you consider using the extended **ping** command and type "yes" when presented with the "Novell Standard Echo [n]:" prompt.

## The show ipx Commands

The are a number of **show** commands available for IPX (see Example 6-1). These commands display information about IPX traffic, routing, access lists, and so on, which is valuable for troubleshooting purposes. The following commands are covered in this section:

- **show ipx interfaces**
- **show ipx traffic**
- **show ipx route**
- **show ipx servers**
- **show ipx eigrp**
- **show ipx nlsp**

**Example 6-1** *show ipx* Commands

```
A_StubR#show ipx ?
  access-lists  IPX access lists
  accounting    The active IPX accounting database
  cache         IPX fast-switching cache
  compression   IPX compression information
  eigrp         IPX EIGRP show commands
  interface     IPX interface status and configuration
  nasi          Netware Asynchronous Services Interface status
  nhrp          NHRP information
  nlsp          Show NLSP information
  ppp-clients   PPP Client list
  route         IPX routing table
  servers       SAP servers
  spx-protocol  Sequenced Packet Exchange protocol status
  spx-spoof     SPX Spoofing table
  traffic       IPX protocol statistics

A_StubR#
```

## show ipx interfaces

**show ipx interfaces** [*type number*]

This command lists the IPX interfaces, and for each interface it shows the status, address, encapsulation, and many other IPX-related parameters and configurations (see Example 6-2).

**Example 6-2** *show ipx interfaces* Command

```
A_StubR#show ipx interface
Ethernet0 is up, line protocol is up
  IPX address is 1100.0060.4740.ebd6, NOVELL-ETHER [up]
  Delay of this IPX network, in ticks is 1 throughput 0 link delay 0
  IPXWAN processing not enabled on this interface.
  IPX SAP update interval is 60 seconds
  IPX type 20 propagation packet forwarding is disabled
  Incoming access list is not set
  Outgoing access list is not set
  IPX helper access list is not set
  SAP GNS processing enabled, delay 0 ms, output filter list is not set
  SAP Input filter list is not set
  SAP Output filter list is not set
  SAP Router filter list is not set
  Input filter list is not set
  Output filter list is not set
  Router filter list is not set
  Netbios Input host access list is not set
  Netbios Input bytes access list is not set
  Netbios Output host access list is not set
  Netbios Output bytes access list is not set
  Updates each 60 seconds aging multiples RIP: 3 SAP: 3
  SAP interpacket delay is 55 ms, maximum size is 480 bytes
```

**Example 6-2**  *show ipx interfaces Command (Continued)*

```
RIP interpacket delay is 55 ms, maximum size is 432 bytes
RIP response delay is not set
IPX accounting is disabled
IPX fast switching is configured (enabled)
RIP packets received 371, RIP packets sent 372
SAP packets received 1488, SAP packets sent 5

Ethernet1 is up, line protocol is up
  IPX address is 1110.0060.4740.ebd7, NOVELL-ETHER [up]
  Delay of this IPX network, in ticks is 1 throughput 0 link delay 0
```

The **show ipx interfaces** command is useful for finding out the settings for various timers such as SAP and RIP update/aging intervals. Also, this command informs you about all the filters that may be active for traffic, routing, and SAP management purposes. You will also discover some packet statistics such as the number of RIP and SAP packets sent and received in the output of this command.

## show ipx traffic

```
show ipx traffic
```

The output of this command is organized into several sections. The first section informs you of the total number of packets received along with a short report including the number of error conditions detected on those packets. Next, the number of broadcasts sent and received, and the number of packets sent, forwarded, and dropped (due to encapsulation failure or no route conditions) are reported. The sections following provide statistics on SAP, RIP, IPX Echo, Watchdog, queue lengths, and any other IPX routing protocols that are active (see Example 6-3).

**Example 6-3**  *show ipx traffic Command*

```
A_StubR#show ipx traffic
System Traffic for 0.0000.0000.0001 System-Name: A_StubR
Rcvd:  1930 total, 0 format errors, 0 checksum errors, 0 bad hop count,
       0 packets pitched, 1930 local destination, 0 multicast
Bcast: 1920 received, 2441 sent
Sent:  2449 generated, 0 forwarded
       0 encapsulation failed, 0 no route
SAP:   0 Total SAP requests, 0 Total SAP replies, 26 servers
       0 SAP general requests, 0 replies
       0 SAP Get Nearest Server requests, 0 replies
       0 SAP Nearest Name requests, 0 replies
       0 SAP General Name requests, 0 replies
       1460 SAP advertisements received, 1452 sent
       16 SAP flash updates sent, 0 SAP format errors
RIP:   0 RIP requests, 0 RIP replies, 4 routes
       364 RIP advertisements received, 727 sent
       3 RIP flash updates sent, 0 RIP format errors
```

*continues*

**Example 6-3** *show ipx traffic Command (Continued)*

```
Echo:    Rcvd 0 requests, 0 replies
         Sent 0 requests, 0 replies
         0 unknown: 0 no socket, 0 filtered, 0 no helper
         0 SAPs throttled, freed NDB len 0
Watchdog:
         0 packets received, 0 replies spoofed
Queue lengths:
         IPX input: 0, SAP 0, RIP 0, GNS 0
         SAP throttling length: 0/(no limit), 0 nets pending lost route reply
         Delayed process creation: 0
EIGRP:   Total received 106, sent 247
         Updates received 2, sent 4
         Queries received 1, sent 2
         Replies received 1, sent 1
         SAPs received 0, sent 0
```

This command is very useful during the course of troubleshooting, as it lets you know if the router under investigation is or is not successfully sending and receiving IPX packets, broadcasts, SAP, RIP, and other IPX-related traffic. Not only can you use these observations to decide on whether the local router is faulty, but you can also focus your attention on more specific transactions and protocols should there be a determination of faulty behavior.

## show ipx route

```
show ipx route
```

The **show ipx route** command is used to display a router's IPX routing table. This table contains information about connected IPX networks, static routes, and dynamic IPX routes leaned through IPX routing protocols in use (see Example 6-4).

**Example 6-4** *show ipx route Command*

```
A_StubR#show ipx route ?
  <1-FFFFFFFE>  IPX network number
  default       Default route
  detailed      Comprehensive display
  <cr>

A_StubR#show ipx route
Codes: C - Connected primary network, c - Connected secondary network
       S - Static,    F - Floating static, L - Local (internal),
       W - IPXWAN,    R - RIP, E - EIGRP, N - NLSP, X - External,
       A - Aggregate, s - seconds, u - uses, U - Per-user static

4 Total IPX routes. Up to 1 parallel paths and 16 hops allowed.

No default route known.

C     1100 (NOVELL-ETHER),  Et0
```

**Example 6-4**  *show ipx route Command (Continued)*

```
C       1110 (NOVELL-ETHER),  Et1
E       1000 [307200/0] via 1100.0060.4740.ef9c, age 00:05:20, 1u,   Et0
E   DEADBEEF [409600/1] via 1100.0060.4740.ef9c, age 00:05:21, 131u, Et0
```

You can use the **show** [*protocol*] **route** command to check the state of the routing table for a specific protocol. You do this in order to ensure that the router is properly configured for the networks it is directly connected to and that it is properly receiving routing information from its routing peers (other routers). If the routing table doesn't display correct connected, static, and local (internal) entries, turn your focus to the local router's configuration. For instance, you could execute the **show ipx interface** command right away. If the expected dynamic routing entries (such as RIP, EIGRP, NLSP) do not appear in the routing table, you must first check the local router's IPX routing configuration. If the local router's IPX routing protocol is configured properly, you then have to shift your focus to its peers.

## show ipx servers

```
show ipx servers
```

The **show ipx servers** command displays the content of the local router's SAP table (see Example 6-5). The local router's SAP table contains a list of IPX servers learned through received SAPs, or those servers that the local router is statically configured to advertise. When you execute the **show ipx servers** command, the entries corresponding to those servers that the local router is statically configured to advertise appear with an "S" in front of them. The entries learned through NLSP have "N," and the entries learned through periodic SAPs appear with a "P" in front of them. Each entry in the SAP table also includes a service type (for example, type 4 is a file server and type 7 is a print server), the name and IPX address of the server offering the service, and, finally, how many hops the server is away from the local router.

**Example 6-5**  *show ipx servers Command*

```
A_StubR#show ipx servers
Codes: S - Static, P - Periodic, E - EIGRP, N - NLSP, H - Holddown, + = detail
U - Per-user static

4 Total IPX Servers

Table ordering is based on routing and server info

  Type  Name       Net       Address     Port   Route    Hops Itf
P    6 FUNNY    DEADBEEF.0000.0000.0007:0451 409600/01   2  Et0
P    6 HAPPY    DEADBEEF.0000.0000.0002:0451 409600/01   2  Et0
P    7 PROUD    DEADBEEF.0000.0000.0002:0451 409600/01   2  Et0
P    7 KIND     DEADBEEF.0000.0000.0003:0451 409600/01   2  Et0
```

If some servers that you expect to see in the local router's SAP table are not displayed, or if some appear that you don't expect to see, the problem would most likely be due to faulty SAP filters or the static SAP configurations of certain routers.

## show ipx eigrp

```
show ipx eigrp
```

The **show ipx eigrp** command must be used with one of the following parameters: **interfaces, neighbors, topology,** or **traffic** (see Example 6-6). Obviously, this **show** command assists you in obtaining information about the IPX-related operation and activities of the EIGRP protocol. Using the **neighbors** option, you can find out if your router has built a neighbor relationship with those intended, and with the **topology** option you may see EIGRP's topology table.

**Example 6-6**   *show ipx eigrp ? Command*

```
A_StubR#show ipx eigrp ?
  interfaces   IPX EIGRP Interfaces
  neighbors    IPX EIGRP Neighbors
  topology     IPX EIGRP Topology Table
  traffic      IPX-EIGRP Traffic Statistics

A_StubR#show ipx eigrp topology
IPX EIGRP Topology Table for process 900

Codes: P - Passive, A - Active, U - Update, Q - Query, R - Reply,
       r - Reply status

P 1110,    1 successors, FD is 281600 via Connected, Ethernet1
P 1000,    1 successors, FD is 307200 via 1100.0060.4740.ef9c (307200/281600),
   Ethernet0
P 1100,    1 successors, FD is 281600 via Connected, Ethernet0
P DEADBEEF, 1 successors, FD is 409600 via 1100.0060.4740.ef9c (409600/128256),
   Ethernet0


A_StubR#show ipx eigrp neighbors

IPX EIGRP Neighbors for process 900
H    Address                    Interface    Hold Uptime    SRTT    RTO  Q  Seq
                                             (sec)          (ms)        Cnt Num
0    1100.0060.4740.ef9c    Et0              12 00:18:40    45      270  0  4

A_StubR#show ipx eigrp interfaces

IPX EIGRP Interfaces for process 900

                     Xmit Queue   Mean   Pacing Time   Multicast    Pending
Interface   Peers   Un/Reliable   SRTT   Un/Reliable   Flow Timer   Routes
Et0          1        0/0         45       0/10          96          0
Et1          0        0/0         0        0/10          0           0
```

**Example 6-6**  *show ipx eigrp ? Command (Continued)*

```
A_StubR#show ipx eigrp traffic
IPX-EIGRP Traffic Statistics for process 900
  Hellos sent/received: 536/247
  Updates sent/received: 4/2
  Queries sent/received: 2/1
  Replies sent/received: 1/1
  Acks sent/received: 3/4
  Input queue high water mark 1, 0 drops
```

## show ipx nlsp

```
show ipx nlsp
```

NetWare Link Services Protocol (NLSP) is a link state routing protocol you may use for IPX routing. This protocol may be activated with or without a process tag. A process tag is useful in cases where you must run multiple copies of the NLSP process on the same router. The **show ipx nlsp** [*process-tag*] command must be used with one of the following parameters: **database, neighbors,** or **spf-log** (see Example 6-7). This command is a specialized command that assists you in obtaining information about the state, database, neighbors, and activities of the NLSP protocol.

**Example 6-7**  *show ipx nlsp ? Command*

```
A_BackR#show ipx nlsp ?
  WORD       Routing process tag
  database   NLSP link state database
  neighbors  NLSP neighbor adjacencies
  spf-log    NLSP SPF log


A_BackR#show ipx nlsp database
NLSP Level-1 Link State Database: Tag Identifier = notag
LSPID            LSP Seq Num  LSP Checksum  LSP Holdtime    ATT/P/OL
A_StubR.00-00    0x00000002   0x213D        7295            0/0/0
A_StubR.01-00    0x00000006   0x4433        7410            0/0/0
A_StubR.01-01    0x00000005   0xD07C        0 (7412)        0/0/0
A_StubR.02-00    0x00000002   0x7E25        7356            0/0/0
A_BackR.00-00  * 0x00000003   0xA1B8        7405            0/0/0
A_BackR.01-00  * 0x00000001   0x8CFB        0 (7404)        0/0/0
A_BackR.02-00  * 0x00000002   0x2D87        7448            0/0/0
A_BackR.03-00  * 0x00000001   0xC680        7390            0/0/0
A_BackR.04-00  * 0x00000001   0xA684        7390            0/0/0
A_BackR.04-01  * 0x00000001   0x389D        7390            0/0/0


A_BackR#show ipx nlsp neighbors
NLSP Level-1 Neighbors: Tag Identifier = notag

System Id    Interface   State  Holdtime  Priority  Cir Adj  Circuit Id
A_StubR      Et0         Up     27        64        mc  mc   A_StubR.01
```

# The Debug IPX Commands

During the course of troubleshooting IPX-related traffic and protocols, you might decide to take advantage of the Cisco IOS **debug ipx** commands. Before executing the required **debug** command, however, you must turn off IPX fast-switching using the **no ipx route-cache** command. Otherwise, assuming that the cache is clear, **debug** will display only one packet for each destination. Because the general recommendations regarding usage of **debug** and its implications are presented in Chapter 4, "Applying Cisco Troubleshooting Tools," in the section named "Handling the Cisco IOS *Debug* Troubleshooting Tool," this section will not discuss those matters again. The complete set of **debug ipx** options can be discovered using the **debug ipx ?** privileged exec command (see Example 6-8). This section presents and briefly discusses a few of the **debug ipx** options. The following commands are covered in this section:

- **debug ipx packet**
- **debug ipx routing**
- **debug ipx sap**
- **debug ipx ipxwan**
- **debug ipx eigrp**
- **debug ipx nlsp**

**Example 6-8**  *debug ipx ? Command*

```
A_BackR#debug ipx ?
  all             IPX activity (all)
  compression     IPX compression
  eigrp           IPX EIGRP packets
  ipxwan          Novell IPXWAN events
  nasi            NASI server functionality
  nlsp            IPX NLSP activity
  packet          IPX activity
  redistribution  IPX route redistribution
  routing         IPX RIP routing information
  sap             IPX Service Advertisement information
  spoof           IPX and SPX Spoofing activity
  spx             Sequenced Packet Exchange Protocol
```

## debug ipx packet

```
debug ipx packet
```

The **debug ipx packet** command displays information about the packets received, transmitted, and forwarded by the local router. The output of this **debug** is simple and easy to understand. Each line displays the source and destination of the IPX packet sent or received. Sometimes the router must send an IPX packet to the destination through a neighboring router; in that case, the neighbor router's address is displayed with a "gw=" in front of it. The "gw=" indicates that the router is forwarding the IPX packet to its destination via a gateway with the displayed address.

## debug ipx routing

```
debug ipx routing
```

The **debug ipx routing** command is used with one of the **activity** or **events** options, and it displays information on IPX-related routing (RIP) traffic that the router generates and also receives (see Example 6-9). Use this **debug** command when you are interested in seeing the IPX routing information your router sends out of and receives from each interface.

**Example 6-9** *debug ipx routing ? Command*

```
A_BackR#debug ipx routing ?
  activity  IPX RIP routing activity
  events    IPX RIP routing events
```

## debug ipx sap

```
debug ipx sap
```

The **debug ipx sap** command displays information about IPX Service Advertisement Protocol (SAP) packets your router sends and receives. You may use the **debug ipx sap** command with the **activity** or the **events** option. To understand the output of this command, you need to be aware of the following:

- Each IPX packet that carries SAP has a source and destination IPX address and socket number.

- Each IPX packet may contain up to seven SAP entries.

- The SAP Update-Type and SAP Response-Type (displayed for each IPX packet that contains SAP) could be shown as 0x1 (General query), 0x2 (General response), 0x3 (Get nearest server request), or 0x4 (Get nearest server response).

- Each SAP entry that is carried within an IPX packet has a service type, the name and IPX address of the server offering the service, and the number of hops to reach the server. Table 6-1 shows some of the popular SAP service types.

**Table 6-1**  *Popular SAP Service Types*

| Service Type Number | Description |
| --- | --- |
| 0 | Unknown |
| 1 | User |
| 2 | User group |
| 3 | Print queue |
| 4 | File server |

*continues*

**Table 6-1**    *Popular SAP Service Types (Continued)*

| Service Type Number | Description |
| --- | --- |
| 5 | Job server |
| 6 | Gateway |
| 7 | Print server |
| 47 | Advertising print server |
| 98 | NetWare access server |
| 23A | NetWare LANalyzer agent |
| FFFF | Wildcard (any SAP service) |

## debug ipx ipxwan

```
debug ipx ipxwan
```

IPXWAN (defined in RFC 1634) allows a router that is running IPX routing to connect via a serial link to another router that is also routing IPX and using IPXWAN. IPXWAN is a connection startup protocol, and once a connection has been established, it is virtually overhead-free. The IPXWAN protocol can be used over PPP or over HDLC (in case of HDLC, both routers must be Cisco routers). The **ipx ipxwan** interface configuration command (with the appropriate parameters) is used to enable IPXWAN on a serial interface. The **debug ipx ipxwan** command displays debug information for interfaces configured to use IPXWAN. This command allows you to see (and verify) the startup negotiations between two routers running the IPX protocol through a WAN, and produces output only during state changes (and during startup).

## debug ipx eigrp

```
debug ipx eigrp
```

The **debug ipx eigrp** command is used to display the packets an EIGRP routing process sends and receives during its operation. With this command you may use the **events** option or the **neighbor** option (see Example 6-10). The **events** option gives you less information, but it has less overhead for the router.

**Example 6-10** *debug ipx eigrp ? Command*

```
A_BackR#debug ipx eigrp ?
  <1-65535>  AS number
  events     IPX EIGRP events
  neighbor   IPX neighbor
  <cr>

A_BackR#debug ipx eigrp events ?
  <cr>
```

**Example 6-10** *debug ipx eigrp ? Command (Continued)*

```
A_BackR#debug ipx eigrp neighbor ?
  <1-65535>  AS number
```

## debug ipx nlsp

```
debug ipx nlsp
```

The **debug ipx nlsp** command is a powerful tool for troubleshooting or monitoring the behavior of an NLSP routing process. With this command you may enter one of many available optional parameters to focus your debug on specific activities such as protocol errors, adjacency, or update packets (see Example 6-11).

**Example 6-11** *debug ipx nlsp ? Command*

```
A_BackR#debug ipx nlsp ?
  <1-FFFFFFFE>     IPX network
  activity         IPX NLSP activity
  adj-packets      NLSP Adjacency related packets
  checksum-errors  NLSP LSP checksum errors
  events           IPX NLSP events
  local-updates    NLSP local update packets
  protocol-errors  NLSP LSP protocol errors
  snp-packets      NLSP CSNP/PSNP packets
  spf-events       NLSP Shortest Path First Events
  spf-statistics   NLSP SPF Timing and Statistics Data
  spf-triggers     NLSP SPF triggering events
  update-packets   NLSP Update related packets
```

# Problem Isolation in IPX Networks

Today's IPX/SPX internetworks are basically composed of a set of IPX servers, IPX clients, and a number of internetworking devices that connect these clients and servers that are placed near or far away from each other. Generally, the job of supporting these types of networks is about discovering the faulty network device(s), client(s), or server(s) and fixing the faulty member—hence, restoring the network to the working state. The following list presents a general set of elements that you must inspect and test:

Check the client's configuration by answering the following questions:

- Is the network adapter card working? Is the correct network adapter driver installed and bound to the IPX/SPX protocol?

- Is the correct IPX frame type specified?

- Has the IPX netx been started on the client?

- Has the user logged on to the IPX server?

- Does NetBIOS over IPX/SPX processing need to be enabled?

Check the router's configuration by answering the following questions:

- Are the router interfaces' IPX addresses correct?

- Are the correct encapsulations set on the IPX interfaces?

- Are there any IPX packet, routing, or SAP filters set on the router?

- Is IPX routing turned on? Are the routing protocols operating properly? Is the IPX routing table showing the expected paths and entries?

- Does the **show ipx servers** command display the expected list of IPX servers and services?

- Do the IPX-enabled interfaces of the router need to forward IPX type 20 packets? Do they need to be configured with an IPX helper address?

- Is the IPX gns-response-delay setting on your router appropriate for your IPX clients?

- Are the timers for the active protocols adequate?

Check the server's configuration by answering the following questions:

- Is the external IPX network number consistent with the IPX network number of the other devices on the same network?

- Is the server's internal IPX network number unique?

- Does the server have a unique name?

- Is the network adapter card working? Is the correct network adapter driver installed and bound to the IPX/SPX protocol?

- Are the amount of free memory, disk space, and CPU utilization adequate on the server?

- Is the server sending SAP updates?

- Based on the server's software license, does the server have enough connections available for its clients?

The following section will discuss a number of common IPX networking issues and some scenario-based cases that intend to help you in your troubleshooting challenges.

# IPX Connectivity Symptoms, Possible Causes, and Suggested Actions

In order to be effective in troubleshooting, in addition to possessing relevant skills and background knowledge, it is also helpful to be familiar with the scenarios that have been dealt with in the past. Some of these cases stem from the special features of certain Cisco

IOS versions (e.g. gns-response-delay), designed to accommodate certain products, protocols, or applications behavior. Other cases are merely those that are worth keeping in mind simply due to their past frequency of occurrence (e.g. encapsulation mismatches).

## The Issue of Frame Type in IPX Networks

For two IPX devices on the same link to be able to communicate directly, there are two requirements:

- The frame type setting on both of the devices on the common link must be identical.

- Both of the devices must agree on the unique IPX network number of the link they share.

Table 6-2 shows the encapsulations supported on Cisco routers.

**Table 6-2**    *IPX Encapsulations Supported by Cisco IOS*

| Common Term | Novell Term | Cisco Term | Characteristics |
|---|---|---|---|
| Ethernet V.2 | Ethernet_II | ARPA | Includes the Ethertype field |
| IEEE 802.3 | Ethernet_802.2 | SAP | Includes the 802.3 Length field, and the LLC header fields (DSAP, SSAP, CNTRL) |
| Novell 802.3 raw | Ethernet_802.3 | NOVELL_ETHER (default on Ethernet interfaces) | Includes the 802.3 Length field, but *not* the LLC header fields (DSAP, SSAP, CNTRL) |
| SNAP | Ethernet_snap | SNAP | Includes both the LLC and the SNAP header fields |

## The gns-response-delay Issue

The default value of the **ipx gns-response-delay** command is 0 ms; but prior to Cisco IOS release 9.1(13), this parameter's default value was equal to 500 ms. The ipx gns-response-delay was set to 500 ms in order to allow a dual-connected NetWare 2.*x* server running in parallel with a Cisco router to reply to GNS requests before the Cisco router. The 500 ms value was also appropriate to compensate for the slow CPU or network adapter card of the client, which would otherwise miss a quicker router response. As you can imagine, if a Cisco router running an IOS release 9.1(13) or later is used in a network where old NetWare clients are present, the reply of the router (at 0 ms) would be too fast for those old clients. Conversely, if your client devices are newer and faster, but your Cisco router is running an IOS release 9.1(13) or older, you might want to decrease the value of the ipx gns-response-delay to improve the response time.

## Specific IPX Symptoms, Causes, and Recommended Actions

The remainder of this section covers specific symptoms, their possible cause(s), and recommended corrective action(s).

- **Symptom: Client cannot make connection to the local LAN's server.**

  Possible Cause #1: Client or server is misconfigured.

  Action: Check the network adapter card and its device driver (on both the client and the server), and the net.cfg file (on the client).

  Possible Cause #2: Encapsulation is mismatched.

  Action: Verify that the encapsulation specified on the client and the server are identical (otherwise, fix it).

  Possible Cause #3: An insufficient number of user licenses is on the server.

  Action: Check the total number of connections available against the number of connections in use (using the Monitor utility on the server).

- **Symptom: Client cannot make connection to the remote LAN's server.**

  Possible Cause #1: Router interface is down.

  Action: Make sure that router interface is connected, is not administratively down, and is configured with the correct IPX network number and encapsulation. The **show ipx interface** command displays all that information.

  Possible Cause #2: There are duplicate IPX network numbers.

  Action: Using the **show ipx servers** and the **show ipx route** privileged exec commands, see if any IPX network number or a server address has been learned from the wrong interface.

  Possible Cause #3: Access list or other filter is misconfigured.

  Action: Use the **show ipx interface** command to check for filters that have been applied to the router interface(s) (you will have to remove or correct these filters).

Possible Cause #4: gns-reply-delay value is too fast.

Action: On the router, adjust the ipx gns-reply-delay (from the interface configuration mode) so that the client can effectively receive and process the GNS reply.

- **Symptom: NetBIOS applications on the client cannot access the remote server(s).**

Possible Cause #1: IPX type-20-propagation is disabled.

Action: Using the **show ipx interface** command, check to see the status of IPX type-20-propagation on the appropriate interface(s). For certain applications (those that need NetBIOS over IPX), IPX type-20-propagation has to be enabled on the appropriate interface (with the **ipx type-20-propagation** interface configuration command). For some other applications (those that send packets with a specification other than type 20, such as type 0 or type 4), the appropriate router interface(s) need the IPX helper address to be configured.

Possible Cause #2: On the client PC, NetBIOS over IPX processing is not enabled (NetBIOS is not bound to the IPX/SPX-compatible protocol).

Action: Make sure that the client has the IPX/SPX loaded and that on the bindings tab of the IPX/SPX-compatible protocol properties sheet (in case of Microsoft Windows 95) the NetBIOS processing over IPX/SPX-compatible protocol box is selected.

- **Symptom: No connectivity over the IPX router.**

Possible Cause #1: IPX routing is not enabled on the router.

Action: Using the **show protocols** exec command, find out if IPX routing is enabled. To enable IPX routing on the router, enter the **ipx routing** command from the global configuration mode.

Possible Cause #2: There is a RIP timer mismatch.

Action: Using the **show ipx interface** command, check the RIP updates and aging timers. By default the IPX RIP update timer is 60 seconds and the aging multiples is 3 (3 times the update time makes it equal to 180 seconds). If the update and aging timers of the local router and the other IPX devices do not match, it is possible that the local router takes certain entries out of its routing table before receiving the next update(s).

Possible Cause #3: Filters are misconfigured.

Action: Observe the output of the **show ipx interface** exec command and look for any access list numbers in front of the input network filter or the output network filter lines. Using the **show ipx access-lists** exec command, see the contents of the access lists used for filtering inbound or outbound routing updates. If any network numbers are filtered, you must investigate their validity and correct or remove the filter based on your findings.

Possible Cause #4: Route redistribution is misconfigured.

Action: Inspect each IPX router's configuration for wrongful **redistribute** statements. Keep in mind that route redistribution is enabled automatically between IPX RIP and Enhanced IGRP and between IPX RIP and NLSP.

- **Symptom: Router does not propagate SAP updates.**

Possible Cause #1: Misconfigured SAP filters.

Action: Check to see if an input-sap-filter or an output-sap-filter is applied to the relevant router interface(s). You may do this by issuing the **show running-config** privileged exec command or the **show ipx interface** exec command. You may have to fix or remove the SAP filters (per your network's policies).

---

**NOTE**     SAP filters only apply when RIP is in use. In other words, if NLSP is in use, SAPs are not sent separately as they are when using RIP. They're part of the LS update messages and SAP filters (access lists) won't block them.

---

Possible Cause #2: Mismatched SAP timer.

Action: Inspect the output of the **show ipx interface** command to see if the SAP update interval has been changed from the default of every 1 minute to another value. Use the **ipx sap-interval** interface configuration command to adjust this parameter to the desired value.

# Foundation Summary

The Foundation Summary is a collection of quick reference information that provides a convenient review of many key concepts in this chapter. For those of you who already feel comfortable with the topics in this chapter, this summary helps you recall a few details. For those of you who just read this chapter, this review should help solidify some key facts. For any of you doing your final prep before the exam, these tables and figures are a convenient way to review the day before the exam.

**Table 6-3**    *Commonly Used IPX **show** Commands*

| Command | Description |
| --- | --- |
| show ipx interface | For each IPX interface, displays the status, address, encapsulation, settings for various timers such as SAP and RIP update/aging intervals, and filters that may be active for traffic, routing, and SAP management purposes. |
| show ipx traffic | Displays the total number of packets received, a short report including the number of error conditions detected on those packets, the number of broadcasts sent and received, the number of packets sent, forwarded, and dropped (due to encapsulation failure or no route conditions), and statistics on SAP, RIP, IPX Echo, Watchdog, queue lengths, and any other IPX routing protocols that are active. |
| show ipx route | Displays the local router's IPX routing table. |
| show ipx servers | Displays the content of the local router's SAP table. |

**Table 6-4**    *Commonly Used IPX **debug** Commands*

| Command | Description |
| --- | --- |
| debug ipx packet | Displays information about the packets received, transmitted, and forwarded by the local router. |
| debug ipx sap {activity \| events} | Displays information about IPX Service Advertisement Protocol (SAP) packets the local router sends and receives. |
| debug ipx routing {activity \| events} | Displays information about IPX-related routing (RIP) traffic that the router generates and receives. |

**Table 6-5**    *SAP Service Types You Should Know*

| Service Type Number | Description |
| --- | --- |
| 0 | Unknown |
| 4 | File server |
| 7 | Print server |
| 47 | Advertising print server |
| 98 | NetWare access server |
| FFFF | Wildcard (any SAP service) |

**Table 6-6**    *IPX Encapsulations Supported by Cisco IOS*

| Common Term | Novell Term | Cisco Term | Characteristics |
| --- | --- | --- | --- |
| Ethernet V.2 | Ethernet_II | ARPA | Includes the Ethertype field |
| IEEE 802.3 | Ethernet_802.2 | SAP | Includes the 802.3 Length field, and the LLC header fields (DSAP, SSAP, CNTRL) |
| Novell 802.3 raw | Ethernet_802.3 | NOVELL_ETHER (default on Ethernet interfaces) | Includes the 802.3 Length field, but *not* the LLC header fields (DSAP, SSAP, CNTRL) |
| SNAP | Ethernet_snap | SNAP | Includes both the LLC and the SNAP header fields |

**Table 6-7**    *Default Values (Settings) of Some IPX-Related Parameters*

| Parameter | Default Setting |
|---|---|
| **Encapsulation** | NOVELL_ETHER |
| **sap interval** | 1 minute |
| **type-20-propagation** | Disabled |
| **helper-address** | None configured |
| **gns-response-delay** | 0 ms[1] |
| **rip update interval** | 60 seconds |
| **sap update interval** | 60 seconds |
| **fast switching** (route-cache) | Enabled |

[1]Prior to Cisco IOS release 9.1(13), this parameter's default value was equal to 500 ms.

**Table 6-8**    *Common IPX Misconfigurations*

| Target | Common Trouble Cause |
|---|---|
| Client | Faulty network adapter card and/or device driver |
| Client | IPX/SPX protocol not loaded |
| Client | NetBIOS over IPX/SPX processing not enabled |
| Server | Non-unique internal network number or name |
| Server | Inappropriate external network number |
| Server | Inappropriate encapsulation |
| Router | IPX routing not enabled |
| Router | Invalid IPX network number or encapsulation |
| Router | Packet, routing, or SAP filter misconfigurations |

## Q&A

The answers to the following questions can be found in Appendix A. Some of the questions in this section are repeated from the "Do I Know This Already" Quiz so that you can gauge the advancement of your knowledge of this subject matter.

1  Can you use **ping** for IPX reachability testing?

 

 

 

2  Are Cisco's implementation of **ping** and Novell's **ping** compatible?

 

 

 

3  Which Cisco IOS global configuration command makes the Cisco routers generate only Novell-compliant pings?

 

 

 

4  How can you **ping** a Novell server from a Cisco router without using the **ipx ping-default novell** command?

 

 

 

5  Name at least three IPX troubleshooting **show** commands.

 

 

 

**6**  Which IPX **show** command displays the IPX address and encapsulation on a router's interface(s)?

_____

_____

_____

**7**  Which IPX **show** command allows you to discover the SAP and RIP update intervals and the applied traffic and routing filters on a router's interface(s)?

_____

_____

_____

**8**  Using which IPX **show** command can you see some statistics regarding the number of IPX packets sent and received (including errors encountered) and the number of SAP, RIP, broadcast, IPX echo, and Watch Dogs generated by a router?

_____

_____

_____

**9**  Name the IPX **show** command that displays the content of the IPX routing table.

_____

_____

_____

**10**  Name the IPX **show** command that displays the local router's SAP table.

_____

_____

_____

**11**  In a router's SAP table, what do the letters S, N, P that may appear in front of the entries stand for?

_____

_____

_____

**12** Is there a Cisco IOS **show** command to help you with troubleshooting IPX Enhanced IGRP routing?

_____

_____

_____

**13** What is the effect of IPX fast switching on debug IPX output?

_____

_____

_____

**14** What is the syntax of the **debug** command that allows you to observe the IPX-related routing updates that are generated/sent and received by a router?

_____

_____

_____

**15** What type of services are represented by the SAP service type numbers 4 and 7?

_____

_____

_____

**16** Are there any **debug ipx** commands available for the IPX Enhanced IGRP and NLSP routing protocols?

_____

_____

_____

**17** What are the three focal points of troubleshooting in IPX/SPX networks?

_____

_____

_____

**18** What are the Cisco IOS encapsulations available for IPX?

_____

_____

_____

**19** What is the current default value for the **gns-reply-delay**, and what was its value prior to Cisco IOS release 9.1(13)?

_____

_____

_____

**20** Why did the IPX **gns-response-delay** of Cisco routers have a different default prior to release 9.1(13) of the IOS?

_____

_____

_____

This chapter covers the following topics that you will need to master to pass the CCNP Support exam:

| Objective | Description |
| --- | --- |
| 1 | List the general requirements for a working AppleTalk network. |
| 2 | Describe the purpose and application of the **ping appletalk** and **test appletalk** commands. |
| 3 | Identify the information displayed by different **show appletalk** commands. |
| 4 | Explain the messages logged by important **debug appletalk** commands. |
| 5 | List the common sources of problems in AppleTalk networks. |
| 6 | Explain how different AppleTalk **show** and **debug** commands can be used to observe the symptoms of and identify the exact source of problems in a troubleshooting scenario. |
| 7 | Suggest actions to be taken for rectifying the identified problems in an AppleTalk network. |

# CHAPTER 7

# Diagnosing and Correcting AppleTalk Problems

Based on the assumption that you have a basic understanding of the AppleTalk protocol suite, this chapter will present a set of troubleshooting commands, tools, techniques, and tips that are essential for supporting AppleTalk networks. The commands and tools presented here are often used to isolate the problem area and determine the exact source of the problem. The "AppleTalk Configuration and Troubleshooting Check List" section summarizes the requirements for a working AppleTalk network. Also, there is a section with a list of common AppleTalk error symptoms, possible cause(s), and suggested corrective action(s).

## "Do I Know This Already?" Quiz

If you wish to evaluate your knowledge of the contents of this chapter before you get started, answer the following questions. The answers are provided in Appendix A, "Answers to Quiz Questions." If you are having difficulty providing correct answers, you should thoroughly review the entire chapter. If all or most of your answers are correct, you might want to skim this chapter for only those subjects you need to review. You can also use the "Foundation Summary" section to quickly review topics. Once you have completed the chapter, you should reevaluate yourself with the questions in the "Q&A" section at the end. Finally, use the companion CD-ROM to evaluate your knowledge of the topics and see if you need a review.

1  True or false: The routers that are connected to a single cable segment must have identical settings with regard to network number/cable range and zone name(s) of that segment.

2  True or false: In an AppleTalk network, a network number or cable range does not have to be unique.

3  True or false: Because Phase II of AppleTalk is completely backward-compatible with Phase I, in a mixed network no special action is necessary and the AppleTalk network will function just fine.

**4** Describe the **ping appletalk** command.

_____

_____

_____

**5** Which AppleTalk **show** command can be used to discover the configured AppleTalk cable range, the AppleTalk address, and the zone(s) an interface falls into?

_____

_____

_____

**6** Which AppleTalk **show** command informs you of the number of entries in the routing and zone information table, whether AppleTalk logging is enabled, the current settings for ZIP, RTMP, and AARP timers, and the routing protocol that is in use?

_____

_____

_____

**7** Provide at least two possible causes for the symptom Zones Missing from Chooser.

_____

_____

_____

**8** What are the default values for AppleTalk (RTMP) timers, and what do they mean?

_____

_____

_____

**9** List at least three of the commonly reported trouble symptoms of the AppleTalk networks.

_____

_____

_____

## Foundation Topics

# AppleTalk Configuration and Troubleshooting Checklist

This section will review the basic requirements for a trouble-free AppleTalk network. Even though network configurations vary from one organization to another, the essential settings needed per the protocol suite's specifications remain the same. The following list specifies those basic requirements:

- All routers connected to a network must agree on the configuration of that network. Those routers (connected to a single cable segment) must have identical settings with regard to network numbers/cable ranges, timers, and zone names.

- Similarly to other protocols, within AppleTalk internetworks network numbers must be unique. If you have more than one segment with the same network number, you will experience initialization, connectivity, performance, and possibly other problems.

- In order to avoid AppleTalk Phase I/Phase II interoperability issues, you should, if possible, upgrade all your AppleTalk networks to Phase II.

- Make the AppleTalk timers consistent, preferably to the default values, across the network. Inconsistent timers can cause route flapping, slow or never-ending convergence, non-optimal packet paths, and other problems.

- Pay special attention to your AppleTalk internetwork's zone mapping. You can minimize Name Binding Protocol (NBP) traffic by careful zone mapping and having as few zones as possible.

# The ping appletalk and test appletalk Commands

The **ping appletalk** command is a useful reachability testing tool, as are its IPX and IP counterparts. The **test appletalk** privileged exec command, available as of IOS Release 11.1, is a tool provided for identifying problem nodes. The NBP options of this command (**confirm**, **lookup**, **poll**) provide information on NBP-registered entities. The **confirm** option sends an NBP confirm packet to the specified entity, the **lookup** option (after prompting for name, type, and zone) looks up a Network Visible Entity (NVE), and the **poll** option searches for all devices in all zones. AppleTalk names comply with the format *object:type@zone*. For instance, a Cisco router called A_BackR in the Azone is specified as: A_BackR:CiscoRouter@Azone (note that AppleTalk names are case sensitive). If you want all objects or all types, you may use an equal sign in place of *object* and *type* fields. In Cisco IOS Release 11.0 and earlier, the privileged **ping** command with the NBP option (known as **nbtest**) served a purpose similar to **test appletalk**.

# AppleTalk show Commands

Cisco IOS offers several **show appletalk** commands. Some of these commands display configuration information (default and configured), some present statistics, and others display dynamically learned information. Example 7-1 displays the **show appletalk** options that are provided by the help feature of Cisco IOS. The following important **show appletalk** commands are listed and briefly explained in this section.

- **show appletalk interface**

- **show appletalk route**

- **show appletalk zone**

- **show appletalk access-lists**

- **show appletalk adjacent-routes**

- **show appletalk arp**

- **show appletalk globals**

- **show appletalk name-cache**

- **show appletalk neighbors**

- **show appletalk traffic**

**Example 7-1**  *show appletalk ? Command Output*

```
A_StubR#show appletalk ?
  access-lists     AppleTalk access lists
  adjacent-routes  AppleTalk adjacent routes
  arp              AppleTalk arp table
  aurp             AURP information
  cache            AppleTalk fast-switching cache
  domain           AppleTalk Domain(s) information
  eigrp            AppleTalk/EIGRP show commands
  globals          AppleTalk global parameters
  interface        AppleTalk interface status and configuration
  macip-clients    Mac IP clients
  macip-servers    Mac IP servers
  macip-traffic    Mac IP traffic
  name-cache       AppleTalk name cache
  nbp              AppleTalk NBP name table
  neighbors        AppleTalk Neighboring router status
  remap            AppleTalk remap table
  route            AppleTalk routing table
  sockets          AppleTalk protocol processing information
  static           AppleTalk static table
  traffic          AppleTalk protocol statistics
  zone             AppleTalk Zone table information
```

# show appletalk interface

This command will display AppleTalk information about all those interfaces that have AppleTalk enabled on them. However, if you specify the interface *type* and *number* along with the **show appletalk interface** command, then the output will be limited to only the specified interface. Example 7-2 shows a sample output of this command.

**Example 7-2**  *show appletalk interface Command Output*

```
A_StubR#show appletalk interface ethernet 0
Ethernet0 is up, line protocol is up
  AppleTalk cable range is 1010-1019
  AppleTalk address is 1018.114, Valid
  AppleTalk zone is "AZone"
  AppleTalk address gleaning is disabled
  AppleTalk route cache is enabled
```

As you can see, the first line of the output displays the status of the physical interface (Up, Down, or Administratively Down) and the state of its link as perceived by the router (Up or Down). The following lines inform you of the configured AppleTalk cable range, AppleTalk address of the interface and its validity (Valid, Invalid), the zone(s) the interface falls into, whether address gleaning is enabled, and, finally, whether AppleTalk route caching is enabled on the interface.

You do not have to statically assign an AppleTalk address to a node. An AppleTalk node can acquire its address dynamically. Upon startup the node selects a network number from the reserved range (65280 to 65534), and it chooses a node number randomly. Next, the node probes for the network information using the Zone-Information Protocol (ZIP). Another device (usually a router) residing on this network replies with the valid cable range for the network to which the node is attached. Then the node selects a valid network number (from the cable range supplied) and a random node number, and it sends a broadcast message(s) to determine whether the selected address is in use by another node. If no other node responds to the broadcast within a specific period of time, the node assumes the selected address. If, however, another node is using the address (i.e. replies to the sent broadcast indicating that the address is in use), the new node must choose another address and repeat the process until it finds an address that is not in use.

AppleTalk Address Resolution Protocol (AARP) is a network layer protocol member of the AppleTalk protocol suite. AARP is in charge of discovering the hardware (MAC) address associated to a network layer AppleTalk address. AARP is media-dependent, but it typically uses broadcasts to perform its hardware address discovery job. When the hardware (MAC) address of a network layer AppleTalk address is discovered, the MAC and Network Layer Address pair is added to an Address-Mapping Table (AMT) we often refer to as *AppleTalk ARP-cache*. Due to the dynamic nature of AppleTalk addresses, the entries within this table are not permanent. In fact, each entry has an associated timer that can eventually age-out that entry. However, an entry may change or be verified at times, and that causes its timer to be reset.

An AppleTalk device with Address Gleaning enabled, examines the AppleTalk Datagram Delivery Protocol (DDP) packets in order to learn the hardware and network addresses of their source (sending) device. The learned information is placed in the AMT (i.e. AppleTalk ARP-cache). This way an AppleTalk device can passively populate its AMT and effectively issue less AppleTalk ARP-Requests. Address gleaning is not widely used, and in fact, it is disabled by default on the AppleTalk interfaces of Cisco routers running current IOS versions.

## show appletalk route

The **show appletalk route** command displays the AppleTalk routing table (see Example 7-3). The routing table displayed in Example 7-3 was obtained from a router called A_BackR connected to a network similar to the one shown in Figure 7-1. If you specify a network number with this command, only the routing table entry corresponding to that network will be displayed. If you specify an interface *type* and *number* after the **show appletalk route** command, only those networks that can be reached through the specified interface will be displayed.

**Example 7-3**  *show appletalk route Command Output*

```
A_BackR#show appletalk route
Codes: R - RTMP derived, E - EIGRP derived, C - connected, A - AURP
       S - static  P - proxy
3 routes in internet

The first zone listed for each entry is its default (primary) zone.

C Net 1000-1009 directly connected, Ethernet1, zone BBZone
C Net 1010-1019 directly connected, Ethernet0, zone AZone
R Net 1030-1039 [1/G] via 1018.114, 3 sec, Ethernet0, zone AZone
```

## show appletalk zone

The **show appletalk zone** command displays the contents of the zone information table (ZIT). Each zone is displayed along with the cable range(s) that fall within that zone. If you specify a zone name along with this command, then only the specified zone and the corresponding cable range(s) will be displayed (of course, if it is in the ZIT). Example 7-4 displays a sample output of the **show appletalk zone** command. Notice that in this instance the zone called AZone includes cable ranges 1010-1019 and1030-1039, while BBZone only includes 1000-1009.

**Example 7-4** *show appletalk zone Command Output*

```
A_BackR#show appletalk zone
Name                Network(s)
AZone               1030-1039 1010-1019
BBZone              1000-1009
Total of 2 zones
```

**Figure 7-1**  *A Sample AppleTalk Network*

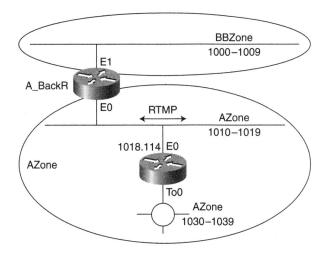

## show appletalk access-lists

The **show appletalk access-lists** command displays all the AppleTalk access lists (and their contents) that your router configuration includes, regardless of whether the access lists are in use (applied to any component) or not.

## show appletalk adjacent-routes

To display the directly connected networks or those networks that are one hop away, use the **show appletalk adjacent-routes** command (see Example 7-5).

**Example 7-5** *show appletalk adjacent-routes Command Output*

```
A_BackR#show appletalk adjacent-route
Codes: R - RTMP derived, E - EIGRP derived, C - connected, A - AURP
       S - static  P - proxy
3 routes in internet

The first zone listed for each entry is its default (primary) zone.
```

*continues*

**Example 7-5** *show appletalk adjacent-routes Command Output (Continued)*

```
C Net 1000-1009 directly connected, Ethernet1, zone BBZone
C Net 1010-1019 directly connected, Ethernet0, zone AZone
R Net 1030-1039 [1/G] via 1018.114, 8 sec, Ethernet0, zone AZone
```

# show appletalk arp

The **show appletalk arp** command displays all the entries of the AppleTalk ARP (Address Resolution Protocol) cache. Example 7-6 displays a sample output of this command. Notice that each ARP entry comprises an AppleTalk address, age, type, hardware address, encapsulation (frame type), and the router interface through which the address was learned.

**Example 7-6** *show appletalk arp Command Output*

```
A_StubR#show appletalk arp
Address    Age (min) Type     Hardware Addr      Encap  Interface
1018.11          -   Hardware 0000.0c04.32e4.0000 SNAP  Ethernet0
1037.90          -   Hardware 0000.3020.4ca7.0000 SNAP  TokenRing0
```

# show appletalk globals

The **show appletalk globals** command displays the AppleTalk global configuration (see Example 7-7). This command informs you of the number of entries in the routing and zone information table; whether AppleTalk logging is enabled; the current settings for ZIP, RTMP, and AARP timers; the routing protocol that is in use; and more. The extent of the valuable information that this command displays makes it very desirable for those instances where you want to see the values of virtually all AppleTalk settings, all from one place.

**Example 7-7** *show appletalk globals Command Output*

```
A_BackR#show appletalk globals
AppleTalk global information:
  Internet is incompatible with older, AT Phase1, routers.
  There are 3 routes in the internet.
  There are 2 zones defined.
  Logging of significant AppleTalk events is disabled.
  ZIP resends queries every 10 seconds.
  RTMP updates are sent every 10 seconds.
  RTMP entries are considered BAD after 20 seconds.
  RTMP entries are discarded after 60 seconds.
  AARP probe retransmit count: 10, interval: 200 msec.
  AARP request retransmit count: 5, interval: 1000 msec.
  DDP datagrams will be checksummed.
  RTMP datagrams will be strictly checked.
  RTMP routes may not be propagated without zones.
  Routes will not be distributed between routing protocols.
  Routing between local devices on an interface will not be performed.
  IPTalk uses the udp base port of 768 (Default).
  AppleTalk EIGRP is not enabled.
  Alternate node address format will not be displayed.
  Access control of any networks of a zone hides the zone.
```

## show appletalk name-cache

This command displays the contents of the router's cache that holds NBP names and services. The **appletalk lookup-type** and **appletalk name-lookup-interval** commands allow you to configure the service types (and periods) for which the router will query and keep names.

## show appletalk neighbors

The **show appletalk neighbors** command displays the list of active AppleTalk routers that reside on the networks the local router is directly connected to (see Example 7-8 for a sample output of this command). Notice that the AppleTalk address of the neighbor, the local router interface through which the neighbor has been learned, and the routing protocol associated with the peering relationship are displayed for each neighbor.

**Example 7-8**  *show appletalk neighbors Command Output*

```
A_BackR#show appletalk neighbors
AppleTalk neighbors:
  1018.114      Ethernet0, uptime 00:06:45, 5 secs
          Neighbor is reachable as a RTMP peer
```

## show appletalk traffic

This command provides a comprehensive set of statistics about AppleTalk traffic. The output is carefully organized into sections that allow you to grasp the activity and errors encountered by different members of the protocol suite (see Example 7-9). The **show appletalk traffic** command can be used as a monitoring, troubleshooting, or network baselining tool.

**Example 7-9**  *show appletalk traffic Command Output*

```
A_BackR#show appletalk traffic
AppleTalk statistics:
  Rcvd:  51 total, 0 checksum errors, 0 bad hop count
         51 local destination, 0 access denied, 0 fast access denied
         0 for MacIP, 0 bad MacIP, 0 no client
         0 port disabled, 0 no listener
         0 ignored, 0 martians
  Bcast: 0 received, 105 sent
  Sent:  107 generated, 0 forwarded, 0 fast forwarded, 0 loopback
         0 forwarded from MacIP, 0 MacIP failures
         0 encapsulation failed, 0 no route, 0 no source
  DDP:   51 long, 0 short, 0 macip, 0 bad size
  NBP:   20 received, 0 invalid, 0 proxies
         0 replies sent, 40 forwards, 20 lookups, 0 failures
  RTMP:  49 received, 0 requests, 0 invalid, 0 ignored
         77 sent, 0 replies
  ATP:   0 received
  ZIP:   2 received, 11 sent, 0 netinfo
```

*continues*

**Example 7-9** *show appletalk traffic Command Output (Continued)*

```
    Echo:   0 received, 0 discarded, 0 illegal
            0 generated, 0 replies sent
  Responder:  0 received, 0 illegal, 0 unknown
            0 replies sent, 0 failures
    AARP:  0 requests, 1 replies, 0 probes
            0 martians, 0 bad encapsulation, 0 unknown
AppleTalk statistics:
            21 sent, 0 failures, 1 delays, 0 drops
  Lost: 0 no buffers
  Unknown: 0 packets
  Discarded: 0 wrong encapsulation, 0 bad SNAP discriminator
  AURP: 0 Open Requests, 0 Router Downs
            0 Routing Information sent, 0 Routing Information received
            0 Zone Information sent, 0 Zone Information received
            0 Get Zone Nets sent, 0 Get Zone Nets received
            0 Get Domain Zone List sent, 0 Get Domain Zone List received
            0 bad sequence
```

# debug apple Commands

Using **debug** commands requires special attention. You should try to use the **debug apple** commands when the traffic in your network is low. Some **debug** commands can produce a large amount of output; hence, you are encouraged to do events debugging when you can. Example 7-10 displays the **debug apple** options. This section contains brief explanations for the following significant **debug apple** commands:

- **debug apple arp**
- **debug apple errors**
- **debug apple events**
- **debug apple nbp**
- **debug apple packet**
- **debug apple routing**
- **debug apple zip**

**NOTE**     Please note that the keywork **apple** used with the **debug** commands listed is not a truncated form of **appletalk**. If you attempt to use the word **appletalk** with these **debug** commands, the Cisco IOS will not accept your command and will give you an error message.

**Example 7-10** *debug apple ? Command Output*

```
A_BackR#debug apple ?
  arp                     Appletalk address resolution protocol
  aurp-connection         AURP connection
  aurp-packet             AURP packets
  aurp-update             AURP routing updates
  domain                  AppleTalk Domain function
  eigrp-all               All AT/EIGRP functions
  eigrp-external          AT/EIGRP external functions
  eigrp-hello             AT/EIGRP hello functions
  eigrp-packet            AT/EIGRP packet debugging
  eigrp-query             AT/EIGRP query functions
  eigrp-redistribution    AT/EIGRP route redistribution
  eigrp-request           AT/EIGRP external functions
  eigrp-target            Appletalk/EIGRP for targeting address
  eigrp-update            AT/EIGRP update functions
  errors                  Information about errors
  events                  Appletalk special events
  fs                      Appletalk fast-switching
  iptalk                  IPTalk encapsulation and functionality
  load-balancing          AppleTalk load-balancing
  macip                   MacIP functions
  nbp                     Name Binding Protocol (NBP) functions
  packet                  Per-packet debugging
  redistribution          Route Redistribution
  remap                   AppleTalk Remap function
  responde                AppleTalk responder debugging
  routing                 (RTMP&EIGRP) functions
  rtmp                    (RTMP) functions
  zip                     Zone Information Protocol functions
```

# debug apple arp

This command enables debugging of the AARP. Use this command to investigate the cases in which the local router has trouble communicating with the other devices on the locally connected network (neighbors). If you see AARP probe replies being received, you may rule out physical layer problems.

# debug apple errors

The **debug apple errors** command is used to display AppleTalk error messages so that you can identify the cause of your network problem. These messages may be generated for many reasons. AppleTalk problems are usually due to mismatching cable range/network number(s), zone name(s), ordering of zone names (Primary, Secondary, and so on), and mixture of AppleTalk Phase I and Phase II among neighbors. The error messages displayed by the **debug apple error** command include:

- Net information mismatch, multicast mismatch, and zones disagree.

- Wrong encapsulation.

- Invalid echo packet, unsolicited AEP echo reply, unknown echo function, invalid ping packet, unknown ping function, and bad responder packet type.

- Invalid NetInfo reply format, NetInfoReply not for me, NetInfoReply from invalid port, and unexpected NetInfoReply.

- Cannot establish primary zone, no primary has been set up, and primary zone invalid.

## debug apple events

The **debug apple events** command is one of the most informative **debug** commands used for troubleshooting AppleTalk networks, yet it imposes less overhead than other commands such as **debug apple packet**. In a stable network, this command does not produce any information. The **debug apple events** command logs messages only about AppleTalk special events such as route changes, neighbors becoming reachable or unreachable, and interfaces going up or down. You may monitor state changes—for instance, those due to an interface being brought up—by enabling **debug apple events**, which reports the following sequence of events:

- Line down

- Restarting

- Probing (for an address using AARP)

- Acquiring (submitting GetNetInfo requests)

- Requesting zones

- Verifying

- Checking zones

- Operational (routing has started)

## debug apple nbp

Use the **debug apple nbp** command to see debugging output about NBP activities. If you want to find out why your router is not receiving NBP lookups from a node, enable this command and, starting from the router closest to the node in question, move towards your own router until you find out where the lookups are being dropped (filtered or otherwise mishandled). Cisco documentation warns that since this **debug** command can generate many messages, it should be used only when the router's CPU utilization is less than 50 percent.

# debug apple packet

The **debug apple packet** command reports output for each AppleTalk packet received and generated/transmitted. This command is often used together with other **debug** commands, such as **debug apple routing**, **debug apple zip**, and **debug apple nbp**, in order to obtain protocol processing information, generic packet details, and successful completion or failure information.

# debug apple routing

Use the **debug apple routing** command to see output about RTMP activities such as sending and receiving of routing information and aging of routing table entries. This command also reports cases of conflicting cable ranges/network numbers existing on the local router's connected (adjacent) networks.

# debug apple zip

The **debug apple zip** command is used to see information pertaining to the activities of the Zone Information Protocol (ZIP). The information displayed by this command includes significant events such as discovery of new zones and zone list queries. You may use the **debug apple zip** command to find out if a ZIP storm is taking place. A ZIP storm is a situation where none of the routers has the zone name corresponding to a network number that exists in all the routers' routing tables. This can happen, for instance, when routers learn of a cable range and in turn send ZIP queries to find out the zone(s) corresponding to the newly learned cable range, but the zones either do not exist or are not distributed as a result of software bugs or misconfigured filters.

# Common AppleTalk Trouble Symptoms, Possible Causes, and Suggested Actions

This section concentrates on common errors and misconfigurations related to AppleTalk settings, the expected symptoms of each problem, and how you can identify the exact reason for the symptoms and rectify the situation. The most common faults found in AppleTalk networks are

- **Configuration mismatch**—Neighboring routers do not have identical specifications for the cable range and zone name(s) of the segment they have in common.

- **Duplicate cable range/network numbers or overlapping cable ranges in the network**—Identical cable range/network numbers or overlapping cable ranges are assigned to distinct segments of the network.

- **Phase I and Phase II incompatibility**—The network is not completely upgraded to AppleTalk Phase II, and the Phase II segments are not using unary (e.g., 100-100) cable ranges or do not have a single zone per segment configuration.

- **ZIP storms**—Misconfigurations or software bugs cause a chain reaction on routers consisting of newly learned cable range(s) advertisements, which in turn triggers ZIP queries (from routers that want to find out the zones corresponding to those cable ranges).

- **Incompatible routing timers causing unstable routing tables**—Routers invalidate certain routing table entries, since they do not receive the periodic updates for those routes on time (before they are marked invalid).

- **Excessive network load causing route flapping**—The AppleTalk timers are not appropriate for the high load of traffic that exists in the network; in other words, congestion and overloading of network devices causes updates to be lost or missed, and hence be aged out of various routing tables.

Most of the problems experienced in AppleTalk networks are caused by one or more of the listed possible faults. The commonly reported trouble symptoms are:

- Zones are missing from Chooser.

- Users cannot see zones and/or services on remote networks.

- The zone list changes every time Chooser is opened.

- Connections to services drop.

- Old zone names appear in Chooser.

- A router port gets stuck in restarting or acquiring mode.

Configuration mismatch and duplicate cable range/network numbers can be the cause of any of the mentioned AppleTalk network's reported symptoms. Use the **show appletalk interface** command to see the configuration of router interfaces. If you suspect that the cable range/network number configured on an interface duplicated the cable range/network number of another segment, temporarily disable the interface and see whether the corresponding entry disappears from the routing tables. You can then find out exactly which segment's cable range is being duplicated by the suspended interface.

The Phase I/Phase II incompatibility issue may cause a lot of misbehavior, too. One common symptom of it is that AppleTalk services in a network do not appear outside that network. Use the **show appletalk globals** command to see if your router can support both AppleTalk Phase I and Phase II. Also, you can use the **show appletalk neighbors** command to see which of the router's neighbors are visible. In other words, if an AppleTalk device does not see a neighboring device, chances are good that there is Phase I/Phase II incompatibility between them.

Unstable routes can be the cause of zones and services not appearing in the Chooser or disappearing from it. They can also cause connection to services to suddenly drop. Use the **show appletalk route** command repeatedly, to observe appearance and disappearance of routes. The **debug apple events** can help you verify that the routes are added and aged correctly. Sometimes unstable routes are merely the result of inconsistency of AppleTalk timers, and the suggested action is obviously to make them consistent.

Another serious possible cause of unstable routes is the existence of routing loops. Routing loops are generally produced as a result of mishandling route redistribution, conflicting dynamic and static routes, and so on. In cases where unstable routes are due to load problems (known as *route flapping*), you may have to adjust routers' timers with the **appletalk timers** command. The default AppleTalk timers are 10, 20, and 60. RTMP updates are sent every 10 seconds; they are considered bad after 20 seconds (without updates), and they are discarded after 60 seconds. It is recommended that the first number remain as 10 and the third number be set to a value three times larger than the second number. Note that the larger the second and third number get, the slower your network convergence gets. Finally, keep in mind that consistency across the network is the most promising, desirable, and rewarding configuration.

ZIP storms may be the result of software bugs, unstable routes, or a bad ZIP reply filter on a router. Though infrequent, ZIP storms are serious because they cause excessive traffic. Cisco routers have a built-in mechanism to deal with ZIP storms: they do not report networks for which the corresponding zone(s) are not known yet. Use the **show appletalk traffic** command repeatedly to see if the number of ZIP requests increases rapidly. If you notice a ZIP storm, your challenge will be to fix the issue of unstable routes.

The symptom of old zone names appearing in the Chooser is usually due to a zone name change. If a zone name is changed, that change takes effect locally, but it does not trigger the other routers to take the old zone name out of their Zone Information Table until it ages out (a phenomenon known as *ghosted zone*). If the old zone name does not disappear eventually, it is probably still being used on some network segment. Use the **show appletalk zones** command to find out the cable range reported for the ghosted zone and then you can find your way (hop by hop) to the router that advertises that zone. Moreover, *ghosted zones* can also result from changing the case of a zone name. Although a zone information table will keep track of multiple spellings of a zone, the zone multicasting hash function actually does treat them the same. However, the misspelled zones can float around for a while until they age out of all routers.

In cases where zones are not visible through the Chooser, you should verify that on the Macintosh client the correct network adapter is selected. Finally, if services are not always visible from the Chooser, or if services are visible but users cannot connect, the reason could be excessive traffic due to ZIP storms or too many AARP broadcast frames. Make routes stable, filter and manage your network's traffic, and use generous cable ranges on your segments.

# Foundation Summary

The Foundation Summary is a collection of quick reference information that provides a convenient review of many key concepts in this chapter. For those of you who already feel comfortable with the topics in this chapter, this summary helps you recall a few details. For those of you who just read this chapter, this review should help solidify some key facts. For any of you doing your final prep before the exam, these tables and figures are a convenient way to review the day before the exam.

**General checklist for a working AppleTalk network:**

- All of the routers connected to a single common segment must specify identical cable range and zone name(s) for that segment.

- The cable range assigned to each segment must be unique throughout the network and cannot overlap with another cable range.

- To avoid AppleTalk Phase I and Phase II incompatibility, it is best to upgrade the entire network to AppleTalk Phase II.

- Make sure the AppleTalk timers are consistent across all routers in the network, and use the default timer values if possible.

- NBP traffic can be minimized by careful zone mapping and having as few zones as possible.

**Table 7-1**    *AppleTalk show Commands*

| Command | Description |
| --- | --- |
| **show appletalk interface** | Displays the status of the AppleTalk interfaces configured in the Cisco IOS software and the parameters configured on each interface. |
| **show appletalk route** | Displays all entries or specified entries in the AppleTalk routing table. |
| **show appletalk zone** | Displays all entries or specified entries in the ZIT. |
| **show appletalk access-lists** | Displays the AppleTalk access lists currently defined. |
| **show appletalk adjacent-routes** | Displays routes to networks that are directly connected or those that are one hop away. |
| **show appletalk arp** | Display the entries in the AppleTalk ARP cache. |

**Table 7-1** *AppleTalk **show** Commands (Continued)*

| Command | Description |
|---|---|
| **show appletalk globals** | Displays AppleTalk global configuration. This command informs you of the number of entries in the routing and zone information table, whether AppleTalk logging is enabled, the current settings for ZIP, RTMP, AARP timers, the routing protocol that is in use, and more. |
| **show appletalk name-cache** | Displays a list of NBP services offered by nearby routers and other devices that support NBP. |
| **show appletalk neighbors** | Displays information about the AppleTalk routers that are directly connected to any of the networks to which this router is directly connected. |
| **show appletalk traffic** | Displays a comprehensive set of statistics about AppleTalk traffic. The output is carefully organized into sections that allow you to grasp the activity and errors encountered by different members of the protocol suite. |

**Table 7-2** *AppleTalk **debug** Commands*

| Command | Description |
|---|---|
| **debug apple arp** | Enables debugging of the AppleTalk AARP. |
| **debug apple errors** | Enables exhaustive logging of AppleTalk error messages (which can be of great assistance in identifying the cause of your network problem). |
| **debug apple events** | Displays information about special AppleTalk events such as neighbors becoming reachable or unreachable and interfaces going up or down. |
| **debug apple nbp** | Displays debugging output about the NBP activities. |
| **debug apple packet** | Reports output for each AppleTalk packet received and generated or transmitted. This command is often used together with other **debug** commands. |

*continues*

**Table 7-2**    *AppleTalk **debug** Commands (Continued)*

| Command | Description |
| --- | --- |
| **debug apple routing** | Displays output about RTMP activities such as sending and receiving of routing information and aging of routing table entries. |
| **debug apple zip** | Displays information pertaining to the activities of the ZIP. |

**Table 7-3**    *Common AppleTalk Symptoms and Possible Sources of the Problem*

| Symptom | Possible Reason |
| --- | --- |
| Users cannot access zones or services | Configuration mismatch. |
|  | Duplicate network numbers or overlapping cable range. |
|  | Phase I and Phase II rule violations. |
|  | Misconfigured access lists or other filters. |
| Zones missing from Chooser | Configuration mismatch. |
|  | Misconfigured access lists or other filters. |
|  | Route flapping (unstable route). |
|  | ZIP storm. |
| No devices in Chooser | Misconfigured access lists. |
| Network services intermittently unavailable | Duplicate network numbers or overlapping cable range. |
|  | Route flapping (unstable route). |
|  | ZIP storm. |
| Old zone names appear in Chooser (phantom zones) | Configuration mismatch. |
|  | Invalid zone names in routing table. |
| Connections to services drop | Route flapping (unstable route). |
| Interface fails to initialize AppleTalk | Configuration mismatch. |
|  | Phase I and Phase II rule violations. |

**Table 7-4**   *Common AppleTalk Problems and Suggested Actions*

| Problem | Suggested Action |
| --- | --- |
| Configuration mismatch | Check the output of the **show appletalk interface** command for a "port configuration mismatch" message. |
| | Alter the parameters (network number or cable range and the zone or zone list) that the neighboring router configurations disagree on to bring all routers into agreement (consistent). |
| Duplicate network numbers or overlapping cable range | Change the network number or cable range of the suspected network to a unique value using the **appletalk cable-range** interface configuration command. |
| | Observe the Appletalk routing table by issuing the **show appletalk route** command. If the network number or cable range continues to appear in the routing table, you have found the duplicate (because the other network using that number will continue to send routing updates). |
| Phase I and Phase II rule violations | Upgrade AppleTalk Phase I routers to AppleTalk Phase II and reconfigure the internetwork. |
| | or |
| | Ensure that all routers are in compliance with the two Phase I and Phase II rules (for example, use unary cable range and make sure there is only one zone per cable range). |
| Misconfigured access lists or other filters | Use the **show appletalk interface** command to find out which access list(s) is/are applied to the router interface(s). |
| | Use the **show appletalk access-lists** command to view the access lists. |
| | Temporarily remove the suspected access list from the target interface to ensure that it is indeed the cause of theproblem. |
| | Fix the access list. |

*continues*

**Table 7-4**    *Common AppleTalk Problems and Suggested Actions (Continued)*

| Problem | Suggested Action |
|---|---|
| Route flapping (unstable route) | Increase the value of the RTMP aging timer, if route flapping is due to excessive traffic. This technique is only effective at 50% utilization rate and lower, but if utilization is over 50%, then network segmentation is the answer. |
| | Make the AppleTalk timer values of routers consistent if route flapping is due to routes being aged faster than they are received. |
| ZIP storm | Use the **show appletalk traffic** command repeatedly (every 30 seconds) to see if the number of ZIP requests increases rapidly. |
| | Since the ZIP storm phenomenon is due to the fact that routers do not have a zone for one or more cable range(s), you must find the router that advertises that cable range and discover why that router does not reply to ZIP requests. The reason maybe a misconfigured ZIP reply filter. |

# Q&A

The answers to the following questions can be found in Appendix A. Some of the questions in this section are repeated from the "Do I Know This Already" Quiz so that you can gauge the advancement of your knowledge of this subject matter.

1  True or false: The routers that are connected to a single cable segment must have identical settings with regard to network number/cable range and zone name(s) of that segment.

2  True or false: In an AppleTalk network, a network number or cable range does not have to be unique.

3  True or false: Because Phase II of AppleTalk is completely backward-compatible with Phase I, in a mixed network no special action is necessary and the AppleTalk network will function just fine.

4  True or false: The AppleTalk timers are only locally significant within a router and hence their values have no effect on the network.

5  True or false: Cisco routers have a built-in mechanism to deal with ZIP storms.

6  Describe the **ping appletalk** command.

7  Which AppleTalk **show** command can be used to discover the configured AppleTalk cable range, AppleTalk address, and the zone(s) an interface falls into?

8  Which AppleTalk **show** command informs you of the number of entries in the routing and zone information table, whether AppleTalk logging is enabled, the current settings for ZIP, RTMP, and AARP timers, and the routing protocol that is in use?

 

9  Which AppleTalk **show** command displays the AppleTalk routing table?

 

10  Which AppleTalk **show** command displays the AppleTalk ZIT?

 

11  Which AppleTalk **show** command displays the directly connected networks or those networks that are one hop away?

 

12  Which AppleTalk **show** command displays the list of active AppleTalk routers that reside on the same networks that the local router is also directly connected to?

 

13  Provide at least two possible causes for the symptom Users cannot access zones or services.

14  Provide at least two possible causes for the symptom Zones missing from Chooser.

_____

_____

_____

15  Provide at least one possible cause for the symptom Network services intermittently unavailable.

_____

_____

_____

16  Provide at least one possible cause for the symptom Old zone names appear in Chooser (phantom/ghosted zones).

_____

_____

_____

17  Provide at least one possible cause for the symptom Interface fails to initialize AppleTalk.

_____

_____

_____

18  What are the default values for AppleTalk (RTMP) timers and what do they mean?

_____

_____

_____

19  List at least three of the commonly reported trouble symptoms of the AppleTalk networks.

_____

_____

_____

**20** Describe the output of **debug apple errors** and provide one example of the error messages that this command displays.

_____

_____

_____

**21** True or false: There will be no questions on AppleTalk troubleshooting in the CCNP Support exam.

_____

This chapter covers the following topics that you will need to master to pass the CCNP Support exam:

| Objective | Description |
|---|---|
| 1 | Understand CiscoWorks for Switched Internetworks (CWSI). |
| 2 | Comprehend embedded RMON agent and SwitchProbe. |
| 3 | Understand using Catalyst switch LEDs. |
| 4 | Know Cable, speed, and media concerns. |
| 5 | Master Catalyst power-on self-test. |
| 6 | Understand Catalyst 5000 Spanning Tree. |
| 7 | Master troubleshooting Catalyst 5000 trunking. |
| 8 | Understand the Catalyst 5000 switch diagnostic tools: **ping** and Cisco Discovery Protocol. |
| 9 | Understand the Catalyst 5000 switch diagnostic tools: **show** commands. |
| 10 | Comprehend Catalyst symptoms, problems, and suggested actions. |

# CHAPTER 8

# Diagnosing and Correcting Catalyst Problems

To diagnose and correct Catalyst switch problems, you need to be familiar with the function and operation of the switches, their IOS's commands, and the troubleshooting tools and commands that assist identifying the source of the reported problems. Proper installation, cabling, and configuration of interfaces, ports, VLANs (Virtual LANs), trunks, Spanning Tree, and VTP (VLAN Trunking Protocol) are the basic requirements of a working switched internetwork. To monitor and support switched internetworks, you must understand the system startup, system LEDs, management software, and many of the IOS **show** commands. This chapter provides a condensed coverage of these topics.

## "Do I Know This Already?" Quiz

If you wish to evaluate your knowledge of the contents of this chapter before you get started, answer the following questions. The answers are provided in Appendix A, "Answers to Quiz Questions." If you are having difficulty providing correct answers, you should thoroughly review the entire chapter. If all or most ofyour answers are correct, you might want to skim this chapter for only those subjects you need to review. You can also use the "Foundation Summary" section to quickly review topics. Once you have completed the chapter, you should reevaluate yourself with the questions in the "Q&A" section at the end. Finally, use the companion CD-ROM to evaluate your knowledge of the topics and see if you need a review.

1 Name the applications that are included in the CWSI Campus package.

_____

_____

_____

2 The structure of the remote network monitoring MIB as outlined in RFC 1757 defines nine groups of objects. Which four of those groups are supported by the Catalyst 5000 embedded RMON agent?

_____

_____

_____

**3** What is SPAN?

_____

_____

_____

**4** Briefly describe Cisco Systems' SwitchProbe product.

_____

_____

_____

**5** Briefly describe the Catalyst 5000 switch's power-on self-test.

_____

_____

_____

**6** At a particular instance, what states can an enabled port be in?

_____

_____

_____

**7** Provide a brief description of VTP.

_____

_____

_____

**8** What roles can a switch have in a VTP domain?

_____

_____

_____

**9** Describe the output of the **show module** [*mod_num*] command.

_____

_____

_____

**10** List at least three important pieces of information that can be gathered by executing the **show vtp domain** command.

_____

_____

_____

## Foundation Topics

# CiscoWorks for Switched Internetworks (CWSI)

CWSI (the Campus version) is a suite of network management applications that together provide remote monitoring, configuration, and management of switched internetworks. The following applications are included in the CWSI Campus package:

- TrafficDirector
- VlanDirector
- AtmDirector
- CiscoView
- UserTracking

These management applications can be used to build the network baseline, identify problem areas (or components), and reconfigure devices from a central point using a GUI (graphical user interface).

CiscoView allows you to view a device's chassis, configuration, and performance information. VlanDirector provides easy VLAN management with a GUI. For instance, the task of adding, deleting, and moving users to and from VLANs is done with a few mouse clicks. TrafficDirector allows you to monitor traffic (on network segments) leading to diagnosis of any abnormalities. It obtains traffic information from embedded RMON agents (of Catalyst switches) and standalone Cisco SwitchProbe products. With this information about different segments, TrafficDirector informs you of collision, error, utilization, and broadcast rates on a port (or port group) basis. You can also set up TrafficDirector to receive threshold-based traps from Catalyst switches. UserTracking provides the means for setting up dynamic VLANs and track location of stations.

CWSI can be integrated with other SNMP-based network management systems, such as SunNet Manager, HP OpenView, and IBM NetView. Protocols such as SNMP, CDP, VTP, and RMON form the foundation of the CWSI application suite. One of the valuable features of CWSI Campus is Network Map. This application provides a map of the physical devices and links in your network. You can then locate specific devices in the network and view how they are linked together. Network Map can also display the network virtual topology (virtual LAN configuration) in relation to the physical topology.

# Embedded RMON Agent and SwitchProbe

The Catalyst 5000 software includes an integrated RMON agent. The structure of the remote network monitoring MIB (Management Information Base), as outlined in RFC

1757, defines nine groups that objects are arranged into. Four of those groups that are supported by the Catalyst 5000 embedded RMON agent are: the (Ethernet) statistics group, the (Ethernet) history group, the alarms group, and the event group.

The (Ethernet) statistics group contains statistics measured for each monitored Ethernet interface (port) on the device (for example, a Catalyst switch). The (Ethernet) history group records periodic statistical samples from an Ethernet network and stores them for later retrieval. The alarm group periodically compares statistics (on monitored variables) to previously configured thresholds; if the monitored variable crosses a threshold, it generates an event. The event group controls the generation and notification of events from the device.

The Catalyst 5000 switches also offer a feature called SPAN (Switched Port Analyzer). SPAN allows mirroring traffic from one port into another port. Network managers can use this feature to capture the groups not supported by the embedded RMON agent. Furthermore, Cisco Systems offers SwitchProbes, which are standalone RMON probes for monitoring any segment (FDDI, CDDI, Token Ring, Ethernet, and Fast Ethernet). While the embedded RMON agent uses in-band network connection, the SwitchProbe can connect to an out-of-band network manager.

# Using Catalyst Switch LEDs

The LEDs on the power supply, supervisor module, and line cards are simple yet important indicators of the working condition of the corresponding component or module. The LEDs indicate whether a component such as a fan, power supply, module, or port is present, whether it is enabled or disabled, and whether it has passed the power-on test. You may also observe the Catalyst LEDs using CiscoView's GUI from a remote location.

On the very left side of the supervisor engine module there is a status LED reporting on the system power and processor status. The Fan, PS1 (power supply 1), and PS2 LEDs are arranged in a column, beside the status LED. The PS1 and PS2 LEDs go on when the power supply is present and is receiving AC source power and providing DC power to the internal system components. A rectangle composed of a series of LEDs in a row, with the title "Switch Load" beside it, provides a visual indication of the current traffic load (as an approximate percentage) over the backplane. The approximate load indicated by this LED can be a significant troubleshooting fact. For instance, if the Switch Load LED steadily reads at 80% or higher, you may have a broadcast storm in progress. Some supervisor modules have two sets of RJ45 and MII connectors and some have two fiber-optic connectors. In either case, every port has a 100 Mbps LED and a link LED.

The line card modules have a module status LED and one link LED for each port. The Ethernet switching modules also have one 100 Mbps LED for each port. The switch performs a series of self-tests and diagnostic tests, and if all the tests pass, the module status LED is green. During the system boot and during the self-test diagnostics, or if the module is disabled, the module status LED is orange. Finally, if a test other than an individual port test fails, the module status LED is red.

Proper insertion of the line card modules is very important—improper insertion is often the source of problems. When the switch is running, if you notice a red status LED on a line card module, check the position of the extractor levers to find out if the red LED status is indeed due to improper insertion of the line card module.

# Cable, Speed, and Media Concerns

The link LED on each individual port of the Catalyst 5000 switch is of great value to you. If this LED, which is often referred to as port integrity LED, is not green on both sides of a connection, you have a problem. If either side is not powered up, has the port disabled, or does not have the cable properly inserted, or if the cable is simply broken, substandard, badly bent or otherwise abused, the link integrity LED does not come on. Hence, checking to make sure that both sides of a link have the green link LED is a simple yet important fact gathering and troubleshooting task.

Speed mismatch on the two sides of a connection could also be a problem. Either both sides of a connection must have the Ethernet 100 Mbps LED on or both should be running at 10 Mbps, which means that the 100 Mbps LED must be off on both sides. It is important to know that Cisco Systems' documentation indicates that some devices do not handle speed autonegotiation correctly, so it is safer to hard-code the speed on both sides of a connection.

Network professionals often indicate that the vast majority of network problems are attributable to cable problems. Hence, as a support professional, you cannot underestimate the importance of being familiar with the distance limitations of different categories of cables and of purchasing and properly installing standards-compliant cables. For instance, it is important to know that Category 3 and Category 5 cables used in either half-duplex or full-duplex mode should not be longer than 100 meters. Multimode fiber (MMF) cables (10BaseFL and 100BaseFX) can be up to 2 kilometers, except for100BaseFX being used in half-duplex mode, which must be kept at or less than 400 meters long. Single-mode fiber (SMF) cables (100BaseFX) can be up to 10 kilometers long regardless of whether they are used in full-duplex or half-duplex mode. The fiber limitations just specified are device dependent; therefore, you may encounter a newer Catalyst module with a more powerful laser beam, which can reliably travel longer distances. Table 8-1 summarizes these distance limitations.

**Table 8-1**  *Cable Length Limitations (Based on Module Type)*

| Switch Module/Port Type Connected To | Half Duplex | Full Duplex |
|---|---|---|
| Copper Category 3 10BaseT | 100 meters | 100 meters |
| Copper Category 5 100BaseTX | 100 meters | 100 meters |

**Table 8-1**    *Cable Length Limitations (Based on Module Type) (Continued)*

| Switch Module/Port Type Connected To | Half Duplex | Full Duplex |
|---|---|---|
| Multimode fiber (MMF) 10BaseFL | 2 kilometers | 2 kilometers |
| Multimode fiber (MMF) 100BaseFX | 400 meters | 2 kilometers |
| Single-mode fiber (SMF) 100BaseFX | 10 kilometers | 10 kilometers |

When copper UTP (unshielded twisted-pair) cable is in use, you need to address the following concerns:

- Category 3 cable should only be used for 10BaseT (10 Mbps throughput). For 100BaseTX (100 Mbps throughput), you must use Category 5 cable.

- When connecting internetworking devices with copper UTP, in some cases you need a straight-through cable, and in other cases, you need crossover cables. For instance, you need a crossover cable to connect one switch's Ethernet port to another switch's Ethernet port. The same rule applies if you connect an Ethernet port from one router to an Ethernet port from another router. However, when connecting a router to a hub or a router to a switch, you must use a straight-through UTP cable.

- If a cable is suspicious or exhibits intermittent open circuit conditions, it is best to replace it with a cable that you know is good. If you have a TDR, cable tester, or scanner, you can test the cable under focus and check its impedance, and see if it is too long, has broken wires, is bent sharply, and so on.

- Finally, remember that if you have a cable plugged into an interface that has multiple connectors, you must ensure that the device is actually using the media type corresponding to the connector you have the cable connected to. Some devices auto-sense the media type and some don't; when in doubt specify the media type manually.

# Catalyst Power-on Self-Test

When you power-on a Catalyst 5000 switch, a self-diagnostics routine (often referred to as the power-on self-test or POST) is performed. This routine performs diagnostics tests on several components, such as ROM, RAM, DRAM, EARL, and BOOTROM. The result of the test performed on each component is displayed on the console (see Example 8-1). If you are not present at the console during the power-on self-test, you may use the output of the

**show test** and **show system** commands to see the status of the components tested by the power-on self-test.

**Example 8-1**  *Catalyst 5000 Power-on Self-Test Output*

```
ATE0
ATS0=1


Power Up Diagnostics

Init NVRAM Log
LED Test
ROM CHKSUM
DUAL PORT RAM r/w
RAM r/w
RAM address test
Byte/Word Enable test
EARL test
EARL test Done


BOOTROM Version 2.1, Dated Jun  4 1996 12:02:33
BOOT date: 06/08/00 BOOT time: 12:43:07
SIMM RAM address test
SIMM Ram r/w 55aa
SIMM Ram r/w aa55
Uncompressing NMP image.  This will take a minute...

Cisco Systems Console
```

# Catalyst 5000 Spanning Tree

You need to be aware of certain facts regarding the operation and behavior of Spanning Tree in Catalyst 5000 switches. The Catalyst 5000 series use IEEE 802.1D Spanning-Tree Protocol. There will be one Spanning Tree per VLAN on a switch. The Spanning Tree corresponding to a particular VLAN is usually enabled on every port that is assigned to that VLAN. However, certain ports that connect to work stations may be in Port-Fast mode or have the Spanning Tree disabled on them.

A port that is configured as a trunk port has as many Spanning Tree instances enabled on it as there are VLANs enabled on that particular trunk. Up to 1000 VLANs are allowed on a Catalyst 5000 switch, but only up to 250 of those can be active on the local switch. This means that if a switched internetwork contains up to 1000 VLANs, the Catalyst switches will not have any problem. However, the collection of all the ports of each switch may not be assigned to more than 250 of the internetwork's VLANs. A port that is enabled (and has Spanning Tree enabled on it), can be in one of Blocking, Listening, Learning, or Forwarding states at a particular instance. When a port is not in the Forwarding state, it does not let frames go through it. A port that is configured to be in one of (Cisco) Port-Fast or Uplink-Fast modes has no timing clock constraints and is moved to the Forwarding state more rapidly than a port that is left in normal mode (with regards to Spanning Tree). These faster modes are appropriate for those ports that handle the traffic from applications that cannot tolerate the normal time it takes for a port to transition from the Blocking state all the way to the Forwarding state. A normal (Spanning Tree) mode port can take up to 20 seconds to transition from Blocking to Listening, plus 15 seconds from Listening to Learning, plus another 15 seconds from Learning to Forwarding state.

A Catalyst 5000 switch has one Spanning-Tree bridge ID per VLAN. If a link layer loop exists in a network topology, it may affect multiple Spanning Trees. You may lower the numeric value of the bridge priority of a Catalyst switch in order to increase its chance of becoming the root. If you want to distribute the load on parallel VLAN InterSwitch Links, change the priority of each of the ports for the appropriate VLAN. The effect of this action is that traffic from some VLANs will travel over one trunk, while traffic from other VLANs will travel over the other trunk. This is clearly a better result than having all traffic travel through one trunk while the other trunk stays in blocking mode.

# Troubleshooting Catalyst 5000 Trunking: VTP and ISL

Interswitch trunk links carry traffic associated with different VLANs. There are two basic requirements for a switch to accept and forward a frame from or to a trunk port. The first requirement is that the switch must recognize the VLAN that the frame is associated with. For instance, if a switch receives a frame associated with VLAN 5, but VLAN 5 has not yet been created on the switch, the switch will not process that frame.

The second requirement is that both of the switches on a trunk (ISL link) must agree on the VLAN numbers that are allowed to traverse that trunk. For instance, if a switch has VLANs 1, 2, and 3 allowed on a trunk, but the other switch connected to this trunk has only VLANs 1 and 2 allowed, VLAN 3 will not be able to travel through this link. As you can imagine, without any automation for creating, deleting, and renaming VLANs and adding or deleting them to or from trunk ports, there can be a substantial amount of manual configuration needed on the part of the network administrator. This also means that there is a potential for misconfigurations, mismatches, loss of connectivity, and many other network problems.

VTP addresses the concerns that were just expressed. VTP is a Layer 2 multicast messaging protocol. This protocol allows switches that are put in a common administrative group, called a VTP domain, to communicate with each other, across the trunk links, regarding creation, deletion, and renaming of VLANs. All VLANs are by default allowed to travel through a trunk port; however, those that are deemed unneeded can be removed from a trunk manually (referred to as manual pruning) or by using an automated process called automated pruning. It is crucial, however, to know that VLAN 1,which is the management VLAN on Catalyst 5000 switches, cannot be pruned out of a trunk.

VTP provides an automated means for having a consistent VLAN configuration throughout a VTP domain. A VTP domain comprises a group of interconnected switches, all of which are configured with a common VTP domain name. Since VTP messages travel through trunk ports, each switch must be connected to the rest of the VTP domain members via at least one trunking link. A switch can be associated with only one VTP domain at a time. VTP uses a reserved VLAN (usually VLAN 1) for sending its advertisements, called *adverts* (according to Cisco documentation, the VLAN number depends on the media type used by the trunk). The VLAN number associated with VTP cannot be changed or deleted. For troubleshooting purposes, remember that VTP relies on the existence of trunks and VLAN 1 (the VLAN that carries VTP information).

Also, make a note that CWSI relies on VTP and that Vlan Director's operation requires at least one VTP server.

A switch can be in one of server, client, or transparent modes with respect to the role it takes within a VTP domain. By default, a switch is in server mode; this means that the administrator of this switch can create and delete VLANs on this switch using CLI (command-line interface), SNMP, or appropriate network management tools. A server generates, accepts (and implements), and forwards VTP adverts. Since a VTP server keeps a copy of VTP information in its NVRAM, it does not lose that information when it is reloaded. On a switch that is in VTP client mode, VLANs cannot be deleted and created. However, clients accept (and implement) VTP adverts received from other switches (that are members of the same VTP domain), and they also forward the information to other switches. Clients do not keep the VTP information in their NVRAM; hence, upon reload they must receive the VTP information from other switches.

You can probably guess why you will need at least one and preferably two VTP servers within a VTP domain. Switches that are members of a domain, but are in transparent mode, receive and forward VTP adverts but do not implement them. In other words, VLANs can be and must be created, deleted, and renamed manually—using CLI, for instance—on a switch in transparent mode. Hence, the consistency of a transparent mode switch's VTP information remains the responsibility of its administrator. If you create, delete, or rename VLANs on a transparent mode switch, the switch will not advertise that information to the other switches that are the members of its VTP domain. As mentioned earlier, though, if this switch (transparent mode) receives an advert, it will forward it, without implementing it.

The VTP information pertaining to a particular VTP domain name has a revision number associated with it. Every time a change (VTP eligible) is implemented in a VTP domain, the revision number is incremented. In a working, interconnected, and consistent VTP domain, the VTP revision number will be the same on all the (non-transparent mode) switches that are members of that VTP domain. Of course, when a change is implemented on a server, the revision number on the other switches will be one behind, due to the fact that the change has incremented the revision number on the server by one. If two switches that are members of the same VTP domain have different revision numbers, the one with the lower revision number (older version) will accept and copy the VTP information from the switch that has the higher VTP revision number (this does not apply to transparent mode switches). It is therefore crucial to know and make sure that VTP information is not changed (adding, deleting, and renaming VLANs) when servers are disconnected (for example, when one or more servers are off line). The reason for this claim is that upon reintroducing a switch (whose VTP-eligible configuration was changed off line), due to the resulting inconsistency between configuration revision number of this switch and others, either this switch's VTP information will be replaced by the VTP information of others, or this switch's VTP information will wipe out and replace the VTP information of the other switches.

The **set vtp** command sets up the VTP management domain, including establishing the management domain name, the VTP mode of operation (server, client, or transparent), the VLAN advertisement interval, and the password value. By default, there is no domain name (it is set to null), the advertisement interval is five minutes, VLAN trunk protocol mode of operation is set to server, and the management domain is set to nonsecure mode without a password. Adding a password sets the management domain to secure mode. A password must be configured on each switch in the management domain when in secure mode. It is essential to know that a management domain does not function properly if the management domain password is assigned to some devices, but it is not assigned to all of the switches in the domain.

Troubleshooting ISL is rather straightforward. When you want to configure a trunk connection between two switches, the port from each switch to be used for this purpose must have trunking enabled. Furthermore, those ports must be consistent (identical) with respect to their native VLAN, port duplexing, port speed, and fiber type (in case of optical links). Also, make sure that the switches are members of the same VTP domain and that they both allow the same set of VLANs to go across the trunk between them. The **show port**, **show trunk**, and **show vlan** commands are among the most useful **show** commands for troubleshooting trunks and ISL.

# Catalyst 5000 Switch Diagnostic Tools: ping and CDP

To make use of ping, the valuable IP connectivity testing tool, on a Catalyst switch, you must assign an IP address and subnet mask to the switch's system console 0 (SC0). Since SC0 is assigned to VLAN number 1 by default (this is modifiable), you have to make sure that the IP address you assign to SC0 is appropriate for VLAN 1. In other words, the IP address of SC0 must be chosen from the address space/IP subnet that corresponds to the VLAN number assigned to SC0. It is a common error to change the IP address of the SC0 for testing purposes, and then to forget to change SC0's VLAN number. Without static routes or a gateway of last resort, a switch with an appropriate IP address, mask, and VLAN number will be able to communicate only with IP nodes that are in the same VLAN as SC0's. Hence, to allow for reachability testing and Telnet to or from remote nodes (residing on other IP subnets or VLANs), you need to also configure static routes and/or a gateway of last resort on your Catalyst switch. If you do all that and still cannot ping a device (IP node), or an IP node cannot ping the switch, you need to check the following:

**Step 1** Ping a device that is connected to your switch and belongs to the same IP subnet and VLAN as your SC0. If the ping is successful, proceed to Step 2. You should always ensure that your switch's SC0 configuration is correct, using the **show interface** command.

If the ping is not successful:

— Make sure that the other device is configured properly (IP address, subnet mask, and so on) and that it is connected to the correct port on the switch.

— Check the link and speed LEDs on the port the IP device is plugged into. If the link LED is not green, the cable, the device, or one of the device components such as its network adapter card may be faulty. If you notice an orange LED, the port is disabled and must be enabled, but a red LED usually means that that particular port is bad.

— Check the status of the port using the **show port** command. Make sure that the port is enabled, assigned to the correct VLAN (same VLAN as your SC0), and configured with the correct speed, duplexing mode, and trunking (on/off).

**Step 2** Ping your router's local interface and remote interface. If you have problems doing either, perform the same tasks as outlined in Step 1 until you can ping your gateway's (router's) local and remote interfaces. Remember that your switch's gateway must be in the same IP subnet (and VLAN) as your switch's SC0. You should always double-check your switch's routing table using the **show IP route** command.

**Step 3** If you can ping an IP device on the remote network, but you cannot ping the device you are interested in, you must check that particular device's connection and IP configuration.

CDP (Cisco Discovery Protocol) is another useful protocol that can help you with your Catalyst switch troubleshooting. Catalyst switches, like other Cisco devices, have the CDP protocol enabled by default. You may see the list of a switch's CDP neighbors with the **show CDP neighbor [detail]** command (see Example 8-2). If you use the **detail** keyword, you will also see the IP address of your switch's neighbor, which can be used for ping, Telnet, and so on. CDP is, to say the least, great for checking that the cabling and hardware connectivity is indeed in place. Please remember that CDP is a Layer 2 protocol and has no dependency on any other protocol (all it needs is basic datalink layer connectivity). However, this also means that CDP might work fine while you get encapsulation errors.

Encapsulation errors could be due to interface hardware faults or the interface cards requiring reseating (the latter is a very common scenario). Obviously, if CDP is disabled for some reason, you must first enable it.

**Example 8-2**  *show cdp neighbor Command Output*

```
BBone_Switch (enable) show cdp neighbor

Capability Codes: R - Router, T - Trans Bridge,
                  B - Source Route Bridge, S - Switch,
                  H - Host, I - IGMP, r - Repeater


Port      Device-I    Port-ID       Platform        Capability


--------  ----------- ------------- --------------- ----------

  3/5     A_BackR     Ethernet1     cisco 4500          R
  3/6     B_BackR     Ethernet1     cisco 4500          R
  3/7     C_BackR     Ethernet1     cisco 4500          R
  3/8     D_BackR     Ethernet1     cisco 4500          R

BBone_Switch (enable)
```

# Catalyst 5000 Switch Diagnostic Tools: show Commands

You are expected to be familiar with the Catalyst switch's **set**, **clear**, and **show** commands. This section will focus on reviewing those commands (mostly **show** commands) that are essential for diagnostics and troubleshooting. First, though, it is important to emphasize the value of the online help utility of Catalyst switch's IOS. One of the great features of the Catalyst switch's IOS help utility is that if you seek help or make a mistake, it provides you with the full syntax of the command you are interested in, instead of just telling you what the next expected parameter is, or that you made a syntactical error. If you know and type part of the configuration command that you need, and type **help** or **?** after that, the help utility will still provide you with the syntax expected. The following commands are covered in this section:

- **set** and **clear**
- **show system**
- **show test**
- **show interface**
- **show log**
- **show mac**
- **show module**

- show port
- show config
- show span and show flash
- show trunk
- show spantree
- show vtp domain

## set and clear Commands

The keyword **set** is used with one or more commands and parameters to create, enable, disable, or modify a component, item, or variable within a switch's anatomy or configuration. For instance, the **set cdp enable 3/1** command enables CDP on module 3/ port 1 of a Catalyst switch. The **set interface sc0 10** command configures the system console interface of a Catalyst switch to be a member of VLAN number 10. The **set ip route** *destination* [*/netmask*] *gateway* command adds an entry to the switch's IP routing table.

The keyword **clear**, depending on the keyword(s) it is used with, allows you to clear a table, delete a previously created item, disable a configured behavior, and more. For example, the **clear cam** command clears the CAM (Content Addressable Memory) table entries. The **clear logging server** deletes a syslog server from the switch's configuration. The **clear vlan** *vlan-number* command deletes a VLAN from a management domain.

There are numerous **set** and **clear** commands within the Catalyst 5000 switch's command set, but discussing the syntax and usage of them is not within the scope of this book. Refer to "Table 1-6: Switch Command Set" in the Cisco Documentation CD-ROM (also available online at Cisco Connection Online, www.cisco.com) for a list and brief explanation of Catalyst 5000 commands.

## The show system Command

This command displays information about the Catalyst switch's system status and other information (see Example 8-3). Table 8-2 has the descriptions of the fields included in the output of this command.

**Example 8-3** *show system Command Output*

```
BBone_Switch (enable) show system

PS1-    PS2-    Fan-    Temp- Sys-   Uptime d,h:m:s Logout
Status  Status  Status  Alarm Status
------  ------  ------  ----- ------ -------------- -------
ok      none    ok      off   ok     2,20:33:06      500 min

PS1-Type  PS2-Type Modem      Baud Traffic Peak Peak-Time
```

**Example 8-3**   *show system Command Output (Continued)*

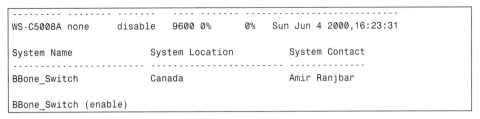

```
--------- -------- -------  ---- -------  ----------------------------
WS-C5008A none     disable  9600 0%       0%   Sun Jun 4 2000,16:23:31

System Name               System Location          System Contact
----------------------    ---------------------    --------------
BBone_Switch              Canada                   Amir Ranjbar

BBone_Switch (enable)
```

**Table 8-2**   *Descriptions for the **show system** Command's Fields*

| Field | Description |
| --- | --- |
| PS1-Status and PS2-Status | Status of power supply 1 and 2 (ok, fan failed, faulty, or none). |
| Fan-Status | Status of the fan (ok, faulty, or other). |
| Temp-Alarm | Status of the temperature alarm (off or on). |
| Sys-Status | System status (ok or faulty). Corresponds to system LED status. |
| Uptime d, h:m:s | Amount of time in days, hours, minutes, and seconds that the system has been up and running. |
| Logout | Amount of time after which an idle session will be disconnected. |
| PS1-Type | Part number of the power supply. |
| PS2-Type | Part number of the redundant power supply, if present. |
| Modem | Modem status (enable or disable). |
| Baud | Baud rate to which the modem is set. |
| Traffic | Current traffic percentage. |
| Peak | Peak percentage of traffic on the backplane. |
| Peak-Time | Time stamp when peak percentage was recorded. |
| System Name | System name. |
| System Location | System location. |
| System Contact | System contact information. |

# The show test Command

```
show test [mod_num]
```

The **show test** command may be entered with or without a module number specified. The purpose of this command is to display the results of the diagnostics tests. If you are interested in seeing only the results of the tests performed on a particular module, then use this command with the number of the module you are interested in. If no module number is specified, the information displayed will correspond to the general system and module 1 (see Example 8-4). Table 8-3 provides the descriptions for the fields displayed by this command.

**Example 8-4** *show test Command Output*

```
BBone_Switch (enable) show test
Environmental Status (. = Pass, F = Fail, U = Unknown)
  PS (3.3V):   .    PS (12V): .    PS (24V):   .    PS1: .    PS2: .
  Temperature: .    Fan:          .

Module 1 : 2-port 100BaseTX Supervisor
Network Management Processor (NMP) Status: (. = Pass, F = Fail,U = Unknown)
  ROM:   .    Flash-EEPROM: .    Ser-EEPROM: .    NVRAM: .    MCPComm: .

  EARL Status :
        NewLearnTest:           .
        IndexLearnTest:         .
        DontForwardTest:        .
        MonitorTest             .
        DontLearn:              .
        FlushPacket:            .
        ConditionalLearn:       .
        EarlLearnDiscard:       .
        EarlTrapTest:           .

Line Card Diag Status for Module 1   (. = Pass, F = Fail, N = N/A)
  CPU        : .    Sprom    : .    Bootcsum : .    Archsum  : N
  RAM        : .    LTL      : .    CBL      : .    DPRAM    : .    SAMBA : N
  Saints     : .    Pkt Bufs : .    Repeater : N    FLASH    : N
MII Status:
  Ports 1  2
  -----------
        N  N

SAINT/SAGE Status :
  Ports 1  2  3
  -------------
        .  .  .

Packet Buffer Status :
  Ports 1  2  3
  -------------
        .  .  .

Loopback Status [Reported by Module 1] :
  Ports  1  2  3
  -------------
         .  .  .

BBone_Switch (enable)
```

**Table 8-3**   *Descriptions for the **show test** Command's Fields*

| Field | Description |
| --- | --- |
| Environmental Status | Test results that apply to the general system environment. |
| PS (3.3V) | Test results for the 3.3V power supply. |
| PS (12V) | Test results for the 12V power supply. |
| PS (24V) | Test results for the 24V power supply. |
| PS1 | Test results for power supply 1. |
| PS2 | Test results for power supply 2. |
| Temperature | Test results for temperature. |
| Fan | Test results for the fan. |
| Module 1 | Test results that apply to module 1. The module type is indicated as well. |
| Network Management Processor (NMP) Status | Test results that apply to the NMP on the supervisor module. |
| ROM | Test results for ROM. |
| Flash-EEPROM | Test results for the Flash EEPROM. |
| Ser-EEPROM | Test results for serial EEPROM. |
| NVRAM | Test results for the NVRAM. |
| EARL Status | Fields that indicate the EARL status. |
| NewLearnTest | Test results for NewLearn test (EARL). |
| IndexLearnTest | Test results for IndexLearn test (EARL). |
| DontForwardTest | Test results for DontForward test (EARL). |
| MonitorTest | Test results for Monitor test (EARL). |
| DontLearn | Test results for DontLearn test (EARL). |
| FlushPacket | Test results for FlushPacket test (EARL). |
| ConditionalLearn | Test results for ConditionalLearn test (EARL). |
| EarlLearnDiscard | Test results for EarlLearnDiscard test (EARL). |
| EarlTrapTest | Test results for EarlTrap test (EARL). |
| LCP Diag Status for Module 1 | Test results for the specified module. |
| CPU | Test results for the CPU. |

*continues*

**Table 8-3**    *Descriptions for the **show test** Command's Fields (Continued)*

| Field | Description |
| --- | --- |
| Sprom | Test results for serial PROM. |
| Bootcsum | Test results for Boot ROM checksum. |
| Archsum | Test results for archive Flash checksum. |
| RAM | Test results for the RAM. |
| LTL | Test results for local target logic. |
| CBL | Test results for color blocking logic. |
| DPRAM | Test results for dual port RAM. |
| SAMBA | Test results for SAMBA chip. |
| Saints | Test results for SAINT chips. |
| Pkt Bufs | Test results for the packet buffers. |
| Repeater | Test results for repeater module. |
| FLASH | Test results for the Flash. |
| MII Status | Test results for MII ports. |
| SAINT/SAGE Status | Test results for individual SAINT/SAGE chip. |
| Packet Buffer Status | Test results for individual packet buffer. |
| Loopback Status | Test results for the loopback test. |

## The show interface Command

This command displays information on network interfaces (see Example 8-5). Use this command to verify SC0's IP address, mask, broadcast address, and VLAN number. The address of the SLIP interface and its destination can also be discovered on this command's output. Table 8-4 provides the descriptions for the fields displayed by this command.

**Example 8-5**    *show interface Command Output*

```
BBone_Switch (enable) show interface

sl0: flags=51<UP,POINTOPOINT,RUNNING>
        slip 0.0.0.0 dest 0.0.0.0

sc0: flags=63<UP,BROADCAST,RUNNING>
        vlan 100 inet 144.251.100.111 netmask 255.255.255.0 broadcast 144.251.100.255

BBone_Switch (enable)
```

**Table 8-4**    *Descriptions for the **show interface** Command's Fields*

| Field | Description |
|-------|-------------|
| sl0 | Information on the SLIP interface. |
| Flags | The interface state (Up, Down, Broadcast, Loopback, Pointopoint, or Running). |
| Slip | The IP address of the SLIP interface. |
| Dest | The IP address of the SLIP destination. |
| VLAN | The VLAN number of the SC0 interface, also known as the management VLAN. |
| sc0 | Information on the in-band interface. |
| Inet | The IP address of the interface. |
| Netmask | The network mask for the interface. |
| Broadcast | The broadcast address for the interface. |

# The show log Command

```
show log [mod_num]
```

This command displays the error log for the system or the specified module. A sample output of this command is displayed in Example 8-6. As you can see, the output is composed of an NMP (Network Management Processor) log section, an NVRAM log section, and a log section for each of the line card modules. The log section for the NMP includes information such as number of resets, history of bootups, exact time and date of last reset, and a set of failure counts. Furthermore, for each module, the number of resets and history of resets are displayed.

**Example 8-6**    *show log Command Output*

```
BBone_Switch (enable) show log
Network Management Processor (ACTIVE NMP) Log:
  Reset count:   192
  Re-boot History:    Jun 04 2000 16:21:06 3, May 14 2000  09:38:42 3
                      May 02 2000 07:25:32 3, May 01 2000  14:30:03 3
                      Apr 28 2000 08:41:54 3, Apr 27 2000  11:11:19 3
                      Apr 26 2000 11:27:43 3, Apr 25 2000  09:14:30 3
                      Apr 24 2000 11:35:14 3, Apr 13 2000  06:57:22 3
  Bootrom Checksum Failures:      0    UART Failures:            0
  Flash Checksum Failures:        0    Flash Program Failures:   0
  Power Supply 1 Failures:        0    Power Supply 2 Failures:  0
  DRAM Failures:                  0

  Exceptions:                     1
```

*continues*

**Example 8-6**  *show log Command Output (Continued)*

```
Last software reset by user: 3/14/0,09:37:00


 Switching bus Timeout NMI

switching bus Last Card Grant(Slot No) = 0
   Last Exception occurred on Apr 29 1999 15:46:27 ...
   Software version = 4.2(1)
   Error Msg:
   PID = 0 Kernel
   PC: 10148668, Status: 2700, Vector: 007C
   sp+00: 27001014 8668007C 113FFF28 10256C76
   ....
   A0: 10AE5952, A1: 103D289E, A2: 10256C4E, A3: 10429D6C
   A4: 10429D6C, A5: 64000000, A6: 113FFF14, sp: 113FFF0C

NVRAM log:


Module 3 Log:
  Reset Count:   190
  Reset History: Sun Jun 4 2000, 16:24:04
                 Sun May 14 2000, 09:41:40
                 Tue May 2 2000, 07:28:30
                 Mon May 1 2000, 14:33:01

BBone_Switch (enable)
```

## The show mac Command

In the output of this command you will find the total number of sent and received unicasts, multicasts, and broadcasts per port of all line card modules (see Example 8-7). The output also includes a table that reports on the following:

- Number of frame transmissions aborted due to MTU being too large or due to excessive deferral (Dely-Exced and MTU-Exced).

- Number of incoming frames that were discarded because the frame did not need to be switched and the number of CAM entries discarded due to page full in EARL (In-Discard and Lrn-Discard).

- Number of incoming and outgoing frames that were lost before being forwarded, due to insufficient buffer space (In-Lost, Out-Lost).

- FDDI and Token Ring data and the date and time of the last clear counters command.

**Example 8-7**  *show mac Command Output*

```
BBone_Switch (enable) show mac

Port     Rcv-Unicast Rcv-Multicast Rcv-Broadcast
-------- ----------- ------------- -------------
 1/1         0            0             0
```

**Example 8-7**  *show mac Command Output (Continued)*

```
1/2        0             0               0
3/1        0             0               0
3/2        0             0               0
3/3        0             0               0
3/4        0             0               0
3/5     72942         29973            8751
3/6     42049         30643            7266
3/7     43987         28918           21236
3/8     58961         30036            9167
3/9     40111           106           84885
3/10       0             0               0
3/11       0             0               0
3/12    14217         18010           36492

Port    Xmit-Unicast Xmit-Multicast Xmit-Broadcast
------- ------------- -------------- --------------
1/1        0             0               0
1/2        0             0               0
3/1        0             0               0
3/2        0             0               0
3/3        0             0               0
3/4        0             0               0
3/5     20075        236170          157301
3/6     14560        237152          159234
3/7     15661        239482          145732
3/8     18737        236120          156504
3/9     89645        264599           82393
3/10       0             0               0
3/11       0             0               0
3/12    14225        189782          100195

Port      Rcv-Octet  Xmit-Octet
------  ------------- -----------
1/1        0             0
1/2        0             0
3/1        0             0
3/2        0             0
3/3        0             0
3/4        0             0
3/5     26535049      54946415
3/6      7320573      45174151
3/7      8763974      43104831
3/8     11017163      43378097
3/9     36017478      53567461
3/10       0             0
3/11       0             0
3/12     6918078      29797639

MAC   Dely- MTU-  In-      Lrn-   In-  Out-
      Exced Exced Discard Discrd Lost Lost
```

*continues*

**Example 8-7** *show mac Command Output (Continued)*

```
----  -----  -----  -------  ------  ----  ----
1/1    0      0       0        0      0     0
1/2    0      0       0        0      0     0
3/1    0      0       0        0      0     0
3/2    0      0       0        0      0     0
3/3    0      0       0        0      0     0
3/4    0      0       0        0      0     0
3/5    0      0      186       0      0     0
3/6    0      0      341       0      0     0
3/7    0      0      140       0      0     0
3/8    0      0      403       0      0     0
3/9    0      0      100       0      0     0
3/10   0      0       0        0      0     0
3/11   0      0       0        0      0     0
3/12   0      0      48        0      0     0

Last-Time-Cleared
-------------------------
Sun Jun 4 2000, 16:23:31
```

# The show module Command

```
show module [mod_num]
```

This command displays the status and other information about the module specified. If no module is indicated, all the switch modules and their corresponding information will be displayed. Using this command, you can discover the range of MAC addresses associated with (reserved for) each line card module of a Catalyst switch. Example 8-8 shows a sample output of the **show module** command and Table 8-5 provides the descriptions for this command's output fields.

**Example 8-8** *show module Command Output*

```
BBone_Switch (enable) show module
Mod Modul-Name Ports Module-Type            Model       Serial-Num   Status
--- ---------- ----- ---------------------- ----------- ----------   ------
1               2    100BaseTX   Supervisor WS-X5009 004896020       ok
3               12   10/100BaseTX Ethernet  WS-X5203 007414676       ok

Mod MAC-Address(es)                        Hw  Fw      Sw
--- --------------- -------------------- --- ------  ------
1   00-e0-fe-80-b8-00 to 00-e0-fe-80-bb-ff 2.0 2.1    4.2(1)
3   00-e0-1e-e8-86-dc to 00-e0-1e-e8-86-e7 1.1 3.1(1) 4.2(1)

BBone_Switch (enable)
```

**Table 8-5**    *Descriptions for the **show module** Command's Fields*

| Field | Description |
| --- | --- |
| Mod | Module number. |
| Module-Name | Name, if configured, of the module. |
| Ports | Number of ports on the module. |
| Module-Type | Module type (such as 10BaseT Ethernet or Token Ring). |
| Model | Model number of the module. |
| Serial-Num | Serial number of the module. |
| Status | Status of the module. Possible status strings are: ok, disable, faulty, other, standby, and error. |
| MAC-Address(es) | MAC address or MAC address range for the module (Token Ring module MAC addresses appear in non-canonical format). |
| Hw | Hardware version of the module. |
| Fw | Firmware version of the module. |
| Sw | Software version of the module. |
| SMT User-Data | User data string defined for the FDDI module. |
| T-Notify | T-Notify timer value configured for the FDDI module. |
| CF-St | Configuration management state of the FDDI module. |
| ECM-St | Entity Coordination Management state of the FDDI module. |
| Bypass | Indicates whether an optical bypass switch is present. |

## The show port Command

```
show port [mod_num[/port_num]]
```

This command provides you with the most comprehensive port information, including status and counters for each of the line card modules' ports. If you do specify the port you are interested in receiving information about, then the output will be limited to that particular port. Otherwise, the output will include information about each and every port of your Catalyst switch. Refer to Example 8-9 for a sample output of the **show port** command. Table 8-6 provides the descriptions of **show port** commands output fields.

**Example 8-9**    *show port Command Output*

```
BBone_Switch (enable) show port
Port  Name             Status     Vlan        Level  Duplex Speed  Type
----- ---------------- ---------- ----------  ------ ------ ------ ----------------
 1/1                   notconnect 1           normal half   100    100BaseTX
 1/2                   notconnect 1           normal half   100    100BaseTX
```

*continues*

**Example 8-9**  *show port Command Output (Continued)*

```
3/1                    notconnect 1          normal  full   100   10/100BaseTX
3/2                    notconnect 1          normal  full   100   10/100BaseTX
3/3                    notconnect 1          normal  full   100   10/100BaseTX
3/4                    notconnect 1          normal  full   100   10/100BaseTX
3/5                    connected  100        normal  half   10    10/100BaseTX
3/6                    connected  100        normal  half   10    10/100BaseTX
3/7                    connected  100        normal  half   10    10/100BaseTX
3/8                    connected  100        normal  half   10    10/100BaseTX
3/9                    connected  100        normal  half   10    10/100BaseTX
3/10                   notconnect 100        normal  half   10    10/100BaseTX
3/11                   notconnect 100        normal  half   10    10/100BaseTX
3/12                   connected  100        normal  half   10    10/100BaseTX

Port  Security Secure-Src-Addr   Last-Src-Addr    Shutdown Trap    IfIndex
----- -------- ----------------  ---------------  -------------    -------
1/1   disabled                   No               disabled         3
1/2   disabled                   No               disabled         4
3/1   disabled                   No               disabled         17
3/2   disabled                   No               disabled         18
3/3   disabled                   No               disabled         19
3/4   disabled                   No               disabled         20
3/5   disabled                   No               disabled         21
3/6   disabled                   No               disabled         22
3/7   disabled                   No               disabled         23
3/8   disabled                   No               disabled         24
3/9   disabled                   No               disabled         25
3/10  disabled                   No               disabled         26
3/11  disabled                   No               disabled         27
3/12  disabled                   No               disabled         28

Port     Broadcast-Limit Broadcast-Drop
-------- --------------- --------------
1/1                 -             -
1/2                 -             -
...
3/12                -             0


Port  Align-Err  FCS-Err    Xmit-Err    Rcv-Err     UnderSize
----- ---------- ---------- ----------  ----------  ---------
1/1            0          0          0           0          0
1/2            0          0          0           0          0
...
3/12           0          0          0           0          0
Port  Single-Col Multi-Coll Late-Coll  Excess-Col Carri-Sen  Runts    Giants
----- ---------- ---------- ----------  ---------- ---------  -------  ------
1/1            0          0          0           0         0        0       0
1/2            0          0          0           0         0        0       0
3/1            0          0          0           0         0        0       0
3/2            0          0          0           0         0        0       0
3/3            0          0          0           0         0        0       0
3/4            0          0          0           0         0        0       0
```

**Example 8-9**  *show port Command Output (Continued)*

```
3/5       3          1         0         0         0         1         0
3/6       0          0         0         0         0         0         0
3/7       3          0         0         0         0         1         0
3/8       6          0         0         0         0         0         0
3/9       0          0         0         0         0         0         0
3/10      0          0         0         0         0         0         0
3/11      0          0         0         0         0         0         0
3/12      0          0         0         0         0         0         0

Last-Time-Cleared
- - - - - - - - - - - - - - - - - - - - - - - - -
Sun Jun 4 2000, 16:23:31
BBone_Switch (enable)
```

**Table 8-6**  *Descriptions for the **show port** Command's Fields*

| Field | Description |
|---|---|
| Port | Module and port number. |
| Name | Name (if configured) of the port. |
| Status | Status of the port (connected, notconnect, connecting, standby, faulty, inactive, shutdown, disabled, or monitor). |
| VLAN | VLANs to which the port belongs. |
| Level | Level setting for the port (normal or high). |
| Duplex | Duplex setting for the port (auto, full, fdx, half, hdx, a-half, a-hdx, a-full, a-fdx). |
| Speed | Speed setting for the port (auto, 10, 100, 155, a-10, a-100, 4, 16, a-4, a-1). |
| Type | Port type (10BaseT, 10BaseFL MM, 100BaseTX, 100BaseT4, 100BaseFX MM, 100BaseFX SM, 10/100BaseTX, TokenRing, FDDI, and so on). |
| Security | Port security status (enabled or disabled). |
| Secure-Src-Addr | The secure MAC address for the security enabled port. |
| Last-Src-Addr | The source MAC address of the last packet received by the port. |
| Shutdown | Indicates whether the port was shut down because of security. |
| Trap | Indicates whether port trap is enabled or disabled. |
| Broadcast-Limit | The broadcast threshold configured for the port. |
| Broadcast-Drop | Number of broadcast/multicast packets dropped because the broadcast limit for the port was exceeded. |

*continues*

**Table 8-6**   *Descriptions for the **show port** Command's Fields (Continued)*

| Field | Description |
| --- | --- |
| Align-Err | Number of frames with alignment errors (frames that do not end with an even number of octets and have a bad CRC) received on the port. |
| FCS-Err | Number of frame check sequence errors that occurred on the port. |
| Xmit-Err | Number of transmit errors that occurred on the port (indicating that the internal transmit buffer is full). |
| Rcv-Err | Number of receive errors that occurred on the port (indicating that the internal receive buffer is full). |
| UnderSize | Number of frames received that are less than 64 octets long (but are otherwise well-formed). |
| Single-Col | How many times one collision occurred before the port successfully transmitted a frame to the media. |
| Multi-Col | How many times multiple collisions occurred before the port successfully transmitted a frame to the media. |
| Late-Col | Number of late collisions (collisions outside the collision domain). |
| Excess-Col | Number of excessive collisions that occurred on the port (indicating that a frame encountered 16 collisions and was discarded). |
| Carrie-Sen | Number of times the port has sensed a carrier (to determine whether the cable is currently being used). |
| Runts | Number of runt frames (frames that are smaller than the minimum IEEE 802.3 frame size) received on the port. |
| Giants | Number of giant frames (frames that exceed the maximum IEEE 802.3 frame size) received on the port. |
| CE-State | Connection entity status. |
| Conn-State | Connection state, one of: Disabled (The port has no line module, or it has been disabled by the user), Connecting (The port is attempting to connect, or is disabled), Standby (The connection is withheld or is the inactive port of a dual homing concentrator), Active (The port has made a connection), or Other (The concentrator is unable to determine the Conn-State). |
| Type | Type of port: A-A port or B-B port. |
| Neig | Type of port attached to this port. The neighbor can be one of the following types: A-A port, B-B port, M-M port, S-Slave port, U-Unknown (The concentrator cannot determine the type of the neighbor port.) |

**Table 8-6**  *Descriptions for the **show port** Command's Fields (Continued)*

| Field | Description |
|---|---|
| Ler Con | Indicates whether the port is currently in a LER (Link Error Rate) condition. |
| Est | Estimated LER. |
| Alm | LER at which a link connection exceeds the LER alarm threshold. |
| Cut | LER cutoff value (the LER at which a link connection is flagged as faulty). |
| Lem-Ct | Number of LEM (Link Error Monitor) errors received on the port. |
| Lem-Rej-Ct | Number of times a connection was rejected because of excessive LEM errors. |
| Tl-Min | TL-min value (the minimum time to transmit a FDDI PHY line state before advancing to the next PCM state). |
| Last-Time-Cleared | Last time the port counters were cleared. |

## The show config Command

The **show config** command displays the current configuration of a Catalyst switch, including many of the default settings. The output includes information about passwords, system, SNMP, interfaces, static route(s), DNS, Tacacs+, VTP, Spanning Tree, modules, ports, and more (see Example 8-10 for a partial sample of the output of this command).

**Example 8-10** *show config Command Output*

```
BBone_Switch (enable) show config

begin
set password $1$FMFQ$HfZR5DUszVHIRhrz4h6V70
set enablepass $1$FMFQ$HfZR5DUszVHIRhrz4h6V70
set prompt BBone_Switch
set length 24 default
set logout 500
set banner motd ^CThe Current Configuration is a Demo Only!^C
!
#system
set system baud  9600
set system modem disable
set system name  BBone_Switch
set system location Canada
set system contact  Amir Ranjbar
!
#snmp
set snmp community read-only        public
set snmp community read-write       private
```

*continues*

**Example 8-10** *show config Command Output (Continued)*

```
set snmp community read-write-all secret
set snmp rmon disable
set snmp trap disable module
set snmp trap disable chassis
set snmp trap disable bridge
set snmp trap disable repeater
set snmp trap disable vtp
set snmp trap disable auth
set snmp trap disable ippermit
set snmp trap disable vmps
set snmp trap disable entity
set snmp trap disable config
set snmp trap disable stpx
!
#ip
set interface sc0 100 144.251.100.111 255.255.255.0 144.251.100.255

set interface sc0 up
set interface sl0 0.0.0.0 0.0.0.0
set interface sl0 up
set arp agingtime 1200
set ip redirect    enable
set ip unreachable    enable
set ip fragmentation enable
set ip route 131.1.0.0       144.251.100.10  1
set ip route 151.50.0.0      144.251.100.20  1
set ip route 181.8.0.0       144.251.100.30  1
set ip route 141.1.0.0       144.251.100.40  1
set ip route 181.8.0.0       144.251.100.202 1
set ip route 141.1.0.0       144.251.100.203 1
set ip route 131.1.0.0       144.251.100.200 1
set ip route 151.50.0.0      144.251.100.201 1
set ip alias default         0.0.0.0
!
#Command alias
!
#vmps
set vmps server retry 3
set vmps server reconfirminterval 60
set vmps tftpserver 0.0.0.0 vmps-config-database.1
set vmps state disable

!
#dns
set ip dns server 144.251.100.90 primary
set ip dns enable
set ip dns domain geotrain.com
!
...
```

## The show span and show flash Commands

The **show span** command displays information about the current setting of the switched port analyzer function. You can find out if SPAN is enabled and, if it is, which port is the source, which port is the destination, and whether receive, transmit, or both receive and transmit traffic are being mirrored from the source port to the destination port. The **show flash** command displays the name, version, and size of the (code) files residing in the Catalyst switch's flash. Example 8-11 displays sample output of the **show span** command and Example 8-12 displays sample output of the **show flash** command.

**Example 8-11** *show span Command Output*

```
BBone_Switch (enable) show span
Status          : disabled
Admin Source    : Port 3/12
Oper Source     : None
Destination     : Port 3/11
Direction       : transmit/receive
Incoming Packets: disabled

BBone_Switch (enable)
```

**Example 8-12** *show flash Command Output*

```
BBone_Switch (enable) show flash
File            Version   Sector    Size      Built
--------------- --------- --------  -------   -----------------
c5000 nmp       4.2(1)    02-11     1879599 09/08/98 17:05:11
      lcp xa2   4.2(1)    12-15       53618 09/08/98 10:05:03
      lcp xa1   4.2(1)    12-15       68440 09/08/98 10:04:55
      lcp atm   4.2(1)    12-15       25257 09/08/98 05:14:03
      mcp 360   4.2(1)    12-15      219988 09/08/98 10:05:10
      lcp tr    4.2(1)    12-15       31069 09/08/98 05:05:15
      lcp c5ip  4.2(1)    12-15       24580 09/08/98 05:07:17
      lcp 64k   4.2(1)    12-15       53859 09/08/98 05:07:15
      atm/fddi  4.2(1)    12-15       25196 09/08/98 05:04:20
      lcp 360   4.2(1)    12-15      129160 09/08/98 10:04:46
      lcp       4.2(1)    12-15       25885 09/08/98 05:04:17
      smcp      4.2(1)    12-15       36864 09/08/98 05:02:06
      mcp       4.2(1)    12-15       24848 09/08/98 05:03:14

BBone_Switch (enable)
```

## The show trunk Command

```
show trunk [mod_num[/port_num]]
```

As its title implies, this command displays trunking information. You may choose to see the trunking information about a particular module/port by typing the module/port number, or you may simply type **show trunk** and receive information about all the ports that are configured for trunking. In the first section of the output, the trunking mode (on, off, auto, or desirable) and the trunking status (trunking or nontrunking) of each port are displayed. The second and third sections display the VLANs allowed for each port, and the VLANs allowed and active on each port, correspondingly. The last section of the **show trunk** command's output displays the range of VLANs that actually go on the trunk with Spanning-Tree Protocol forwarding state (see Example 8-13 for a sample output of the **show trunk** command).

**Example 8-13** *show trunk Command Output*

```
BBone_Switch (enable) show trunk
Port      Mode    Encapsulation  Status    Native vlan
--------  ------  -------------  --------  -----------
  3/1     on      isl            trunking      1
  3/2     on      isl            trunking      1
  3/3     on      isl            trunking      1
  3/4     on      isl            trunking      1


Port      Vlans allowed on trunk
--------  -----------------------------------------------
  3/1     1-1005
  3/2     1-1005
  3/3     1-1005
  3/4     1-1005


Port      Vlans allowed and active in management domain
--------  -----------------------------------------------
  3/1     1-7,100
  3/2     1-7,100
  3/3     1-7,100
  3/4     1-7,100


Port      Vlans in spanning tree forwarding state and not pruned
--------  -----------------------------------------------------
  3/1     1,3-7,100
  3/2     1-7,100
  3/3     1-7,100
  3/4     1,3-7,100
BBone_Switch (enable)
```

## The show spantree Command

```
show spantree [vlan]
```

This command displays detailed Spanning Tree information for the VLAN specified. The other parameters that can be used to further qualify the output, as well as a sample output of this command, are shown in Example 8-14. Table 8-7 is provided as a reference for interpreting the displayed fields.

**Example 8-14** *show spantree Command Output*

```
BBone_Switch (enable) show spantree ?

Usage: show spantree [vlan] [active]
```

**Example 8-14** *show spantree* Command Output (Continued)

```
        show spantree <mod_num/port_num>
        show spantree backbonefast
        show spantree blockedports [vlan]
        show spantree portstate <trcrf>
        show spantree portvlancost <mod_num/port_num>
        show spantree statistics <mod_num/port_num> [vlan]
        show spantree statistics <trcrf> <trbrf>
        show spantree summary
        show spantree uplinkfast

BBone_Switch (enable) show spantree 100
VLAN 100
Spanning tree enabled
Spanning tree type            ieee

Designated Root               00-e0-fe-80-b8-63
Designated Root Priority      32768
Designated Root Cost          0
Designated Root Port          1/0
Root Max Age   20 sec    Hello Time 2  sec   Forward Delay 15 sec

Bridge ID MAC ADDR            00-e0-fe-80-b8-63
Bridge ID Priority            32768
Bridge Max Age 20 sec    Hello Time 2  sec   Forward Delay 15 sec

Port   Vlan  Port-State      Cost   Priority  Fast-Start  Group-Method
------ ----  -------------   -----  --------  ----------  -----------
 3/5   100   forwarding       10       32     disabled
 3/6   100   forwarding       10       32     disabled
 3/7   100   forwarding       10       32     disabled
 3/8   100   forwarding       10       32     disabled
 3/9   100   forwarding       10       32     disabled
 3/10  100   not-connected    10       32     disabled
 3/11  100   not-connected    10       32     disabled
 3/12  100   forwarding       10       32     disabled

BBone_Switch (enable)
```

**Table 8-7**   *Descriptions for the* **show spantree** *[vlan] Command's Fields*

| Field | Description |
| --- | --- |
| VLAN | VLAN for which Spanning Tree information is being shown. |
| Spanning Tree | Spanning Tree status: enabled or disabled. |
| Designated Root | MAC address of the root bridge. |
| Designated Root Priority | Priority of the root bridge. |
| Designated Root Cost | Total (path) cost to reach the root. |

*continues*

**Table 8-7** *Descriptions for the **show spantree** [vlan] Command's Fields (Continued)*

| Field | Description |
|---|---|
| Designated Root Port | The port chosen for reaching the root. |
| Root MAX Age | How long a BPDU1 packet is considered valid. |
| Hello Time | How often the root bridge sends BPDUs (Sec). |
| Forward Delay | The amount of time the root bridge spends in listening or learning mode. |
| Bridge ID MAC ADDR | (Local) bridge's MAC address. |
| Bridge ID Priority | (Local) bridge's priority. |
| Bridge Max Age | (Local) bridge's maximum age. |
| Hello Time | How often the (local) bridge sends BPDUs. |
| Forward Delay | The amount of time the (local) bridge spends in listening or learning mode. |
| Port | Port number. |
| VLAN | The VLAN that the port belongs to. |
| Port-State | One of: disabled, inactive, not-connected, blocking, listening, learning, forwarding, or bridging. |
| Cost | Cost associated with the port. |
| Priority | Priority associated with the port. |
| Fast-Start | Whether the port is configured to use the Spanning-Tree Fast-Start feature. |

## The show vtp domain Command

Use this command to display VTP information (see Example 8-15) such as:

- VTP domain name

- Mode of the switch (server, client, or transparent)

- Number of VLANs currently in the VTP domain

- Configuration revision number

- The device (IP address) that submitted the last VTP update

**Example 8-15** *show vtp domain Command Output*

```
BBone_Switch (enable) show vtp domain

Domain Name  Domain Index VTP Version Local Mode  Password
------------ ------------ ------------ --------------------
```

**Example 8-15** *show vtp domain* Command Output (Continued)

```
CITCOURSE          1        2              server        .

Vlan-count Max-vlan-storage Config Revision Notifications
---------- ---------------- --------------- -------------
11              1023                82         disabled

Last Updater   V2 Mode  Pruning  PruneEligible on Vlans
-------------- -------- -------- ----------------------
181.8.128.140  disabled disabled  2-1000

BBone_Switch (enable)
```

# Catalyst Symptoms, Problems, and Suggested Actions

This section presents three common Catalyst switch–related troubleshooting symptoms, the possible causes of the problems, and the suggested actions for each case.

## Case 1: Users Report that the Connection to Their Designated Local Switch is Not Working

In this case, users report that the connection between their devices (workstations) and their designated local switch is not working. It is very possible that the switch has lost power, perhaps due to failure of its power supply or a blown fuse. If the fuse is blown, refer to the user guide for your LAN switch for information on replacing the fuse. If the power supply is working (the LED is green), you must check the system LED (on the supervisor), the appropriate module status LED, and, finally, the appropriate port link and speed LED. If the system LED is red, you must find out (for instance, from logs) what major component has failed and think about replacing the supervisor module or perhaps even the switch.

If the system LED is green (OK) and the module LED is not on, there is a possibility that the module needs to be reseated. If the module status LED is/becomes green but the port link LED is not green, you may have a cable problem or the workstation might be faulty, and hence both items need to be examined. The cable may be broken, inappropriate (for example, crossover instead of straight, or Category 3 instead of Category 5), or simply not plugged in. It is best to use a cable known to be good to test the validity of cable suspicion. Finally, remember that if the port LED is orange, it means that either the port is disabled and you need to enable it or the port is in a non-existent VLAN. The latter case could happen if the VLAN existed but was removed by a VTP server somewhere in the network while the port is still in that VLAN.

## Case 2: Trouble Regarding Communication of the Terminal or Modem with the Switch

This problem is most likely due to baud rate or character format mismatch between the switch and the connecting device. It is also possible that an incorrect cable has been used. For modem connections, straight-through cable must be used, and for terminal connections, null-modem cable must be used.

## Case 3: Switch Cannot Be Accessed from Remote Devices

This case is usually due to one or some of the following problems:

- Invalid or unassigned IP address on the SC0.

- Invalid subnet mask on the SC0, no default gateway, inappropriate static route(s).

- Invalid VLAN number assigned to the SC0.

The IP address on the switch's SC0 must be a unique IP address from a valid IP subnet. Use the **show interface** command to verify SC0's IP address, mask, and VLAN number. Correct these parameters using the **set interface sc0** command. Also, check the switch's routing table with the **show ip route** command, and correct or delete any entries with the **set ip route** or **clear ip route** commands.

# Foundation Summary

The Foundation Summary is a collection of quick reference information that provides a convenient review of many key concepts in this chapter. For those of you who already feel comfortable with the topics in this chapter, this summary helps you recall a few details. For those of you who just read this chapter, this review should help solidify some key facts. For any of you doing your final prep before the exam, these tables and figures are a convenient way to review the day before the exam.

**Table 8-8**    *Catalyst 5000 **show** Commands Summary*

| Command | Description |
| --- | --- |
| **show system** | Displays system, power supply, fan, general traffic, and information. |
| **show test** [*mod_num*] | Displays the results of diagnostic tests. |
| **show interface** | Displays information on network interfaces (SC and SLIP). |
| **show log** [*mod_num*] | Displays the error log for the system or a specific module. |
| **show mac** | Displays various MAC counters (stats). |
| **show module** [*mod_num*] | Displays module status and information (including the modules' ports). |
| **show port** [*mod_num*[/*port_num*]] | Displays port status, settings (speed and duplexing), VLAN, and counters. |
| **show config** | Displays the current system configuration. |
| **show span** | Displays SPAN information. |
| **show flash** | Lists Flash information, including file code names, version numbers, and sizes. |
| **show trunk** [*mod_num*[/*port_num*]] | For each displayed port, the port trunking mode, status, VLANs allowed, and VLANs active are shown. |
| **show spantree** [*vlan*] | Displays Spanning Tree information for a VLAN. |
| **show vtp domain** | Displays VTP information (VTP domain name, switch's role, last updater, configuration revision number, and number of VLANs). |

## Q&A

The answers to the following questions can be found in Appendix A. Some of the questions in this section are repeated from the "Do I Know This Already" Quiz so that you can gauge the advancement of your knowledge of this subject matter.

1  Name the applications that are included in the CWSI Campus package.

_____

_____

_____

2  Describe the functions of TrafficDirector.

_____

_____

_____

3  What is the VlanDirector application component of CWSI used for?

_____

_____

_____

4  What does CiscoView allow you to do?

_____

_____

_____

5  Name at least two of the protocols that form the foundation of the CWSI application suite.

_____

_____

_____

6  What does the Network Map feature of CWSI provide you with?

_____

_____

_____

**7** True or false: You need to purchase and install RMON as an added feature to Catalyst 5000 IOS.

_____

**8** The structure of the remote network monitoring MIB as outlined in RFC 1757 defines nine groups that objects are arranged into. Which four of those groups are supported by the Catalyst 5000 embedded RMON agent?

_____

_____

_____

**9** What is SPAN?

_____

_____

_____

**10** Briefly describe Cisco Systems' SwitchProbe product.

_____

_____

_____

**11** Provide a general description for the Catalyst 5000 switches' LEDs.

_____

_____

_____

**12** List and describe the supervisor engine module's LEDs.

_____

_____

_____

**13** Provide a brief description for the Catalyst 5000 switch line card module status LED.

_____

_____

_____

**14** How would you interpret the fact that the port link integrity LED on a line card module is not green?

_____

_____

_____

**15** What is the most common source of network problems?

_____

_____

_____

**16** What is the distance (length) limitation for the Category 3 and Category 5 cables?

_____

_____

_____

**17** What is the distance (length) limitation for the fiber-optic cables?

_____

_____

_____

**18** If you find a particular cable segment suspicious, what courses of action can you take?

_____

_____

_____

**19** Briefly describe Catalyst 5000 switch's power-on self-test.

_____

_____

_____

**20** Which Spanning-Tree Protocol is used by the Catalyst 5000 switch?

_____

_____

_____

**21** How many Spanning Trees are associated with one VLAN?

_____

_____

_____

**22** How many Spanning Tree instances are enabled on a port that is in trunking mode?

_____

_____

_____

**23** What is the maximum number of VLANs that a Catalyst 5000 switch can handle?

_____

_____

_____

**24** At a particular instance, what states can an enabled port be in?

_____

_____

_____

**25** What are the normal/estimated times that a port spends in one state before moving to another state?

_____

_____

_____

**26** How can you influence the chance of a Catalyst switch to become the root of a Spanning Tree?

_____

_____

_____

**27** What are the two basic requirements for a switch to accept and forward a frame from or to a trunk port?

_____

_____

_____

**28** Provide a brief description for VTP.

_____

_____

_____

**29** What is the purpose of VTP and how many VTP domains can a Catalyst switch be associated with?

_____

_____

_____

**30** What are the possible modes for a switch in a VTP domain?

_____

_____

_____

**31** What is the default VTP mode of a Catalyst 5000 switch?

_____

_____

_____

**32** What is the VTP configuration revision number?

_____

_____

_____

**33**  What are some of the basic settings required for an ISL trunk connection between two Catalyst 5000 switches to work?

_____

_____

_____

**34**  What configuration is required to make a switch an IP node?

_____

_____

_____

**35**  To which VLAN does the Catalyst 5000 switch's system console 0 interface belong? Can the VLAN number of SC0 be changed?

_____

_____

_____

**36**  Which Catalyst 5000 IOS command displays SC0's IP address, mask, and VLAN number?

_____

_____

_____

**37**  Which Catalyst 5000 IOS command displays its configured IP routes?

_____

_____

_____

**38**  Provide at least three significant pieces of information displayed by the Catalyst 5000 **show system** command.

_____

_____

_____

**39** Describe the purpose and methods of using the **show test** command.

_____

_____

_____

**40** Which command displays the error log for the system or for a specified module?

_____

_____

_____

**41** Which command displays a complete report of MAC-related statistics?

_____

_____

_____

**42** Describe the output of the **show module** [_mod_num_] command.

_____

_____

_____

**43** Which command displays the status, speed, VLAN, and duplexing mode of a switch's port?

_____

_____

_____

**44** Which command displays the current configuration of a Catalyst switch, including many of the default settings?

_____

_____

_____

**45** Which command displays information about the current setting of the switched port analyzer function?

_____

_____

_____

**46** What does the **show flash** command display?

_____

_____

_____

**47** Describe the information that may be gathered through usage of the **show trunk** [*mod_num*[/*port_num*]] command.

_____

_____

_____

**48** Which command can you use to see detailed Spanning Tree information about a VLAN?

_____

_____

_____

**49** List at least three important pieces of information that can be gathered by executing the **show vtp domain** command.

_____

_____

_____

**50** On a Catalyst 5000 switch, if you disable a port, what will be the LED status of that particular port?

_____

_____

_____

This chapter covers the following topics that you will need to master to pass the CCNP Support exam:

| Objective | Description |
| --- | --- |
| 1 | Troubleshooting Cisco IOS configuration. |
| 2 | VLAN design issues for troubleshooting. |
| 3 | Switch/router configuration consistency. |
| 4 | Router VLAN diagnostic tools: **show** commands. |
| 5 | Router VLAN diagnostic tools: **debug** commands. |
| 6 | Problem isolation in router/switch VLAN networks. |

# CHAPTER 9

# Troubleshooting VLANS on Routers and Switches

This chapter's focus is on routers used in switched internetworks to provide communication between VLANs and access to remote sites across wide area networks. In this context, routers not only facilitate integration of switching products, but they also make VLAN-based architectures scalable and flexible. This chapter discusses how VLANs must be implemented on Cisco routers, what the key configuration issues are, and which commands can help diagnose related errors and faults.

A router may play different roles in a switched internetwork. A router may be connected to a switch through a trunk connection, in which case the router interface that is on the trunk connection will have one subinterface for each VLAN that goes through the trunk. The router is typically used to route packets between the VLANs and the other networks (including wide-area connections) to which it connects. This setup is usually referred to as the router on a stick (see Figure 9-1). The term "router on a stick" is used for a scenario in which an external router is connected to a LAN switch via trunk connection(s) and performs routing between the VLANs that belong to the trunk connection(s). On the other hand, a Router Switch Module (RSM), sometimes referred to as a "router on a blade," is also commonly used in Catalyst switches for the purpose of routing between VLANs.

In certain scenarios the router may be configured to perform bridging between certain ports, including the subinterfaces of the interface that is configured for trunking. This function is called VLAN switching. Naturally the router's Spanning-Tree Protocol must then match and communicate with the Spanning-Tree Protocols of the other devices (switches and bridges) on the network. Finally, if a router has multiple trunk connections via different media (ISL over Fast Ethernet, 802.1Q over Fast Ethernet, 802.10 over FDDI, LANE over ATM) it can also provide transparent connectivity between them. This function, called VLAN translation, was introduced as of Cisco IOS Release 11.1 and it is fast switched. In summary, a router may perform VLAN routing, VLAN switching, and VLAN translation in a network.

**Figure 9-1** *Router on a Stick*

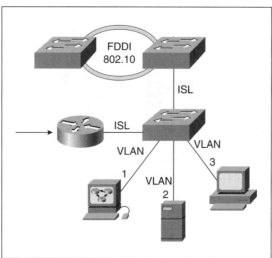

# "Do I Know This Already?" Quiz

If you wish to evaluate your knowledge of the contents of this chapter before you get started, answer the following questions. The answers are provided in Appendix A, "Answers to Quiz Questions." If you are having difficulty providing correct answers, you should thoroughly review the entire chapter. If all or most of your answers are correct, you might want to skim this chapter for only those subjects you need to review. You can also use the "Foundation Summary" section to quickly review topics. Once you have completed the chapter, you should reevaluate yourself with the questions in the "Q&A" section at the end. Finally, use the companion CD-ROM to evaluate your knowledge of the topics and see if you need a review.

  1  Name three of the functions routers perform in a VLAN switching environment.

  _____

  _____

  _____

**2**   Which type of router interface is used for ISL trunking?

_____

_____

_____

**3**   How many VLANs can a subinterface of an interface used for trunking correspond to?

_____

_____

_____

**4**   Which command functions are configured on the main interface of the (Fast Ethernet) interface for the purpose of trunking?

_____

_____

_____

**5**   What is the general recommendation for the bridged networks in terms of the number of hops?

_____

_____

_____

**6**   How many default VLANs are preconfigured on a Catalyst 5000 switch?

_____

_____

_____

**7**   What is the recommended usage of VLAN number 1?

_____

_____

_____

**8**   What role can a Cisco router play in a VTP domain?

_____

_____

_____

9 What information can one obtain from the output of the **show vlans** command?

_____

_____

_____

# Foundation Topics

# Troubleshooting Cisco IOS Configuration

The Fast Ethernet interface of a router is used to connect a router to a switch for trunking purpose. Example 9-1 shows a sample configuration for the Fast Ethernet interface of a router for this case.

**Example 9-1**  *Sample Configuration of Fast Ethernet Interface for Trunking*

```
interface FastEthernet0
 no ip address
 full-duplex
!
interface FastEthernet0.1
 encapsulation isl 1
 ip address 10.1.1.44 255.255.0.0
 ipx network 36dd
!
interface FastEthernet0.2
 encapsulation isl 2
 ip address 10.2.1.40 255.255.0.0
 bridge-group 60
!
interface FastEthernet0.3
 encapsulation isl 3
 ip address 10.3.1.40 255.255.0.0
  bridge-group 60
!
interface FastEthernet0.100
 encapsulation isl 100
 ip address 144.251.100.40 255.255.255.0
!
```

If a Fast Ethernet interface is used for trunking purposes, it should not have any Layer 3 (OSI network layer) address or any bridging commands configured on the main interface. These types of commands must be appropriately entered on the subinterfaces. Each subinterface will correspond to one VLAN member of the trunk.

The main interface configuration commands that may be necessary on the Fast Ethernet interface are **media-type** and **full-duplex**. Those router interfaces that have multiple connectors for different types of connections (such as MII and100BaseTx) consider one of the media as the default media. If you connect your cable to the default connector (for example, MII), then you do not need to enter the media-type command. However, if the 100BaseTx connection is used, then you have to enter  the **media-type 100basetx** command on the main (Fast Ethernet) interface. Because a trunk connection is point-to-point, it is possible and very advantageous to configure the trunk connection with the full-duplex command (also done on the main interface).

If you forget to configure, or misconfigure, the media type on an interface, the symptom will be easy to spot. If the interface is not administratively shut down, then the physical layer will show as UP, but the link layer will show as DOWN, since the router's keepalive will fail. If an interface is configured with the **no keepalive** command, both the physical and link layers will show as UP, even though the cable is connected to the wrong connector! This makes troubleshooting more difficult. Fortunately, there are three methods to discover that. You may enter the **show controller fastethernet** *interface-number* command and find out the media type from its output. Some interfaces (for instance, the FASTETHERNET cards of the Cisco 4500 routers) have a LED that tells you the media type the router is configured for. You may also look at the running-config of a router to find out the media type configured on an interface. Keep in mind that the default media type is not shown on the running-config and startup-config.

The duplexing configuration of a trunk port can be tricky. Catalyst switches are supposed to autosense the duplexing (full versus half) and Cisco routers have a default setting. If you are troubleshooting a trunk connection between a router and a switch, it is best if you decide on the duplexing mode and do a manual configuration on both devices. Relying on the auto-sensing feature is usually discouraged.

As mentioned earlier, each subinterface of a Fast Ethernet interface used for trunking corresponds to one VLAN. On each subinterface you need to enter the **encapsulation isl** *vlan-number* command. A subinterface may have a Layer 3 (OSI network layer) address such as an IP address, and it may have a **bridge-group** *bridge-group-number*.

The interface shown in Example 9-1 has four subinterfaces, each with an IP address (for each interface you may configure up to 255 subinterfaces). The subinterfaces correspond to VLANs 1, 2, 3, and 100, and each VLAN matches one IP subnet. Note that the fa0.2 and fa0.3 subinterfaces are configured to bridge any packet other than IP. When the router receives an ISL frame on its Fast Ethernet interface, it first recognizes the VLAN number of the frame from the ISL header. It then de-encapsulates the original frame from the ISL frame and processes it based on the assumption that the original frame was received from the subinterface that corresponds to the VLAN ID of the ISL frame.

You must now realize why it is important to have one subinterface for each VLAN that belongs to the trunk. After the router selects the subinterface the frame corresponds to, it will then route, bridge, or drop the received packet. For example, assume that the router (using Example 9-1 as the guide) receives an ISL frame with VLAN ID of 100 encapsulating an Ethernet frame, which in turn encapsulates an IPX packet. The router processes the de-encapsulated Ethernet frame as if it has arrived from a real Ethernet interface. However, because the Fast Ethernet 0.100 interface shown in Example 9-1 does not have an IPX address and is not configured to bridge IPX either, the frame will be dropped.

There are some important facts you need to remember about the limitations of VLAN processing and trunking on a router. For example, the ISL encapsulation is available only on the Fast Ethernet interfaces of certain routers (4500 and 7000 series Cisco routers). IP and IPX routing between VLANs is only allowed by specific IOS releases (and the IPX frame-type must be Novell-Ethernet). Some IOS releases, in addition to transparent bridging, support integrated routing and bridging (IRB) between the VLANs, for IPX (with SAP and SNAP frame types) and AppleTalk.

# VLAN Design Issues for Troubleshooting

One important topic of interest in switched internetworks is the convergence time of the spanning tree. Two factors, the diameter of a network measured in terms of the number of hops (bridges/switches), and the values of the spanning tree timers, affect the time it takes for the bridged/switched internetwork to converge. The general rule for the bridged networks is that the number of hops (bridges/switches) should not exceed seven.

When a port that is in the Forwarding state fails, the other ports (of the other devices) on that segment wait for a period equal to three times the HELLO period before they consider that port gone (dead). Because the spanning tree may have to be reexecuted, the change notification BPDU must first be sent to ALL of the switches. This notification might have to traverse through all of the network segments hop by hop via BPDUs that are released as often as the HELLO period (the default HELLO period is 2 seconds).

Hence, from the instant that a port fails to the moment that all switches are notified of the change can take up to 20 seconds (assuming the maximum of 7 hops). The default value of the MAX_AGE parameter of the spanning tree is set to 20 (seconds) for this reason. Next, the spanning tree is executed for a period equal to the fwddelay parameter, which is equal to 15 seconds by default. During this period the ports are in the Listening state and are NOT forwarding received frames.

After completion of the spanning tree, each port spends a period equal to the fwddelay parameter in the Learning mode during which it builds the initial MAC table and does not forward received frames. Hence, the convergence of a switched internetwork (seven hops assumed) can take up to 50 seconds (20 + 15 + 15). The values of the HELLO, MAX_AGE, and Forward Delay (fwddelay) parameters are imposed on all other switches by the root device. In other words, changing any of these parameters on any device other than the root device is not practical, as the non-root device will revert to the values imposed by the root device. Changing these parameters on the root device, on the other hand, practically means changing the parameters on all of the devices.

# Switch/Router Configuration Consistency

There are five default VLANs preconfigured on a Catalyst 5000 switch for different media types. Table 9-1 shows these VLANs along with their associated MTU, ISL VLAN ID, and 802.10 Security Association Identifier (SAID). Numbers 1 though 1000 may be used for the VLANs created on a Catalyst 5000 family switch. You are encouraged to leave VLAN number 1 for management and troubleshooting and use VLANs 2 through 1000 for user (traffic) VLANs. When you connect a router and a switch via a trunk connection, you must make sure that the Media type and MTU of each VLAN are consistent between these devices.

**Table 9-1**   *Default VLANs on a Catalyst 5000 Family Switch*

| VLAN Name | Type | MTU | ISL VLAN-id | 802.10 SAID |
| --- | --- | --- | --- | --- |
| Default | Ethernet | 1500 | 0001 | 100001 |
| Fddi-default | Fddi | 4352 | 1002 | 101002 |
| Token-ring-default | Token-ring | 2048 | 1003 | 101003 |
| Fddinet-default | Fddi-net | 4352 | 1004 | 101004 |
| Trnet-default | Tr-net | 2048 | 1005 | 101005 |

As mentioned earlier, on a (an ISL-capable) Cisco router, you have the option to bridge between the subinterfaces of the ISL (trunk) interface. This may very well be necessary; however, you must realize that this action combines the spanning trees associated with the VLANs of those subinterfaces that you bridge. Moreover, when you do bridging on a router, you must also ensure that the Spanning-Tree Protocol used on the router (IEEE or DEC) is identical to the Spanning-Tree Protocol used on your switches. Usage of incompatible Spanning-Tree Protocols has serious implications, including loss of BPDUs (drops), loops, broadcast storms, and ultimately network meltdown.

An important factor in management and troubleshooting of switched internetworks is having a map of the network showing the connections (loops), bridge and port priorities, and the root bridge. In most cases automatic election of root device, designated port, and root port, as per the Spanning-Tree Protocol's algorithm, does not yield the most efficient and effective topology. You must make use of manual bridge priority, port priority, and port cost configuration for the most desirable Layer 2 topology.

Keep in mind that spanning tree timers are dictated by the root device to all of the other participating members of the spanning tree (the non-root devices). In periods of instability it is wise to reduce the spanning tree activities of the devices. One way of achieving this is by setting the spanning tree timers at their maximum values on the root device. The forward delay (fwddelay) parameter can be set to the maximum value of 30 seconds, and the maximum age (MAX_AGE) parameter can be set to the maximum value of 40 seconds. In a stable network, on the other hand, using shorter timer values assist in swift detection of a failure and a faster network convergence.

Cisco routers do not yet support VTP (VLAN Trunking Protocol). Positioning a router between a bunch of switches segregates a VTP domain. If there is only one switch behind a router, it is probably wise to configure that switch in a VTP transparent mode. If there is more than one switch behind a router, however, it is probably easier to have them configured with a different VTP domain (name).

# Router VLAN Diagnostic Tools: show Commands

In this section a few of the Cisco router IOS **show** commands that help diagnose VLAN-related cases are presented. You need to know the syntax of each command and what information each command's output makes available. The following sections each provide a sample output for the presented **show** command to help you better understand the usage and benefits of it.

## show vlans

The **show vlans** command lists all the VLANs configured on a router. Example 9-2 shows a sample output of this command. For each VLAN, the corresponding subinterface and its configured addresses (for instance, IP and IPX) are displayed. For each protocol configured on a subinterface, this command also shows the number of packets sent and received.

**Example 9-2**  *A Sample Output for the **show vlans** Command*

```
D_BackR#show vlans

Virtual LAN ID:  1 (Inter Switch Link Encapsulation)

 vLAN Trunk Interface:    FastEthernet0.1
 Protocols Configured:    Address:            Received:    Transmitted:
 IP                       10.1.1.44           67           104


Virtual LAN ID:  2 (Inter Switch Link Encapsulation)

 vLAN Trunk Interface:    FastEthernet0.2
 Protocols Configured:    Address:            Received:    Transmitted:
 IP                       10.2.1.40           134          87
 IPX (NOVELL-ETHER)       2000.00e0.1454.cf19 10           10


Virtual LAN ID:  3 (Inter Switch Link Encapsulation)

 vLAN Trunk Interface:    FastEthernet0.3
 Protocols Configured:    Address:            Received:    Transmitted:
 IP                       10.3.1.40           20           44
 IPX (NOVELL-ETHER)       3000.00e0.1454.cf19 14           13


Virtual LAN ID:  100 (Inter Switch Link Encapsulation)

 vLAN Trunk Interface:    FastEthernet0.100
 Protocols Configured:    Address:            Received: Transmitted:
 IP                       144.251.100.40      367       98


D_BackR#
```

# show span [*vlan-number*]

This command first appeared in Cisco IOS Release 10.3 and it shows the Spanning-Tree Protocol information known to the router (see Example 9-3). The first part of this command's output shows the type of Spanning-Tree Protocol in use, the bridge ID (priority and address) of the local device (the router), the ID of the root device, and the timer parameters of the spanning tree. Next, the interfaces that participate in the spanning tree (associated to the VLAN number typed in) are listed. For each interface, its associated state (for example, Forwarding), priority, cost, timers, as well as the ID of the designated root and bridge are displayed. It is noteworthy that the Catalyst switch's IOS command counterpart for displaying information about Spanning Tree is **show spantree**; the **show span** command on a Catalyst switch displays SPAN (switched port analyzer) information.

**Example 9-3**  *A Sample Output for the* **show span** [*vlan-number*] *Command*

```
D_BackR_J#show span 1

Bridge Group 1 is executing the IEEE compatible Spanning Tree protocol
  Bridge Identifier has priority 32768, address 00e0.1454.cf1b
  Configured hello time 2, max age 20, forward delay 15
  We are the root of the spanning tree
  Topology change flag set, detected flag set
  Times:  hold 1, topology change 30, notification 30
          hello 2, max age 20, forward delay 15, aging 300
  Timers: hello 2, topology change 25, notification 0

Port 3 (Ethernet1) of bridge group 1 is forwarding
   Port path cost 100, Port priority 128
   Designated root has priority 32768, address 00e0.1454.cf1b
   Designated bridge has priority 32768, address 00e0.1454.cf1b
   Designated port is 3, path cost 0
   Timers: message age 0, forward delay 0, hold 0

Port 19 (FastEthernet0.100 ISL) of bridge group 1 is forwarding
   Port path cost 10, Port priority 128
   Designated root has priority 32768, address 00e0.1454.cf1b
   Designated bridge has priority 32768, address 00e0.1454.cf1b
   Designated port is 19, path cost 0
   Timers: message age 0, forward delay 0, hold 0
```

You can construct a map of your Spanning-Tree Protocol network from the key information displayed by the **show span** command. A network map is one of the essential parts of the set of facts you need to support and troubleshoot a network (see Figure 9-2). When you read the output of this command, you need to be aware of the following facts:

- When the MAC address of the designated bridge is the same as the MAC address of the root bridge, the port or interface of the bridge being examined and the root bridge are attached to the same network.

- When the MAC address of the designated bridge is different from the MAC address of the bridge being examined, the designated bridge is in the path to the root bridge.

- When the MAC address of the designated bridge is the same as the bridge identifier of the bridge being examined, the port or interface points away from the root bridge.

- The bridge port value specified for a particular port belongs to the bridge associated with the designated bridge shown in the port listing.

**Figure 9-2**    *Spanning-Tree Map of a Network*

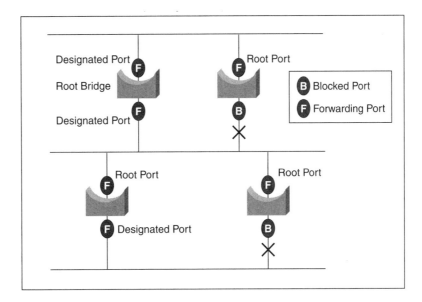

## show bridge [*bridge-number*]

The **show bridge** command displays the contents of your router's bridge forwarding database for all the bridge groups defined (see Example 9-4). If you specify a bridge number, then of course the output will show only the information pertaining to the bridge group specified.

**Example 9-4**    *A Sample Output for the **show bridge** Command*

```
D_BackR_J#show bridge

Total of 300 station blocks, 295 free
Codes: P - permanent, S - self

Bridge Group 1:
```

*continues*

**Example 9-4**    *A Sample Output for the* **show bridge** *Command (Continued)*

```
Address          Action    Interface    Age    RX count    TX count
0010.7b2c.5b1b   forward   Ethernet1    0      6           0
00e0.fe80.bbff   forward   Ethernet1    0      119         0
00e0.1ee8.86e3   forward   Ethernet1    0      2           0
00e0.1454.cf49   forward   Ethernet1    0      4           0
0080.c885.54a2   forward   Ethernet1    0      5           0
D_BackR_J#
```

## show interface fastethernet 0

The Fast Ethernet interface can be used to build a trunk connection to a switch or another router with ISL. The **show interfaces fastethernet 0** command displays information about this interface's state (up, down, administratively down) and other information that you see when you issue this command for any interface. However, when you observe the output of this command, pay special attention to the duplexing mode, speed, and the media reported. Example 9-5 provides a sample output of this command. As you can see, the sixth line of the output shows Full-duplex, 100 Mbps, and 100BaseTX/FX, which is a common configuration for a trunk/ISL connection between a router and a Catalyst switch.

**Example 9-5**    *A Sample Output of the* **show interfaces fastethernet 0** *Command*

```
D_BackR_J#show interfaces fastethernet 0
FastEthernet0 is up, line protocol is up
  Hardware is DEC21140, address is 00e0.1454.cf19 (bia00e0.1454.cf19)
  Description: For ISL trunking
  MTU 1500 bytes, BW 100000 Kbit, DLY 100 usec, rely 255/255, load 1/255
  Encapsulation ARPA, loopback not set, keepalive set (10 sec)
  Full-duplex, 100Mb/s, 100BaseTX/FX
  ARP type: ARPA, ARP Timeout 04:00:00
  Last input 00:00:00, output 00:00:00, output hang never
  Last clearing of "show interface" counters never
  Queueing strategy: fifo
  Output queue 0/40, 0 drops; input queue 0/75, 0 drops
  5 minute input rate 1000 bits/sec, 2 packets/sec
  5 minute output rate 2000 bits/sec, 4 packets/sec
     1651 packets input, 126990 bytes, 0 no buffer
     Received 1194 broadcasts, 0 runts, 0 giants, 0 throttles
     0 input errors, 0 CRC, 0 frame, 0 overrun, 0 ignored, 0 abort
     0 watchdog, 0 multicast
     0 input packets with dribble condition detected
     2536 packets output, 272626 bytes, 0 underruns
     41 output errors, 41 collisions, 7 interface resets
     0 babbles, 0 late collision, 0 deferred
     41 lost carrier, 0 no carrier
     0 output buffer failures, 0 output buffers swapped out
D_BackR_J#
```

# Router VLAN Diagnostic Tools: debug Commands

There are two **debug** commands particularly useful for troubleshooting VLANs on a router. The **debug VLAN packets** command helps diagnose a trunk/ISL connection on a Fast Ethernet interface, and the **debug span** command with the **tree** or **events** option is helpful for diagnosing spanning tree issues.

## debug vlan packets

The **debug vlan packet** command displays messages about virtual LAN (VLAN) packets that the router receives (off the trunk connection) but is not configured to support (see Example 9-6). In other words, if an ISL packet with a VLAN ID of 6 is received, but none of the subinterfaces of the input interface are configured for VLAN 6, the router cannot process the encapsulated frame and the debug process displays a message indicating what has just happened. As mentioned earlier, you may use the **show vlans** command to see the list of all the VLANs configured on your router.

**Example 9-6**  *A Sample Output of the **debug vlan packets** Command*

```
D_BackR#debug vlan packets
Virtual LAN packet information debugging is on
D_BackR#
05:20:45: vLAN: Received ISL encapsulated UNKNOWN packet bearing colour ID 100
       on interface FastEthernet0.100 which is not configured to
       route or bridge this packet type.

05:20:45: vLAN: Received ISL encapsulated UNKNOWN packet bearing colour ID 3
       on interface FastEthernet0.3 which is not configured to
       route or bridge this packet type.

05:20:45: vLAN: ISL packet received bearing colour ID 4 on FastEthernet0
       which has no subinterface configured to route or bridge ID 4.

05:20:45: vLAN: ISL packet received bearing colour ID 5 on FastEthernet0
       which has no subinterface configured to route or bridge ID 5.

05:20:45: vLAN: ISL packet received bearing colour ID 6 on FastEthernet0
       which has no subinterface configured to route or bridge ID 6.

05:20:45: vLAN: ISL packet received bearing colour ID 7 on FastEthernet0
       which has no subinterface configured to route or bridge ID 7.

05:20:45: vLAN: Received ISL encapsulated UNKNOWN packet bearing colour ID 100
       on interface FastEthernet0.100 which is not configured to
       route or bridge this packet type.
```

The first entry in the output of Example 9-6 notifies you that an ISL frame was received from the fastethernet 0.100 subinterface. That ISL frame's VLAN ID was 100, but it encapsulated a frame that in turn encapsulated a packet that the fastethernet 0.100 subinterface is not configured to route or bridge.

The third entry in the output of Example 9-6 tells you that an ISL frame was received from the fastethernet 0 interface. The ISL frame's VLAN ID was 4, and the fastethernet 0 interface does not have a subinterface to handle this VLAN's frames. In scenarios like this, it is usually wise to configure the device on the other side of the trunk not to send certain VLANs' frames in this direction. On the Catalyst 5000 switch, you may use the **clear trunk** command to take a VLAN out of a trunk port.

## debug span tree and debug span events

The **debug span** command can be used with either the **tree** or the **events** parameter. The **events** option is more user-friendly because it tells you in words the meaning of the BPDU packets that the router is receiving (see Example 9-7). The **tree** option, on the other hand, displays each BPDU received from each interface in its raw format.

For instance, the first entry in the output of the debug span tree (Example 9-7) shows the following line: 00:15:42: ST: Fa0.100 00000080. This line tells you that at 3:42 p.m. a spanning-tree packet was received from the fastethernet 0.100 subinterface. This BPDU packet starts with four zeros (field A), which means that this packet is an IEEE spanning-tree BPDU. The following two zeros (field B) indicate the version, and the 80 at the end (field C) indicates that the received BPDU is a Topology Change Notification (TCN). As you can see, either of these commands can be used to track and verify the operation of the spanning tree.

**Example 9-7** *Sample Output of* **debug span ?***,* **debug span tree***, and* **debug span events**

```
D_BackR_J#debug span ?
  events  Spanning-tree topology events
  tree      Spanning-tree protocol data units

D_BackR_J#debug span tree
Spanning Tree BPDU debugging is on
D_BackR_J#
00:15:42: ST: Fa0.100 00000080
00:16:19: ST: Ethernet1 00000080
00:16:27: ST: Fa0.100 00000080
00:16:37: ST: Ethernet1 00000080

D_BackR_J#debug span events
Spanning Tree event debugging is on
D_BackR_J#
00:16:57: ST: Topology Change rcvd on FastEthernet0.100
00:16:57: ST: Topology Change rcvd on FastEthernet0.100
00:17:19: ST: Topology Change rcvd on Ethernet1
00:17:29: ST: Topology Change rcvd on FastEthernet0.100

D_BackR_J#
```

# Problem Isolation in Router/Switch VLAN Networks

To ensure that a router is properly connected to a switch through a trunk and that it is receiving the desired data units and processing them, you need to do the following:

- Check the physical link between the router and the switch. For instance, make sure that the cable between the router and switch is straight-through, is of the correct type/category, and is properly connected using proper connectors. The LEDs and the output of appropriate **show** commands can help you determine the state of the physical link between a switch port and a router's Fast Ethernet interface. Also make sure that the correct media type is specified (if applicable).

- Make sure that the router and the switch are both configured for the same speed and duplexing mode.

- Make sure that the router's Fast Ethernet interface has the correct subinterfaces and VLANs configured on it. On each subinterface, make sure that the network layer addressing or any bridging commands are appropriately configured.

- Those VLANs that do not need to be relayed to the router should be taken out of the trunk (with the **clear trunk** command).

- Make sure that the Spanning-Tree Protocol configured on the router matches the spanning tree of the connected switch.

# Foundation Summary

The Foundation Summary is a collection of quick reference information that provides a convenient review of many key concepts in this chapter. For those of you who already feel comfortable with the topics in this chapter, this summary helps you recall a few details. For those of you who just read this chapter, this review should help solidify some key facts. For any of you doing your final prep before the exam, these tables and figures are a convenient way to review the day before the exam.

**Example 9-8**  *Sample Configuration for the Fast Ethernet Interface of a Router*

```
interface FastEthernet0
 no ip address
 media-type mii
 full-duplex
!
interface FastEthernet0.1
 encapsulation isl 1
 ip address 10.1.1.44 255.255.0.0
 ipx network 36dd
!
interface FastEthernet0.2
 encapsulation isl 2
 ip address 10.2.1.40 255.255.0.0
 bridge-group 60
 !
interface FastEthernet0.3
 encapsulation isl 3
 ip address 10.3.1.40 255.255.0.0
  bridge-group 60
!
```

**Table 9-2**  *Default Values for the IEEE Spanning-Tree Protocol Timers*

| Parameter | Default Value |
|---|---|
| HELLO | 2 |
| MAX_AGE | 20 |
| Fwddelay | 15 |
| Convergence | 50 |
| MAX_AGE + Listening (fwddelay) + Learning (fwddelay) | |

**Table 9-3**  *Default VLANs on a Catalyst 5000 Family Switch*

| VLAN Name | Type | MTU | ISL VLAN-id | 802.10 SAID |
|---|---|---|---|---|
| Default | Ethernet | 1500 | 0001 | 100001 |
| Fddi-default | FDDI | 4352 | 1002 | 101002 |
| Token-ring-default | Token Ring | 2048 | 1003 | 101003 |
| Fddinet-default | FDDI-net | 4352 | 1004 | 101004 |
| Trnet-default | Tr-net | 2048 | 1005 | 101005 |

**Table 9-4**  *Router VLAN Diagnostic Tools: **show** Commands*

| Command | Description |
|---|---|
| **show vlans** | Lists all the VLANs configured on a router. For each VLAN, the corresponding subinterface and its configured addresses are displayed. |
| **show span** [*vlan-number*] | Shows the Spanning-Tree Protocol information known to the router. The first part of this command's output shows the type of Spanning-Tree Protocol in use, the bridge ID (priority and address) of the local device (the router), the ID of the root device, and the timer parameters of the spanning tree. Next, the interfaces that participate in the spanning tree (associated with the VLAN number typed in) are listed. |
| **show bridge** [*bridge-number*] | Displays contents of your router's bridge forwarding database for all the bridge groups defined. |

**Table 9-5**  *Router VLAN Diagnostic Tools: **debug** Commands*

| Command | Description |
|---|---|
| **debug vlan packets** | The **debug vlan packet** command displays messages about virtual LAN (VLAN) packets that the router receives (off the trunk connection) but is not configured to support. |
| **debug span tree** | Displays messages about the BPDU packets that the router is receiving (in text format). |
| **debug span events** | Displays the BPDU packets that the router is receiving (in its raw format). |

# Q&A

The answers to the following questions can be found in Appendix A. Some of the questions in this section are repeated from the "Do I Know This Already" Quiz so that you can gauge the advancement of your knowledge of this subject matter.

**1** Name three of the functions routers perform in a VLAN switching environment.

_____

_____

_____

**2** Which type of router interface is used for ISL trunking?

_____

_____

_____

**3** True or false: If a Fast Ethernet interface is used for trunking purposes, it should not have any Layer 3 address or any bridging commands configured on the main interface.

_____

**4** How many VLANs can a subinterface of an interface used for trunking correspond to?

_____

_____

_____

**5** Which command functions are configured on the main interface of the interface used for trunking?

_____

_____

_____

**6** What IOS command configures a multiport Fast Ethernet interface to operate from its RJ45 (100BaseTX) connector?

_____

_____

_____

7  What IOS command configures a multi-port Fast Ethernet interface to operate in full-duplex mode?

_____

_____

_____

8  Which command shows the media type configured on a Fast Ethernet interface?

_____

_____

_____

9  Which command would configure a subinterface of a Fast Ethernet interface to be in VLAN number 10 (in ISL format)?

_____

_____

_____

10  Routing between VLANs is supported for which protocols on Cisco 4500 and 7000 series routers running IOS Release 11.3?

_____

_____

_____

11  What is the general rule for the bridged networks in terms of the number of hops?

_____

_____

_____

12  What is the default HELLO interval in the IEEE Spanning-Tree Protocol?

_____

_____

_____

**13**   What is the default MAX_AGE interval in the IEEE Spanning-Tree Protocol?

_____

_____

_____

**14**   What is the default fwddelay interval in the IEEE Spanning-Tree Protocol?

_____

_____

_____

**15**   What is the maximum convergence time of the IEEE Spanning-Tree Protocol in a network with a seven-hop diameter and default IEEE spanning tree timer values?

_____

_____

_____

**16**   How many default VLANs are preconfigured on a Catalyst 5000 switch?

_____

_____

_____

**17**   What is the recommended usage of VLAN number 1?

_____

_____

_____

**18**   What are the possible implications of using different (inconsistent) Spanning-Tree Protocols for a VLAN in the same network?

_____

_____

_____

**19** What is the suggested setting for the spanning tree timers during periods of instability?

_____

_____

_____

**20** What role can a Cisco router play in a VTP domain?

_____

_____

_____

**21** What information can one obtain from the output of the **show vlans** command?

_____

_____

_____

**22** Describe the output of the **show span** *vlan-number* command.

_____

_____

_____

**23** Discuss the output of the **show bridge** [*bridge-number*] command.

_____

_____

_____

**24** What messages does the **debug vlan packets** command display?

_____

_____

_____

**25** What are the two forms of the Cisco IOS's **debug span** command?

_____

_____

_____

This chapter covers the following topics that you will need to master to pass the CCNP Support exam:

| Objective | Description |
|-----------|-------------|
| 1 | Frame Relay troubleshooting process. |
| 2 | The IETF frame structure for Frame Relay. |
| 3 | The Frame Relay diagnostic **show** commands. |
| 4 | Frame Relay loopback testing. |
| 5 | The Frame Relay diagnostic **debug** commands. |
| 6 | Frame Relay problem isolation. |

# CHAPTER 10

# Diagnosing and Correcting Frame Relay Problems

Frame Relay is a connection-oriented OSI Layer 2 protocol. Frame Relay fits in the packet-switching category for wide-area network technology. Currently most of the implementations use permanent virtual circuits (PVCs) to connect remote offices, and many organizations are testing switched virtual circuits (SVCs). This chapter's focus is on diagnosing and correcting Frame Relay PVC networking on Cisco serial interfaces. Even though the chapter is not intended to provide a course on Frame Relay configuration, the troubleshooting tips discussed involve many of the Frame Relay configuration commands. A comprehensive list of related Cisco IOS **show** and **debug** commands is presented to enhance your diagnostic skills to support Frame Relay networks.

## "Do I Know This Already?" Quiz

If you wish to evaluate your knowledge of the contents of this chapter before you get started, answer the following questions. The answers are provided in Appendix A, "Answers to Quiz Questions." If you are having difficulty providing correct answers, you should thoroughly review the entire chapter. If all or most of your answers are correct, you might want to skim this chapter for only those subjects you need to review. You can also use the "Foundation Summary" section to quickly review topics. Once you have completed the chapter, you should reevaluate yourself with the questions in the "Q&A" section at the end. Finally, use the companion CD-ROM to evaluate your knowledge of the topics and see if you need a review.

1 What is the default frame type for the serial interfaces of Cisco routers that have been configured with the **encapsulation frame-relay** command?

_____

_____

_____

**2** What are the two frame types supported on the Frame Relay (serial) interfaces of a Cisco router?

_____

_____

_____

**3** Can the LMI type be autosensed by any of the IOS releases?

_____

_____

_____

**4** What are the LMI types supported by Cisco IOS?

_____

_____

_____

**5** Does the LMI type have to be identical on both ends of a Frame Relay connection?

_____

_____

_____

**6** What are the main pieces of information that you can obtain from the output of the **show interface serial** _n_ command?

_____

_____

_____

**7** If the LMI type of Cisco is used on a Cisco router's serial interface, which DLCI number is used on that interface for LMI purposes?

_____

_____

_____

**8**  If the LMI type of ANSI is used on a Cisco router's serial interface, which DLCI number is used on that interface for LMI purposes?

_____

_____

_____

**9**  Give at least two reasons for a Frame Relay serial interface being reported as up and its line protocol reported as down.

_____

_____

_____

**10**  Discuss the reasons for a serial interface being reported as down.

_____

_____

_____

**11**  Which **show** command displays Local Management Interface (LMI) statistics about a Cisco router's Frame Relay interface(s)?

_____

_____

_____

**12**  Which Frame Relay **show** command lists all of the PVCs that the router is aware of on all of its Frame Relay interfaces (and subinterfaces) along with their status, creation time, last status-change time, and statistics regarding the sent/received packets/bytes and the congestion notification flags?

_____

_____

_____

**13**  Provide at least two pieces of information given for each interface on the output of the **show frame-relay map** command.

_____

_____

_____

**14** Which generic **debug** command displays real-time information about the activities (such as keepalives) and status of serial interfaces?

_____

_____

_____

**15** Which Frame Relay troubleshooting **debug** command displays the LMI messages that are exchanged between your router and the Frame Relay switch?

_____

_____

_____

## Foundation Topics

# Frame Relay Troubleshooting (Checklist)

There are some steps that you need to be aware of and make sure are in effect with respect to the configuration of the Cisco routers involved in a Frame Relay connection.

One of the very basic commands that needs to be entered in the interface configuration mode is:

```
encapsulation frame-relay [ietf]
```

As you can see, with this command you have the option to specify the IETF frame type. If you do not enter the **ietf** optional parameter, the IOS implements the **cisco** frame type. In other words, **cisco** is the default frame type on the serial interfaces of Cisco routers that are configured with the **encapsulation frame relay** command. The frame type used on one end of a circuit must match the frame type used at the other end of that circuit. Mismatched frame types are a common source of problems on a Frame Relay circuit. Upper layer protocols that rely on delivery of their packets through Frame Relay PDUs will work only if the frame types match on both ends of a Frame Relay circuit.

As of version 11.2 of the Cisco IOS, the LMI type that the service provider switch uses is auto-sensed by the router connecting to it. This means that if your IOS is older than version 11.2, you must hard-code the LMI type on your router's serial interface using the following command:

```
frame-relay lmi-type {cisco ¦ ansi ¦ q933a}
```

If your router's IOS version supports auto-sensing the LMI, you may still enter the LMI type if you wish to do so. In any case, however, you must make sure that the LMI type you enter is indeed the LMI type used by the service provider's switch. It is a common misunderstanding that the LMI type must be identical on both ends of a connection circuit. That is not true; the LMI type must only be consistent between the router and the service provider switch it is connected to. If the DTE device's (router's) LMI type does not match the LMI type used by the service provider's switch, the link will not come up (keepalive mismatch).

If Frame Relay LMI is not turned off on an interface (using the **no keepalive** interface configuration command), the router can learn the DLCI (Data Link Connection Identifier) numbers and the status of each DLCI from the service provider's switch (through LMI) dynamically. The LMI (keepalive) also allows the service provider's switch to be aware of the presence of your router and reflect its knowledge of your router's presence to other devices by means of status reporting.

It is crucial for the router to be able to associate each of the Frame Relay DLCI numbers to the appropriate upper layer protocols' addresses. On a connection that uses the main serial interface (subinterfaces are not used), the routers send their upper layer address(es) to each other every 60 seconds (this is called Frame Relay inverse ARP), and they are hence able to build a dynamic map table that matches each DLCI number to one or more upper layer address(es).

When subinterfaces are used, the router is not able to associate the received Frame Relay inverse-arps (if any) to the appropriate subinterfaces. Hence, on a Frame Relay point-to-point subinterface you must hard-code the DLCI number. The syntax for hard-coding the DLCI number is:

```
frame-relay interface-dlci dlci-number
```

On the other hand, with a Frame Relay multipoint you must either hard-code the DLCI number(s) or provide a **frame-relay map** statement for each DLCI and the appropriate upper layer address. The syntax for the **frame-relay map** statement is:

```
frame-relay map protocol address dlci-number
```

On a point-to-point subinterface, broadcasting is supported and no special configuration is required. However, if you want broadcasts to be sent to the opposite ends of a multipoint connection, you must enter the keyword **broadcast** at the end of each **frame-relay map** statement.

Frame Relay is a nonbroadcast multiaccess (NBMA) network. This link layer technology does not offer a broadcast address. When an upper layer protocol (such as IP) generates a broadcast such as a RIP update, since there is no Frame Relay equivalent address for a broadcast, Frame Relay will not be able to deliver those broadcast packets. With the **frame-relay map** statement, you map an upper layer unicast address to a Frame Relay DLCI number. If you use the keyword **broadcast** with the **frame-relay map** statement, you are effectively instructing the router to map the broadcast address of the upper layer protocol to the same DLCI number that the map statement uses for the unicast address. For instance, the following **frame-relay map** statement maps the IP address 10.162.71.1 to the DLCI number 35. However, the keyword **broadcast** instructs the router to also map the IP broadcast address 255.255.255.255 to DLCI 35:

```
frame-relay map ip 10.162.71.1 35 broadcast
```

# The IETF Frame Structure for Frame Relay

Based on the IETF specification, the header of the Frame Relay frame is 2 bytes (16 bits) long. 10 bits of the header's 16 bits form a field called DLCI (Data Link Connection Identifier). The DLCI number that a router places on a frame identifies where the frame is ultimately forwarded to.

The basic implementation of DLCIs does not require that two different routers sending frames to the same destination (a third router) necessarily use the same DLCI number. This means that DLCI numbers have only local significance and that, generally speaking, you should not be comparing the DLCI numbers and map statements used on one router to the DLCI numbers and the map statements used on another. Three of the remaining bits on the

IETF Frame Relay header are used for congestion notification and control. These bits are called FECN (Forward Explicit Congestion Notification), BECN (Backward Explicit Congestion Notification), and DE (Discard Eligibility). FECN and BECN bits are set by the Frame Relay network to notify the sending and receiving devices that the network is experiencing congestion and that frames (especially those from devices that are bursting beyond their CIRs) will/may be dropped. The discard eligibility bit is intended to be set by the DTE device (the router, for instance) so that certain frames are dropped before other ones.

When a router bursts beyond its CIR and receives congestion notification from the service provider's network, it has a number of options. The first option is to reduce traffic submission to the CIR value. The second option is for the router to continue bursting beyond the CIR and let its frames be dropped (if necessary) by the service provider at random. The third option is to set the discard eligibility bit to 0 on some frames (up to the CIR value) and set it to 1 on other frames. The service provider will try to deliver the frames with DE bit equal to 0 as long as their volume does not exceed the CIR. The frames with the DE bit set to 1 are not guaranteed to be dropped, but they certainly have a higher chance of being dropped than the frames with the DE bit set to 0.

# The Frame Relay Diagnostic Tools: show

There are a number of Cisco IOS **show** commands that are especially useful in diagnosing Frame Relay issues. In this section, four of those **show** commands—the most significant **show** commands for Frame Relay troubleshooting—are discussed. Also, the Support exam expects you to be fully familiar with the usage and output of these commands. A sample output and a brief discussion of how the output should be interpreted are presented for each command.

## show interface serial *n*

The output of the **show interface serial** *n* command gives you some information similar to the output of the **show** command for other types of interfaces. However, with this command you must also concentrate on the type of information that is particular to Frame Relay. Example 10-1 displays a sample output of this command for a Serial interface that is configured with the **encapsulation frame-relay** command and has three point-to-point subinterfaces. The line numbers in Example 10-1 were added for the purpose of this discussion. On the bottom of Example 10-1 the configuration of the serial interface 1 is also displayed.

**Example 10-1** *A Sample Output of the **show interface serial n** Command*

```
B_StubR_FRNorm#sho int s1
01  Serial1 is up, line protocol is up
02  Hardware is HD64570
03  MTU 1500 bytes, BW 1544 Kbit, DLY 20000 usec, rely 255/255, load 1/255
```

*continues*

**Example 10-1** *A Sample Output of the **show interface serial n** Command (Continued)*

```
04  Encapsulation FRAME-RELAY, loopback not set, keepalive set (10 sec)
05  LMI enq sent  463, LMI stat recvd 457, LMI upd recvd 0, DTE LMI up
06  LMI enq recvd 0, LMI stat sent  0, LMI upd sent  0
07  LMI dlci 0  LMI type is ANSI Annex D  frame relay DTE
08  FR SVC disabled, LAPF state down
Broadcast queue 0/64, broadcasts sent/dropped 831/0, interface broadcasts
603
Last input 00:00:07, output 00:00:00, output hang never
Last clearing of "show interface" counters never
Input queue: 0/75/0 (size/max/drops); Total output drops: 0
Queueing strategy: weighted fair
Output queue: 0/1000/64/0 (size/max total/threshold/drops)
  Conversations  0/2/256 (active/max active/max total)
  Reserved Conversations 0/0 (allocated/max allocated)
5 minute input rate 0 bits/sec, 0 packets/sec
5 minute output rate 0 bits/sec, 0 packets/sec
1307 packets input, 199385 bytes, 0 no buffer
Received 608 broadcasts, 0 runts, 0 giants, 0 throttles
  0 input errors, 0 CRC, 0 frame, 0 overrun, 0 ignored, 0 abort
  1318 packets output, 186520 bytes, 0 underruns
  0 output errors, 0 collisions, 4 interface resets
  0 output buffer failures, 0 output buffers swapped out
  6 carrier transitions
 DCD=up  DSR=up  DTR=up  RTS=up  CTS=up

interface Serial1
 no ip address
 encapsulation frame-relay
!
interface Serial1.1 point-to-point
 ip address 192.50.18.21 255.255.255.252
 ipx network 5400
 frame-relay interface-dlci 755
!
interface Serial1.2 point-to-point
 ip address 192.50.18.25 255.255.255.252
 ipx network 5500
 frame-relay interface-dlci 655
!
interface Serial1.4 point-to-point
 ip address 192.50.18.6 255.255.255.252
 ipx network 5000
 frame-relay interface-dlci 156
```

Line number 01 of the output indicates that the physical interface is up (it is not down or administratively shut down) and the link (line protocol) is also up. This means that the serial interface is properly connected to the CSU (and is receiving the clock signal), and it is also communicating with the service provider's switch through the local access loop. The fourth line of the output says that the interface is configured for Frame Relay encapsulation (it is the Cisco format since it does not say IETF), is not looped (loopback), and is sending keepalives every 10 seconds. The fifth line displays the number of LMI inquiries (enq) sent and the number of LMI status messages received.

The seventh line indicates that the ANSI annex D LMI is in use, that this interface is acting as a Frame Relay DTE device, and that the reserved DLCI number 0 is being used for LMI purposes. Finally, the eighth line of the output shows that Frame Relay SVC is disabled (LAPF, the protocol that is used with SVCs for call setup, is down). In other words, this connection is PVC based.

In summary, the **show interface serial** *n* command allows you to check the status of the interface hardware, the link status, the encapsulation used, whether keepalives are being sent, the LMI type, the standard statistics on the sent and received data, queue accounting, and so on.

The LMI type, as said earlier, may be set as one of Cisco, ANSI, or Q933a. The LMI type configured on the router must match the LMI type configured on the service provider switch to which the router connects. The LMI type at the other end of a connection—between the destination router and its service provider's switch—may be different. Table 10-1 illustrates how the seventh line of the **show interface serial** *n* would be different based on the LMI type configured on that interface. Notice that, depending on the LMI type used, a special DLCI number is reserved for the local LMI usage. If Cisco LMI is used, dlci 1023 shall be used for LMI purposes. If ANSI or Q933a LMI is used, dlci 0 will be dedicated to LMI.

**Table 10-1**   *Indication of the Configured LMI Type on a Serial Interface*

| The Configured LMI type | What the output of the show interface serial *n* indicates: |
| --- | --- |
| Cisco | LMI dlci 1023  LMI type is Cisco |
| ANSI | LMI dlci 0  LMI type is ANSI Annex D |
| Q933a | LMI dlci 0  LMI type is CCITT |

The number of resets and the number of carrier transitions are two important indicators to check while troubleshooting. In Example 10-1, line number 23 reports four interface resets and line number 25 indicates six carrier transitions. Because line number 11 of the output states that the interface counters have never been cleared, the shown numbers have accumulated since the last router reload. You may discover the router's uptime using the **show version** command.

The number of interface resets reported on the output of any **show interface** command tells you how many times the interface buffers have been flushed (since the last time the interface counters were cleared or the router has reloaded). An interface reset may be forced by an administrator—through execution of the **clear interface** command, for instance—or it may happen for any of the following reasons:

- An interface has packets queued for transmission, but those packets are not sent within a reasonable amount of time (a few seconds).

- There is a hardware problem (on the interface, cable, or the CSU).

- There are clocking problems.

- The interface is looped.

- The router is attempting to restart an interface that has line protocol problems (the router tries to do that periodically).

The carrier transitions counter tells you how many times the DCD (Data Carrier Detect) has changed state. A large number of carrier transitions, or at least a number much different from the baseline value, should make you curious about the carrier's facility. You must know that every carrier transition causes the line to drop and the interface to reset.

Now take a deeper look at the first line of the output from the **show interface serial** *n* command. This line may be reported as one of the following:

- Serial1 is up, line protocol is up

- Serial1 is up, line protocol is down

- Serial1 is up, line protocol is down (looped)

- Serial1 is administratively down, line protocol is down

- Serial1 is down, line protocol is down

The first possible output tells you that the physical interface is up and that the link (line protocol) is up. It means that the serial interface is properly connected to the CSU (and is receiving the clock signal). You also can conclude that the interface is communicating with the service provider's switch (using LMI) via the local loop.

The second possible output indicates that the router considers the serial interface (physical hardware) as good, that the interface is not administratively shut down or looped, and that this interface's connection is properly clocked. The line protocol being reported as down, however, is usually due to lack of synchronization between the Frame Relay DTE (usually the router) and DCE device (usually the service provider's switch). This is usually the result of LMI mismatch between the router and the switch. On the other hand, if your **show** command specified a subinterface (for example, **show interfaces serial 1.3**), then the line protocol being down is directly related to whether that particular subinterface's DLCI is active or not. Other possible reasons for the line protocol to be down are:

- The interface is not sending keepalives (keepalives can be stopped using the **no keepalive** interface configuration command).

- The service provider's switch has failed or has been misconfigured.

- The leased line is experiencing trouble such as too much noise.

- The CSU is not working properly.

**NOTE**    Note that in all of the preceding cases the bottom line result is that the router and the service provider's switch lose their communication path, which is why the router reports the line protocol as down. One way of finding out the exact point of failure is to perform loopback testing. This is discussed in the next section.

The third possible output also indicates that the serial interface is up and the line protocol is down. However, the output indicates that the interface is looped. Obviously, if an interface is looped it will not be able to communicate with the service provider's switch.

The fourth possible output indicates that the interface has been administratively shut down. Again, while in this state, of course, the router cannot communicate with the switch.

Finally, the fifth possible condition of a serial interface that the **show interface serial** $n$ would indicate is: Serial1 is down, line protocol is down. This condition is usually the result of a bad connection (or a lack of connection) between the router and the CSU. If a serial interface with the DTE end of the serial cable does not receive clocking on that connection, it will go or stay down until the DCE device starts clocking. The problem could be entirely due to the cable being faulty or improper, as well. This condition is clearly an indicator of a physical problem on the router's serial interface, or a bad serial cable used between the router and the CSU (usually a V.35 Cisco cable), or a faulty CSU. You must also check the CD LED on the CSU to make sure that CD is active. If the CD is not active, you must contact the service provider, so that they can rectify the problem. CSU is usually considered the border item/equipment between CPE (customer premises equipment) and the service provider's equipment. The service provider (Telco) manages/provisions the local (access) loop, which connects CPE's egress point to the service provider's equipment.

## Frame Relay Loopback Testing

Loopback testing is a commonly employed technique to identify the exact problem area in an end-to-end connection such as a Frame Relay. The end-to-end Frame Relay connection comprises the following segments:

- The segment between the local router and its CSU (local CPE)

- The segment between the local CSU and the service provider's switch (local loop)

- The Frame Relay network (the WAN cloud)

- The segment between the remote CSU and the service provider's switch at the remote location

- The segment between the CSU and the router in the remote location (remote CPE)

It is a good idea to rule out the possibility of the problems listed in the first and last bullets of the previous list (local and remote CPEs) before contacting the service provider.

A simple and effective way to do that is to loop the CSU at each end. When the CSU is looped, your router receives the frames it has sent, back again. The DTE status will remain up on the first, second, and third status inquiries, but it will go down after. However, that is nothing to worry about. The main purpose of this exercise is to see the frames come back. Example 10-2 displays the output of the **debug frame-relay lmi** command during loopback testing.

**Example 10-2** *A Sample Output of the* **debug frame-relay Lmi** *Command during Loopback Testing*

```
Serial1(out): StEnq, myseq 1, yourseen 0, DTE up
datagramstart = 0x668480, datagramsize = 13
FR encap = 0xFCF10309
00 75 01 01 00 03 02 01 00

RT IE 1, length 1, type 0
KA IE 3, length 2, yourseq 1 , myseq 0
Serial1(in): Unexpected StEnq

Serial1(out): StEnq, myseq 2, yourseen 0, DTE up
datagramstart = 0x668480, datagramsize = 13
FR encap = 0xFCF10309
00 75 01 01 00 03 02 02 00

RT IE 1, length 1, type 0
KA IE 3, length 2, yourseq 2, myseq 0
Serial1(in): Unexpected StEnq

Serial1(out): StEnq, myseq 3, yourseen 0, DTE up
datagramstart = 0x668480, datagramsize = 13
FR encap = 0xFCF10309
00 75 01 01 00 03 02 03 00

RT IE 1, length 1, type 0
KA IE 3, length 2, yourseq 3, myseq 0
Serial1(in): Unexpected StEnq

Serial1(out): StEnq, myseq 1, yourseen 0, DTE down
datagramstart = 0x668480, datagramsize = 13
FR encap = 0xFCF10309
```

If the interface hardware is up, and the frames that your router sends arrive at the CSU and come back to the router (due to the fact that the CSU is looped), you may naturally conclude that there are no problems within that segment. The same exercise must also be deployed on the remote location to verify that the connection between the remote router and its CSU is working. If that is the case, you must then contact your service provider and notify them of your problems. Mention to them that you have successfully completed the loopback testing on your local and remote segments (between the router and the CSU). The service provider will then perform its own loopback testing to find out where in the Frame Relay network problems exist. You may have to cooperate with your service provider when they decide to test the segment between your CSU and their switch in the local and remote locations (often called local access loops).

## show frame-relay lmi [*interface*]

This command displays LMI statistics about the interface under investigation. If you do not use the interface parameter, this information will be displayed for each and every Frame Relay interface (see Example 10-3).

**Example 10-3** *A Sample Output of the* **show frame-relay lmi** *Command*

```
A_StubR#sho frame-relay lmi

LMI Statistics for interface Serial1 (Frame Relay DTE) LMI TYPE = CISCO
  Invalid Unnumbered info 0          Invalid Prot Disc 0
  Invalid dummy Call Ref 0           Invalid Msg Type 0
  Invalid Status Message 0           Invalid Lock Shift 0
  Invalid Information ID 0           Invalid Report IE Len 0
  Invalid Report Request 0           Invalid Keep IE Len 0
  Num Status Enq. Sent 371           Num Status msgs Rcvd 326
  Num Update Status Rcvd 0           Num Status Timeouts 44
```

The first line of this command's output tells you of the role of the router's serial interface (DTE/UNI or NNI) and the LMI type it is configured for (UNI is the acronym for User Network Interface and NNI is the acronym for Network Node Interface). The following lines of the output provide error statistics on the LMI. It is a good idea to clear the counters on an interface (with the **clear counters** [**serial**] command) and see the amount of time it takes for those statistics to grow. On the last two lines of the **show frame-relay lmi** command's output, you will see the number of status inquiry (Status Enq.) messages sent, number of status messages (Status msgs) received, and number of status messages timed out. When there is an LMI mismatch between the router and the service provider's switch, the number of status messages timed out grows as fast as the number of status inquiry messages sent.

## show frame-relay map

This command displays the following information about each of the Frame Relay interfaces (see Example 10-4):

- The status of the interface (up, down, administratively down).

- The destination Layer 3 address (IP address). However, in the case of a point-to-point connection, the destination is identified with the phrase point-to-point dlci.

- The DLCI number in decimal, hexadecimal, and facility format.

- Whether the mapping is static or dynamic. In the case of a point-to-point connection, neither static nor dynamic is mentioned.

- Whether broadcast is supported.

- The encapsulation type (CISCO or IETF). The encapsulation type is shown for multipoint subinterfaces that have map statement(s).

- Whether the status of the connection (PVC) is defined or deleted. A connection with a defined status may be active or inactive.

**Example 10-4** *A Sample Output of the show* **frame-relay map** *Command*

```
B_StubR_FRNorm#sho frame-relay map

Serial0 (up): ipx 5200.00e0.b064.4cff dlci 356(0x164,0x5840), dynamic,
              broadcast,, status defined, active
Serial0 (up): ip 192.50.18.13 dlci 356(0x164,0x5840), dynamic,
              broadcast,, status defined, active
Serial0 (up): ipx 5500.00e0.b064.4cd3 dlci 656(0x290,0xA400), dynamic,
              broadcast,, status defined, active
Serial0 (up): ip 192.50.18.25 dlci 656(0x290,0xA400), dynamic,
              broadcast,, status defined, active
Serial0 (up): ipx 5800.0010.7b37.b95f dlci 956(0x3BC,0xECC0), dynamic,
              broadcast,, status defined, active
Serial0 (up): ip 192.50.18.37 dlci 956(0x3BC,0xECC0), dynamic,
              broadcast,, status defined, active
Serial1.4 (up): ip 192.50.18.5 dlci 156(0x9C,0x24C0), static,
              broadcast,
              CISCO, status defined, active
Serial1.1 (up): point-to-point dlci, dlci 755(0x2F3,0xBC30), broadcast
            status defined, active
Serial1.2 (up): point-to-point dlci, dlci 655(0x28F,0xA0F0), broadcast
            status defined, active
Serial1.3 (down): point-to-point dlci, dlci 555(0x22B,0x88B0), broadcast
            status deleted

B_StubR_FRNorm#
```

It is very useful to know that even though a DLCI number is reported as active (by the switch), your router may not be configured to correctly map that active connection's DLCI number to an appropriate upper layer address. Those DLCIs that are active but cannot be mapped to an upper layer address do not show up in the output of the **show frame-relay map** statement. In a situation where a DLCI is shown in the output of the **show frame-relay pvc** statement (and is reported as active) but does not appear in the output of the **show frame-relay map** statement, chances are good that all you are missing is a **frame-relay map** statement on the corresponding Frame Relay interface (or multipoint subinterface).

## show frame-relay pvc

The **show frame-relay pvc** command lists all of the PVCs that the router is aware of on all of its Frame Relay interfaces (and subinterfaces), along with their status, creation time, last status change time, and statistics regarding the sent/received packets/bytes and the congestion notification flags (see Example 10-5).

**Example 10-5** *A Sample Output of the **show frame-relay pvc** Command*

```
B_StubR_FRNorm#show frame-relay pvc
PVC Statistics for interface Serial0 (Frame Relay DTE)

dlci = 356, dlci USAGE = LOCAL, PVC STATUS = ACTIVE, INTERFACE = Serial0
  input pkts 102          output pkts 152          in bytes 25972
  out bytes 31896         dropped pkts 0           in FECN pkts 0
  in BECN pkts 0          out FECN pkts 0          out BECN pkts 0
  in DE pkts 0            out DE pkts 0
  out bcast pkts 152       out bcast bytes 31896
  pvc create time 00:54:23, last time pvc status changed 00:54:23
:
PVC Statistics for interface Serial1 (Frame Relay DTE)

dlci = 156, dlci USAGE = LOCAL, PVC STATUS = ACTIVE, INTERFACE = Serial1.4
  input pkts 355          output pkts 112          in bytes 86779
  out bytes 13288         dropped pkts 0           in FECN pkts 0
  in BECN pkts 0          out FECN pkts 0          out BECN pkts 0
  in DE pkts 0            out DE pkts 0
  out bcast pkts 108       out bcast bytes 12508
  pvc create time 02:05:20, last time pvc status changed 00:54:30

dlci = 555, dlci USAGE = LOCAL, PVC STATUS = DELETED, INTERFACE = Serial1.3
  input pkts 0            output pkts 11           in bytes 0
  out bytes 1832          dropped pkts 0           in FECN pkts 0
  in BECN pkts 0          out FECN pkts 0          out BECN pkts 0
  in DE pkts 0            out DE pkts 0
  out bcast pkts 11        out bcast bytes 1832
  pvc create time 02:05:39, last time pvc status changed 01:54:40
```

You may specify an interface or subinterface number along with the **show frame-relay pvc** command to limit the output of this command to the interface you are investigating. Another method of using the **show frame-relay pvc** command is to enter a PVC number along with it so that the output is limited to that specific PVC number. Example 10-6 shows the syntax and samples for the proper usage of this command.

**Example 10-6** *Various Methods of Using the **show frame-relay pvc** Command*

```
B_StubR_FRNorm#show frame-relay pvc ?
  interface
  <16-1022> dlci
  <cr>

B_StubR_FRNorm#show frame-relay pvc interface serial 1.1

B_StubR_FRNorm#show frame-relay pvc 755
```

In the output of the **show frame-relay pvc** command, DLCI USAGE is shown as SWITCHED when the router is used as a switch, or LOCAL when the router is used as a Frame Relay DTE device. PVC STATUS is reported as ACTIVE, INACTIVE, or DELETED. These are explained in the following paragraph. Furthermore, this command displays statistics regarding the amount of information that has been sent and received via a connection. For a PVC, the amount of received congestion control flags (FECNs, BECNs, and DEs) reported might be an important part of your fact gathering when troubleshooting Frame Relay. Finally, from the output of this command you may also learn when a PVC was created, and when its status changed last.

The PVC status (corresponding to each DLCI) that the service provider's switch provides to your router may be reported as ACTIVE, INACTIVE, or DELETED. If the status is reported as ACTIVE, the service provider's switch is claiming that it can deliver a frame to the final destination/end point of the DLCI; this is good news. If the status is reported as INACTIVE, it means that the service provider's switch is programmed to handle/forward frames that your router sends with that DLCI number, but is not aware/informed that your destination router is ready to receive them. Finally, the DELETED status means that the service provider's switch is not programmed to handle this DLCI, at least not from this channel (sent from your router). You have probably configured your router with the wrong static DLCI or **frame-relay map** statement. In other words, in cases where you encounter the DELETED status, your troubleshooting focus must turn to your local router. When the status of a PVC is reported as INACTIVE, on the other hand, you should turn your troubleshooting attention to the remote router.

# The Frame Relay Diagnostic Tools: debug

There are many **debug** command options available for Frame Relay. Example 10-7 shows the **debug frame-relay** options available with Cisco Router IOS Version 11.2 (13). This section presents a subset of the **debug** command options available for troubleshooting Frame Relay PVC connections.

**Example 10-7** *debug frame-relay* Options

```
B_StubR_FRNorm#debug frame-relay ?

  detailed  Detailed Debug: Only for Lab use
  dlsw      Frame Relay dlsw
  events    Important Frame Relay packet events
  ip        Frame Relay Internet Protocol
  l3cc      Frame Relay Layer 3 Call Control
  l3ie      Frame Relay IE parsing/construction
  lapf      Frame Relay SVC Layer 2
  llc2      Frame Relay llc2
  lmi       LMI packet exchanges with service provider
  nli       Network Layer interface
  packet    Frame Relay packets
  rsrb      Frame Relay rsrb
  verbose   Frame Relay
```

## debug serial interface

This command is not limited to troubleshooting Frame Relay only. Indeed, any serial interface can be diagnosed with this command. If a serial interface is operating properly and is exchanging keepalives with the switch that it is connected to, the debug serial interface displays the keepalives that are being sent and received. If anything goes wrong and the exchange of keepalives gets interrupted, the debug serial interface displays a message that with luck will lead you to the cause. Example 10-8 shows a sample capture of the **debug serial interface** command's output; the output pertains to a Frame Relay serial interface.

**Example 10-8** *A Sample Output of the* **debug serial interface** *Command*

```
B_StubR_FRNorm#debug serial interface
Serial network interface debugging is on
B_StubR_FRNorm#

Serial1(out): StEnq, myseq 199, yourseen 198, DTE up
Serial1(in): Status, myseq 199

Serial1(out): StEnq, myseq 200, yourseen 199, DTE up
Serial1(in): Status, myseq 200

HD(1): got an interrupt state = 0x814A
HD(1): New serial state = 0x014A
HD(1): DCD is down.

HD(1): got an interrupt state = 0x815F
HD(1): New serial state = 0x015F
HD(1): DCD is up.

Serial1(out): StEnq, myseq 201, yourseen 200, DTE up
```

*continues*

**Example 10-8** *A Sample Output of the **debug serial interface** Command (Continued)*

```
Serial1(in): Status, myseq 201

Serial1(out): StEnq, myseq 202, yourseen 201, DTE up
Serial1(in): Status, myseq 202

Serial1(out): StEnq, myseq 203, yourseen 202, DTE up
Serial1(in): Status, myseq 203
```

Depending on the type of encapsulation used and the hardware platform, the output of the **debug serial interface** command might be a little different.

This command is very useful during loopback testing as well, where your intention is to see whether a frame is released from the interface and, if it is, whether it goes to the CSU and returns to the router.

## debug frame-relay lmi

When you execute the **debug frame-relay lmi** command, you should see the status enq. (inquiry) that your router sends out every 10 seconds and the status message (type 1) that your router receives (in) from the Frame Relay switch every 10 seconds (see Example 10-9). Also, every 60 seconds the switch sends a FULL LMI message to your router (type 0), which includes a list of PVC DLCIs along with the status of each DLCI and its corresponding CIR (Committed Information Rate). The status of each DLCI reported on the LMI type 1 status message can be 0x02 (added/active), 0x00 (added/inactive), 0x08 (new/inactive), or 0x0a (new/active).

If you don't see these incoming and outgoing messages, check for LMI-type compatibility between your router and the switch. Also, make sure that keepalive has not been turned off (with the **no keepalive**, or the **no frame-relay keepalive** command) on your router, and that the interface is not looped or shut down. If your loopback testing results tell you that the connection between your router and the CSU is fine, and your link still does not come up, you should contact your service provider.

**Example 10-9** *A Sample Output of the **debug frame-relay lmi** Command*

```
B_StubR_FRNorm#debug frame-relay lmi
Frame Relay LMI debugging is on
Displaying all Frame Relay LMI data
B_StubR_FRNorm#

Serial1(in): Status, myseq 35
RT IE 1, length 1, type 1
KA IE 3, length 2, yourseq 35, myseq 35

Serial1(out): StEnq, myseq 36, yourseen 35, DTE up
datagramstart = 0x668CB4, datagramsize = 13
FR encap = 0xFCF10309
```

**Example 10-9** *A Sample Output of the **debug frame-relay lmi** Command (Continued)*

```
00 75 01 01 01 03 02 24 23

Serial1(in): Status, myseq 36
RT IE 1, length 1, type 1
KA IE 3, length 2, yourseq 36, myseq 36

Serial1(out): StEnq, myseq 37, yourseen 36, DTE up
datagramstart = 0x668CB4, datagramsize = 13
FR encap = 0xFCF10309
00 75 01 01 00 03 02 25 24

Serial1(in): Status, myseq 37
RT IE 1, length 1, type 0
KA IE 3, length 2, yourseq 37, myseq 37
PVC IE 0x7 , length 0x6 , dlci 156, status 0x2 , bw 0
PVC IE 0x7 , length 0x6 , dlci 655, status 0x2 , bw 0
PVC IE 0x7 , length 0x6 , dlci 755, status 0x2 , bw 0
```

# The debug frame-relay and the debug frame-relay events Commands

The **debug frame-relay** command is no longer a supported IOS command. However, if you use the **verbose** parameter with this command, the IOS starts Frame Relay debugging for incoming traffic (see Example 10-10). This command will then display debugging information about the packets that are being received on Frame Relay interface(s). The Cisco Documentation CD suggests that because the **debug frame-relay** command generates a lot of output, you should use it only when traffic on the Frame Relay network is less than 25 packets per second. Example 10-10 shows a sample output of the **debug frame-relay verbose** command. As you can see, each line of the output corresponds to one received packet, and each line has a corresponding DLCI number and a packet type that identifies the payload (see the Cisco Documentation CD for a listing of packet types). This command would be useful for verifying the flow of incoming traffic related to different upper layer protocols.

**Example 10-10**  *A Sample Output of the **debug frame-relay verbose** Command*

```
B_StubR_FRNorm# debug frame-relay verbose

Serial0(i): dlci 500(0x7C41), pkt type 0x800,  datagramsize 24
Serial1(i): dlci 1023(0xFCF1), pkt type 0x309, datagramsize 13
Serial0(i): dlci 500(0x0x7C41), pkt type 0x800,  datagramsize 24
Serial1(i): dlci 1023(0xFCF1), pkt type 0x309, datagramsize 13
Serial0(i): dlci 500(0x7C41), pkt type 0x800,  datagramsize 24

B_StubR_FRNorm#
```

The **debug frame-relay events** command displays debugging information about Frame Relay ARP activities (on networks that support dynamic addressing). Because the **debug frame-relay events** command does not generate much output, the Cisco Documentation CD states that you can use it at any time, even during periods of heavy traffic, without adversely affecting other users on the system. Example 10-11 displays a sample capture of the **debug frame-relay events** command's output.

**Example 10-11**    *A Sample Output of the **debug frame-relay events** Command*

```
A_StubR_FRNorm#debug frame-relay events
Frame Relay events debugging is on
A_StubR_FRNorm#

Serial1.1: FR ARP input
datagramstart = 0x666E00, datagramsize = 30
FR encap = 0x24B10300
80 00 00 00 08 06 00 0F 08 00 02 04 00 08 00 00
C0 32 12 06 24 C1 00 00 00 00

Serial1.1: FR ARP input
datagramstart = 0x6659D8, datagramsize = 46
FR encap = 0x24B10300
80 00 00 00 08 06 00 0F 81 37 02 0A 00 08 00 00
00 00 50 00 00 E0 B0 64 4C D3 24 C1 00 00 00 00
00 00 00 00 00 00 3B 9F C0 C0
```

**NOTE**    The CIT course's student training book does not acknowledge that **debug frame-relay** is not a supported command anymore. Unfortunately, the text also confuses the **debug frame-relay events** command with the **debug frame-relay** command.

# debug frame-relay packet

The **debug frame-relay packet** command displays the packets that have been sent (out) on a Frame Relay interface (see Example 10-12). This command helps you to analyze the packets that have been sent on a Frame Relay interface. Because the **debug frame-relay packet** command generates large amount of output, the Cisco Documentation CD suggests that you use it only when traffic on the Frame Relay network is less than 25 packets per second.

**Example 10-12**    *A Sample Output of the **debug frame-relay packet** Command*

```
B_StubR_FRNorm#debug frame-relay packet
Frame Relay packet debugging is on
B_StubR_FRNorm#

Serial1.4: broadcast search
Serial1.4(o): dlci 156(0x24C1), pkt type 0x8137(NOVELL),
    datagramsize 148 broadcast dequeue
```

**Example 10-12**  *A Sample Output of the **debug frame-relay packet** Command (Continued)*

```
Serial1.4(o):Pkt sent on dlci 156(0x24C1), pkt type 0x8137(NOVELL),
    datagramsize 148
Serial1.4: broadcast search
Serial1.4(o): dlci 156(0x24C1), pkt type 0x8137(NOVELL),
    datagramsize 356 broadcast dequeue
Serial1.4(o):Pkt sent on dlci 156(0x24C1), pkt type 0x8137(NOVELL),
    datagramsize 356

Serial1.1: broadcast search
Serial1.1(o): dlci 755(0xBC31), pkt type 0x800(IP), datagramsize 120

Serial1.2: broadcast search
Serial1.2(o): dlci 655(0xA0F1), pkt type 0x800(IP), datagramsize 120

Serial1.4: broadcast search
Serial1.4(o): dlci 156(0x24C1), pkt type 0x800(IP),
    datagramsize 176 broadcast dequeue
```

In Example 10-12 you should notice that the router sends four NOVELL packets of
different sizes out of serial 1.4 to DLCI number 156. Following the NOVELL packets, the
router then sends three IP packets of different sizes to DLCI numbers 755, 655, and 156 out
serial 1.1, serial 1.2, and serial 1.4 subinterfaces. This debug command is useful for
investigating whether the local router sends packets of different kinds to the different
destination points (DLCIs). Hence this debug command is considered an end-to-end Frame
Relay diagnostic tool.

**NOTE**    The keyword **packet** is not a short form for "packets." In other words, if you type **debug
frame-relay packets** instead of **debug frame-relay packet**, you will receive an error
message.

# Frame Relay Problem Isolation

To check/diagnose a Frame Relay connection, you must perform the following tests (using
the troubleshooting commands you have learned) in sequence:

- Check the status of your router's (Frame Relay) serial interface (for example, Serial 1
  interface) using the **show interface serial** *n* command. The output must show:

  ```
  Serial1 is up, line protocol is up
  ```

  If serial 1 is down, you must check and correct the connection between your
  router's serial interface and the CSU. If the serial interface is up and the line
  protocol is down, either the local loop between the CSU and the service

provider's switch is bad, the service provider's switch is not functioning, or there is an LMI-type mismatch between your router and the service provider's switch.

On the output of the **show interface serial 1** command, check to make sure that encapsulation is stated as Frame Relay and you have configured the correct LMI type. Moreover, make sure that your interface is not looped and is sending keepalives.

- Using the **show frame-relay pvc** command, check the status of the DLCIs. If a DLCI is shown as active, you have an end-to-end Frame Relay (Layer 2) connectivity. Of course, this does not necessarily mean that your router is fully configured to deliver upper layer protocols' packets via this circuit. However, at this stage you want to make sure that the Layer 2 connection is properly in place. If the status of a DLCI is reported as inactive, then the troubleshooting approach for this stage must be focused at the other end of the connection. If a DLCI status is reported as deleted, the DLCI number configured on your router is not being acknowledged by the switch and you must revisit your configuration and correct it. Some people do not fully appreciate the concept of Local DLCI numbers and configure a local router with a DLCI number that must indeed be used at the other end of the connection.

- You must now make sure that the upper layer protocols' addresses can be and are properly mapped to the appropriate DLCI numbers. The command that would help you do that is **show frame-relay map**. Depending on whether you are using Frame Relay subinterfaces or not, have inverse-arp turned off or not, and have point-to-point or multipoint connections, the output of the **show frame-relay map** command varies. The following is a list of possible entries from the output of the **show frame-relay map** command:

```
Serial0 (up): ip 192.50.18.37 dlci 956(0x3BC,0xECC0), dynamic,
              broadcast,, status defined, active
Serial1.4 (up): ip 192.50.18.5 dlci 156(0x9C,0x24C0), static,
              Broadcast, CISCO, status defined, active
Serial1.1 (up): point-to-point dlci, dlci 755(0x2F3,0xBC30),
broadcast status defined, active
```

The first line shows that on the serial 0 interface, Frame Relay inverse-arp has DLCI 956 mapped to IP address 192.50.18.37 dynamically and that this connection's status is active.

The second line shows that on the serial 1.4 subinterface (since it is not point-to-point, it is multipoint), DLCI 156 is statically (using a **frame-relay map** statement) mapped to IP address 192.50.18.5 and that this connection's status is active as well.

The third line show that on the serial 1.3 subinterface (point-to-point), DLCI 755 is configured (using the **frame-relay interface-dlci** command) and that this connection's status is also active. You must also make sure that this interface's IP address has been correctly configured, using the **show ip interface serial 1.3** command.

Figure 10-1 shows the commands that are used for Frame Relay troubleshooting. This figure also illustrates which command is most appropriate for testing a specific section of the Frame Relay connection. You are advised to study this figure thoroughly.

**Figure 10-1**  *Review of Frame Relay Troubleshooting Commands*

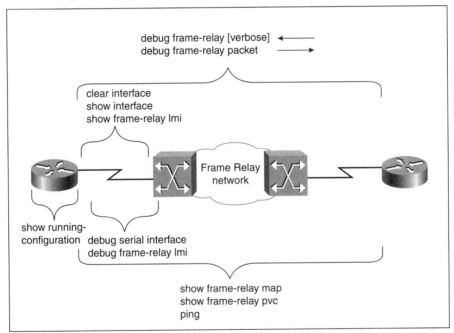

# Foundation Summary

The Foundation Summary is a collection of quick reference information that provides a convenient review of many key concepts in this chapter. For those of you who already feel comfortable with the topics in this chapter, this summary helps you recall a few details. For those of you who just read this chapter, this review should help solidify some key facts. For any of you doing your final prep before the exam, these tables and figures are a convenient way to review the day before the exam.

**Frame Relay Troubleshooting checklist:**

- Make sure that the router is properly connected to the CSU and that the CSU is operational and is receiving CD on the line that connects it to the service provider's switch.

- Make sure that the serial interface is not shut down, is not looped, and sends keepalives.

- Make sure that you have configured the serial interface with the correct encapsulation.

- Make sure that the LMI type configured on your router's serial interface matches the LMI type of the service provider's switch to which your router is connected.

- Make sure that you have configured the serial interface with the appropriate upper layer address(es).

- If you want to or have to use the **frame-relay map** statement, make sure that the local DLCI number is mapped to the appropriate destination upper layer (IP) address.

- If you use point-to-point subinterface(s), make sure they are configured with the correct local DLCI number (using the **frame-relay interface-dlci** command).

**Table 10-2**  *Summary of Basic Frame Relay Configuration Commands*

| Action | Configuration Mode | Command |
|---|---|---|
| Specify Frame Relay encapsulation<br><br>Default frame type is **cisco**<br><br>Option: Specify ietf frame format | Interface configuration mode | **encapsulation frame-relay [ietf]** |
| Specify Layer 3 address (for example, the IP and IPX address) | Interface configuration mode | **ip address 192.50.18.6 255.255.255.0**<br><br>**ipx network 5000** |
| Turn off Frame Relay inverse arp | Interface configuration mode | **no frame-relay inverse-arp** |

**Table 10-2**  *Summary of Basic Frame Relay Configuration Commands (Continued)*

| Action | Configuration Mode | Command |
|---|---|---|
| Specify the DCLI to Layer 3 address mapping (for example, DLCI to destination IP Address mapping)<br><br>This command is one of the two options on a multipoint subinterface. The other option is the **interface-dlci** command.<br><br>Use the **broadcast** option if you want Frame Relay to handle the upper layer broadcasts—for example, to forward them to the same DLCI. | Interface configuration mode<br><br>(a subinterface command also) | **frame-relay map ip 192.50.18.5 156 [ietf] [broadcast]** |
| Turn keepalive on<br><br>(By default it is.) | Interface configuration mode | **keepalive**<br><br>(This is the physical interface keepalive. Frame Relay–specific keepalives, such as the LMI, are controlled with the **frame-relay keepalive** command.) |
| Specify Frame Relay LMI type<br><br>(As of IOS ver 11.2, LMI type is autosensed.) | Interface configuration mode | **frame-relay lmi-type [cisco \| ansi \| q933a]** |
| Specify the local DLCI number | Interface configuration mode | **frame-relay local-dlci 156** |
| Specify the local DLCI number<br><br>(This command is required on point-to-point subinterfaces and is one of the two options on a multipoint subinterface.) | Subinterface configuration mode | **frame-relay interface-dlci 156** |
| Create a point-to-point subinterface | Global configuration mode | **interface serial 1.1 point-to-point** |
| Create a multipoint subinterface | Global configuration mode | **interface serial 1.1 multipoint** |

*continues*

**Table 10-2**    *Summary of Basic Frame Relay Configuration Commands (Continued)*

| Action | Configuration Mode | Command |
|---|---|---|
| Set interface into Loopback state | Interface configuration mode | **loopback** |
| Specify bandwidth of the interface (usually set to the value of CIR) | Interface configuration mode | **bandwidth 64** |

**Table 10-3**    *Summary of Basic Frame Relay **show** Commands*

| Command | Purpose/Use |
|---|---|
| **show interface serial 1** | To see the status of the interface and the line protocol, encapsulation type, LMI type, whether keepalives are being sent, whether the interface is shut down or looped. Also to see packet and error statistics for that interface. |
| **show frame-relay pvc** | To see lists of all the PVCs that the router is aware of, on all of its Frame Relay interfaces (and subinterfaces) along with their status, creation time, last status change time, and statistics regarding the sent/received packets/bytes and the congestion notification flags. |
| **show frame-relay map** | To see the following information about each of the Frame Relay interfaces: <br><br>The status of the interface (up, down, administratively down). <br><br>The destination Layer 3 address (in the case of a point-to-point connection, the destination is identified with the phrase **point-to-point dlci**). <br><br>The DLCI number. <br><br>Whether the mapping is static or dynamic. <br><br>Whether broadcast is supported. <br><br>The encapsulation type (CISCO or IETF). <br><br>Whether the status of the connection (PVC) is defined or deleted. A connection whose status is defined may be active or inactive. |
| **show frame-relay lmi** | To see the following information for each Frame Relay interface: <br><br>The first line indicates the role of the router's serial interface (DTE/UNI or NNI) and the LMI type it is configured for. The following lines provide error statistics on the LMI. |

**Table 10-4**  *Summary of Basic Frame Relay **debug** Commands*

| Command | Description |
|---|---|
| **debug serial interface** | If a serial interface is operating properly and is exchanging keepalives with the switch that it is connected to, **debug serial interface** displays the keepalives that are being sent and received. If anything goes wrong and the exchange of keepalives gets interrupted, **debug serial interface** displays a message that usually lead you to the cause. |
| **debug frame-relay lmi** | To see the status enq. (inquiry) that your router sends out every 10 seconds and the status message (type 1) that your router receives (in) from the Frame Relay switch every 10 seconds. Also, every 60 seconds the switch sends a FULL LMI message to your router (type 1), which includes a list of PVC DLCIs along with the status of each DLCI and its corresponding CIR. |
| **debug frame-relay [verbose]** | The **debug frame-relay** command is not a supported IOS command any more, but if you use the **verbose** parameter along with it, the IOS informs you that Frame Relay debugging has been turned on. You will then see debugging information about the packets that are being received on Frame Relay interfaces. |
| **debug frame-relay events** | To see debugging information about Frame Relay ARP activities (on networks that support dynamic addressing). |
| **debug frame-relay packet** | To see and analyze the packets that are sent out of the Frame Relay interface(s). |

# Q&A

The answers to the following questions can be found in Appendix A. Some of the questions in this section are repeated from the "Do I Know ThisAlready" Quiz so that you can gauge the advancement of your knowledge of this subject matter.

1 To which layer of the OSI model does the Frame Relay technology correspond?

_____

_____

_____

2 Is Frame Relay a connectionless or a connection-oriented service?

_____

_____

_____

3 Are most of the current Frame Relay implementations PVC based or are they SVC based?

_____

_____

_____

4 What is the default frame type for the serial interfaces of Cisco routers that have been configured with the **encapsulation frame-relay** command?

_____

_____

_____

5 What are the two frame types supported on the Frame Relay (serial) interfaces of a Cisco router?

_____

_____

_____

**6** Does the frame type have to be consistent across a Frame Relay connection?

_____

_____

_____

**7** Which command would configure a serial interface with the Frame Relay encapsulation and the Cisco frame type?

_____

_____

_____

**8** Can the LMI type be autosensed by any of the IOS releases?

_____

_____

_____

**9** What are the LMI types supported by Cisco IOS?

_____

_____

_____

**10** What command would configure a Cisco router's serial interface for the q933a LMI type?

_____

_____

_____

**11** Which command completely turns off LMI on a Cisco router's serial interface?

_____

_____

_____

**12** Does the LMI type have to be identical on both ends of a Frame Relay connection?

_____

_____

_____

**13** What is the purpose of LMI?

_____

_____

_____

**14** What is the process that allows routers that are at the two ends of a Frame Relay circuit to learn each other's upper layer address(es) and associate them with the appropriate DLCI number?

_____

_____

_____

**15** What is the default frequency at which a router sends Frame Relay inverse-arp packets?

_____

_____

_____

**16** What command would hard-code the DLCI number 55 on a Frame Relay subinterface?

_____

_____

_____

**17** What command would map the destination IP address 192.50.18.5 to DLCI number 156 on a Frame Relay interface or a multipoint subinterface and enable broadcasting on that DLCI?

_____

_____

_____

**18** What is the size of the IETF Frame Relay frame header? And what is the purpose of the FECN and BECN bits/fields?

_____

_____

_____

19  Using which **show** command can you discover the status of a serial interface (for example, s 1) configured for a Frame Relay connection?

_____

_____

_____

20  Using which **show** command can you check the encapsulation and the LMI type configured on interface serial 1?

_____

_____

_____

21  Would the **show interface serial 1** command's output display whether this interface is sending keepalives?

_____

_____

_____

22  What are the main pieces of information that you can obtain from the output of the **show interface serial *n*** command?

_____

_____

_____

23  If the Frame Relay LMI type entered for the serial 1 interface of a Cisco router is Q933a, what LMI type is reported for that interface on the output of the **show interface serial 1** command?

_____

_____

_____

24  If the LMI type of Cisco is used on a Cisco router's serial interface, which DLCI number is used on that interface for LMI purposes?

_____

_____

_____

**25** If the LMI type of ANSI is used on a Cisco router's serial interface, which DLCI number is used on that interface for LMI purposes?

_____

_____

_____

**26** Provide at least two reasons for an interface reset to occur.

_____

_____

_____

**27** What does the number of transitions reported on the output of the **show interface serial n** command signify? If this number is too large for your network's baseline, where should you turn your attention?

_____

_____

_____

**28** Give at least two reasons for a Frame Relay serial interface being reported as up and its line protocol reported as down.

_____

_____

_____

**29** Discuss the reasons for a serial interface being reported as down.

_____

_____

_____

**30** What is loopback testing?

_____

_____

_____

**31**  Which command displays Local Management Interface statistics about a Cisco router's Frame Relay interface(s)?

_____

_____

_____

**32**  If the number of status messages timed out and the number of status inquiry messages sent grow every time you enter the **show frame-relay** command, what could be the reason?

_____

_____

_____

**33**  Which Frame Relay **show** command lists all of the PVCs that the router is aware of on all of its Frame Relay interfaces (and subinterfaces) along with their status, creation time, last status change time, and statistics regarding the sent/received packets/bytes and the congestion notification flags?

_____

_____

_____

**34**  Provide at least two pieces of information given for each interface on the output of the **show frame-relay map** command.

_____

_____

_____

**35**  How would you interpret a situation in which a DLCI is shown in the output of the **show frame-relay pvc** statement (and is reported as active), but it does not appear in the output of the **show frame-relay map** statement?

_____

_____

_____

**36** Which generic **debug** command displays real-time information about the activities (keepalives) and status of serial interfaces?

_____

_____

_____

**37** How often does a router send the LMI enq. message and receive a normal LMI status? How often does the router receive the FULL LMI message?

_____

_____

_____

**38** Which Frame Relay troubleshooting **debug** command displays the LMI messages that are exchanged between your router and the Frame Relay switch?

_____

_____

_____

**39** If you enter the **debug frame-relay lmi** command and you do not see a proper flow/ exchange of LMI messages between your router and the Frame Relay switch (or you see no LMI at all), assuming that the interface is up, what could be wrong?

_____

_____

_____

**40** Which command displays debugging information about the packets that are being received on Frame Relay interface(s)?

_____

_____

_____

**41** Which Cisco router IOS command displays debugging information about Frame Relay ARP activities?

_____

_____

_____

**42**  Which Frame Relay **debug** command displays the packets that have been sent (out) on Frame Relay interface(s)?

_____

_____

_____

**You need to refer to the following figure to answer the remaining questions (on Frame Relay troubleshooting commands):**

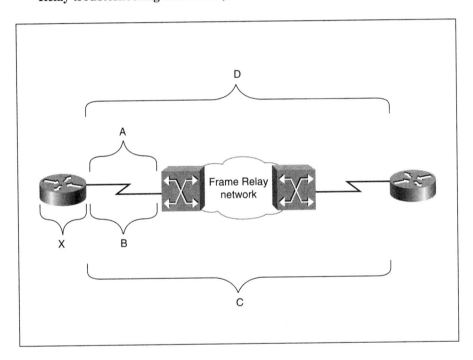

**43**  Provide the two most appropriate **show** commands to test the area marked by the letter A.

_____

_____

_____

**44** Provide the two most appropriate **debug** commands to test the area marked by the letter B.

_____

_____

_____

**45** Provide the two most appropriate **show** commands to test the area marked by the letter C.

_____

_____

_____

**46** Provide the two most appropriate **debug** commands to test the area marked by the letter D.

_____

_____

_____

This chapter covers the following topics that you will need to master to pass the CCNP Support exam:

| Objective | Description |
|-----------|-------------|
| 1 | ISDN components and reference points. |
| 2 | ISDN BRI channels. |
| 3 | ISDN BRI Layer 1 specifications and activation. |
| 4 | ISDN BRI Layer 1 troubleshooting commands. |
| 5 | ISDN Layer 2 initialization. |
| 6 | Troubleshooting ISDN Layer 2. |
| 7 | Troubleshooting DDR for triggering an ISDN call. |
| 8 | ISDN Layer 3 specifications. |
| 9 | ISDN switch types. |
| 10 | ISDN SPID numbers. |
| 11 | ISDN call screening. |
| 12 | PPP over B channels. |
| 13 | PPP negotiation, authentication, and multilink. |

# Diagnosing and Correcting ISDN BRI Problems

ISDN is a circuit-switched wide-area service that provides end-to-end digital connection between remote devices. Similarly to other WAN services, the ISDN service is used to provide connectivity between remote offices through a service provider's network. The physical devices and media that provide this complete connectivity fall into one of three categories: customer premises equipment (CPE), local access loops, and service provider networks. The communication between these devices is a formalized and standardized process. Our focus will be on customer premises equipment and the local access loop. It is important to know the different types of equipment that may be involved, the ISDN reference points, and, most importantly, how these devices can be connected and configured to get all three layers of ISDN up and running. Once all layers of ISDN layers are functional, an end-to-end circuit is built on demand. An end-to-end ISDN circuit is made of at least one B channel, which by nature is a point-to-point physical link. Data-link and upper layer protocols can then be configured at both ends of the connection to transmit data over the B channel(s).

This chapter provides a detailed coverage of how initialization, working condition, and configuration of each component and functional layer of an ISDN connection can be examined. The results of various misconfigurations are discussed to help you learn to more effectively troubleshoot ISDN connections. A comprehensive set of related IOS **show** and **debug** commands are presented along with their sample output to help you fully appreciate the purpose of each command.

## "Do I Know This Already?" Quiz

If you wish to evaluate your knowledge of the contents of this chapter before you get started, answer the following questions. The answers are provided in Appendix A, "Answers to Quiz Questions." If you are having difficulty providing correct answers, you should thoroughly review the entire chapter. If all or most of your answers are correct, you might want to skim this chapter for only those subjects you need to review. You can also use the "Foundation Summary" section to quickly review topics. Once you have completed the chapter, you should reevaluate yourself with the questions in the "Q&A" section at the end.

Finally, use the companion CD-ROM to evaluate your knowledge of the topics and see if you need a review.

**1** How are TE1 and TE2 different?

_____

_____

_____

**2** What kind of wiring is used between the TE and the network termination (NT) devices?

_____

_____

_____

**3** In North America, is NT1 considered part of CPE or is it considered part of the service provider's equipment?

_____

_____

_____

**4** What is the difference between ISDN BRI B channels and the ISDN D channel?

_____

_____

_____

**5** Which two ISDN **show** commands allow you to discover the status of ISDN Layer 1?

_____

_____

_____

**6** Which **show** command displays the ISDN switch type you have configured your router for?

_____

_____

_____

**7** Which **debug** command allows you to observe the activation process of ISDN BRI Layer 1?

_____

_____

_____

**8** Which **show** command allows you to discover the true state of the ISDN BRI Layer 2?

_____

_____

_____

**9** Which **show** command displays information about all BRI and Dialer interfaces (if there are any) of a router?

_____

_____

_____

**10** If you are troubleshooting an ISDN call, which **debug** command allows you to observe the cause of the call (dialing cause), the interface used for the call, and the string (number) that was used to make the call?

_____

_____

_____

**11** Which **debug** command provides detail information on ISDN Layer 3 activities such as call setup?

_____

_____

_____

**12** Provide one **show** and one **debug** command that are useful for ISDN Service Profile Identifier (SPID) troubleshooting.

_____

_____

_____

**13** Which **debug** command allows you to observe PPP's LCP, authentication, and NCP process?

_____

_____

_____

**14** Which **debug** command displays information on the ppp authentication process?

_____

_____

_____

**15** Which command displays the status of both of the B channels of the BRI0 interface of a Cisco router?

_____

_____

_____

**16** Which command allows you to examine the status of your Cisco router's active Multilink PPP sessions?

_____

_____

_____

# Foundation Topics

## ISDN Components and Reference Points

When ISDN is the choice of wide-area connection, the customer equipment may include terminal equipment (TE) (types 1 and 2), terminal adapters (TAs), and network termination (NT) equipment (types 1 and 2). A common two-wire facility forms the local access loop for ISDN. The line termination (LT) and exchange termination (ET) equipment are located at the edge of the service provider's network (see Figure 11-1).

**Figure 11-1**  *ISDN Components and Reference Points*

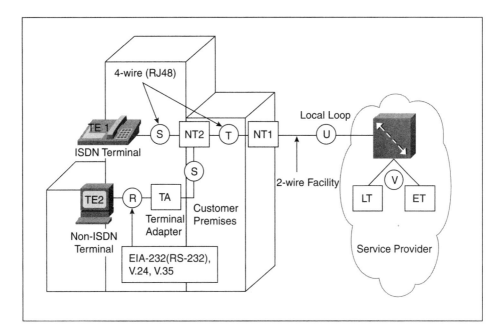

The ISDN (TE) is classified into two types: TE2 and TE1. TE2 devices are non-ISDN terminals such as a standard telephone, a personal computer, or a router with no ISDN interface. TE1s are ISDN devices such as an ISDN telephone, or a router with a BRI interface. A TE2 device needs (to be connected to) an ISDN TA to get connected to an ISDN network. The TA may be an external device or a board that can be plugged into the TE2. If the TA is an external device, the TE2 connects to it with a standard serial cable/connection such as EIA/TIA-232-C (formerly RS-232-C), V.24, or V.35.

The TE1 (and TA) connects to NT1 using a four-wire cable (RJ48). You can also use a straight-through RJ45 cable for this purpose, knowing that only the inner four wires out of the eight wires of the RJ45 cable will be used. ISDN standards allow multiple terminals

(TE1s and TAs) to share an NT1 device (technically the S/T bus), one at a time, through a contention control mechanism provided by the NT2 device. The NT2 device naturally appears before the NT1 device. NT2 is typically found in digital private branch exchanges (PBXs). There are NT1/NT2 boxes also, which provide the functionality of both an NT1 and an NT2 device. The multiple TE1s (and/or TAs) connect to NT2 using a four-wire facility, and the NT2 device connects to the NT1 device with a four-wire cable as well. The NT1 device, however, connects to the LT equipment in the carrier network using the conventional two-wire (local loop) facility. In North America, it is the customer's responsibility to provide or pay for the NT1 device, while in Europe NT1 falls in the service provider's realm of responsibility.

As a result, the routers with ISDN BRI interface(s) that are produced for the North American market usually have the NT1 functionality built-in the BRI interface, whereas the routers produced for the European market don't. When the NT1 functionality is built into the BRI interface, this interface has a U label. On the other hand, if the NT1 functionality is not built into the interface, the interface has the S/T label. Table 11-1 provides four examples of 800 series Cisco routers, two of which (801 and 802) target the European market and the other two (803 and 804) target the North American market.

**Table 11-1**   *Examples of 800 Series Routers with S/T and U BRI Interfaces*

| Model | BRI Interface | Ethernet Interface | Comment |
|-------|---------------|--------------------|---------|
| 801 | S/T | Single RJ45 10BaseT port | Target Europe |
| 802 | S/T | 4 port internal 10BaseT hub | Target Europe |
| 803 | U | Single RJ45 10BaseT port | Target North America |
| 804 | U | 4 port internal 10BaseT hub | Target North America |

ISDN reference points define logical interfaces between functional groupings such as TEs and NTs. Refer to Table 11-2 for a list of ISDN reference points. Figure 11-1 also shows where the reference points fit on the ISDN network.

**Table 11-2**   *ISDN Reference Points*

| Reference Point | Place |
|-----------------|-------|
| R | Between terminal equipment type 2 (TE2) and terminal adapter (TA). |
| S | Between terminal equipment type 1 (TE1) or terminal adapter (TA) and the network termination type 2 (NT2) device. |
| T | Between the network termination type 2 (NT2) and the network termination type 1 (NT1) device. |
| U | Between the network termination type 1 (NT1) and the service provider's (carrier's) local termination (LT) device. |
| V | Between the service provider's (carrier's) local termination (LT) device and their exchange termination (ET) device. |

A Cisco router may have no BRI interfaces, in which case you will have to connect its serial interface to an ISDN TA. If the router has a BRI interface with the S/T label on it, it means that you must connect the BRI interface to an external NT (NT2, NT2/NT1, or NT1) device. If the BRI interface of a router has NT1 built in, then the interface is marked with the U label. If the BRI interface of a router has the NT1 built in, it can then be directly connected to the service provider's switch (using the two-wire facility). If you connect a BRI interface that has an NT1 built in (one that has the U label) to an external NT1 device, the router's BRI interface and/or the external NT1 box may get damaged severely.

# BRI Channels

The ISDN BRI interface offers two B channels (B1 and B2) and a D channel (2B+D). The B channels are 64 kbps and the D channel is 16 kbps (see Figure 11-2). The D channel is used for carrying control and signaling information. If the service provider allows it, the D channel may also carry user data. The B channels are meant to carry user data.

**Figure 11-2** *ISDN BRI Channels and the ISDN Layer 1 Frame*

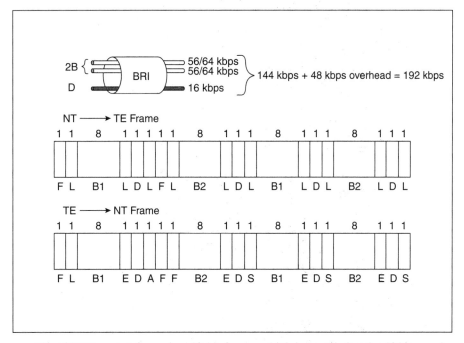

The ISDN Layer 1 frame is a 48-bit frame, which is sampled at the 4000-samples-per-second rate, providing a 192-kbps pipe. However, since 12 bits out of the 48 are used for purposes such as DC line balancing, synchronization, activation, and collision avoidance, 48 kbps of the 192 kbps is considered to be the BRI's overhead bandwidth. 16 B1 bits, 16

B2 bits, and 4 D bits occupy the other 36 bits of the 48-bit ISDN Layer 1 frame (see Figure 11-2). All of the communication between the router and the service provider's ISDN switch happens over the D channel. The protocol used for this purpose is called Link Access Procedure on the D channel (LAPD). The specifications for ISDN numbering plan, concepts, devices, wiring, connectors, interfaces, and protocols are all provided by the ITU-T (formerly CCITT) technical specification documents (E, I, and Q series). For instance, the Q.921 specification is about ISDN Layer 2, and Q.931 provides the detail of the ISDN signaling over the D channel.

# ISDN BRI Layer 1

To set up and activate ISDN Layer 1, you need to have the proper equipment, cables, and connectors in place. As mentioned earlier, the cable used between the S/T interface and the NT1 device is a four-wire (straight) cable (RJ48). You may also use a straight RJ45 cable for this purpose, knowing that only wires 3, 4, 5, and 6 will be used. The connector used for this purpose is an RJ45 connector. The mechanical specifications for the ISDN connector are presented by ISO 8877 standard. The line coding specification used by ISDN is Alternate Mark Inversion (AMI).

The very first and basic step in the initialization of an ISDN communication is activation of Layer 1. Assuming that the physical layer is in place—in other words, your devices, cables, and connectors are good and properly connected—the stage is set for Layer 1 activation. If your router's BRI is administratively shut down, type the IOS **no shutdown** command at the interface configuration mode. Through usage of the synchronization bits (these are some of the 12 overhead bits on the ISDN Layer 1 frame that was mentioned earlier), the router (TE1) and the NT1 will synchronize and the NT1 will send a frame with the **A** bit set to 1, to the router. At this point, Layer 1 ISDN is reported as active by your router. You may check the status of ISDN Layer 1 using two commands:

```
show controller bri bri-number
show isdn status
```

Example 11-1 shows sample outputs of these commands: in both examples, the ISDN Layer 1 is reported as active. When troubleshooting ISDN BRI connections, after you ensure that the BRI interface under investigation is not shut down and that proper cabling is in place, the very first fact you must gather is the status of ISDN Layer 1. Please notice (Example 11-1) and remember that the first line of the **show ISDN status** command displays the ISDN switch type you have configured the router for. The status of ISDN Layer 2 and Layer 3 are also reported by the **show ISDN status** command. Hence, engineers and support personnel find this command very convenient and informative.

**Example 11-1** *Checking the Status of ISDN Layer 1*

```
B_BackR#show controller bri 0
BRI slot 1 unit 0 subunit 0
Layer 1 is ACTIVATED. (ISDN L1 State F7)
Master clock for slot 1 is bri subunit 0.
```

**Example 11-1** *Checking the Status of ISDN Layer 1 (Continued)*

```
Total chip configuration successes: 94, failures: 0, timeouts: 0
D Channel Information:


B_BackR#show isdn status
The current ISDN Switchtype = basic-5ess
ISDN BRI0 interface
    Layer 1 Status:
        ACTIVE
    Layer 2 Status:
        TEI = 71, Ces = 1, SAPI = 0, State = MULTIPLE_FRAME_ESTABLISHED
    Layer 3 Status:
        1 Active Layer 3 Call(s)
    Activated dsl 0 CCBs = 1
        CCB:callid=0x8001, sapi=0x0, ces=0x1, B-chan=1
B_BackR#
```

The **debug bri-interface** command allows you to observe the process of activation of the BRI interface (physical). With all the physical devices, cables, and connectors in place and plugged in, if you enter this **debug** command and see the output on the console after entering the **no shutdown** command on the BRI0 interface of your router, the results will look similar to those displayed by Example 11-2. During initialization, two timers are used: Power Up (PUP) timer and the T3 timer. The T3 timer is generally a one- to two-second interval during which the BRI interface must become active.

**Example 11-2** *Sample Output of the **debug bri-interface** Command*

```
B_BackR#debug bri-interface
Basic Rate network interface debugging is on

B_BackR#conf t
Enter configuration commands, one per line.  End with CNTL/Z.
B_BackR(config)#int bri 0
B_BackR(config-if)#no shut
B_BackR(config-if)#^Z
B_BackR#
BRI: write_sid: wrote 1 for subunit 0, slot 1.
...
BRI: write_sid: wrote 20 for subunit 0, slot 1.
BRI: Starting Power Up timer for unit = 0.
BRI: write_sid: wrote FF for subunit 0, slot 1.
BRI: write_sid: wrote 3 for subunit 0, slot 1.
BRI: Starting T3 timer for unit = 0.
BRI: Activation Pending for unit = 0, current state is F6.
BRI: write_sid: wrote FF for subunit 0, slot 1.
BRI: Activation for unit = 0, current state is F7.

22:58:56: %LINK-3-UPDOWN: Interface BRI0, changed state to up
```

*continues*

**Example 11-2** *Sample Output of the **debug bri-interface** Command (Continued)*

```
22:58:56: %SYS-5-CONFIG_I: Configured from console by console

22:58:58: %ISDN-6-LAYER2UP: Layer 2 for Interface BR0, TEI 103 changed to up
```

As you can see, when the T3 timer starts, the status of the BRI interface is reported as F6 State (Pending), and shortly after, the state is reported as F7 (Active). This is good news! The next example output was captured as follows: with the cable unplugged from the BRI0 interface of the router and with the **debug bri-interface** still on, the **no shutdown** command was entered on the BRI0 interface (see Example 11-3).

**Example 11-3** *Output of the **debug bri-interface** Command with the Cable Unplugged from the BRI0 Interface*

```
B_BackR#debug bri-interface
Basic Rate network interface debugging is on
B_BackR#conf t
Enter configuration commands, one per line.  End with CNTL/Z.
B_BackR(config)#int bri0
B_BackR(config-if)#no shut
B_BackR(config-if)#^Z
B_BackR#
BRI: write_sid: wrote 1 for subunit 0, slot 1.
...
BRI: write_sid: wrote 20 for subunit 0, slot 1.
BRI: Starting Power Up timer for unit = 0.
BRI: write_sid: wrote 3 for subunit 0, slot 1.
BRI: Starting T3 timer after expiry of Power Up timeout forunit = 0,
     current state is F4.
23:59:11: %LINK-3-UPDOWN: Interface BRI0, changed state to up
BRI: write_sid: wrote 92 for subunit 0, slot 1.
BRI: write_sid: wrote 93 for subunit 0, slot 1.
BRI: T3 timer expired for unit = 0, current state is F2.
BRI: write_sid: wrote 1 for subunit 0, slot 1.
BRI: write_sid: wrote 0 for subunit 0, slot 1.
BRI: Forced interrupt for subunit 0, slot 1 is F .
BRI: write_sid: wrote FF for subunit 0, slot 1.
BRI: write_sid: wrote 1 for subunit 0, slot 1.
BRI: write_sid: wrote 0 for subunit 0, slot 1.
BRI: Deactivation for unit = 0, current state is F2.
```

Notice that this time, the PUP timer has expired and after that the T3 timer started with the state reported as F4 (PUP expired, T3 started). The logging message indicates that the BRI0 has changed state to UP. As discussed later in this chapter, the state of the BRI interface is spoofed as UP for the sake of the routing table. As you can see, the T3 timer expires a little later and the state is then reported as F2 (T3 expired, state is DEACTIVATED). In a situation like this, the status of Layer 1 is reported as DEACTIVATED on the output of the **show ISDN status** command.

# ISDN Layer 2

ISDN Layer 2 is concerned with the communication between the TE and the ISDN switch over the D channel. The LAPD protocol is used for this purpose. LAPD delivers control and signaling information between the TE (the router, for instance) and the ISDN switch. The LAPD protocol is formally specified in ITU-T Q.920 and ITU-T Q.921.

The **show isdn status** command can be used to discover the status of ISDN Layer 2. If ISDN Layer 2 is reported as NOT Activated, you must first find out if ISDN Layer 1 is ACTIVE or DEACTIVATED (see Example 11-4). If ISDN Layer 1 is not active, you should naturally focus on bringing Layer 1 up first. As stated earlier, Layer 1 will not come up if the physical connectivity is not in place, any of the relevant physical components are faulty, or if the BRI interface is shutdown (or not up for any reason, including faulty interface hardware).

**Example 11-4** *Sample Output of the* **show isdn status** *Command*

```
B_BackR#show isdn status

The current ISDN Switchtype = basic-5ess

ISDN BRI0 interface

    Layer 1 Status:
        DEACTIVATED

    Layer 2 Status:
        Layer 2 NOT Activated

    Layer 3 Status:
        0 Active Layer 3 Call(s)

    Activated dsl 0 CCBs = 0

    Total Allocated ISDN CCBs = 0

B_BackR#
```

Another command that is useful at this stage is the **show interface BRI** *number* command. If the BRI interface under investigation (say, BRI0) is not shut down, the first line of the output should say: BRI0 is up, line protocol is up (spoofing). Even though the BRI interface being reported as up and the line protocol being reported as up (spoofing) is necessary, it is not a sufficient condition for you to assume Layer 1 to be intact and operational. For instance, if you disconnect the cable from the BRI0 interface of your router and enter the **show interfaces bri 0** command, you will find out that even though the BRI0 interface is not connected to anything, it is still reported as up, line protocol up (spoofing) (see Example 11-5).

I suggest that you use the **show interfaces bri** *number* command to make sure that the interface is not shutdown and more importantly, to read the throughput, error statistics and carrier transitions accounting information that it provides. The real status of Layer 2 is reported by the **show isdn status** command. See the second part of Example 11-5 for the output of the **show isdn status** that you would see if you entered the command immediately after the **show interfaces bri 0** command, whose output is shown on the top portion of Example 11-5.

**Example 11-5** *Checking ISDN Layer 2's Status*

```
B_BackR#show interfaces bri 0
BRI0 is up, line protocol is up (spoofing)
  Hardware is BRI
  Internet address is 172.61.10.22/24
  MTU 1500 bytes, BW 64 Kbit, DLY 20000 usec, rely 255/255, load 1/255
  Encapsulation PPP, loopback not set
  Last input 00:22:23, output 00:22:23, output hang never
  Last clearing of "show interface" counters never
  Input queue: 0/75/0 (size/max/drops); Total output drops: 0
  Queueing strategy: weighted fair
  Output queue: 0/1000/64/0 (size/max total/threshold/drops)
     Conversations  0/1/256 (active/max active/max total)
     Reserved Conversations 0/0 (allocated/max allocated)
  5 minute input rate 0 bits/sec, 0 packets/sec
  5 minute output rate 0 bits/sec, 0 packets/sec
     58 packets input, 265 bytes, 0 no buffer
     Received 9 broadcasts, 0 runts, 0 giants, 0 throttles
     0 input errors, 0 CRC, 0 frame, 0 overrun, 0 ignored, 0 abort
     60 packets output, 271 bytes, 0 underruns
     0 output errors, 0 collisions, 7 interface resets
     0 output buffer failures, 0 output buffers swapped out
     6 carrier transitions


B_BackR#show isdn status
The current ISDN Switchtype = basic-5ess
ISDN BRI0 interface
    Layer 1 Status:
        DEACTIVATED
    Layer 2 Status:
        TEI = 99, Ces = 1, SAPI = 0, State = TEI_ASSIGNED
    Layer 3 Status:
        0 Active Layer 3 Call(s)
    Activated dsl 0 CCBs = 0
    Total Allocated ISDN CCBs = 0
B_BackR#
```

Now it is important to discuss two issues. The first is the reason that the output of the **show interfaces bri 0** command displays (spoofing) on the first line of its output where it claims line protocol is up. To understand why the status of the line protocol being up must be spoofed, think about how this affects the routing table. Say that you have entered a static command in your router's configuration, forcing the router to send packets that are destined to some network X, out of its BRI0 interface. In this case, the static route entered will not be installed into the routing table, unless the BRI0 is UP (physical and link layer).

To make sure that the routing process always considers the BRI0 as up (operationally available), the status of this interface is spoofed (as up) regardless of the status of its ISDN connection(s). The exceptions to this rule are when the interface is faulty and when the interface is administratively shut down.

The second issue to be discussed is the requirements for the ISDN Layer 2 to become active. The short answer to this question is: ISDN Layer 2 is reported as active once a terminal equipment (the BRI interface of a router, for instance) that has successfully received a TEI (terminal endpoint identifier) from the ISDN switch, submits a SABME (set asynchronous balanced mode extended) request to the ISDN switch and receives an unnumbered acknowledgement (UA) back!

To understand this process a little better, it is useful to be familiar with the LAPD frame format and see the entire Layer 2 initialization process, using the output of the **debug isdn q921** command.

As Cisco Documentation CD truly states, the LAPD frame format is very similar to that of HDLC and, like HDLC, LAPD uses supervisory, information, and unnumbered frames. Figure 11-3 shows the format of the LAPD frame. Keep in mind that the purpose of the LAPD frame is to carry (encapsulate) signaling and control information within the D channel between the TE (the router's BRI, for instance) and the ISDN switch.

Because the ISDN switch usually communicates with multiple TEs, the very first task it performs is assigning an address to the TE that has just become active. The ISDN switch will use the assigned TE address (formally called TEI, or terminal equipment identifier), later, to identify the source of the LAPD frames it shall be receiving. The terminal equipment sends LAPD frames with TEI=127 (this is a broadcast address) and SAPI=63 (SAPI 63 identifies the TEI assignment process) until the switch assigns the terminal a TEI. See the top portion of Example 11-6.

**Figure 11-3** *The LAPD Frame Format*

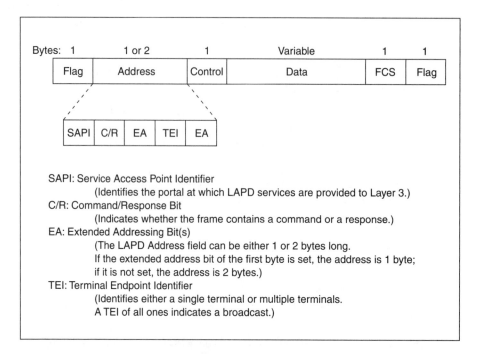

Upon receiving a TEI, in an attempt to bring Layer 2 up—in other words, to establish a session for future delivery (sending) of Layer 3 signaling information—the terminal sends a SABME request to the switch. The LAPD frame carrying the SABME request has the terminal's assigned TEI address, and its SAPI number is 0 (SAPI 0 identifies ISDN Layer 3 signaling—Q.931). If the switch responds to the SABME request with a UA, ISDN Layer 2 on the router has successfully come up. At this time, if you issue the **show isdn status** command, below the Layer 2 status line on the output, the value of the TEI (a number between 64 and 126) is shown along with SAPI = 0, and State = MULTIPLE_FRAME_ ESTABLISHED. However, if the switch responds to the SABME request with DM (Disconnect Mode), the Layer 2 initialization has failed. If the problem persists, the very first action suggested is clearing the BRI interface or reloading your router if possible. Clearing the BRI interface or reloading your router will cause your router's BRI interface to acquire a new TEI that should have better luck in receiving a UA upon submission of the SABME request.

**Example 11-6** *ISDN Layer 2 Activation Process*

```
B_BackR#debug isdn q921

ISDN Q921 packets debugging is on
```

**Example 11-6** *ISDN Layer 2 Activation Process (Continued)*

```
6d01h: ISDN BR0: TX -> IDREQ  ri = 4042  ai = 127
6d01h: ISDN BR0: RX <- IDASSN  ri = 4042  ai = 78
6d01h: ISDN BR0: TX -> SABMEp sapi = 0  tei = 78
6d01h: ISDN BR0: RX <- UAf sapi = 0  tei = 78

6d01h: ISDN BR0: TX -> RRp sapi = 0  tei = 78 nr = 0
6d01h: ISDN BR0: RX <- RRf sapi = 0  tei = 78  nr = 0
...

6d01h: ISDN BR0: TX -> SABMEp sapi = 0  tei = 78
6d01h: ISDN BR0: RX <- IDCKRQ  ri = 0  ai = 127
6d01h: ISDN BR0: TX -> IDCKRP  ri = 3179  ai = 78

6d01h: ISDN BR0: RX <- IDREM  ri = 0  ai = 78

6d01h: ISDN BR0: TX -> IDREQ  ri = 1245  ai = 127
6d01h: ISDN BR0: RX <- IDASSN  ri = 1245  ai = 79
6d01h: ISDN BR0: TX -> SABMEp sapi = 0  tei = 79
6d01h: ISDN BR0: RX <- UAf sapi = 0  tei = 79
```

As you can imagine, activation of Layer 2 sets the stage for ISDN Layer 3 actions (Call Setup and so on) to take place when the need arises. Indeed, that is exactly the meaning behind the UA that the ISDN switch sends back to the router in response to the SABME request. However, while there are no ISDN Layer 3 (Q.931) actions taking place, the router (TE in general) and the switch exchange their own flavor of keepalives called Receiver Ready (RR) messages.

In Example 11-6, the two lines following the UA message that the router has received from the switch are examples of the RR messages that are continuously exchanged between the TE and the ISDN switch. RRp is Receiver Ready Poll and RRf means Receiver Ready Final. As you can see, the router transmits (TX) the RRp and then it receives (RX) the RRf from the ISDN switch. It is worthwhile mentioning that sometimes the ISDN switch sends ID Check Request Messages (IDCKRQ) to its clients (TEs) to check the value of their TEIs. The switch then expects ID Check Response (IDCKRP) back from the TEs. Finally, the switch might send an ID Remove (IDREM) message to a TE, asking the TE to give up its TEI and request a new one (see the last lines of the output shown in Example 11-6).

**NOTE**    I was quite curious to find out when and why a switch would ask a router to give up its TEI and request a new one. To find an answer to my question, I enabled ISDN Q.921 debugging (using the **debug isdn q921** command), and watched the RR messages get exchanged between my router and the ISDN switch. Then I decided to (all of a sudden!) shut down my router's BRI0 interface and see the result. Of course, the ISDN layers and the BRI0 interface all went down and the RR messages stopped. Interestingly, after doing a no shutdown on my router's BRI0 interface, I noticed that the router did not request a new TEI from the ISDN switch this time. However, since the keepalive process between the router and the switch was interrupted during the period that I had the BRI0 interface shut down, immediately after the router sent a LAPD frame with its old TEI and SAPI=0 to the ISDN switch, the switch sent an IDCKRQ to the router and immediately after that it asked the router to give up its old ID and request a new one. I captured this whole process for you and used it in Example 11-6!

I conducted the same exercise by typing the **clear interface bri0** command and the results were identical to doing a shutdown and no shutdown. I am not by any means claiming, however, that these are the only situations that cause the switch to ask the terminal to give up its TEI and request a new one.

---

The other types of LAPD frames that are exchanged between the TE (the router's BRI0, for instance) and the ISDN switch are INFO frames, RNR, REJ, and DISC messages. The INFO frames that you may see on the output of the **debug isdn q921**, carry/encapsulate ISDN Q.931 information/mesages. Examples of Q.931 messages are CallSetup, Connect, Disconnect, and Release. Example 11-7 shows a sample output of the **debug isdn q921**. Initially there is no end-to-end circuit, and you can see that RR messages are only exchanged. Then I triggered a call using a ping. As you can see, the call setup–related information is exchanged between the router and the switch using the INFO frames.

**Example 11-7** *LAPD INFO Frames Carry Q.921 Messages*

```
B_BackR#debug isdn q921
ISDN Q921 packets debugging is on
B_BackR#
ISDN BR0: TX -> RRp sapi = 0  tei = 110 nr = 24
ISDN BR0: RX <- RRf sapi = 0  tei = 110  nr = 18
B_BackR#ping  172.61.10.21

Type escape sequence to abort.
Sending 5, 100-byte ICMP Echos to 172.61.10.21, timeout is 2 seconds:
.!!!!
Success rate is 80 percent (4/5), round-trip min/avg/max =28/30/32 ms
B_BackR#
ISDN BR0: TX -> INFOc sapi = 0  tei = 110  ns = 18  nr = 24 i = 0x08010D050402
889018018320C0735353532303031
ISDN BR0: RX <- INFOc sapi = 0  tei = 110  ns = 24  nr = 19  i= 0x08018D02180189
ISDN BR0: TX -> RRr sapi = 0  tei = 110  nr = 25
ISDN BR0: RX <- INFOc sapi = 0  tei = 110  ns = 25  nr = 19  i= 0x08018D07
ISDN BR0: TX -> RRr sapi = 0  tei = 110  nr = 26
```

**Example 11-7** *LAPD INFO Frames Carry Q.921 Messages (Continued)*

```
%LINK-3-UPDOWN: Interface BRI0:1, changed state to up
ISDN BR0: TX ->  INFOc sapi = 0  tei = 110  ns = 19  nr = 26 i = 0x08010D0F
ISDN BR0: RX <-  RRr sapi = 0  tei = 110  nr = 20
%LINEPROTO-5-UPDOWN: Line protocol on Interface BRI0:1, changed state to up
B_BackR#
%ISDN-6-CONNECT: Interface BRI0:1 is now connected to 5552001 A_BackR
B_BackR#
```

If your router has trouble making a call, look for Receiver Not Ready (RNR), Reject (REJ), and the Disconnect (DISC) messages in the output of the **debug isdn q921**. Many errors may cause these, and of course, you need to investigate. When Q.931 is discussed later, you will learn the importance of configuring the correct ISDN switch type and Service Profile Identifier (SPID) numbers, for instance, to make sure that Q.931 can operate properly.

# DDR Triggers an ISDN Call

Before discussing or investigating ISDN Q.931 and establishment of an end-to-end circuit over the B channel(s), one must ensure that the router is properly configured to trigger the ISDN call for the appropriate traffic. To get Dial on Demand Routing (DDR) to function properly, your router needs to be configured with the following information:

- The routing table must direct the appropriate traffic to the desired BRI interface (BRI is an example of an on-demand interface) as the exit point. This usually entails configuration of static routes.

- The interesting traffic (the type of traffic for which a call is made/triggered) must be defined with a dialer list, and linked to the interface with the **dialer group** command.

- A dialer map (or a dialer string) that defines the dialer information (number to be dialed) must exist for each destination.

- If nondefault values for DDR timers (idle-timeout, fast-idle, and so on) are desired, they must be defined accordingly.

Example 11-8 shows a (DDR-related) partial configuration of a router that has been configured with all the necessary commands mentioned. Figure 11-4 displays a scenario in which Router B_BackR would require a configuration similar to the configuration shown in Example 11-8.

**Figure 11-4** *A Sample ISDN Diagram for the Configuration Shown in Example 11-8*

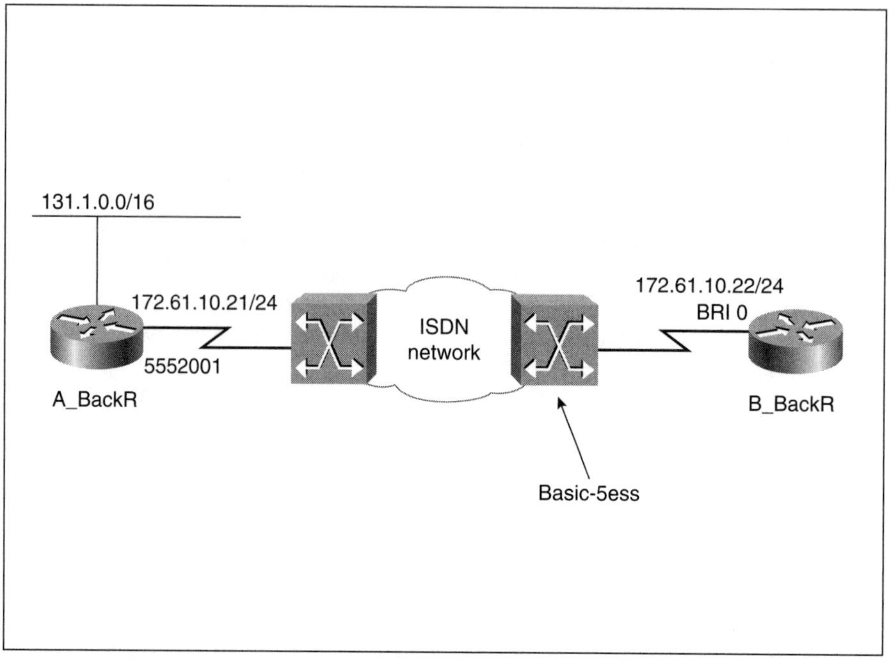

**Example 11-8** *DDR Configuration Commands*

```
0 hostname B_BackR
!
1  username A_BackR password 0 cisco
 !
2 isdn switch-type basic-5ess
 !
3 interface BRI0
4 ip address 172.61.10.22 255.255.255.0
5 encapsulation ppp
6 dialer idle-timeout 2147483
7 dialer map ip 172.61.10.21 name A_BackR broadcast 5552001
8 dialer-group 1
9 ipx network 6000
10 ppp authentication chap
 !
11 ip route 131.1.0.0 255.255.0.0 172.61.10.21
 !
12 dialer-list 1 protocol ip permit
 !
```

The line numbers shown in Example 11-8 are added for the purpose of this discussion. Line number 11 shows the static route that has been configured to tell the router that when it receives packets that are destined for the 131.1.0.0 network, it should forward them to the 172.61.10.21 address. Line number 4 indicates that the IP address for the routers BRI0 is 172.61.10.22 255.255.255.0 and line number 7 indicates that the address 172.61.10.21 is the IP address of the device on the destination of the ISDN connection. Line number 8, dialer-group 1, indicates that the interesting traffic for the BRI0 interface is defined by dialer-list 1, shown on line number 12. Once a packet that is destined for the 131.1.0.0 network is received, and is considered interesting, the router will call the number specified on line number 7 (5552001). After the flow of interesting traffic ends, the router will hang up after 2147483 seconds (during this period any non-interesting traffic may be flowing through the ISDN connection), based on the idle-timeout value specified on line number 6.

When troubleshooting DDR, in addition to looking at the routers configuration (**show running-config**), you may use other Cisco IOS **show** and **debug** commands as well to check the status of the DDR elements that were just discussed. The **show ip route** command, for instance, displays your router's IP routing table. Look for the appropriate static routes in your routing table and make sure that they are configured correctly. One common mistake I have noticed my students make is that they use the BRI number instead of the next-hop address on the static route statement that they configure for (legacy) DDR purposes. Even though using one of the router's local interfaces on a static route is perfectly legitimate and can be quite appropriate at times, it will not work with BRI interfaces (for example, legacy DDR configurations).This claim is true regardless of the number of map statements configured on the BRI interface. A legacy DDR configuration is one that does not make use of dialer profiles, and configures the BRI interfaces directly.

The **show dialer** command is a very useful DDR diagnostic **show** command. This command can be used on its own, or along with either the **interface** (interface BRI0) option or the **maps** option (see Example 11-9). If the **show dialer** command is entered without any parameters, it shows DDR information about all BRI and Dialer interfaces (if there are any).

**Example 11-9** *The show dialer Command*

```
B_BackR#show dialer ?
  interface  Show dialer information on one interface
  maps       Show dialer maps
  <cr>

B_BackR#show dialer interface bri 0
BRI0 - dialer type = ISDN

Dial String Successes Failures    Last called   Last status
5552001       13        0         01:17:20      successful
0 incoming call(s) have been screened.
0 incoming call(s) rejected for callback.

BRI0:1 - dialer type = ISDN
Idle timer (2147483 secs), Fast idle timer (20 secs)
Wait for carrier (30 secs), Re-enable (15 secs)
Dialer state is idle
```

*continues*

**Example 11-9** *The show dialer Command (Continued)*

```
BRI0:2 - dialer type = ISDN
Idle timer (2147483 secs), Fast idle timer (20 secs)
Wait for carrier (30 secs), Re-enable (15 secs)
Dialer state is idle


B_BackR#show dialer maps
Static dialer map ip 172.61.10.21 name A_BackR broadcast (5552001) on BRI0
```

As you can see (in Example 11-9), the output of the **show dialer interface bri 0** has displayed the string (ISDN number) that the BRI0 interface has called along with the number of successes and failures, last time called, and screening and callback rejection statistics for that interface. Furthermore, for each of the B channels of the BRI0 interface, its state and the configured values for its idle-timeout, fast-idle, wait for carrier, and re-enable timers are shown. On the bottom of Example 11-9 you can see the output of the **show dialer maps** command, which enables you to examine all of the map statements configured on your router's BRI interfaces.

When troubleshooting DDR, the **debug dialer** command also comes in very handy. The output of this command shows why a call was made (dialing cause), what interface was used for the call, and the string (number) that was used to make the call. Of course, in a case where the string has not been defined (configured), the output clearly states that no dialer string was defined, and dialing cannot occur. Two samples of the output of the debug dialer command are shown in Example 11-10. The first sample shows the output for a successful call, and the second sample output displays a case where the string was missing.

**Example 11-10** *Sample Outputs of the debug dialer Command*

```
B_BackR#debug dialer
Dial on demand events debugging is on
B_BackR#ping 172.61.10.21
Type escape sequence to abort.
Sending 5, 100-byte ICMP Echos to 172.61.10.21, timeout is 2 seconds:
.!!!!
Success rate is 80 percent (4/5), round-trip min/avg/max = 28/31/32 ms
BRI0: Dialing cause ip (s=172.61.10.22, d=172.61.10.21)
BRI0: Attempting to dial 5552001
%LINK-3-UPDOWN: Interface BRI0:1, changed state to up
dialer Protocol up for BR0:1
%LINEPROTO-5-UPDOWN: Line protocol on Interface BRI0:1, changed state to up
%ISDN-6-CONNECT: Interface BRI0:1 is now connected to 5552001 A_BackR


B_BackR#
B_BackR#ping 131.1.1.1
Type escape sequence to abort.
Sending 5, 100-byte ICMP Echos to 131.1.1.1, timeout is 2 seconds:
.....
Success rate is 0 percent (0/5)
```

**Example 11-10**  *Sample Outputs of the **debug dialer** Command (Continued)*

```
BRI0: Dialing cause ip (s=172.61.10.22, d=131.1.1.1)
BRI0: No dialer string, dialing cannot occur
BRI0: Dialing cause ip (s=172.61.10.22, d=131.1.1.1)
BRI0: No dialer string, dialing cannot occur
BRI0: Dialing cause ip (s=172.61.10.22, d=131.1.1.1)
BRI0: No dialer string, dialing cannot occur
```

In summary, the **show debug** and the **debug dialer** commands can be used to diagnose DDR configurations. These commands help you determine if you have misconfigured or if you are missing commands related to:

- Defining interesting traffic (dialer lists, and access lists)
- Linking interesting traffic (dialer list) to the interface (dialer group)
- Specifying map or string commands
- DDR timer-values.

# ISDN Layer 3

ISDN Layer 3 is about signaling between the TE and the ISDN switch (ET). The ISDN Layer 3 signaling specifications are provided by ITU-T I.450 (also known as ITU-T Q.930) and ITU-T I.451 (also known as ITU-T Q.931). Although the purpose of Layer 3 signaling is to establish an end-to-end circuit, the signaling itself is not a user-to-user process; it operates over the D channel between the terminal and the switch (TE and ET). Signaling essentially facilitates call establishment and call termination, and exchange of information and messages. ISDN Q.931 messages include CALL SETUP, CALL PROCEEDING, CONNECT, CONNECT ACK, DISCONNECT, RELEASE, RELEASE COMPLETE, INFORMATION, CANCEL, STATUS, and so on (see Figure 11-5).

It is best if you save your ISDN Layer 3 troubleshooting effort for after you have fixed all the Layer 2 issues and Layer 2 has become active. Call setup can fail for any of the following reasons:

- The ISDN switch type is not configured, or it is configured incorrectly, on either the caller's or the called party's side (or both!).
- The called party has no B channel free to accept an incoming call (i.e., the called party is busy).
- Due to some form of call screening (based on called number or the calling party's number), the called party rejects the call.

**Figure 11-5** *ISDN Call Setup and Teardown*

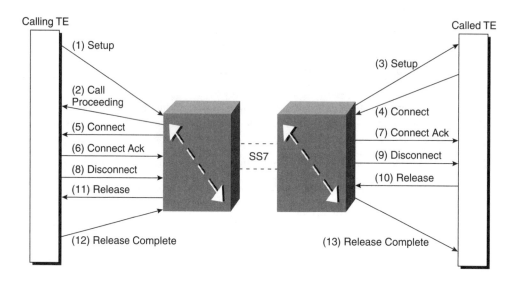

Many ISDN switch manufacturers developed products before the Q.931 specifications were completed. These products differ in the way they interpret the Layer 3 (signaling) frames. It is crucial that you specify/configure the switch type precisely and double-check with your service provider to make sure that it is indeed the type of switch to which your router is connected. Prior to version 12 of Cisco IOS, the ISDN switch type was only a global configuration command; as of version 12.0, the switch type can be configured separately for each interface. Some of the ISDN (BRI) switch types that are supported by Cisco IOS are listed in Table 11-3.

**Table 11-3** *ISDN (BRI) Switch Types (Cisco-Supported)*

| Type | Description |
| --- | --- |
| basic-1tr6 | 1TR6 switch type for Germany |
| basic-5ess | AT&T 5ESS switch type for the U.S. |
| basic-dms100 | Northern DMS-100 switch type |
| basic-net3 | NET3 switch type for U.K. and Europe |
| basic-ni1 | National ISDN-1 switch type |
| basic-nwnet3 | NET3 switch type for Norway |
| basic-nznet3 | NET3 switch type for New Zealand |

**Table 11-3**    *ISDN (BRI) Switch Types (Cisco-Supported) (Continued)*

| Type | Description |
|------|-------------|
| basic-ts013 | TS013 switch type for Australia |
| ntt | NTT switch type for Japan |
| vn2 | VN2 switch type for France |
| vn3 | VN3 and VN4 switch types for France |

The ISDN switch type is configured using the following command in global configuration mode:

```
isdn switch-type switch-type
```

As of Release 12.0 of Cisco IOS, however, each individual BRI interface may be individually configured with an ISDN switch type using the same command syntax in interface configuration mode.

To find out the switch type configured on your router, you may look at your router's running configuration (using the **show running-config** command). The simpler option you have is to issue the **show isdn status** command, which also displays the ISDN switch type your router is configured for. Remember that if you change the ISDN switch type on your router, the change will not take effect until you reload your router.

One effective method for troubleshooting ISDN Layer 3 is through usage of the **debug isdn q931** command. A sample output of this debug during call setup is shown in Example 11-11. The top portion of Example 11-11 shows the output for the calling router and the bottom portion shows the output for the called router.

**Example 11-11**    *Sample Outputs of the **debug isdn q931** Command*

```
B_BackR#debug isdn q931
ISDN Q931 packets debugging is on

ISDN BR0: TX -> SETUP pd = 8  callref = 0x14
        Bearer Capability i = 0x8890
        Channel ID i = 0x83
        Keypad Facility i = '5552001'
ISDN BR0: RX <- CALL_PROC pd = 8  callref = 0x94
        Channel ID i = 0x89
ISDN BR0: RX <- CONNECT pd = 8  callref = 0x94
ISDN BR0: TX -> CONNECT_ACK pd = 8  callref = 0x14

%LINK-3-UPDOWN: Interface BRI0:1, changed state to up
%LINEPROTO-5-UPDOWN: Line protocol on Interface BRI0:1, changed state to up
%ISDN-6-CONNECT: Interface BRI0:1 is now connected to 5552001 A_BackR

ISDN BR0: RX <- SETUP pd = 8  callref = 0x28
        Bearer Capability i = 0x8890
        Channel ID i = 0x89
```

*continues*

**Example 11-11** *Sample Outputs of the **debug isdn q931** Command (Continued)*

```
              Called Party Number i = 0xC1, '5552001'
ISDN BR0: TX ->  CONNECT pd = 8  callref = 0xA8
ISDN BR0: RX <-  CONNECT_ACK pd = 8  callref = 0x28

%LINK-3-UPDOWN: Interface BRI0:1, changed state to up
%LINEPROTO-5-UPDOWN: Line protocol on Interface BRI0:1, changed state to up
%ISDN-6-CONNECT: Interface BRI0:1 is now connected to 5552002B_Back
```

When reading the output of the **debug isdn q931** command, you must pay attention to the callref (call reference) number that is used on the messages that are sent back and forth between the router and the ISDN switch. This will allow you to analyze the distinct conversations that are occurring between the router and the switch regarding different calls. The callref is an 8-bit field (2 hex digits—0x14) and its left most bit is a flag bit that indicates the flow direction of the message. The flag bit on the call ref of messages that go from the router to the switch are 0, and the flag is set to 1 when the switch sends a message to the router. For instance, in Example 11-11 (the top portion), when the router transmits (TX) a setup for the number 5552001 to the switch, it gives it a call ref number of 0x14. When the switch responds to the router regarding callref 0x14, the switch flips the leftmost bit of the callref from 0 to 1, resulting in callref 0x94.

The output of the **debug isdn q931** command can help you find out the reason for a call setup failure. The top portion of Example 11-12 shows a case in which the call made by the local router was rejected. Notice that below the Release message the cause information (cause i) is shown to be =0x8295, which is also stated in words as **Call rejected**. The reason for a call rejection could be any of the following:

- Remote router's call screening

- Remote router is out of channels (has no B channel available)

- Bad SPID number configuration

**Example 11-12** *Determining Call Rejected and Call Release Causes*

```
B_BackR#debug isdn q931
ISDN Q931 packets debugging is on

ISDN BR0: TX ->  SETUP pd = 8  callref = 0x18
        Bearer Capability i = 0x8890
        Channel ID i = 0x83
        Keypad Facility i = '5552001'
ISDN BR0: RX <-  CALL_PROC pd = 8  callref = 0x98
        Channel ID i = 0x89
ISDN BR0: RX <-  RELEASE pd = 8  callref = 0x98
        Cause i = 0x8295 - Call rejected
ISDN BR0: TX ->  RELEASE_COMP pd = 8  callref = 0x18

B_BackR#
ISDN BR0: RX <-  DISCONNECT pd = 8  callref = 0x9D
```

**Example 11-12**  *Determining Call Rejected and Call Release Causes (Continued)*

```
                Cause i = 0x8290 - Normal call clearing
%ISDN-6-DISCONNECT: Interface BRI0:1  disconnected from 5552001 A_BackR,
call lasted 17 seconds
%LINK-3-UPDOWN: Interface BRI0:1, changed state to down
ISDN BR0: TX -> RELEASE pd = 8  callref = 0x1D
        Cause i = 0x8090 - Normal call clearing
ISDN BR0: RX <- RELEASE_COMP pd = 8  callref = 0x9D
B_BackR#
%LINEPROTO-5-UPDOWN: Line protocol on Interface BRI0:1, changed state to down
B_BackR#
```

On the bottom portion of Example 11-12, another capture of the **debug isdn q931** command's output is shown. In that case, a DISCONNECT message is received by the router and the cause information is stated to be =0x8290, which is also stated in words as **Normal call clearing**. The router replies with a RELEASE message (causei=0x8090) and it restates the cause as **Normal call clearing**.

## The Importance of SPID Numbers

ISDN Service Profile Identifier (SPID) is a configuration parameter that may or may not have to be configured on your router. This merely depends on the type of switch your service provider has and the software version on that switch. What is important to know, however, is that if the router does not need to have SPID number(s) configured, then it should not have any configured. In other words, having a SPID number configured when it is not needed should not be considered as a harmless extra piece of configuration code. On the other hand, if the router needs to have SPIDs configured you should make sure that it does and it is entered (configured) 100% accurately. SPID numbers are entered from the interface configuration mode using **isdn spid1** and **isdn spid2** commands:

```
B_BackR#configure terminal
Enter configuration commands, one per line.  End with CNTL/Z.
B_BackR(config)#interface bri 0
B_BackR(config-if)#isdn spid1 555200201
B_BackR(config-if)#isdn spid2 555200202
```

The SPID allows the router (the TE in general) to identify the connection profile it needs to the service provider's switch. For instance, SPID2 (the second SPID) number might indicate that the second B channel will only be used for voice. Once ISDN Layer 1 and Layer 2 have completed their activation, if you recall, the TE sends a SABME request and waits for a UA from the ET. If the TE receives the UA, it means that the TE and ET can, from this point on, engage in Q.931 (Layer 3 signaling) activities. However, missing or misconfigured SPID number(s) paralyze this process. If the SPID number is correctly configured, when Layer 3 is initializing the TE sends its SPID number(s) to the switch (ET). The switch validates the SPID(s) and sends back EIDs (EndPoint Identifiers) to the TE (the router).

The DMS-100 switch and the National ISDN 1 (NI-1) are examples of the type of switches that expect the TE to be configured with and submit SPIDs to the switch upon Layer 3 initialization. If the switch type is 5ess, the requirement for SPID is dependent on its software version. When required, the service provider will furnish two SPIDs (one for each BRI B channel) to you, and you must make sure to enter them into your router's configuration accurately. It is noteworthy that the SPID numbers may or may not resemble your ISDN number. Therefore you should merely enter the SPID numbers that the service provider gives you (and not argue about it!), regardless of how similar to your ISDN number they are.

How can the SPID configurations be checked and debugged? First of all, the invaluable **show isdn status** command tells whether SPID number(s) are configured on each of the BRI interfaces (see Example 11-13) and whether they are valid. Notice that in the example presented by Example 11-13 the BRI0 interface is reported to have SPID numbers entered for both of its B channels and they are both rejected by the switch. It is important to keep in mind that the BRI0 interface, in this example, has successfully received TEIs (118 and 119) for its B channels. However, due to the incorrect configuration of its SPIDs, it will not be able to place any calls.

**Example 11-13**  *Using the **show isdn status** Command to See the SPID Configuration on BRI Interfaces*

```
B_BackR#show isdn status
The current ISDN Switchtype = basic-dms100
ISDN BRI0 interface
    Layer 1 Status:
        ACTIVE
    Layer 2 Status:
        TEI = 118, Ces = 1, SAPI = 0, State = MULTIPLE_FRAME_ESTABLISHED
        TEI = 119, Ces = 2, SAPI = 0, State = MULTIPLE_FRAME_ESTABLISHED
    Spid Status:
        TEI 118, ces = 1, state = 4(await init)
            spid1 configured, no LDN, spid1 sent, spid1 NOT valid
        TEI 119, ces = 2, state = 4(await init)
            spid2 configured, no LDN, spid2 sent, spid2 NOT valid
    Layer 3 Status:
        0 Active Layer 3 Call(s)
    Activated dsl 0 CCBs = 0

    Total Allocated ISDN CCBs = 0
B_BackR#
```

Example 11-14 presents the output of the **debug isdn q931** command for a router, with bad SPIDs, during initialization (the **clear interface bri0** command was entered to force initialization for this simulation), and later, when it attempted to place a call. As you can see, during initialization, ISDN Layer 2 came up and TEIs 122 and 123 were assigned to the B channels. Next, the router transmitted (TX) its SPID information (555200201 and 555200202). Finally, the Q.931 messages (ISDN BR0: Invalid EID/SPID, Spid failure) can be seen. These state that EIDs were not received for the submitted SPIDs. As a result, the

SPID numbers are considered invalid. On the bottom portion of Example 11-14, note that a call was triggered with a ping to address 172.61.10.21, and the router generated a Q.931 error message (setup) stating that due to invalid SPID it cannot process the call to 5552001.

**Example 11-14**    *Using the **debug isdn q931** Command to Test the SPID Configuration on BRI Interfaces*

```
B_BackR#debug isdn q931
ISDN Q931 packets debugging is on
B_BackR#clear int bri0
B_BackR#
%ISDN-6-LAYER2UP: Layer 2 for Interface BR0, TEI 122 changed to up
%ISDN-6-LAYER2UP: Layer 2 for Interface BR0, TEI 123 changed to up

ISDN BR0: TX ->  INFORMATION pd = 8  callref = (null)
        SPID Information i = '555200201'
ISDN BR0: TX ->  INFORMATION pd = 8  callref = (null)
        SPID Information i = '555200202'

ISDN BR0: Invalid EID/SPID, Spid failure
ISDN BR0: Invalid EID/SPID, Spid failure

B_BackR#ping 172.61.10.21
Type escape sequence to abort.
Sending 5, 100-byte ICMP Echos to 172.61.10.21, timeout is 2 seconds:
.....
Success rate is 0 percent (0/5)
B_BackR#
ISDN cannot send Setup: Event: Invalid SPID, ces 1624369412 call_id 0x1
ISDN BR0: Error: Cannot process the call to 5552001
B_BackR#
```

## Call Rejection May Be Caused by Call Screening

On each BRI interface, you may enter two numbers (using the **ISDN answer1** and **ISDN answer2** interface configuration commands) to force the router to answer an incoming call on a particular BRI interface, but only if the number dialed by the other party matches the numbers you specify. Naturally, this technique will be effective only if the switch hands that information over to your router. When troubleshooting ISDN call setup failures, keep in mind that this BRI interface configuration command may be causing the call setup failure.

Another BRI interface configuration command, the **ISDN caller** command, allows an administrator to specify from which sources (based on their ISDN number) a BRI interface should accept calls. Again, this will only work if the switch provides the caller's number to your router (when an incoming call is received). A few points to remember about this command follow:

- The specified numbers are the only numbers from which incoming calls will be accepted and all other calls will be rejected.

- If you use this command on your router, but the switch does not supply the caller's number, your router will reject all calls.

- You can use the wildcard character X in place of digits, and where X is used, any digit will match it.

# ISDN End-to-End Circuit

If ISDN Layers 1 and 2 are active on a router, and Layer 3 has successfully been initialized, when DDR triggers a call to a certain destination the router sends a call setup request to the service provider's switch. If the destination device can and is willing to accept the call, an end-to-end circuit will be built between the local and the remote device (routers) by the service provider's circuit-switched network. An end-to-end ISDN circuit is composed of at least one B channel, over which the local and the remote devices must mutually agree upon an OSI data-link layer protocol (encapsulation). The supported ISDN BRI B channel protocols on Cisco routers are CPP (Combinet Packet Protocol), frame-relay, HDLC (Cisco's Serial HDLC synchronous), LAPB (X.25 Level 2), PPP (Point-to-Point Protocol), and X25 (X.25). PPP, with CHAP (Challenge Handshake Authentication Protocol) authentication, is used the most often, and is the recommended protocol for ISDN connections.

## PPP over B Channel

Before PPP starts delivering upper layer protocol packets between two devices, it goes through a series of negotiations regarding link options and network protocols. The PPP frame format is shown in Figure 11-6.

During link options negotiation, the PPP frame's protocol number is 0xC021 (LCP). LCP negotiates link options such as Authentication, Multilinking, Callback, Compression, and line Quality Protocol. For a link option to be implemented, both parties must agree on it. Disagreement on a link option does not make the link fail, it only means that the option will not be used. The exception to this rule is Authentication. Authentication must be agreed upon and it must immediately take place and succeed, or the circuit will be dropped.

After authentication successfully completes (if there was any), several PPP frames with the PPP protocol field identifying them as IPCP, IPXCP, CDPCP, and so on (commonly called Network Control Protocols or NCPs) are exchanged between the two parties. The purpose of exchanging NCPs is to negotiate whether the two ends of the PPP connection will run protocols such as CDP, IP, and IPX between them or not and, if they do, to determine what addressing scheme they will use (where applicable) for each protocol.

**Figure 11-6**  *PPP Frame Format*

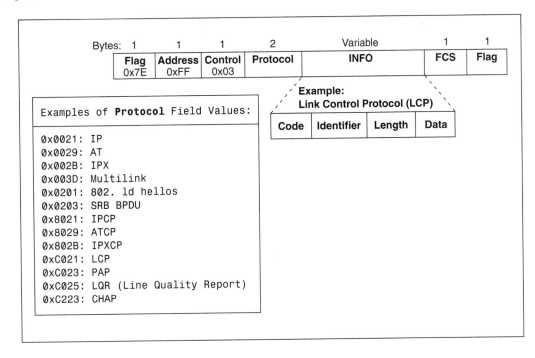

Example 11-15 shows the ppp negotiation process, which was captured using the **debug ppp negotiation** command. Notice how each side sends its desired option (by submitting CONFREQ, which means configuration request) and the other party either agrees with that option (by sending the CONFACK message) or disagrees with that option (by sending CONFNACK, which means that the option is recognized, but not accepted, or by sending CONFREJ, which means that the option is not recognized and therefore is not acceptable). Also notice that once PPP CHAP authentication was agreed upon, it immediately (and successfully) took place. If Authentication is not agreed upon, or if it fails, the link immediately goes down and the circuit is dropped.

**Example 11-15**  *Sample Output of the **debug ppp negotiation** Command*

```
B_BackR#debug ppp negotiation
PPP protocol negotiation debugging is on
B_BackR#
%LINK-3-UPDOWN: Interface BRI0:1, changed state to up
BR0:1 PPP: Treating connection as a callout
BR0:1 PPP: Phase is ESTABLISHING, Active Open
BR0:1 LCP: O CONFREQ [Closed] id 17 len 15
BR0:1 LCP:    AuthProto CHAP (0x0305C22305)
BR0:1 LCP:    MagicNumber 0x2FD17F49 (0x05062FD17F49)
BR0:1 LCP: I CONFREQ [REQsent] id 22 len 15
BR0:1 LCP:    AuthProto CHAP (0x0305C22305)
```

*continues*

**Example 11-15** *Sample Output of the **debug ppp negotiation** Command (Continued)*

```
BR0:1 LCP:    MagicNumber 0xFF646A49 (0x0506FF646A49)
BR0:1 LCP: O CONFACK [REQsent] id 22 len 15
BR0:1 LCP:    AuthProto CHAP (0x0305C22305)
BR0:1 LCP:    MagicNumber 0xFF646A49 (0x0506FF646A49)
BR0:1 LCP: I CONFACK [ACKsent] id 17 len 15
BR0:1 LCP:    AuthProto CHAP (0x0305C22305)
BR0:1 LCP:    MagicNumber 0x2FD17F49 (0x05062FD17F49)
BR0:1 LCP: State is Open
BR0:1 PPP: Phase is AUTHENTICATING, by both
BR0:1 CHAP: O CHALLENGE id 16 len 28 from "B_BackR"
BR0:1 CHAP: I CHALLENGE id 16 len 28 from "A_BackR"
BR0:1 CHAP: O RESPONSE id 16 len 28 from "B_BackR"
BR0:1 CHAP: I SUCCESS id 16 len 4
BR0:1 CHAP: I RESPONSE id 16 len 28 from "A_BackR"
BR0:1 CHAP: O SUCCESS id 16 len 4
BR0:1 PPP: Phase is UP
BR0:1 IPCP: O CONFREQ [Closed] id 6 len 10
BR0:1 IPCP:    Address 172.61.10.22 (0x0306AC3D0A16)
BR0:1 CDPCP: O CONFREQ [Closed] id 6 len 4
BR0:1 IPXCP: O CONFREQ [Closed] id 6 len 18
BR0:1 IPXCP:    Network 0x00006000 (0x010600006000)
BR0:1 IPXCP:    Node 00e0.1e58.de18 (0x020800E01E58DE18)
BR0:1 IPCP: I CONFREQ [REQsent] id 6 len 10
BR0:1 IPCP:    Address 172.61.10.21 (0x0306AC3D0A15)
BR0:1 IPCP: O CONFACK [REQsent] id 6 len 10
BR0:1 IPCP:    Address 172.61.10.21 (0x0306AC3D0A15)
BR0:1 CDPCP: I CONFREQ [REQsent] id 6 len 4
BR0:1 CDPCP: O CONFACK [REQsent] id 6 len 4
BR0:1 IPCP: I CONFACK [ACKsent] id 6 len 10
BR0:1 IPCP:    Address 172.61.10.22 (0x0306AC3D0A16)
BR0:1 IPCP: State is Open
BR0 IPCP: Install route to 172.61.10.21
BR0:1 CDPCP: I CONFACK [ACKsent] id 6 len 4
BR0:1 CDPCP: State is Open
BR0:1 LCP: I PROTREJ [Open] id 23 len 24 protocol IPXCP
BR0:1 LCP:    (0x802B0106001201060000600002800E0)
BR0:1 LCP:    (0x1E58DE18)
BR0:1 IPXCP: State is Closed
```

When performing ISDN troubleshooting, if you notice that a circuit is built, but it immediately drops, you should keep in mind that the authentication failure might be causing it. The **debug ppp authentication** command displays the PPP authentication process. Example 11-16 shows a sample output of the **debug PPP authentication** command's output, where two routers both authenticate each other using CHAP.

CHAP is a three-way handshake authentication protocol. The authenticating node (server) sends a challenge (input code=1) to the other side (the client). The client sends a response (input code=2). Finally, the server either accepts the response by sending a success message (input code=3), or it rejects the response by sending a failure message (input code=4) back.

Another reason for a circuit that is dropped too quickly could be the value of the dialer idle-timeout parameter (it is too small) on either side of the ISDN connection. To check the value of this timer and any other ISDN-related timer, use the **show dialer** command (see Example 11-9). Of course, you can use the **show running-config** command too, but remember that if a parameter's value is not different from its default value, it will not be displayed in the output of the **show running-config** or **show startup-config** commands.

**Example 11-16** *Sample Output of the **debug ppp authentication** Command*

```
B_BackR# debug ppp authentication
PPP authentication debugging is on

B_BackR#

BR0:1 PPP: Treating connection as a callout
BR0:1 PPP: Phase is AUTHENTICATING, by both
BR0:1 CHAP: O CHALLENGE id 17 len 28 from "B_BackR"
BR0:1 CHAP: I CHALLENGE id 17 len 28 from "A_BackR"
BR0:1 CHAP: O RESPONSE id 17 len 28 from "B_BackR"
BR0:1 CHAP: I SUCCESS id 17 len 4
BR0:1 CHAP: I RESPONSE id 17 len 28 from "A_BackR"
BR0:1 CHAP: O SUCCESS id 17 len 4

%LINEPROTO-5-UPDOWN: Line protocol on Interface BRI0:1, changed state to up

B_BackR#
```

While ISDN troubleshooting, if you want to check and see the active Layer 3 calls on a router you may use the **show isdn status** command. You can also check the status of each BRI interface's B channel using the **show interface BRI** *n* **1 2** command (where n is the BRI number). Example 11-17 shows the output of both of these commands while the router under focus had a single B channel circuit with another router.

**Example 11-17** *Sample Outputs of the **show isdn status** and the **show interface bri 0 1** Commands During an Active Layer 3 Call*

```
%ISDN-6-CONNECT: Interface BRI0:1 is now connected to 5552001A_BackR
B_BackR# show isdn status
The current ISDN Switchtype = basic-5ess
ISDN BRI0 interface
    Layer 1 Status:
        ACTIVE
    Layer 2 Status:
        TEI = 125, Ces = 1, SAPI = 0, State = MULTIPLE_FRAME_ESTABLISHED
    Layer 3 Status:
        1 Active Layer 3 Call(s)
    Activated dsl 0 CCBs = 1
        CCB:callid=0x8001, sapi=0x0, ces=0x1, B-chan=1
    Total Allocated ISDN CCBs = 1

B_BackR# show interface bri 0 1
BRI0:1 is up, line protocol is up
```

*continues*

**Example 11-17** *Sample Outputs of the **show isdn status** and the **show interface bri 0 1** Commands During an Active Layer 3 Call (Continued)*

```
Hardware is BRI
MTU 1500 bytes, BW 64 Kbit, DLY 20000 usec, rely 255/255, load 1/255
Encapsulation PPP, loopback not set, keepalive set (10 sec)
LCP Open
Closed: IPXCP
Open: IPCP, CDPCP
Last input 00:00:03, output 00:00:03, output hang never
Last clearing of "show interface" counters never
```

One of the powerful features of PPP is its multilink option (Multilink PPP, or MLP). When used with ISDN, this feature allows aggregation of B channels over single or multiple interfaces that are configured with the **ppp multilink** command. Aggregation of B channels from different interfaces requires those interfaces to be configured as part of a rotary group. The B channels of a single interface are considered members of a common rotary group, and therefore do not require any special configuration. For Multilink PPP to kick in, however, both ends of the PPP connection must agree to it during the initial LCP negotiation phase, and there must be a **dialer load-threshold** command configured at either or both ends of a connection to trigger the multilink to kick in and request another circuit. To check the status of your router's multilink connection, use the **show ppp multilink** troubleshooting command.

Example 11-18 displays a sample output of the **show ppp multilink** command during an active MLP session. Below the output of the **show ppp multilink** command, on Example 11-18, the output of the **show interface bri 0 1 2** is also included. This command's output indicates whether a B channel is involved in an MLP session. On both B channels of the BRI0 interface in Example 11-18, the output has the **multilink open** flag beside the LCP open phrase.

**Example 11-18** *Sample Outputs of the **show ppp multilink** and the **show interface bri 0 1 2** Commands during an Active Multilink PPP Session*

```
B_BackR#show ppp multilink
Bundle A_BackR, 2 members, Master link is Virtual-Access1
Dialer Interface is BRI0
  0 lost fragments, 0 reordered, 0 unassigned, sequence 0x2/0x2 rcvd/sent
  0 discarded, 0 lost received, 1/255 load
Member Links: 2 (max not set, min not set)
BRI0:2
BRI0:1

B_BackR#sho int bri 0 1 2
BRI0:1 is up, line protocol is up
  Hardware is BRI
  MTU 1500 bytes, BW 64 Kbit, DLY 20000 usec, rely 255/255, load 1/255
  Encapsulation PPP, loopback not set, keepalive set (10 sec)
  LCP Open, multilink Open
  Last input 00:00:07, output 00:00:07, output hang never
```

**Example 11-18** *Sample Outputs of the **show ppp multilink** and the **show interface bri 0 1 2** Commands during an Active Multilink PPP Session (Continued)*

```
...
BRI0:2 is up, line protocol is up
  Hardware is BRI
  MTU 1500 bytes, BW 64 Kbit, DLY 20000 usec, rely 255/255, load 1/255
  Encapsulation PPP, loopback not set, keepalive set (10 sec)
  LCP Open, multilink Open
  Last input 00:00:00, output 00:00:00, output hang never
  Last clearing of "show interface" counters never
...
```

# Review of ISDN Troubleshooting Commands

Figure 11-7 displays some of the commands that are used for ISDN troubleshooting. This figure also illustrates which commands are more appropriate for testing specific segments of the ISDN connection (or layer). You are advised to study this figure thoroughly.

**Figure 11-7** *Review of ISDN Troubleshooting Commands*

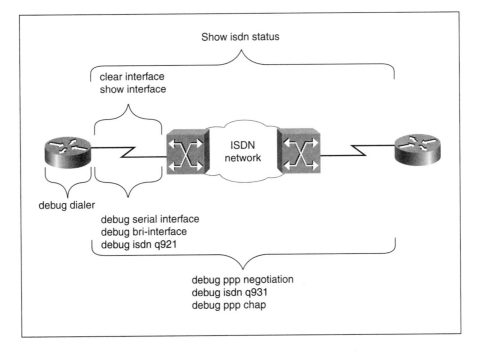

# Foundation Summary

The Foundation Summary is a collection of quick reference information that provides a convenient review of many key concepts in this chapter. For those of you who already feel comfortable with the topics in this chapter, this summary helps you recall a few details. For those of you who just read this chapter, this review should help solidify some key facts. For any of you doing your final prep before the exam, these tables and figures are a convenient way to review the day before the exam.

**Table 11-4**   *ISDN Reference Points*

| Reference Point | Place |
| --- | --- |
| R | Between terminal equipment type 2 (TE2) and terminal adapter (TA). |
| S | Between terminal equipment type 1 (TE1) or terminal adapter (TA) and the network termination type 2 (NT2) device. |
| T | Between the network termination type 2 (NT2) and the network termination type 1 (NT1) device. |
| U | Between the network termination type 1 (NT1) and the service provider's (carrier's) local termination (LT) device. |
| V | Between the service provider's (carrier's) local termination (LT) device and their exchange termination (ET) device. |

**Table 11-5**   *ISDN (BRI) Switch Types (Cisco-Supported)*

| Switch Type | Description |
| --- | --- |
| basic-1tr6 | 1TR6 switch type for Germany |
| basic-5ess | AT&T 5ESS switch type for the U.S. |
| basic-dms100 | Northern DMS-100 switch type |
| basic-net3 | NET3 switch type for U.K. and Europe |
| basic-ni1 | National ISDN-1 switch type |
| basic-nwnet3 | NET3 switch type for Norway |
| basic-nznet3 | NET3 switch type for New Zealand |
| basic-ts013 | TS013 switch type for Australia |
| ntt | NTT switch type for Japan |
| vn2 | VN2 switch type for France |
| vn3 | VN3 and VN4 switch types for France |

**Table 11-6**   *Summary of This Chapter's **show** Commands*

| Command | Description |
| --- | --- |
| **show controller bri 0** | Use this command to see the Layer 1 status of ISDN BRI0. |
| **show isdn status** | Displays the configured ISDN switch type and information on all three ISDN layers (status and error information). |
| **show interface bri 0** | Displays D channel information of the BRI0 interface along with its status and the error, i/o, and carrier transition statistics. |
| **show dialer** | Displays dialer information on all interfaces. |
| **show dialer interface bri 0** | Displays dialer information on the BRI0 interface. |
| **show dialer maps** | Displays configured dialer maps. |
| **show interface bri 0 1 2** | Displays information on interface BRI0's B channels. |
| **show ppp multilink** | Displays Information on current Multilink PPP sessions. |

**Table 11-7**   *Summary of This Chapter's **debug** Commands*

| Command | Description |
| --- | --- |
| **debug bri-interface** | Use this command to see the process of ISDN Layer 1 activation. |
| **debug isdn q921** | Use this command to see the ISDN Q.921 (Layer 2) conversations. |
| **debug dialer** | Use this command to troubleshoot DDR problems. |
| **debug isdn q931** | Use this command to see the ISDN Q.931 (signaling) messages. |
| **debug ppp negotiation** | Use this command to see the entire process of PPP's Initialization (LCP, Authentication, and NCPs). |
| **debug ppp authentication** **debug ppp chap** | Use these commands to observe the PPP Authentication Process. |

# Q&A

The answers to the following questions can be found in Appendix A. Some of the questions in this section are repeated from the "Do I Know This Already" Quiz so that you can gauge the advancement of your knowledge of this subject matter.

**1** List at least two generic types of devices that are classified as ISDN customer premises equipment in North America.

**2** What kind of wiring facility is used for ISDN local access loop?

**3** Are the line termination (LT) and exchange termination (ET) part of CPE or are they components of the service provider's (telco's) equipment?

**4** How are TE1 and TE2 different?

**5** Which one of TE1 and TE2 needs to be connected to a TA?

**6** If the TA is an external device, how is the TE connected to it?

_____

_____

_____

**7** What kind of wiring is used between the TE and the NT1 device?

_____

_____

_____

**8** In North America, is NT1 considered part of CPE or is it considered part of the service provider's equipment?

_____

_____

_____

**9** Name the ISDN reference point for the interface between TE2 andTA.

_____

_____

_____

**10** Name the ISDN reference point for the interface between the NT2 and the NT1 device.

_____

_____

_____

**11** Name the ISDN reference point for the interface between the NT1 and the service provider's (carrier's) LT device.

_____

_____

_____

12 Name the ISDN reference point for the interface between TE1 or TA and the NT2 device.

_____

_____

_____

13 What does the label U mean on a BRI interface?

_____

_____

_____

14 Name the ISDN BRI channels and specify each channel's bandwidth.

_____

_____

_____

15 What is the difference between ISDN BRI B channels and the ISDN D channel?

_____

_____

_____

16 What is the protocol that runs over ISDN D channel?

_____

_____

_____

17 Which two ISDN **show** commands allow you to discover the status of ISDN Layer 1?

_____

_____

_____

18 Which **show** command displays the ISDN switch type you have configured your router for?

_____

_____

_____

**19** Which **debug** command allows you to observe the activation process of ISDN BRI Layer 1?

_____

_____

_____

**20** Which **show** command allows you to discover the true state of the ISDN BRI Layer 2?

_____

_____

_____

**21** Which **show** command displays information about all BRI and Dialer interfaces (if there are any) of a router?

_____

_____

_____

**22** Which **show** command displays all of the map statements configured on your router's BRI interfaces?

_____

_____

_____

**23** If you are troubleshooting an ISDN call, which **debug** command allows you to observe the cause of the call (dialing cause), the interface used for the call, and the string (number) that was used to make the call?

_____

_____

_____

**24** Name at least three ISDN Q.931 messages.

_____

_____

_____

**25** Provide an example of the failure cause of an ISDN Q.931 SETUP failure.

_____

_____

_____

**26** Name at least 2 ISDN BRI switch types that are supported by Cisco router IOS?

_____

_____

_____

**27** Which command configures a Cisco router (IOS-based) for the ISDN switch type ntt?

_____

_____

_____

**28** Which **debug** command provides detail information on ISDN Layer 3 activities such as call setup?

_____

_____

_____

**29** Provide one **show** and one **debug** command that are useful for ISDN SPID troubleshooting.

_____

_____

_____

**30** Name at least two ISDN B channel protocols (on Cisco routers).

_____

_____

_____

**31** Name at least two of the link options that PPP's LCP negotiates.

_____

_____

_____

**32** Which **debug** command allows you to observe PPP's LCP, authentication, and NCP process?

_____

_____

_____

**33** Which **debug** command displays information on the ppp authentication process?

_____

_____

_____

**34** Which command displays the status of both of the B channels of the BRI0 interface of a Cisco router?

_____

_____

_____

**35** Which command allows you to examine the status of your Cisco router's active Multilink PPP sessions?

_____

_____

_____

**36** Using the following figure, for each of the segments identified by the letters A through E, provide the appropriate ISDN troubleshooting command(s) requested as follows:

For Segment A, Provide 1 **debug** command
For Segment B, Provide 1 **show** command
For Segment C, Provide 3 **debug** commands
For Segment D, Provide 1 **show** command

For Segment E, Provide 3 **debug** commands

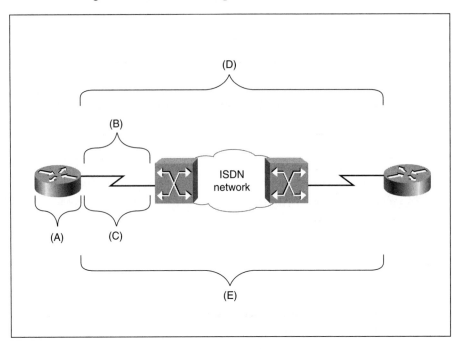

# Answers to Quiz Questions

This appendix contains the answers to each chapter's "Do I Know This Already" quiz questions and "Q&A" questions.

## Chapter 1

### "Do I Know This Already?" Quiz

**1** Name three classes of network media test equipment.

**Volt/Ohm meters, cable testers (scanners), and time domain reflectometers (TDRs) and optical time domain reflectometer (OTDRs).**

**2** What are the tasks network monitors can perform?

**Network monitors allow you to capture, display, and save (store) network traffic data from a network segment.**

**Depending on the brand, further functionalities such as traffic statistics, alarms, and others may also be provided.**

**3** Name the tool that does multilayer analysis of network traffic.

**Protocol analyzer.**

**4** What are the five functional areas of network management?

**Fault management, accounting management, performance management, security management, and configuration and name management.**

**5** What is Cisco Systems' flagship network management software called?

**CiscoWorks.**

**6** List at least three members of the CWSI Campus Application.

**TrafficDirector, VlanDirector, AtmDirector, CiscoView, and UserTracking.**

**7** Name Cisco's network simulation and modeling tool.

**Netsys.**

**8** What does the acronym CCO stand for, and what is the URL address for CCO?

**Cisco Connection Online at www.cisco.com.**

**9** Name at least two tools or resources from CCO available for problem prevention.

**The Documentation CD (also available online), CCO MarketPlace, and CCO Software Center.**

**10** Name at least three tools or resources that CCO provides for problem correction and troubleshooting.

**The Bug Toolkit, Troubleshooting Engine, Stack Decoder, Open Forum, and Case Management Toolkit.**

# Q&A

**1** What parameters do Volt/Ohm meters test?

**Resistance, current, capacitance, voltage, and continuity.**

**2** Give two examples of the cable conditions reported by Scanners.

**NEXT (near-end crosstalk), attenuation, continuity, and impedance.**

**3** Which cable-testing function is offered only by the high-end equipment?

**Time domain reflectometer (TDR).**

**4** Name the tasks testing equipment with TDR functionality can perform.

**Locate kinks, opens, shorts, sharp bends, crimps, and other physical problems on a cable.**

**5** Which OSI Reference Model layer does the information gathered by network monitors correspond to?

**Data link layer (Layer 2).**

**6** What is one of the major applications of network monitors?

**Network baselining, network capacity planning (based on observed patterns of traffic), and problem detection (alarms set based on predetermined thresholds).**

**7**  Which application that can be bundled with CiscoWorks provides real-time device monitoring?

**CiscoView.**

**8**  What does the acronym CRM stand for?

**Cisco Resource Manager.**

**9**  Name the components of CRM.

**Inventory Manager, Availability Manager, Syslog Analyzer, and Software Image Manager.**

**10**  What does the TrafficDirector work with in order to obtain traffic information about different segments?

**RMON agents and standalone switch probes.**

**11**  Which tasks are generally facilitated by network simulation and modeling tools? (Name at least two.)

**Network design, testing, performance analysis, and stress testing.**

**12**  Which Cisco component, also available online, provides the IOS command reference, product reference, and other valuable information?

**The Cisco Documentation CD-ROM.**

**13**  Which tasks do you need to complete before ordering direct from Cisco using the Internet Commerce Apps?

— **Obtain a valid Cisco purchase order or sales order number for your company, as well as your company billing information.**

— **Complete the online registration form to become a CCO user.**

— **Complete and send a hard copy of an Internet Commerce Agreement (ICA) to the appropriate Cisco Systems personnel.**

**14**  What does CCO MarketPlace allow you to do?

**MarketPlace provides for online ordering of Cisco networking products, promotional merchandise, and training materials.**

**15**  Name at least one major service that the CCO Software Library makes available.

**CCO Software Library has major upgrades and maintenance releases of Cisco software products, as well as network management and security applications for workstation servers, selected demo and beta distributions, software upgrade planners, software checklists, and custom-file-access postings of various software.**

**16**   What are the member components of Cisco Bug Toolkit?

**Bug Navigator II, Bug Watcher, and alert agents**

**17**   Who can submit questions to the CCO Open Forum, and who provides answers to questions on CCO Open Forum?

**Registered customers can submit questions and the Open Forum CCIEs (whose opinions do not necessarily reflect those of Cisco Systems) reply to the questions.**

**18**   What are the four general pieces of information that the customer must provide to TAC when opening a case?

— **The maintenance contract number for the product that needs service, as well as the product's serial number.**

— **A brief description of the problem.**

— **The relevant facts surrounding the network and the case.**

— **The priority level of the problem.**

**19**   How many priority levels are available to be assigned to a new case to be opened with TAC?

**Four**

**20**   What are the tasks that the Case Management Toolkit allows you to do?

**CCO Case Management Toolkit allows registered customers with the appropriate service or contract agreement with Cisco Systems to open, query, and update cases online.**

**21**   Name three classes of network media test equipment.

**Volt/Ohm meters, cable testers (scanners), and time domain reflectometers (TDRs) and optical time domain reflectometer (OTDRs).**

**22**   What are the tasks network monitors can perform?

**Network monitors allow you to capture, display, and save (store) network traffic data from a network segment.**

**Depending on the brand, further functionalities such as traffic statistics, alarms, and others may also be provided.**

**23**   Name the tool that does multilayer analysis of network traffic?

**Protocol analyzer.**

**24** What are the five functional areas of network management?

**Fault management, accounting management, performance management, security management, and configuration and name management.**

**25** What is Cisco Systems' flagship network management software called?

**CiscoWorks.**

**26** List at least three members of the CWSI Campus Application.

**TrafficDirector, VlanDirector, AtmDirector, CiscoView, and UserTracking.**

**27** Name Cisco's network simulation and modeling tool.

**Netsys.**

**28** What does the acronym CCO stand for, and what is the URL address for CCO?

**Cisco Connection Online at www.cisco.com.**

**29** Name at least two tools or resources from CCO available for problem prevention.

**The Documentation CD (also available online), CCO MarketPlace, and CCO Software Center.**

**30** Name at least three tools or resources that CCO provides for problem correction and troubleshooting.

**The Bug Toolkit, Troubleshooting Engine, Stack Decoder, Open Forum, and Case Management Toolkit.**

# Chapter 2

## "Do I Know This Already?" Quiz

**1** Explain the importance of using a systematic troubleshooting method.

**A systematic troubleshooting method guarantees progress—the time and effort spent produce results. The step-by-step and methodological nature of this approach continuously allows you to discover more facts and eliminate false hypotheses and possibilities.**

**The documentation produced will aid current and future network maintenance efforts.**

**If you do not use a systematic troubleshooting method, you may waste a substantial amount of time, effort, and money.**

**2** Draw a flow diagram of a systematic troubleshooting model.

**The following figure is a flow diagram of a systematic troubleshooting model.**

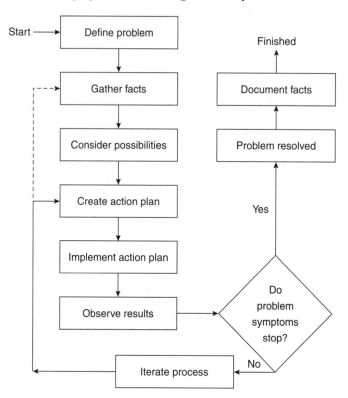

**3** What are the general tasks performed during the problem definition step?

**During the problem definition step you make a clear statement of the problem in terms of the associated symptoms and possible causes. The problem definition would preferably reference the network baseline.**

**4** What tools/resources can assist you during the fact gathering step?

**Information provided/reported by the end-user(s) is of value. It is also useful to obtain information from network engineers and administrators, managers, and so on. You can use basic fact gathering techniques with commands such as**

**traceroute or show ip route or various debug traces. You may use more sophisticated tools such as network monitors, protocol analyzers, and network management systems to gather facts as well.**

5   Based on what information do you eliminate possibilities (those you considered during the problem definition step) and consider new possibilities?

**You consider certain possibilities for further examination and eliminate others based on gathered facts, plus your knowledge of the network (baseline), devices, operating systems, and any relevant tips, reported bugs, and compatibility issues.**

6   What do you do if you hypothesize many possibilities for the network problem?

**If many hypotheses are formed, you must order them based on their likelihood and examine them one at a time and individually in that order.**

7   Name a common technique that is deployed when you plan actions.

**Divide and conquer, or using a partitioning effect.**

8   What kind of mistakes can happen during the action implementation step?

**The following are common mistakes during the action implementation step:**
— **More than one change made at a time**

— **Changes not documented**

— **Configurations not saved/backed up before changes made**

9   What do you do if none of the possibilities you hypothesized ends up being the cause of your network problem?

**You must think of more possibilities by gathering more facts. There is also a chance that the IOS has a bug specific to the problem you are experiencing. Use CCO's Bug Toolkit to check this out.**

10   What are some of the benefits of documenting a solved problem?

**The main benefit of documenting your work after you solve a problem is that the experience can be transferred to others. Otherwise, it is possible that in the future someone else will spend as much time as you did—or more—solving a similar problem.**

**Furthermore, by studying the documentation, others can understand what you did exactly, and why you did it.**

# Q&A

1  Write the title of each of the systematic troubleshooting method's steps in the appropriate box on the diagram below:

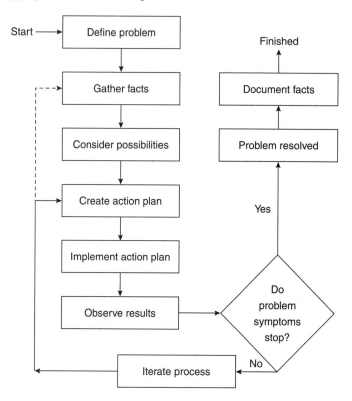

2  Explain the importance of using a systematic troubleshooting method.

**A systematic troubleshooting method guarantees progress—the time and effort spent produce results. The step-by-step and methodological nature of this approach continuously allows you to discover more facts and eliminate false hypotheses and possibilities.**

**The documentation produced will aid current and future network maintenance efforts.**

**If you do not use a systematic troubleshooting method, you may waste a substantial amount of time, effort, and money.**

**3**  What are the general tasks performed during the problem definition step?

**During the problem definition step, you make a clear statement of the problem in terms of the associated symptoms and possible causes. The problem definition would preferably reference the network baseline.**

**4**  What tools/resources can assist you during the fact gathering step?

**Information provided/reported by the end-user(s) is of value. It is also useful to obtain information from network engineers and administrators, managers, and so on. You can use basic fact gathering techniques with commands such as traceroute or show ip route or various debug traces. You may use more sophisticated tools such as network monitors (for example, sniffers), protocol analyzers, and network management systems to gather facts as well.**

**5**  Based on what information do you eliminate possibilities (those you considered during the problem definition step) and consider new possibilities?

**You consider certain possibilities for further examination and eliminate others based on gathered facts, plus your knowledge of the network (baseline), devices, operating systems, and any relevant tips, reported bugs, and compatibility issues.**

**6**  What do you do if you hypothesize many possibilities for the network problem?

**If many hypotheses are formed, you must order them based on their likelihood and examine them one at a time and individually in that order.**

**7**  Name a common technique that is deployed when you plan actions.

**Divide and conquer, or, using a partitioning effect.**

**8**  What kind of mistakes can happen during the action implementation step?

**The following are common mistakes during the action implementation step:**
— **More than one change made at a time.**

— **Changes not documented.**

— **Configurations not saved/backed up before changes made.**

**9**  What do you do if none of the possibilities you hypothesized ends up being the cause of your network problem?

**You must think of more possibilities by gathering more facts. There is also a chance that the IOS has a bug specific to the problem you are experiencing. Use CCO's Bug Toolkit to check this out.**

10 What are some of the benefits of documenting a solved problem?

**The main benefit of documenting your work after you solve a problem is that the experience can be transferred to others. Otherwise, it is possible that in the future someone else will spend as much time as you did—or more—solving a similar problem.**

**Furthermore, by studying the documentation, others can understand what you did exactly, and why you did it.**

# Chapter 3

## "Do I Know This Already?" Quiz

1 What is a key point in identifying troubleshooting targets, with respect to internetwork component dependencies?

**A key point in identifying troubleshooting targets is recognizing the dependency of each component on the correct functioning of the other components or protocols. For instance, if a user has trouble logging on to a server, you should first ensure that the underlying networking protocol (such as TCP/IP) permits communication between the user's device and the authenticating server, before you focus the troubleshooting effort on the user's device or on the server. If the underlying internetworking protocol is indeed TCP/IP, you can test the connection path between the user's device and the server using simple tools such as ping. Yet, if TCP/IP connectivity is not in place, before focusing on troubleshooting TCP/IP, you must ensure that the underlying data link layer is in working order.**

2 Before starting to troubleshoot the data link layer, what must you assure yourself of?

**You must make sure that the underlying physical layer (cables, connectors, repeaters, hubs, terminators, and so on) are not faulty.**

3 Name two of the router components that are often examined when troubleshooting the data link layer.

**Interface and controller.**

4 What information does the output of the **show interfaces** command provide?

**The output of the show interfaces command gives you a great amount of information about the state of the interface (physical and logical) and also some statistics about the data sent/received, errors encountered, and so on.**

**5** List at least two types of information displayed by the **show controllers** command.

**This command displays a variety of data such as firmware versions, memory management, error counters, and some configuration information for each controller's interface card(s).**

**6** How is the MAC address of an interface card formed? How can you see it? Where is it stored? Is it always identical to the bia?

**The MAC (Media Access Control) address of an interface is stored in its RAM and it can be seen on the second line of the show interfaces command output. The MAC address of an interface is copied from its ROM (the address stored in ROM is called the burned-in address, or bia for short) during the initialization of the interface card. Hence, the bia and the MAC address are usually identical. However, in the following cases the bia and the MAC address may not be the same:**

— **The administrator of the router hard-codes the MAC address (the ability to do this is IOS/version dependent).**

— **An upper-layer protocol modifies the MAC address (DECNET does that).**

**7** Why would an Ethernet interface be reported as up and the line protocol be reported as down?

**In this case the interface keepalive is failing. One reason might be that the interface is not (or is improperly) connected to the media. In certain types of interfaces where two connectors are provided—for example, an AUI and an RJ-45connector—the AUI is usually the default medium. Hence, another reason for this condition could be that the media type is not auto-sensed and the administrator failed to specify the correct media type.**

**In certain circumstances—when IPX is in use, for instance—encapsulation mismatch between the setting of your router's Ethernet interface and the other devices on that Ethernet segment can cause this as well.**

**8** List at least two types of errors that are common in Token Ring networks.

**The line errors, burst errors, and the receive-congested errors are among the most common errors reported in Token Ring networks.**

**9** What information does a CDP device send out about itself?

**A device sends (multicasts) the following information about itself in its CDP updates:**

— **Device name**

— **Device capabilities**

— **Hardware platform**

— **The port type and number through which CDP information is being sent out**

— **One address per upper layer protocol**

**10**  What are the two general classes of networking protocols? (Briefly explain each one.)

**Network protocols are divided into two classes based on their characteristics: connection-oriented protocols and connectionless protocols. Connection-oriented protocols are those that establish an end-to-end connection before submitting data. Connectionless protocols, on the other hand, do not establish a connection prior to sending data.**

# Q&A

**1**  Why is the correct function of the data link layer so significant, and if this layer is faulty, what kinds of symptoms will you experience?

**All networking layers, except the physical layer, rely on the correct operation of the data link (control). If there are faults at this layer, reports will be made of problems such as application failures, inability to make connections, network slowdowns, distorted data, and so on.**

**2**  List a few methods that can be used to test proper functioning of the physical layer.

**Look at the first line of the** show interface *x* **command output and make sure that the interface is up and line protocol is up.**

**Look at the Link LED of the appropriate interface.**

**Manually check and observe for yourself the condition and type of cables, jacks, and connectors. Look for damage, standards violation, compatibility, and appropriateness.**

**Use physical media test equipment.**

**3**  What is the term used to refer to devices that are on a common data link?

**Adjacent (or connected) devices.**

**4**  How does a router check the state of its link on an Ethernet interface?

**An Ethernet interface sends (transmits) keepalives every 10 seconds and it also listens for traffic (such as keepalives) in order to discover and report on the state of its link.**

5   The interpretation of the performance (I/O) and error statistics displayed by the **show interfaces** command depends on what other pieces of information?

**When those counters were cleared last.**

**Knowing the time period through which those counters have accumulated, how those statistics compare to your baseline.**

6   What is a router's IOS response to the **show interfaces ethernet** command?

**On the Cisco 7000 series, if you type the show interfaces ethernet command, the ethernet keyword is ignored and your command is interpreted as show interfaces. On the other hand, if you type show interfaces ethernet on a Cisco 2502 router, you get the "% Incomplete command." response.**

7   If you enter the **show interfaces** command for an interface that has been removed, what will the command output show?

**On the output you will see interface statistics and the "Hardware has been removed" message. On the other hand, removed software interfaces (for example, a subinterface) will be reported as deleted.**

8   Why would the first line of the **show interfaces ethernet 0** output display Ethernet0 to be disabled?

**If the interface experiences more than 5000 errors during the keepalive interval (10 seconds by default), it will be reported as disabled.**

9   Which command must you enter to specify which one of the available physical connectors of a router's interface should be used?

**The media-type interface configuration command.**

10   How do you check current settings of the **media-type** command on an Ethernet 0 interface?

**Use the show controller ethernet 0 command.**

11   What is the bia of an interface? How can you see it? Where is it stored? And what is it composed of?

**The bia is the burned-in address of a LAN interface card. It can be seen on the second line of the show interfaces command output and it is stored in the ROM of the interface. The bia is 12 hex digits (48 bits) long. The leftmost 6 hex digits of the bia identify the manufacturer of the card (OUI), and the rightmost 6 hex digits of the bia are referred to as the serial number.**

**12** How is the MAC address of an interface card formed? How can you see it? Where is it stored? And is it always identical to the bia?

**The MAC address of an interface is stored in its RAM and it can be seen on the second line of the show interfaces command output. The MAC address of an interface is copied from its ROM/bia during the initialization of the interface card. Therefore, the bia and the MAC address are usually identical. However, in the following cases the bia and the MAC address may not be the same:**

— **The administrator of the router hard-codes the MAC address (the ability to do this is IOS/Version dependent).**

— **An upper-layer protocol modifies the MAC address (for example, DECNET does this).**

**13** What is the format that the output of the **show interfaces ethernet 0** uses for displaying the reliability and load parameters? Over what time interval are these parameters measured?

**Reliability (Rely) of the interface is displayed as a fraction of 255 (255/255 is 100% reliability), calculated as an exponential average over 5 minutes. Load on the interface is also displayed as a fraction of 255 (255/255 is completely saturated) and calculated as an exponential average over 5 minutes.**

**14** Provide a reason for a **show interfaces** command output showing a nonzero value for the No Buffer counter.

**Broadcast storms on Ethernets and bursts of noise on serial lines are often responsible for no input buffer events.**

**15** What do the Total Runts and the Total Giants counters inform you about?

**Total Runts is the number of packets that are discarded because they are smaller than the medium's minimum packet size. For instance, any Ethernet packet that is less than 64 bytes is considered a runt. Total Giants is the number of packets that are discarded because they exceed the medium's maximum packet size. For example, any Ethernet packet that is greater than 1518 bytes is considered a giant. (Note: Frames that are larger than 1518 bytes but less than or equal to 1522 bytes are called baby giants, and when encountered, they cause the counter for giants to increment, but they are not discarded.)**

**16** The Total Errors counter includes the number of occurrences of which error conditions?

**Runts, giants, no buffer, CRC, frame, overrun, and ignored counts.**

**17** What does a high number of reported CRC errors on an interface usually indicate?

**On a LAN, CRC errors usually indicate noise or transmission problems on the LAN interface or the LAN bus itself. A high number of CRCs is usually the result of collisions or a station transmitting bad data.**

**18** What is a generally acceptable rate of collisions on an Ethernet? What are late collisions?

**The rule of thumb is that a segment has too many collisions if the number of collisions exceeds approximately 0.1% of the total number of the output packets. Late collisions usually happen in overextended LANs (Ethernet or transceiver cable too long, more than two repeaters between stations, or too many cascaded multi-port transceivers).**

**19** Explain the reason(s) why a router interface would report resets.

**Interface resets can happen if packets queued for transmission were not sent within several seconds. On a serial line, this can be caused by a malfunctioning modem that is not supplying the transmit clock signal, or by a cable problem. If the system notices that the carrier detect line of a serial interface is up, but the line protocol is down, it periodically resets the interface in an effort to restart it. Interface resets also occur when an interface is looped back or shut down.**

**20** What will the first line of the **show interfaces tokenring** *n* output report about the state of the Token Ring interface if the cable is not plugged into the interface card?

**In contrast to the Ethernet case, if you disconnect the cable from the Token Ring interface, the show interfaces tokenring *n* output will not report the interface being up and the line protocol as down. What you will see is: "Interface is Initializing" and "Line Protocol is Down."**

**21** What does the Single ring/multiring node field on the output of the **show interfaces tokenring** *n* indicate?

**It indicates whether a node is enabled to collect and use source routing information (RIF) for routable Token Ring protocols. It shows Multiring when RIF processing is enabled and it shows Single ring when RIF processing is disabled.**

**22** On the output of the **show interfaces tokenring** *n* command, what does the field Group Address indicate?

**It tells you the interface's group address (multicast address), if any.**

**23** Provide a short description for the line errors, burst errors, and receive-congested errors of Token Ring networks. Suggest a troubleshooting action to be taken in case these counters are reported with nonzero values.

**The line error counter increments as CRC check failures occur. The burst error counters report on signaling errors seen (these are usually due to noise and/or crosstalk). The receive-congested error counter tells if the station has had difficulty keeping up with processing of the received traffic.**

**In cases where these counters are nonzero and require investigation, use a network monitor or protocol analyzer to capture traffic and investigate which stations are acting up or to find out if you need to test the media or Token Ring hardware and cabling.**

**24** Specify the two classes of soft errors in Token Ring and briefly describe each.

**The Token Ring soft errors are divided into two classes: isolating soft errors and non-isolating soft errors. Isolating soft errors are those that are caused by the local station, its NAUN (Nearest Active Upstream Neighbor), or the medium in between the two. The non-isolating soft errors are not necessarily caused by the local station or its NAUN; these errors can be caused by device(s) anywhere in the ring.**

**25** On the output of the **show interfaces fddi** command, what are the key fields and their expected values for a dual attached device that is in good working condition and reports no errors?

**The Phy-A and Phy-B are reported as Active, status is usually in ILS (idle line state), ECM (Entity Coordination Management) is in, CFM (ConFiguration Management) is thru, and RMT (Ring ManagemenT) is ring_op.**

**26** List two of ATM interface encapsulation types.

**AAL5, PVC, or SVC mode.**

**27** What do the TX Buffers and RX Buffers fields of the **show interfaces atm** command output report on?

**TX Buffer's counter reports on the maximum number of transmit buffers for simultaneous packet fragmentation (set using the atm txbuff interface configuration command) and the RX Buffer's counter reports on the maximum number of receive buffers for simultaneous packet reassembly (set using the atm rxbuff interface configuration command).**

**28** How is the value of the Maximum active VCs field from the **show interfaces atm** command output interpreted?

**This field reports on the maximum number of supported virtual circuits; it is set using the atm maxvc interface configuration command. Valid values are 256, 512, 1024, or 2048. The default is 2048.**

**29**  How is the value of the VCs per VP field from the **show interfaces atm** command output interpreted?

**This field reports on the maximum number of VCIs to support per VPI; it is set using the atm vc-per-vp interface configuration command.**

**30**  How can you display the content of a device's CDP table?

**The CDP table of a device is displayed using the show cdp neighbor [detail] command.**

**31**  List the general actions of a connection-oriented protocol.

**The sequence of steps performed by a connection-oriented protocol are:**

**1. Establish a connection**

**2. Send (and perhaps receive) data**

**3. Terminate (tear down) the connection**

**32**  What is the IP ARP table? How can you display it?

**The MAC addresses discovered as a result of ARP requests are stored in the ARP table (cache) for a predetermined period of time. The purpose of the ARP table is to prevent repeating ARP requests that are for the same IP address (at least in a short period of time). To display the Address Resolution Protocol (ARP) cache, use the show ip arp EXEC command.**

**33**  What would a high number of format errors on the output of the **show novell traffic** indicate?

**A high number of format errors can be a sign of encapsulation mismatch on the local network.**

**34**  What is the normal value for the Checksum Errors field on the output of the **show novell traffic** command?

**Checksum errors should not be reported because IPX does not use a checksum.**

**35**  Explain the meaning of the Encapsulation failed field on the output of the **show appletalk traffic** command.

**This field reports the number of times packets were received for a connected network but the node was not found (for example, AppleTalk ARP address resolution failed).**

**36**  What is the most common reason for routers to report Wrong encapsulation on the output of the **show appletalk traffic** command?

**Nonextended AppleTalk packet on an extended AppleTalk port (or vice versa).**

**37** Based on the captured traffic displayed as follows, specify the frame type and explain its purpose.

```
DLC: -----DLC Header -----
DLC:
DLC: Frame 2 arrived at 14:53:37.6592; frame size is 60 (003C hex) bytes.
DLC: Destination = FF FF FF FF FF FF
DLC: Source = Station cisco 01 56 A8
DLC: Ethertype = 0806 (ARP)
DLC:
DLC: ----- ARP/RARP frame -----
DLC:
DLC: Hardware type = 1 (10 MB ETHERNET)
DLC: Protocol type = 0800 (IP)
DLC: Length of hardware address = 6 bytes
DLC: Length of protocol address = 4 bytes
DLC: Opcode 1 (ARP Request)
DLC: Sender's hardware address = cisco 0156A8
DLC: Sender's protocol address = [144.251.100.204]
DLC: Target hardware address = 00 00 00 00 00 00
DLC: Target protocol address = [144.251.100.100]
```

**Ethernet II (Cisco ARPA) frame, Ethernet data link broadcast.**

**Carrying ARP (Request).**

**An IP device with IP address 144.251.100.204 is searching for the MAC address of the IP device with IP address 144.251.100.100.**

**38** Based on the captured traffic displayed as follows, specify the frame type and explain its purpose.

```
DLC: ----- DLC Header -----
DLC:
DLC: Frame 3 arrived at 15:06:34.789; frame size is 141 (008D hex) bytes..
DLC: Destination = 09 00 07 FF FF FF
DLC: Source = cisco 059AC2
DLC: Length = 127

LLC: ----- LLC Header -----
LLC:
LLC: DSAP = AA, SSAP = AA, Command, Unnumbered frame: UI
LLC:

SNAP: --- SNAP Header ----
SNAP:
SNAP: OUI = 080007 (Apple)
SNAP: Type = 809B (AppleTalk)
SNAP:
DDP:----- DDP Header -----
DDP:
DDP:  Hop Count = 0
DDP:  Length = 119
```

```
DDP:  Checksum = 396A (correct)
DDP: Destination network number = 0
DDP: Destination node = 255
DDP: Destination socket = 1 (RTMP)
DDP: Source network number = 1140
DDP: Source node = 100
DDP: Source socket = 1 (RTMP)
DDP: DDP protocol type = 1 (RTMP data)
DDP:
RTMP: ----- RTMP Data -----
RTMP:
RTMP: Extended packet, Version 2
RTMP: Net = 1140
RTMP: Node ID Length = 8 Bits
RTMP: Node ID = 100
RTMP: Tuple 1 (Extended): Cable range = 1140 TO 1140, Distance = 0
RTMP: Tuple 2 (Extended): Range = 47 TO 47, Distance = 2
RTMP: Tuple 3 (Extended): Range = 1000 TO 1005, Distance = 1
RTMP: Tuple 4 (Extended): Range = 1010 TO 1010, Distance = 2
...
```

**Ethernet SNAP frame, Ethernet data link multicast.**

**Carrying Apple AppleTalk (Extended, Version 2).**

**An AppleTalk device with address 1140.100 is broadcasting a DDP packet that encapsulates RTMP data (routing table).**

**39** Based on the captured traffic displayed as follows, specify the frame type and explain its purpose.

```
DLC: ----- DLC Header -----
DLC:
DLC: Frame 4 arrived at 15:07:13.281; frame size is 238 (00EE hex) bytes.
DLC: Destination = Broadcast
DLC: Source = 3Com C25C79
DLC: 802.3 length = 224

IPX: ----- IPX Header -----
IPX:
IPX: Checksum = FFFF
IPX: Length = 224
IPX: Transport control = 00
IPX:     0000 .... = Reserved
IPX:     .... 0000 = Hop Count
IPX: Packet type = 0 (Novell)
IPX:
IPX: Dest Network.Node = 1000.FFFFFFFFFFFF Socket=1106(SAP)
IPX: Source Network.Node = 1000.02 60 8C C2 5C 79 Socket=1106(SAP)
```

**Novell 802.3 (Cisco Novell_Ether), Ethernet data link broadcast.**

**Carrying IPX packet.**

**An IPX device with address 1000.0260.8CC2.5C79 is sending a broadcast on the local IPX network 1000 (1000.FFFF.FFFF.FFFF) encapsulating SAP.**

**40** Based on the captured traffic displayed as follows, specify the frame type and explain its purpose.

```
DLC: ----- DLC Header -----
DLC:
DLC: Frame 1 arrived at 15:05:33.389; frame size is 62 (003E hex) bytes.
DLC: AC: Frame priority 0, Reservation priority 0, Monitor count 0
DLC: FC: LLC frame, PCF attention code: None
DLC: FS: Addr recognized indicators: 00, Frame copied indicators: 00
DLC: Destination = Station cisco A05903
DLC: Source      = Station IBM 0AE591
DLC:
LLC: ----- LLC Header -----
LLC:
LLC: DSAP = AA, SSAP = AA, Command, Unnumbered frame: UI
LLC:
SNAP: ----- SNAP Header -----
SNAP:
SNAP: Type = 0800 (IP)
SNAP:
```

**Token Ring SNAP frame, data link unicast.**

**Encapsulating an IP packet.**

# Chapter 4

## "Do I Know This Already?" Quiz

**1** Briefly explain why Cisco IOS troubleshooting commands/tools need proper handling.

**Despite their importance in terms of the valuable information they provide, these tools inevitably utilize some processing cycles and memory of the router. Furthermore, they may disable or at least have a negative effect on some of router's internal (optimized) operations, such as fast switching.**

**2**  What does proper handling of troubleshooting tools entail?

**Proper usage of troubleshooting tools means that you should be selective in your use of tools and should use them with appropriate focus to gather the desired information. You must stop using these tools immediately after you attain your objective. This also means that you should limit the period of time during which these tools are used.**

**3**  Provide a generic explanation for route caching (or fast switching) and the motivation behind it.

**During a time interval, the packets that are arriving into a router can be divided into a number of groups (called streams), each of which comprises a bunch of packets with a common destination. A router usually forwards packets that belong to the same stream in a similar way. In other words, it forwards them out from the same interface. The result of the routing decision made is based on the processing of the first packet of the stream. The result of processing the first packet of a stream can be reapplied to the packets following the first one. This is called route caching. Since the routing task is complex and resource consuming, and it introduces latency, skipping this operation on all the packets except the first (from the same stream) is very advantageous and efficient.**

**4**  Which of the route caching methods are not enabled by default? And from which configuration mode (prompt level) can they be enabled?

**All of the switching (route caching) features, except fast switching (and optimum switching for IP on supported interfaces), need to be turned on manually. Enabling a specific type of switching is an interface configuration task and is done for each protocol individually. Of course, the type of switching that is available is router/component dependent.**

**5**  With regard to speed and switching optimization, how did Cisco Systems improve the Cisco 7500 routers (in comparison to the 7000 series)?

**The internal bus of the 7500 router (CyBus) operates at 1 Gbps, which is about twice as fast as the 7000 router's CxBus.**

**Instead of having two components (SSP and RP, or SP and RP) as in 7000 routers, the 7500 router is equipped with one component called the Route/Switch Processor (which eliminates the slow 153 Mbps system bus connecting the RP and SSP).**

**The switch cache of the 7500 router, called Optimum Switch Cache, is faster than the Silicon Switch Cache of the 7000 router.**

**6** Briefly describe the advantages of Netflow switching. Also specify whether there should be any precautions with respect to enabling Netflow switching.

**Netflow switching caches security information and accounting information as well as routing information for each flow. Hence, once a network flow is identified and the first packet (of the flow) is processed, for the following packets the access list checks are bypassed and packet switching and statistics captures are performed in tandem. Netflow also allows for exporting captured data to management utilities. Netflow switching, especially with the export option, can be quite resource consuming, so caution must be exercised when enabling this feature in production network routers.**

**7** Provide at least three examples of operations or packet types that are process switched.

**Data-link layer broadcasts**

**Packets subjected to Debug**

**Packets delivering error log messages to syslog**

**SNMP packets**

**Protocol translations**

**Tunneling**

**Custom and priority queuing**

**Link compression**

**Keepalives**

**8** Before you activate Debug, what are some of its characteristics that you should consider?

**Debug is treated as a very high priority task, it can consume a significant amount of resources, and the router is forced to process-switch the packets being debugged.**

**9** Before you enable debugging on a router, you are encouraged to check the router's CPU utilization. What is the command that allows you to do that? If the utilization is above 50%, are you encouraged to debug packets or to debug events?

**Before starting to use the debug command, see the CPU utilization of your router using the show processes cpu exec command. If your router's CPU utilization is consistently at 50% or more, you are advised to debug events instead of packets.**

**10** What is the default setting (for example, enabled/disabled, default destination) for message logging?

**Message logging is enabled by default and it is directed to the console line and the internal buffer.**

**11** What information does the output of the **show logging** Cisco IOS exec command display?

**It displays the state of syslog error and event logging, which type of logging (destination) is enabled, and the messages that are currently stored in the internal buffer.**

**12** The outputs of the **show memory** and the **show processes [cpu]** commands will most likely be asked for in which situation (loss of functionality, crash, or performance degradation)?

**Performance degradation.**

**13** If the output of **show buffer** command displays a large number of misses, increasing the value of which one of the buffer management parameters (Permanent, Min-Free, Max-Free, Initial) will most likely remedy the situation?

**Permanent and Min-Free.**

**14** The **show processes** command's output provides two numbers separated by a slash (for example, 4%/4%) for the CPU utilization over the last five seconds. How are those numbers interpreted?

**The first number is the total CPU utilization, and the second one is the utilization due to interrupt routines (in the last five seconds).**

**15** Which command causes the router to attempt to produce a core dump when it crashes?

**The exception dump *ip-address* global configuration command (*ip-address* is the address of your TFTP, FTP, or RCP server) causes the router to attempt to produce a core dump when it crashes.**

# Q&A

**1** Briefly explain why Cisco IOS troubleshooting commands and tools need proper handling.

**Despite their importance in terms of the valuable information they provide, these tools inevitably utilize some processing cycles and memory of the router. Furthermore, they may disable or at least have a negative effect on some of the router's internal (optimized) operations such as fast switching.**

**2** What does proper handling of troubleshooting tools entail?

**Proper usage of troubleshooting tools means that you should be selective about which one you use and use it with appropriate focus to gather the desired information. You must stop using these tools immediately after you attain your objective. You should also limit the period of time during which these tools are used.**

**3** Define switching and specify whether it is considered a complex task.

**Switching is commonly defined as the process that takes charge of moving data units (in other words, frames or packets) through the anatomy of an internetworking device. The mere task of moving a data unit (a packet, in the context of routers) from one internal component to another is one of the simplest and least resource-consuming tasks.**

**4** Define routing and compare its complexity to switching.

**Routing can be simply defined as the operation that attempts to select an output interface and perhaps a next hop for a packet, usually based on the packet's destination address. Routing is considered more complex and resource consuming than switching.**

**5** List the sources of information used by a routing process for building its routing table.

— **The network segments that the router is actively connected to**

— **The usable static routes available in the router configuration**

— **The dynamic routing entries that the routing protocols offer**

— **The routing policies or restrictions that are imposed**

— **The usable default routes available**

**6** When a packet is process-switched, what major tasks are performed?

**Both routing and switching.**

**7** Provide a short and generic explanation for route caching (or fast switching) and the purpose behind it.

**During a time interval, the packets that are arriving into a router can be divided into a number of groups, each of which comprises a bunch of packets with a common destination. Because a router usually forwards those packets with the same destination in a similar way (i.e., out from the same interface), the result of the routing decision made based on processing of the first packet of a particular group (all those with the same destination) can be reused on the following packets (with the same destination address). This is called route caching. Since**

the routing task is complex and resource consuming and introduces latency, skipping this operation on all the packets except the first (from the group, all of which have the same destination address) is very advantageous and efficient.

**8** Which of the route caching methods are not enabled by default? And from which configuration mode (prompt level) can they be enabled?

**All of the switching (route caching) features, except fast switching (and optimum switching for IP on supported interfaces), need to be turned on manually. Enabling a specific type of switching is an interface configuration task and it is done for each protocol individually. Of course, the type of switching available is router dependent.**

**9** On which component of the Cisco 7000 router is the Fast Switch Cache located?

**Route Processor (RP).**

**10** Name the two major components that participate in the routing and switching tasks within a Cisco 7000 router.

**Route Processor and Silicon Switch Processor (or Switch Processor).**

**11** What is the difference between the Silicon Switch Processor (SSP) and the Switch Processor (SP) with respect to the switching cache options?

**The early models of the Cisco 7000 routers had RP and SP. The Switch Processor (in the earlier models) had an Autonomous Switch Cache only. The SSP (later introduced by Cisco Systems) is equipped with both an Autonomous Switch Cache and a Silicon Switch Cache.**

**12** What is the command for enabling IP fast switching on an interface?

**ip route-cache**

**13** What is the command for enabling IP autonomous switching on a Cisco 7000 series router interface?

**ip route-cache cbus**

**14** What is the command for enabling IP silicon switching on a Cisco 7000 series router (with SSP) interface?

**ip route-cache sse**

**15** With regard to speed and switching optimization, how did Cisco Systems improve the Cisco 7500 routers in comparison to the 7000 series?

**The internal bus of the 7500 router (CyBus) operates at 1 Gbps, which is about twice as fast as the 7000 router's CxBus.**

Instead of having two components (SSP and RP) as in 7000 routers, the 7500 router is equipped with one component called the Route/Switch Processor (which eliminates the slow 153 Mbps system bus connecting the RP and SSP).

The switch cache of the 7500 router, called Optimum Switch Cache, is faster than the Silicon Switch Cache of the 7000 router.

**16**  What switching method (route caching) can be enabled on the 7000/7500 series routers' VIP cards?

**Distributed switching.**

**17**  On which Cisco router models is Netflow switching supported? (Specify the IOS version.)

**Netflow switching was introduced with Cisco IOS version 11.1(2) for the Cisco 7000, 7200, and 7500 routers with an RSP.**

**18**  What information does Netflow use as the basis of identifying a flow?

**Netflow identifies a flow based on the source and destination IP address, source and destination port, protocol type (number), type of service (TOS), and input interface.**

**19**  Briefly describe the advantages of Netflow switching. Also specify whether there should be any precautions with respect to enabling Netflow switching.

**Netflow switching caches security information and accounting information as well as routing information for each flow. Hence, once a network flow is identified and the first packet (of the flow) is processed, for the following packets the access list checks are bypassed and packet switching and statistics capture are performed in tandem. Netflow also allows for exporting captured data to management utilities. Netflow switching, especially with the export option, can be quite resource consuming, so caution must be exercised when enabling this feature in production network routers.**

**20**  What is the command for enabling IP Netflow switching on a supported router interface?

**ip route-cache flow**

**21**  What are the only switching (route caching) options on the 4000, 3000, and 2500 series routers?

**Fast switching (performed on the shared memory) and process switching (which means no route caching is done).**

**22**  The output of which command includes information about whether fast switching is enabled/disabled for a particular protocol on a particular interface?

**router# show [*protocol*] interface**

**23** Which command can be used to see the statistics on the number of packets that are process switched and fast switched?

**router# show interface stats**

**24** Provide at least three examples of operations or packet types that are process switched.

— **Data-link layer broadcasts**

— **Packets subjected to debug**

— **Packets delivering error log messages to syslog**

— **SNMP packets**

— **Protocol translations**

— **Tunneling**

— **Custom and priority queuing**

— **Link compression**

— **Keepalives**

**25** What are some facts about the **debug** privileged exec mode command that one must keep in mind before using it?

**debug is treated as a very high priority task, it can consume a significant amount of resources, and the router is forced to process-switch the packets being debugged.**

**26** Which service must be loaded if you need to see a timestamp with each of the **debug** output lines? (Also provide the command syntax.)

**If you want to see a timestamp along with each line of the debug output, you must load the timestamp service with the following command:**

**router(config)#service timestamps debug [*datetime* | *uptime*]**

**27** What command enables you to see the debug output from within a Telnet session?

**The terminal monitor privileged exec mode command.**

**28** Compare debugging with the packet option to debugging with the events option.

**Event debugging is less resource intensive than packet debugging, but packet debugging produces more information.**

**29** Which command enables debugging for all protocols and activities? Are there any concerns regarding usage of this command?

**Turning debugging on for everything (using the debug all privileged exec mode command) is seriously discouraged in production networks. This command causes a tremendous amount of information to be generated and displayed (very fast), and it can severely diminish your router's performance or even render the router unusable.**

30 Before you enable debugging on a router, you are encouraged to check the router's CPU utilization. What is the command that allows you to do that? If the utilization is above 50%, are you encouraged to debug packets or to debug events?

**Before starting to use the debug command, see the CPU utilization of your router using the show processes cpu exec command. If your router's CPU utilization is consistently at 50% or more, you are advised to debug events instead of packets.**

31 Specify the command syntax for enabling debugging for those IP packets that satisfy (are permitted by) an access list 100.

**Router# debug ip packet detail 100**

32 What is the default setting (for example, enabled/disabled, default destination) for message logging?

**Message logging is enabled by default and it is directed to the console line and the internal buffer.**

33 How do the logging message destination options compare in terms of the overhead they introduce to a router?

**The following relationship demonstrates how different methods of logging compare in terms of the overhead they produce:**

**Buffered logging < Syslog < Virtual terminal < Console logging**

34 Which Cisco IOS router command turns console logging on and specifies the level of logging to be directed to the console?

**Router(config)# logging console [*level*]**

35 By using which Cisco IOS router command can you enable sending logging messages to the internal buffer and specify the level of logging desired to be buffered?

**Router(config)# logging buffered [*level*]**

36 Specify the Cisco IOS router command that enables sending logging messages to the virtual terminal sessions and specifies the level of logging desired to be directed to the virtual terminal lines.

**Router(config)# logging monitor [level]**

**37** What Cisco IOS router command would you use to make a router's logging messages be sent to a syslog server at IP address 10.1.2.3?

**Router(config)# logging 10.1.2.3**

**38** What Cisco IOS router command would you use to make virtual terminal lines receive logging messages at the errors level and higher (i.e., errors, critical, alerts, emergencies)?

**Router(config)# logging monitor error**

**39** What is the severity of the following logging message?

`%TR-3-WIREFAULT:Unit[0],wirefault:check the lobe cable MAU connection`

**3 (error)**

**40** What information does the output of the **show logging** Cisco IOS exec command display?

**It displays the state of syslog error and event logging, which type of logging (destination) is enabled, and the messages that are currently stored in the internal buffer.**

**41** What are your choices in order to make your Cisco IOS router generate Novell-compliant (ipx) pings?

**If you want your Cisco router to generate Novell-compliant (ipx) pings, you can do so using the global configuration command ipx ping-default novell. But if you want to be able to ping (IPX) Cisco devices as well as non-Cisco (Novell-compliant) devices, you should not use the ipx ping-default novell command. When you use the privileged exec mode ping (IPX), one of the questions you will be prompted with is whether you want a Novell standard echo. Hence, with the privileged mode ping (IPX) you can ping Cisco devices and have the choice of generating a Novell standard ping.**

**42** In which situation (loss of functionality, crash, or performance degradation) will the output of the **show stack** command most likely be asked for?

**Crash.**

**43** The outputs of the **show memory** and the **show processes** [**cpu**] commands will most likely be asked for in which situation (loss of functionality, crash, or performance degradation)?

**Performance degradation.**

**44** In which situation (loss of functionality, crash, or performance degradation) will you most likely be asked to produce and provide a core dump for the technical support representative?

**Crash.**

**45**  Which **show** command conveniently produces output equivalent to the output of **show version**, **show running-config**, **show controllers**, and a few other **show** commands?

**show tech-support**

**46**  Which Cisco IOS router command's output displays the current setting (value) of the config-register?

**show version**

**47**  What is the outcome of not having an allocated and free buffer available for a packet?

**A buffer must be allocated and free at the time a packet arrives or the packet will be dropped.**

**48**  Explain the role of the parameter called Permanent in buffer management.

**This parameter is the minimum number of buffers allocated. Buffers are de-allocated (trimmed) at times, but the number of allocated buffers will not go below the value of Permanent.**

**49**  Explain the role of the parameter called Max-Free in buffer management.

**When the number of buffers that are allocated but not used (free) reaches this value, a trim (de-allocation) is triggered. The memory is returned to the shared pool and can be used for other purposes.**

**50**  Explain the role of the parameter called Min-Free in buffer management.

**As the allocated (free) buffers are used up, the number of free buffers is naturally reduced. When the number of free buffers reduces to be equal to the Min-Free parameter, buffer allocation (create) is triggered.**

**51**  Explain the role of the parameter called Initial in buffer management.

**This parameter indicates how many buffers should be allocated (for a particular packet size) at the router initialization time.**

**52**  If the output of **show buffer** command displays a large number of misses, increasing the value of which one of the buffer management parameters (Permanent, Min-Free, Max-Free, Initial) will most likely remedy the situation?

**Permanent and Min-Free.**

**53**  What does the number of failures displayed on the output of **show buffer** command indicate?

**The number of failures indicates how many times the allocation of more buffers has been unsuccessful.**

**54** Using what command can you find out the allocation of interface buffers on the Switch Processor of the Cisco 7x00 series routers?

**Router# show controllers cxbus**

**55** What does the **show buffers** command display?

**This command displays information (statistics) on buffer elements, public buffer pools, and interface buffer pools.**

**56** Which Cisco IOS command's output displays statistics about router memory (for example, amount of free processor memory)?

**Router# show memory**

**57** What information does the output of the Cisco IOS **show processes** exec command display?

**It displays the CPU utilization and a list of active processes along with their corresponding process ID, priority, scheduler test (status), CPU time used, number of times invoked, and so on.**

**58** The **show processes** command's output provides two numbers separated by a slash (for example, 4%/4%) for the CPU utilization over the last five seconds. How are those numbers interpreted?

**The first number is the total cpu utilization, and the second one is the utilization due to interrupt routines (in the last five seconds).**

**59** Specify the command (with appropriate parameters) that displays the five-seconds, one-minute, and five-minute CPU utilization for each of the active processes.

**Router# show processes cpu**

**60** What information can be gathered from the output of the Cisco IOS **show stacks** exec command?

**This command's output displays stack utilization of processes and interrupt routines, and the reason for the last system reboot. When a system crash happens, failure type, failure program counter (PC), address (operand address), and a stack trace are saved by the ROM Monitor. All that information (saved by the ROM Monitor at the system failure point) is displayed on the show stacks command's output.**

**61** Which command allows you to generate a core dump without reloading?

**Router# write core**

**62** To ensure that a core dump can be sent to a server and saved successfully, what are some of the preliminary tasks and tests you must perform?

**You must make sure that your server (TFTP, FTP, or RCP server) is reachable and has enough storage space. You must also learn the file-naming convention that the server's operating system supports. Finally, find out whether you need to create an empty file (with the desired name) on the server in advance.**

**63** Which command causes the router to attempt to produce a core dump when it crashes?

**The exception dump** *ip-address* **global configuration command (***ip-address* **is the address of your TFTP, FTP, or RCP server) causes the router to attempt to produce a core dump when it crashes.**

**64** By default, what is the name of the file that the core dump is written to?

**The file is named** *hostname***-core, where** *hostname* **is the name of the router that has sent the core dump.**

**65** Which command allows you to change the name of the core file?

**The exception core-file** *filename* **global configuration command allows you do that.**

# Chapter 5

## "Do I Know This Already?" Quiz

**1** Name the main TCP/IP tool used for path discovery between IP nodes. Specify the full Cisco IOS command for this tool.

**The tool is called trace. The IOS command is traceroute, but its shortened form, trace, is often all that is typed.**

**2** What is the IP path discovery command available with Microsoft's Windows 95 and Windows NT TCP/IP stack?

**tracert**

**3** Specify the Cisco IOS command that allows you to see if an IP inbound access list is applied to a router's ethernet 0 interface (note that this is not a command that displays a router's startup or running configuration).

**show ip interface ethernet 0**

**4** How can you see the content of an IP access list without looking at a router's startup or running configuration?

**show ip access-list** [*access-list-number* | *name*]

5   Which Cisco IOS command allows you to see the IP static routes that are configured on a router (without looking at startup or running configuration)?

**show ip route static**

6   Which Cisco IOS command displays the active IP routing protocols and how they are configured to operate (without looking at startup or running configuration)?

**show ip protocols**

7   Which Cisco IOS command displays the state of each debugging option?

**show debugging**

8   What is the command that allows you to see the IP configuration of a Windows NT machine from the CMD window's prompt?

**ipconfig [/all]**

9   What is the command that allows you to see the content of the NetBIOS cache of a Windows NT machine from the CMD window's prompt?

**nbtstat -c**

10  When you redistribute routing information from one protocol into another, what is a major source of concern?

**Assignment of the metric (or default-metric) parameter. The reason for the concern is that different routing protocols use different metrics.**

# Q&A

1   Name the main TCP/IP tool used for reachability testing.

**Ping.**

2   Name the main TCP/IP tool used for path discovery between IP nodes. Also specify the full Cisco IOS command for this tool.

**The tool is called** trace. **The IOS command is** traceroute, **but its shortened form, trace, is often all that is typed.**

3   Can the extended **ping** and **trace** be used from the user exec mode?

**No, you need to be in the privileged exec mode for that.**

4   What is the IP path discovery command available with Microsoft's Windows 95 and Windows NT TCP/IP stack?

**tracert**

5  Name two Cisco IOS commands that allow you to see the IP address and subnet mask configured on a router's ethernet 0 interface (not a command that displays a router's startup or running configuration).

**show interface ethernet 0**

**show ip interface ethernet 0**

6  Specify the Cisco IOS command that allows you to see if an IP inbound access list is applied to a router's ethernet 0 interface (not a command that displays a router's startup or running configuration).

**show ip interface ethernet 0**

7  Name the Cisco IOS command that allows you to see if IP Proxy-ARP is enabled/disabled on a router's ethernet 0 interface (not a command that displays a router's startup or running configuration).

**show ip interface ethernet 0**

8  If a router's ethernet 0 interface is equipped with both AUI and RJ45 connectors, how can you find out which is the active one?

**The show controllers ethernet 0 command provides that information by specifying the media type (also, the interface hardware might have an LED that indicates the active connector).**

9  How can you see the content of an IP access list without looking at a router's startup or running configuration?

**show ip access-list [*access-list-number* | *name*]**

10  Which Cisco IOS command allows you to see the IP static routes that are configured on a router (without looking at startup or running configuration)?

**show ip route static**

11  Which Cisco IOS command is used to see the entire IP routing table of a router?

**show ip route**

12  Which Cisco IOS command is used to display the IP Address Resolution Protocol cache of a router?

**show ip arp**

13  Specify the Cisco IOS command that displays IP statistics such as the number of packets sent and received, error counts, and the number of broadcasts/multicasts sent and received.

**show ip traffic**

14  Which Cisco IOS command displays the active IP routing protocols and how they are configured to operate (not a command that displays a router's startup or running configuration)?

**show ip protocols**

15  How can you find out whether a Cisco router has been configured with the **no ip forward-protocol udp** command?

**show running-config**

16  How can you check whether the IP helper address is correctly configured on a Cisco router's ethernet 0 interface?

**show ip interface ethernet 0 or show running-config**

17  What is the command that allows you to see the IP configuration of a Windows NT machine from the CMD window's prompt?

**ipconfig [/all]**

18  What is the command/utility that allows you to see the IP configuration of a Windows 95 device?

**winipcfg**

19  What is the command that allows you to see the contents of the NetBIOS cache of a Windows NT machine from the CMD window's prompt?

**nbtstat -c**

20  When you redistribute routing information from one protocol into another, what is a major source of concern?

**Assignment of the metric (or default-metric) parameter. The reason for the concern is that different routing protocols use different metrics.**

# Chapter 6

## "Do I Know This Already?" Quiz

1  Can you use **ping** for IPX reachability testing?

**Yes, ping for IPX has been available since IOS release 8.2.**

2  Which Cisco IOS global configuration command makes the Cisco routers generate only Novell-compliant pings?

**ipx ping-default novell**

**3** Which IPX **show** command displays the IPX address and encapsulation on a router's interface(s)?

**show ipx interface [*type number*]**

**4** Name the IPX **show** command that displays the contents of the IPX routing table.

**show ipx route**

**5** Name the IPX **show** command that displays the local router's SAP table.

**show ipx servers**

**6** What is the effect of IPX fast-switching on **debug ipx** output?

**Before executing a required debug command you must turn IPX fast-switching off using the no ipx route-cache command. Otherwise, even if you assume that the cache is clear, debug will display only one packet for each destination.**

**7** What are the Cisco IOS encapsulations available for IPX?

**Arpa, Novell_ether, SAP, and SNAP.**

**8** What is the current default value for the **ipx gns-response-delay** command, and what was its value prior to Cisco IOS release 9.1(13)?

**The default value of ipx gns-response-delay is 0 ms; prior to Cisco IOS release 9.1(13), this parameter's default value was equal to 500 ms.**

## Q&A

**1** Can you use **ping** for IPX reachability testing?

**Yes, ping for IPX has been available since IOS release 8.2.**

**2** Are Cisco's implementation of **ping** and Novell's **ping** compatible?

**No, these two ping for IPX implementations are not compatible.**

**3** Which Cisco IOS global configuration command makes the Cisco routers generate only Novell-compliant pings?

**ipx ping-default novell**

**4** How can you **ping** a Novell server from a Cisco router without using the **ipx ping-default novell** command?

**By using extended ping.**

**5**  Name at least three IPX troubleshooting **show** commands.

**Answers can vary, and may include:**

— **show ipx interface**

— **show ipx traffic**

— **show ipx route**

— **show ipx servers**

— **show ipx access-lists**

**6**  Which IPX **show** command displays the IPX address and encapsulation on a router's interface(s)?

**show ipx interface [*type number*]**

**7**  Which IPX **show** command allows you to discover the SAP and RIP update intervals and the applied traffic and routing filters on a router's interface(s)?

**show ipx interface [*type number*]**

**8**  Using which IPX **show** command can you see some statistics regarding the number of IPX packets sent and received (including errors encountered) and the number of SAP, RIP, broadcast, IPX echo, and Watch Dogs generated by a router?

**show ipx traffic**

**9**  Name the IPX **show** command that displays the content of the IPX routing table.

**show ipx route**

**10**  Name the IPX **show** command that displays the local router's SAP table.

**show ipx servers**

**11**  In a router's SAP table, what do the letters S, N, P that may appear in front of the entries stand for?

**S: Static (statically configured on the local router)**

**N: NLSP (learned through NLSP advertisements)**

**P: Periodic (learned through periodic SAP updates)**

**12**  Is there a Cisco IOS **show** command to help you with troubleshooting IPX Enhanced IGRP routing?

**show ipx eigrp {interface | neighbor | topology | traffic}**

**13**   What is the effect of IPX fast switching on debug IPX output?

**Before executing a required debug command, you must turn IPX fast switching off using the no ipx route-cache command. Otherwise, even if you assume that the cache is clear, debug will display only one packet for each destination.**

**14**   What is the syntax of the **debug** command that allows you to observe the IPX-related routing updates that are generated/sent and received by a router?

**debug ipx routing {activity | events}**

**15**   What type of services are represented by the SAP service type numbers 4 and 7?

**File server (4) and print server (7).**

**16**   Are there any **debug ipx** commands available for the IPX Enhanced IGRP and NLSP routing protocols?

**Yes, they are debug ipx eigrp and debug ipx nlsp.**

**17**   What are the three focal points of troubleshooting in IPX/SPX networks?

**IPX clients, IPX servers, and the internetworking devices (mainly routers).**

**18**   What are the Cisco IOS encapsulations available for IPX?

**ARPA, NOVELL_ETHER, SAP, and SNAP.**

**19**   What is the current default value for the **ipx gns-response-delay**, and what was its value prior to Cisco IOS release 9.1(13)?

**The default value of ipx gns-response-delay is 0 ms; prior to Cisco IOS release 9.1(13), this parameter's default value was equal to 500 ms.**

**20**   Why did the **ipx gns-response-delay** of Cisco routers have a different default prior to release 9.1(13) of the IOS?

**The ipx gns-response-delay was set to 500 ms in order to allow a dual connected NetWare 2.x server running in parallel with a Cisco router to reply to GNS requests before the Cisco router. The 500 ms value was also appropriate to compensate for the slow CPU or Network Adapter Card of the client, who would otherwise miss a quicker router response.**

# Chapter 7

## "Do I Know This Already?" Quiz

1 True or false: The routers that are connected to a single cable segment must have identical settings with regard to network number/cable range and zone name(s) of that segment.

   **True. A Cisco router's AppleTalk interface will not become active on a network segment if the zone name(s) and cable range it is configured with do not agree with those of other devices on that segment.**

2 True or false: In an AppleTalk network, a network number or cable range does not have to be unique.

   **False. In other words, in AppleTalk networks a cable range cannot be associated with more than one (non-overlapping) zone. Otherwise, routing inconsistencies and, ultimately, routing loops will be the result.**

3 True or false: Because Phase II of AppleTalk is completely backward-compatible with Phase I, in a mixed network no special action is necessary and the AppleTalk network will function just fine.

   **False. For instance, due to usage of different Layer 2 frame types, Phase I and Phase II AppleTalk devices cannot, by default, communicate on the same segment.**

4 Describe the **ping appletalk** command.

   **The ping appletalk command is a reachability testing tool similar to its IPX and IP counterparts.**

5 Which AppleTalk **show** command can be used to discover the configured AppleTalk cable range, the AppleTalk address, and the zone(s) an interface falls into?

   **show appletalk interface [*type number*]**

6 Which AppleTalk **show** command informs you of the number of entries in the routing and zone information table, whether AppleTalk logging is enabled, the current settings for ZIP, RTMP, and AARP timers, and the routing protocol that is in use?

   **show appletalk globals**

7 Provide at least two possible causes for the symptom Zones Missing from Chooser.

   **The following are the most likely causes:**

   **— Configuration mismatch.**

   **— Misconfigured access lists or other filters.**

— **Route flapping (unstable route).**

— **ZIP storm.**

8  What are the default values for AppleTalk (RTMP) timers, and what do they mean?

**The default AppleTalk timers are 10, 20, and 60. RTMP updates are sent every 10 seconds; they are considered bad after 20 seconds (without updates), and they are discarded after 60 seconds.**

9  List at least three of the commonly reported trouble symptoms of the AppleTalk networks.

**Commonly reported trouble symptoms of the AppleTalk networks include the following:**

— **Zones are missing from Chooser.**

— **Users cannot see zones and/or services on remote networks.**

— **Zone list changes every time Chooser is opened.**

— **Connections to services drop.**

— **Old zone names appear in Chooser.**

— **Router port gets stuck in restarting or acquiring mode.**

# Q&A

1  True or false: The routers that are connected to a single cable segment must have identical settings with regard to network number/cable range and zone name(s) of that segment.

**True. A Cisco router's AppleTalk interface will not become active on a network segment if the zone name(s) and cable range it is configured with do not agree with those of other devices on that segment.**

2  True or false: In an AppleTalk network, a network number or cable range does not have to be unique.

**False. In other words, in AppleTalk networks, a cable range cannot be associated with more than one (non-overlapping) zones. Otherwise, routing inconsistencies and ultimately, routing loops will be the result.**

3  True or false: Because Phase II of AppleTalk is completely backward-compatible with Phase I, in a mixed network no special action is necessary and the AppleTalk network will function just fine.

**False. For instance, due to usage of different layer 2 frame types, Phase I and Phase II AppleTalk devices cannot, by default, communicate on the same segment.**

4  True or false: The AppleTalk timers are only locally significant within a router and hence their values have no effect on the network.

**False. Routers invalidate the routing table entries for which they do not receive periodic updates on time.**

5  True or false: Cisco routers have a built-in mechanism to deal with ZIP storms.

**True. Cisco routers do not report networks for which the corresponding zone(s) are not yet known.**

6  Describe the **ping appletalk** command.

**The ping appletalk command is a reachability testing tool similar to its IPX and IP counterparts.**

7  Which AppleTalk **show** command can be used to discover the configured AppleTalk cable range, AppleTalk address, and the zone(s) an interface falls into?

**show appletalk interface [*type number*]**

8  Which AppleTalk **show** command informs you of the number of entries in the routing and zone information table, whether AppleTalk logging is enabled, the current settings for ZIP, RTMP, and AARP timers, and the routing protocol that is in use?

**show appletalk globals**

9  Which AppleTalk **show** command displays the AppleTalk routing table?

**show appletalk route**

10  Which AppleTalk **show** command displays the AppleTalk ZIT?

**show appletalk zone**

11  Which AppleTalk **show** command displays the directly connected networks or those networks that are one hop away?

**show appletalk adjacent-routes**

12  Which AppleTalk **show** command displays the list of active AppleTalk routers that reside on the same networks that the local router is also directly connected to?

**show appletalk neighbors**

13  Provide at least two possible causes for the symptom Users cannot access zones or services.

**Possible causes include the following:**

— **Configuration mismatch.**

— **Duplicate network numbers or overlapping cable range.**

— **Phase I and Phase II rule violations.**

— **Misconfigured access lists or other filters.**

14  Provide at least two possible causes for the symptom Zones missing from Chooser.

**Possible causes include the following:**

— **Configuration mismatch.**

— **Misconfigured access lists or other filters.**

— **Route flapping (unstable route).**

— **ZIP storm.**

15  Provide at least one possible cause for the symptom Network services intermittently unavailable.

**Possible causes include the following:**

— **Duplicate network numbers or overlapping cable range.**

— **Route flapping (unstable route).**

— **ZIP storm.**

16  Provide at least one possible cause for the symptom Old zone names appear in Chooser (phantom/ghosted zones).

**Possible causes include the following:**

— **Configuration mismatch.**

— **Invalid zone names in routing table.**

17  Provide at least one possible cause for the symptom Interface fails to initialize AppleTalk.

**Possible causes include the following:**

— **Configuration mismatch.**

— **Phase I and Phase II rule violations.**

18  What are the default values for AppleTalk (RTMP) timers and what do they mean?

**The default AppleTalk timers are 10, 20, and 60. RTMP updates are sent every 10 seconds; they are considered bad after 20 seconds (without updates), and they are discarded after 60 seconds.**

19  List at least three of the commonly reported trouble symptoms of the AppleTalk networks.

**Commonly reported trouble symptoms of the AppleTalk networks include the following:**

— **Zones are missing from Chooser.**

— **Users cannot see zones and/or services on remote networks.**

— **Zone list changes every time Chooser is opened.**

— **Connections to services drop.**

— **Old zone names appear in Chooser.**

— **Router port gets stuck in restarting or acquiring mode.**

20  Describe the output of **debug apple errors** and provide one example of the error messages that this command displays.

**The debug apple errors command is used to display AppleTalk error messages so that the cause of network problem can be identified. These messages may be generated for many reasons. The error messages displayed by the debug apple error command include:**

— **Net information mismatch and zones disagree.**

— **Wrong encapsulation.**

— **Cannot establish primary zone, no primary has been set up, primary zone invalid.**

21  True or false: There will be no questions on AppleTalk troubleshooting in the CCNP Support exam.

**False.**

# Chapter 8

## "Do I Know This Already?" Quiz

1  Name the applications that are included in the CWSI Campus package.

**The following applications are included in the CWSI Campus package:**

— **TrafficDirector**

— **VlanDirector**

— **AtmDirector**

— **CiscoView**

— **UserTracking**

**2** The structure of the remote network monitoring MIB as outlined in RFC 1757 defines nine groups of objects. Which four of those groups are supported by the Catalyst 5000 embedded RMON agent?

**Statistics Group, History Group, Alarms Group, and Event Group.**

**3** What is SPAN?

**SPAN (Switched Port Analyzer) is a feature offered by the Catalyst 5000 IOS. SPAN allows mirroring traffic from one port into another port. Network managers can use this feature to capture the groups not supported by the embedded RMON agent.**

**4** Briefly describe Cisco Systems' SwitchProbe product.

**SwitchProbes are standalone RMON probes for monitoring any segment (FDDI, CDDI, Token Ring, Ethernet, and Fast Ethernet). While the embedded RMON agent uses in-band network connection, the SwitchProbe can connect to an out-of-band network manager.**

**5** Briefly describe the Catalyst 5000 switch's power-on self-test.

**When you power up a Catalyst 5000 switch, a self-diagnostics routine (often referred to as power-on self-test) is performed. This routine performs diagnostics tests on several components, such as ROM, RAM, DRAM, EARL, and BOOTROM. The result of the test performed on each component is displayed on the console.**

**6** At a particular instance, what states can an enabled port be in?

**Blocking, listening, learning, or forwarding.**

**7** Provide a brief description of VTP.

**VTP (VLAN Trunking Protocol) is a Layer 2 multicast messaging protocol. This protocol allows switches that are put in a common administrative group, called a VTP domain, to communicate with each other across the trunk links, regarding creation, deletion, and renaming of VLANs. VTP provides an automated means for having a consistent VLAN configuration throughout a VTP domain.**

**8** What roles can a switch have in a VTP domain?

**A switch can be in one of server, client, or transparent modes with respect to the role it takes within a VTP domain.**

**9** Describe the output of the **show module** [*mod_num*] command.

This command displays the status and other information about the module specified. If no module is indicated, all the switch modules and their corresponding information will be displayed. Using this command, you can also discover the range of MAC addresses associated with (reserved for) each line card module of a Catalyst switch.

**10** List at least three important pieces of information that can be gathered by executing the **show vtp domain** command.

**Important information that can be gathered by executing the show vtp domain includes the following:**

— **VTP domain name**

— **Mode of the switch (server, client, or transparent)**

— **Number of VLANs currently in the VTP domain**

— **Configuration revision number**

— **The device which has submitted the last VTP update**

# Q&A

**1** Name the applications that are included in the CWSI Campus package.

**The following applications are included in the CWSI Campus package:**

— **TrafficDirector**

— **VlanDirector**

— **AtmDirector**

— **CiscoView**

— **UserTracking**

**2** Describe the functions of TrafficDirector.

**TrafficDirector allows you to monitor traffic (on network segments) leading to the diagnosis of any abnormalities. It obtains traffic information from embedded RMON agents (of Catalyst switches) and standalone Cisco SwitchProbe products. With this information about different segments, TrafficDirector informs you of collision, error, utilization, and broadcast rates on a port (or port group) basis. You can also set up TrafficDirector to receive threshold-based traps from Catalyst switches. UserTracking provides the means for setting up dynamic VLANs and track location of stations.**

**3** What is the VlanDirector application component of CWSI used for?

**VlanDirector provides easy VLAN management with a GUI (Graphic User Interface). For instance, the task of adding, deleting, and moving users to and from VLANs is done with a few mouse clicks.**

**4** What does CiscoView allow you to do?

**CiscoView allows you to view a device's chassis (and LEDs), configuration, and performance information from a remote management workstation.**

**5** Name at least two of the protocols that form the foundation of the CWSI application suite.

**Protocols such as SNMP, CDP, VTP and RMON form the foundation of the CWSI application suite.**

**6** What does the Network Map feature of CWSI provide you with?

**This application provides a map of the physical devices and links in your network. You can then locate specific devices in the network and view how they are linked together. Network Map can also display the network virtual topology (virtual LAN configuration) in relation to the physical topology.**

**7** True or false: You need to purchase and install RMON as an added feature to Catalyst 5000 IOS.

**False. The Catalyst 5000 software includes an integrated RMON agent.**

**8** The structure of the remote network monitoring MIB as outlined in RFC 1757 defines nine groups that objects are arranged into. Which four of those groups are supported by the Catalyst 5000 embedded RMON agent?

**Statistics Group, History Group, Alarms Group, and Event Group.**

**9** What is SPAN?

**SPAN (Switched Port Analyzer) is a feature offered by the Catalyst 5000 IOS. SPAN allows mirroring traffic from one port into another port. Network managers can use this feature to capture the groups not supported by the embedded RMON agent.**

**10** Briefly describe Cisco Systems' SwitchProbe product.

**SwitchProbes are standalone RMON probes for monitoring any segment (FDDI, CDDI, Token Ring, Ethernet, and Fast Ethernet). While the embedded RMON agent uses in-band network connection, the SwitchProbe can connect to an out-of-band network manager.**

**11** Provide a general description for the Catalyst 5000 switches' LEDs.

**The LEDs on the power supply, supervisor module, and line cards are simple yet important indicators of the working condition of the corresponding component or module. The LEDs indicate whether a component such as a fan, power supply, module, or port is present, whether it is enabled or disabled, and whether it has passed the power-up test. You may also observe the Catalyst LEDs using CiscoView's GUI from a remote location.**

**12**  List and describe the supervisor engine module's LEDs.

**The LEDs are: Status, PS1, PS2, Fan, and Switch Load.**

**On the very left side of the supervisor engine module there is a status LED reporting the system power and processor status. The Fan, PS1 (power supply 1), and PS2 LEDs are arranged in a column, beside the status LED. The PS1 and PS2 LEDs go on when the power supply is present and is receiving AC source power and providing DC power to the internal system components. A rectangle composed of a series of LEDs in a row with the title "Switch Load" provides a visual indication of the current traffic load (as an approximate percentage) over the backplane.**

**13**  Provide a brief description for the Catalyst 5000 switch line card module status LED.

**The line card modules have a module status LED and a link LED for each port. The Ethernet switching modules also have a 100 Mbps LED for each port. The switch performs a series of self-tests and diagnostic tests, and if all the tests pass, the module status LED is green. During the system boot and during the self-test diagnostics, or if the module is disabled, the module status LED is orange. Finally, if a test other than an individual port test fails, the module status LED is red.**

**14**  How would you interpret the fact that the port link integrity LED on a line card module is not green?

**If this LED is not green on both sides of a connection, you have a problem. If either side of the connection is not powered up, has the port disabled, or does not have the cable properly inserted, or if the cable in use is simply broken, substandard, badly bent, or otherwise abused, the link integrity LED does not come on. Checking to make sure that both sides of a link have the green link LED is a simple yet important fact-gathering and troubleshooting task. Speed mismatch on the two sides of a connection could also be a problem. Either both sides of a connection must have the Ethernet 100 Mbps LED on or both should be running at 10 Mbps, which means that the 100 Mbps LED must be off on both sides. It is important to know that Cisco Systems' documentation indicates that some devices do not handle speed auto-negotiation correctly, so it is safer to hard-code the speed on both sides of a connection.**

**15**  What is the most common source of network problems?

**Network professionals often indicate that the vast majority of network problems are attributable to cable problems.**

**16** What is the distance (length) limitation for the Category 3 and Category 5 cables?

**Category 3 and Category 5 cables used in either half-duplex or full-duplex mode should not be longer than 100 meters.**

**17** What is the distance (length) limitation for the fiber-optic cables?

**Multimode fiber (MMF) cables (10BaseFL and 100BaseFX) can be up to 2 kilometers, except for 100BaseFX being used in half-duplex mode, which must be kept at or less than 400 meters long. Single-mode fiber (SMF) cables (100BaseFX) can be up to 10 kilometers long regardless of whether they are used in full-duplex or half-duplex mode. Note that the fiber limitations just specified are device/module dependent; therefore, you may encounter a newer Catalyst module with a more powerful laser beam, which can reliably travel longer distances.**

**18** If you find a particular cable segment suspicious, what courses of action can you take?

**If possible, use a known good cable, momentarily, instead of the suspicious cable to see if the connection starts to work with the good cable and fails with the bad cable. Cable-testing equipment can help you find out if you have a bad cable, and also what exactly the problem is with that cable.**

**Remember that if you have a cable plugged into an interface (such as a Cisco 4500 router's Ethernet interface) that has multiple connectors, you must ensure that the device is actually using the media type corresponding to the connector you have the cable plugged into.**

**19** Briefly describe Catalyst 5000 switch's power-on self-test.

**When you power up a Catalyst 5000 switch, a self-diagnostics routine (often referred to as the power-on self-test) is performed. This routine performs diagnostics tests on several components, such as ROM, RAM, DRAM, EARL, and BOOTROM. The result of the test performed on each component is displayed on the console.**

**20** Which Spanning-Tree Protocol is used by the Catalyst 5000 switch?

**The Catalyst 5000 series use IEEE 802.1D Spanning-Tree Protocol.**

**21** How many Spanning Trees are associated with one VLAN?

**One.**

**22** How many Spanning Tree instances are enabled on a port that is in trunking mode?

**By default, a port that is configured as a trunk port has as many Spanning Tree instances enabled on it as there are VLANs enabled and active on that particular trunk.**

**23**  What is the maximum number of VLANs that a Catalyst 5000 switch can handle?

**Catalyst 5000 switches support up to 1000 VLANs, but only up to 250 of those can exist on the switch itself (called native VLANs).**

**24**  At a particular instance, what states can an enabled port be in?

**Blocking, Listening, Learning, or Forwarding.**

**25**  What are the normal/estimated times that a port spends in one state before moving to another state?

**A normal (Spanning-Tree) mode port can take up to 20 seconds to transition from Blocking to Listening, plus 15 seconds from Listening to Learning, plus another 15 seconds from Learning to Forwarding state.**

**26**  How can you influence the chance of a Catalyst switch to become the root of a Spanning Tree?

**You may lower the numeric value of the bridge priority of a Catalyst switch in order to increase its chance of becoming the root.**

**27**  What are the two basic requirements for a switch to accept and forward a frame from or to a trunk port?

**There are two basic requirements for a switch to accept and forward a frame from or to a trunk port. The first requirement is that the switch must recognize the VLAN that the frame is associated with. The second requirement is that both of the switches on a trunk (ISL link) must agree on the VLAN numbers that are allowed to traverse that trunk. Note that this answer assumes the VTP configuration does not use a password; if passwords are used, the devices must also have matching VTP passwords.**

**28**  Provide a brief description for VTP.

**VTP (VLAN Trunking Protocol) is a Layer 2 multicast messaging protocol. This protocol allows switches that are put in a common administrative group, called a VTP domain, to communicate with each other across the trunk links, regarding creation, deletion, and renaming of VLANs. VTP provides an automated means for having a consistent VLAN configuration throughout a VTP domain.**

**29**  What is the purpose of VTP and how many VTP domains can a Catalyst switch be associated with?

**VTP provides an automated means for having a consistent VLAN configuration throughout a VTP domain. A Catalyst switch can be associated with only one VTP domain.**

**30**  What are the possible modes for a switch in a VTP domain?

**A switch can be in one of server, client, or transparent modes.**

**31**   What is the default VTP mode of a Catalyst 5000 switch?

**Server.**

**32**   What is the VTP configuration revision number?

**The VTP information pertaining to a particular VTP domain name has a revision number associated with it. Every time a change is implemented in a VTP domain, the revision number is incremented. (Note that a change implemented on a switch in server mode does not affect [increment the revision number of] a switch in transparent mode and vice versa.)**

**33**   What are some of the basic settings required for an ISL trunk connection between two Catalyst 5000 switches to work?

**On the two ports of the two switches you need to configure a trunk between them that is consistent with respect to trunking (enabled), port duplexing, port speed, and fiber type (for optical links). For VTP to work across this trunk, make sure that the two switches are members of the same VTP domain and that they both allow the same set of VLANs to go across the trunk between them. The show port, show trunk, and show vlan commands are among the most useful show commands for troubleshooting trunks and ISL. Note that this answer assumes the VTP configuration does not use a password; if passwords are used, the devices must also have matching VTP passwords.**

**34**   What configuration is required to make a switch an IP node?

**You must assign an IP address and subnet mask to the switch's system console 0 (SC0). For internetwork accessibility and reachability, the switch will also need a default gateway and/or some static routes configured.**

**35**   To which VLAN does the Catalyst 5000 switch's system console 0 interface belong? Can the VLAN number of SC0 be changed?

**The Catalyst 5000 switch's system console 0 interface belongs to VLAN number 1, but that can be changed.**

**36**   Which Catalyst 5000 IOS command displays SC0's IP address, mask, and VLAN number?

**show interface**

**37**   Which Catalyst 5000 IOS command displays its configured IP routes?

**show ip route**

**38**   Provide at least three significant pieces of information displayed by the Catalyst 5000 **show system** command.

**PS1-Status, PS2-Status, Fan-Status, Temp-Alarm (on/off), Sys-Status, Uptime, Logout (similar to idle-timeout), Modem (enabled/disabled), Baud (rate), Traffic (percentage), Peak (level), Peak-Time, System Name, System Location, and System Contact are all provided by the Catalyst 5000 show system command.**

**39**  Describe the purpose and methods of using the **show test** command.

**The** show test **command may be entered with or without a module number specified. The purpose of this command is to display the results of the diagnostics tests performed on various system and modules components. If you want to see only the results of the tests performed on a particular module, then use this command with the number of the module you are interested in. If no module number is specified, the information displayed will correspond to the general system, and of module 1.**

**40**  Which command displays the error log for the system or for a specified module?

**show log [*mod_num*]**

**41**  Which command displays a complete report of MAC-related statistics?

**show mac**

**42**  Describe the output of the **show module** [*mod_num*] command.

**This command displays the status and other information about the module specified. If no module is indicated, all the switch modules and their corresponding information will be displayed. Using this command you can also discover the range of MAC addresses associated with (reserved for) each line card module of a Catalyst switch.**

**43**  Which command displays the status, speed, VLAN, and duplexing mode of a switch's port?

**show port [*mod_num*[*/port_num*]]**

**44**  Which command displays the current configuration of a Catalyst switch, including many of the default settings?

**show config**

**45**  Which command displays information about the current setting of the switched port analyzer function?

**show span**

**46**  What does the **show flash** command display?

**It displays the name, version, and size of the (code) files residing in the Catalyst switch's Flash.**

47 Describe the information that may be gathered through usage of the **show trunk** [*mod_num*[/*port_num*]] command.

**This command displays trunking information. You may choose to see the trunking information about a particular module/port by typing the module/port number, or you may simply type show trunk and receive information about all the ports that are configured for trunking. In the first section of the output, the trunking mode (on, off, auto, or desirable) and the trunking status (trunking or nontrunking) of each port are displayed. The second and third sections display the VLANs allowed for each port, and the VLANs allowed and active on each port, correspondingly. The last section of the show trunk command's output displays the range of VLANs that actually go on the trunk along with Spanning-Tree Protocol forwarding state.**

48 Which command can you use to see detailed Spanning Tree information about a VLAN?

**show spantree [*vlan*]**

49 List at least three important pieces of information that can be gathered by executing the **show vtp domain** command.

**The** show vtp domain **command gives you the following information:**

— **VTP domain name**

— **Mode of the switch (server, client, or transparent)**

— **Number of VLANs currently in the VTP domain**

— **Configuration revision number**

— **The device that submitted the last VTP update**

50 On a Catalyst 5000 switch, if you disable a port, what will be the LED status of that particular port?

**The port LED will be orange.**

# Chapter 9

## "Do I Know This Already?" Quiz

1 Name three of the functions routers perform in a VLAN switching environment.

**VLAN switching, VLAN translation, VLAN routing.**

2 Which type of router interface is used for ISL trunking?

**Fast Ethernet.**

**3** How many VLANs can a subinterface of an interface used for trunking correspond to?

**A subinterface can correspond to only one VLAN.**

**4** Which command functions are configured on the main interface of the (Fast Ethernet) interface for the purpose of trunking?

**Commands for configuring the speed, duplexing, and media type.**

**5** What is the general recommendation for the bridged networks in terms of the number of hops?

**The number of hops should not exceed seven.**

**6** How many default VLANs are preconfigured on a Catalyst 5000 switch?

**There are five default VLANs preconfigured on a Catalyst 5000 switch for different media types: default (ISL VLAN # 0001), fddi-default (ISL VLAN # 1002), token-ring-default (ISL VLAN # 1003), fddinet-default (ISL VLAN # 1004), trnet-default (ISL VLAN # 1005).**

**7** What is the recommended usage of VLAN number 1?

**You are encouraged to leave VLAN number 1 for management and troubleshooting and use VLANs 2 through 1000 for user (traffic) VLANs.**

**8** What role can a Cisco router play in a VTP domain?

**None. Cisco routers do not yet support VTP (VLAN Trunking Protocol).**

**9** What information can one obtain from the output of the **show vlans** command?

**It lists all the VLANs configured on a router. For each VLAN, the corresponding subinterface and its configured addresses are displayed. For each protocol configured on a subinterface, this command also shows the number of packets sent and received.**

# Q&A

**1** Name three of the functions routers perform in a VLAN switching environment.

**VLAN switching, VLAN translation, VLAN routing.**

**2** Which type of router interface is used for ISL trunking?

**Fast Ethernet.**

**3** True or false: If a Fast Ethernet interface is used for trunking purposes, it should not have any Layer 3 address or any bridging commands configured on the main interface.

**True.**

**4** How many VLANs can a subinterface of an interface used for trunking correspond to?

**A subinterface can correspond to only one VLAN.**

**5** Which command functions are configured on the main interface of the interface used for trunking?

**Commands for configuring the speed, duplexing, and media type.**

**6** What IOS command configures a multiport Fast Ethernet interface to operate from its RJ45 (100BaseTX) connector?

**The media-type 100basetx interface configuration command.**

**7** What IOS command configures a multi-port Fast Ethernet interface to operate in full-duplex mode?

**full-duplex**

**8** Which command shows the media type configured on a Fast Ethernet interface?

**show controller fastethernet** *interface-number*

**9** Which command would configure a subinterface of a Fast Ethernet interface to be in VLAN number 10 (in ISL format)?

**encapsulation isl 10**

**10** Routing between VLANs is supported for which protocols on Cisco 4500 and 7000 series routers running IOS Release 11.3?

**IP and IPX (the IPX frame type must be Novell Ethernet).**

**Note: This answer is IOS release and feature set dependent, but since it is in line with the CIT course material, it will be appropriate should it be encountered in the Support exam.**

**11** What is the general rule for the bridged networks in terms of the number of hops?

**The number of hops should not exceed seven.**

**12** What is the default HELLO interval in the IEEE Spanning-Tree Protocol?

**2 seconds.**

**13** What is the default MAX_AGE interval in the IEEE Spanning-Tree Protocol?

**20 seconds.**

**14** What is the default fwddelay interval in the IEEE Spanning-Tree Protocol?

**15 seconds.**

**15**  What is the maximum convergence time of the IEEE Spanning-Tree Protocol in a network with a seven-hop diameter and default IEEE spanning tree timer values?

**MAX_AGE + Listening(fwddelay) + Learning(fwddelay) = 20+15+15 = 50.**

**16**  How many default VLANs are preconfigured on a Catalyst 5000 switch?

**There are five default VLANs preconfigured on a Catalyst 5000 switch for different media types.**

**17**  What is the recommended usage of VLAN number 1?

**You are encouraged to leave VLAN number 1 for management and troubleshooting and use VLANs 2 through 1000 for user (traffic) VLANs.**

**18**  What are the possible implications of using different (inconsistent) Spanning-Tree Protocols for a VLAN in the same network?

**Usage of incompatible Spanning-Tree Protocols has serious implications including loss of BPDUs (drops), loops, broadcast storms, and ultimately network meltdown.**

**19**  What is the suggested setting for the spanning tree timers during periods of instability?

**In periods of instability it is wise to reduce the spanning tree activities of the devices. One way of achieving this is by setting the spanning tree timers at their maximum values on the root device.**

**20**  What role can a Cisco router play in a VTP domain?

**None. Cisco routers do not yet support VTP (VLAN Trunking Protocol).**

**21**  What information can one obtain from the output of the **show vlans** command?

**It lists all the VLANs configured on a router. For each VLAN, the corresponding subinterface and its configured addresses are displayed. For each protocol configured on a subinterface, this command also shows the number of packets sent and received.**

**22**  Describe the output of the **show span** *vlan-number* command.

**The first part of this command's output shows the type of Spanning-Tree Protocol in use, the bridge ID (priority and address) of the local device (the router), the ID of the root device, and the timer parameters of the spanning tree. Next, the interfaces that participate in the spanning tree (associated to the VLAN number typed in) are listed. For each interface, its associated state (for example, Forwarding), priority, cost, and timers, as well as the ID of the designated root and bridge, are displayed.**

23  Discuss the output of the **show bridge** [*bridge-number*] command.

**The show bridge command displays contents of your router's bridge forwarding database for the bridge group requested (bridge-number).**

24  What messages does the **debug vlan packets** command display?

**The debug vlan packets command displays messages about virtual LAN (VLAN) packets that the router receives (off the trunk connection) but is not configured to support.**

25  What are the two forms of the Cisco IOS's **debug span** command?

**debug span tree and debug span events**

# Chapter 10

## "Do I Know This Already?" Quiz

1  What is the default frame type for the serial interfaces of Cisco routers that have been configured with the **encapsulation frame-relay** command?

**Cisco.**

2  What are the two frame types supported on the Frame Relay (serial) interfaces of a Cisco router?

**Cisco and IETF.**

3  Can the LMI type be autosensed by any of the IOS releases?

**Yes. As of IOS release 11.2 the LMI type is auto-sensed.**

4  What are the LMI types supported by Cisco IOS?

**Cisco, ANSI, Q933a.**

5  Does the LMI type have to be identical on both ends of a Frame Relay connection?

**No. You must only make sure that the LMI type on a router matches the LMI type on the service provider switch to which it connects.**

6  What are the main pieces of information that you can obtain from the output of the **show interface serial** *n* command?

**The show interface serial *n* command allows you to check the status of the interface hardware, the link status, the encapsulation used, whether keepalives are being sent, the LMI type, the standard statistics on the sent and received data, and queue accounting.**

**7** If the LMI type of Cisco is used on a Cisco router's serial interface, which DLCI number is used on that interface for LMI purposes?

**dlci 1023**

**8** If the LMI type of ANSI is used on a Cisco router's serial interface, which DLCI number is used on that interface for LMI purposes?

**dlci 0**

**9** Give at least two reasons for a Frame Relay serial interface being reported as up and its line protocol reported as down.

**LMI type mismatch between the router and the switch.**

**The interface is not sending keepalives.**

**The service provider's switch has failed or has been misconfigured.**

**The leased line is experiencing trouble such as too much noise.**

**The CSU is not working properly.**

**10** Discuss the reasons for a serial interface being reported as down.

**This condition is usually the result of a bad connection (or lack of connection) between the router and the CSU. If a serial interface with the DTE end of the serial cable does not receive clocking on that connection, it will go or stay down until the DCE device starts clocking. The problem could be entirely due to cable being faulty or improper, as well. This condition is clearly an indicator of a physical problem on the router's serial interface, or a bad serial cable used between the router and the CSU (usually a V.35 Cisco cable), or a faulty CSU. You must also check the Carrier Detect (CD) LED on the CSU to make sure that CD is active. If CD is not active, you must contact the service provider, as a problem on that side is their responsibility to look after.**

**11** Which **show** command displays Local Management Interface (LMI) statistics about a Cisco router's Frame Relay interface(s)?

**show frame-relay lmi**

**12** Which Frame Relay **show** command lists all of the PVCs that the router is aware of on all of its Frame Relay interfaces (and subinterfaces) along with their status, creation time, last status-change time, and statistics regarding the sent/received packets/bytes and the congestion notification flags?

**show frame-relay pvc**

**13** Provide at least two pieces of information given for each interface on the output of the **show frame-relay map** command.

**The status of the interface (up, down, administratively down).**

The destination Layer 3 address (IP address). However, in the case of a point-to-point connection, the destination is identified with the phrase point-to-point dlci.

The DLCI number in decimal, hexadecimal, and facility format.

Whether the mapping is static or dynamic. In case of a point-to-point connection, neither static nor dynamic is mentioned.

Whether broadcast is supported.

The encapsulation type (CISCO or IETF). Encapsulation type is shown for multipoint subinterfaces that have map statement(s).

Whether the status of the connection (PVC) is defined or deleted. (A connection whose status is defined may be active or inactive.)

**14**  Which generic **debug** command displays real-time information about the activities (such as keepalives) and status of serial interfaces?

**debug serial interface**

**15**  Which Frame Relay troubleshooting **debug** command displays the LMI messages that are exchanged between your router and the Frame Relay switch?

**debug frame-relay lmi**

# Q&A

**1**  To which layer of the OSI model does the Frame Relay technology correspond?

**Layer 2 (data link layer).**

**2**  Is Frame Relay a connectionless or a connection-oriented service?

**Connection-oriented.**

**3**  Are most of the current Frame Relay implementations PVC based or are they SVC based?

**Most of the current Frame Relay implementations are PVC based.**

**4**  What is the default frame type for the serial interfaces of Cisco routers that have been configured with the **encapsulation frame-relay** command?

**Cisco.**

**5**  What are the two frame types supported on the Frame Relay (serial) interfaces of a Cisco router?

**Cisco and IETF.**

**6** Does the frame type have to be consistent across a Frame Relay connection?

**Yes.**

**7** Which command would configure a serial interface with the Frame Relay encapsulation and the Cisco frame type?

**encapsulation frame-relay**

**8** Can the LMI type be autosensed by any of the IOS releases?

**Yes. As of IOS release 11.2, the LMI type is auto-sensed.**

**9** What are the LMI types supported by Cisco IOS?

**Cisco, ANSI, Q933a.**

**10** What command would configure a Cisco router's serial interface for the q933a LMI type?

**frame-relay lmi-type q933a**

**11** Which command completely turns off LMI on a Cisco router's serial interface?

**no keepalive OR no frame-relay keepalive**

**12** Does the LMI type have to be identical on both ends of a Frame Relay connection?

**No. You must only make sure that the LMI type on a router matches the LMI type on the service provider switch that it connects to.**

**13** What is the purpose of LMI?

**LMI can be defined as the Frame Relay keepalive that takes place between a router and the Frame Relay service provider's switch. Through LMI the Frame Relay switch sends the router the list of DLCIs it is programmed for, and the status of each DLCI.**

**14** What is the process that allows routers that are at the two ends of a Frame Relay circuit to learn each other's upper layer address(es) and associate them with the appropriate DLCI number?

**frame-relay inverse-arp.**

**15** What is the default frequency at which a router sends Frame Relay inverse-arp packets?

**Every 60 seconds.**

**16** What command would hard-code the DLCI number 55 on a Frame Relay subinterface?

**frame-relay interface-dlci 55**

**17** What command would map the destination IP address 192.50.18.5 to DLCI number 156 on a Frame Relay interface or a multipoint subinterface and enable broadcasting on that DLCI?

**frame-relay map ip 192.50.18.5 156 broadcast**

**18** What is the size of the IETF Frame Relay frame header? And what is the purpose of the FECN and BECN bits/fields?

**The IETF frame's header is 2 bytes (16 bits) long. The FECN and BECN bits are set by the Frame Relay network to notify the sending and receiving devices that the network is experiencing congestion and that frames (specially those from devices that are bursting beyond their CIRs) will/may be dropped.**

**19** Using which **show** command can you discover the status of a serial interface (for example, s 1) configured for a Frame Relay connection?

**show interface serial 1**

**20** Using which **show** command can you check the encapsulation and the LMI type configured on interface serial 1?

**show interface serial 1**

**21** Would the **show interface serial 1** command's output display whether this interface is sending keepalives?

**Yes.**

**22** What are the main pieces of information that you can obtain from the output of the **show interface serial *n*** command?

**The show interface serial *n* command allows you to check the status of the interface hardware, the link status, the encapsulation used, whether keepalives are being sent, the LMI type, the standard statistics on the sent and received data, and queue accounting.**

**23** If the Frame Relay LMI type entered for the serial 1 interface of a Cisco router is Q933a, what LMI type is reported for that interface on the output of the **show interface serial 1** command?

**CCITT.**

**24** If the LMI type of Cisco is used on a Cisco router's serial interface, which DLCI number is used on that interface for LMI purposes?

**DLCI 1023.**

**25** If the LMI type of ANSI is used on a Cisco router's serial interface, which DLCI number is used on that interface for LMI purposes?

**DLCI 0.**

**26**   Provide at least two reasons for an interface reset to occur.

**A reset is forced by an administrator, through execution of the** clear interface **command.**

**An interface has packets queued for transmission, but those packets are not sent within a reasonable amount of time (a few seconds).**

**There is a hardware problem (on the interface, cable, or CSU).**

**There are clocking problems.**

**The interface is looped.**

**The router attempting to restart an interface that has line protocol problems (the router tries to do that periodically).**

**27**   What does the number of transitions reported on the output of the **show interface serial n** command signify? If this number is too large for your network's baseline, where should you turn your attention?

**The carrier transitions counter tells you how many times the DCD (Data Carrier Detect) has changed state. A large number of carrier transitions, or at least a number much different from the baseline value, should make you curious about the carrier's facility.**

**28**   Give at least two reasons for a Frame Relay serial interface being reported as up and its line protocol reported as down.

**There is an LMI-type mismatch between the router and the switch.**

**The interface is not sending keepalives.**

**The service provider's switch has failed or has been misconfigured.**

**The leased line is experiencing trouble such as too much noise.**

**The CSU is not working properly.**

**29**   Discuss the reasons for a serial interface being reported as down.

**This condition is usually the result of a bad connection (or lack of connection) between the router and the CSU. If a serial interface with the DTE end of the serial cable does not receive clocking on that connection, it will go or stay down until the DCE device starts clocking. The problem could be entirely due to the cable being faulty or improper, as well. This condition is clearly an indicator of a physical problem on the router's serial interface, or a bad serial cable used between the router and the CSU (usually a V.35 Cisco cable), or a faulty CSU. You must also check the CD LED on the CSU to make sure that CD is active. If CD is not active, you must contact the service provider, as a problem on that side is their responsibility to look after.**

**30** What is loopback testing?

**Loopback testing is a commonly employed technique to identify the exact problem area in an end-to-end connection such as a Frame Relay that comprises a number of segments. Certain devices such as CSUs can be looped to test a specific segment, and if that segment operates successfully, it will be eliminated from the list of suspicious areas.**

**31** Which command displays Local Management Interface statistics about a Cisco router's Frame Relay interface(s)?

**show frame-relay lmi**

**32** If the number of status messages timed out and the number of status inquiry messages sent grow every time you enter the **show frame-relay** command, what could be the reason?

**The most common reason for this symptom is LMI-type mismatch between the router and the service provider's switch.**

**33** Which Frame Relay **show** command lists all of the PVCs that the router is aware of on all of its Frame Relay interfaces (and subinterfaces) along with their status, creation time, last status change time, and statistics regarding the sent/received packets/bytes and the congestion notification flags?

**show frame-relay pvc**

**34** Provide at least two pieces of information given for each interface on the output of the **show frame-relay map** command.

**The status of the interface (up, down, administratively down).**

**The destination Layer 3 address (IP address). However, in the case of a point-to-point connection, the destination is identified with the phrase point-to-point dlci.**

**The DLCI number in decimal, hexadecimal, and facility format.**

**Whether the mapping is static or dynamic. In the case of a point-to-point connection, neither static nor dynamic is mentioned.**

**Whether broadcast is supported.**

**The encapsulation type (CISCO or IETF). Encapsulation type is shown for multipoint subinterfaces that have map statement(s).**

**Whether the status of the connection (PVC) is defined or deleted. (A connection whose status is defined may be active or inactive.)**

**35** How would you interpret a situation in which a DLCI is shown in the output of the **show frame-relay pvc** statement (and is reported as active), but it does not appear in the output of the **show frame-relay map** statement?

The router is not able to map the active DLCI number to any upper layer address. The mapping between a DLCI number and an upper layer address can be made as a result of the dynamic inverse-arp process, or a static map statement entered by the administrator. Obviously, in this case neither of the mentioned techniques is in place. However, when a point-to-point subinterface is in use, even though the corresponding DLCI number appears in the output of the show frame-relay map statement, it is merely shown as a point-to-point DLCI and it is not shown to be mapped to a specific upper layer address (in a point-to-point connection a specific mapping is not necessary).

**36**  Which generic **debug** command displays real-time information about the activities (keepalives) and status of serial interfaces?

**debug serial interface**

**37**  How often does a router send the LMI enq. message and receive a normal LMI status? How often does the router receive the FULL LMI message?

**The simple LMI messages are exchanged every 10 seconds by default. The router receives the FULL LMI message (containing the list of DLCIs and the status of each DLCI) every 60 seconds from the switch.**

**38**  Which Frame Relay troubleshooting **debug** command displays the LMI messages that are exchanged between your router and the Frame Relay switch?

**debug frame-relay lmi**

**39**  If you enter the **debug frame-relay lmi** command and you do not see a proper flow/exchange of LMI messages between your router and the Frame Relay switch (or you see no LMI at all), assuming that the interface is up, what could be wrong?

**One likely cause is LMI-type incompatibility between the router and the switch. Also, keepalive may be turned off (with the no keepalive command). If loopback testing results indicate that the connection between the router and the CSU is fine, and the link (line protocol) still does not come up, the service provider must be contacted.**

**40**  Which command displays debugging information about the packets that are being received on Frame Relay interface(s)?

**debug frame-relay verbose**

**41**  Which Cisco router IOS command displays debugging information about Frame Relay ARP activities?

**debug frame-relay events**

**42**  Which Frame Relay **debug** command displays the packets that have been sent (out) on Frame Relay interface(s)?

**debug frame-relay packet**

**You need to refer to the following figure to answer the remaining questions (on Frame Relay troubleshooting commands):**

Quiz: Frame Relay Troublehooting Commands

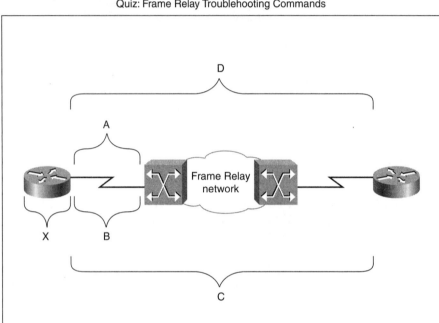

**43**  Provide the two most appropriate **show** commands to test the area marked by the letter A.

**show interface**

**show frame-relay lmi**

**44**  Provide the two most appropriate **debug** commands to test the area marked by the letter B.

**debug serial interface**

**debug frame-relay lmi**

**45** Provide the two most appropriate **show** commands to test the area marked by the letter C.

**show frame-relay map**

**show frame-relay pvc**

**46** Provide the two most appropriate **debug** commands to test the area marked by the letter D.

**debug frame-relay verbose**

**debug frame-relay packet**

# Chapter 11

## "Do I Know This Already?" Quiz

**1** How are TE1 and TE2 different?

**The ISDN terminal equipment (TE) is classified into two types: TE2 and TE1. TE2 devices are non-ISDN terminals such as a standard telephone, a personal computer, or a router with no ISDN interface. TE1s are ISDN devices such as an ISDN telephone or a router with a BRI interface.**

**2** What kind of wiring is used between the TE and the network termination (NT) devices?

**The TE1 (and TA) connects to Network Termination type 1 (NT1) using a four-wire cable (RJ48). You can also use a straight-through RJ45 cable for this purpose.**

**3** In North America, is NT1 considered part of CPE or is it considered part of the service provider's equipment?

**In North America, the NT1 device is considered part of CPE.**

**4** What is the difference between ISDN BRI B channels and the ISDN D channel?

**The D channel is used for carrying control and signaling information. The B channels are meant to carry user data.**

**5** Which two ISDN **show** commands allow you to discover the status of ISDN Layer 1?

**show controller bri** *bri-number*

**show isdn status**

**6** Which **show** command displays the ISDN switch type you have configured your router for?

**The first line of the show ISDN status command displays the ISDN switch type you have configured the router for.**

**7** Which **debug** command allows you to observe the activation process of ISDN BRI Layer 1?

**debug bri-interface (This command can be shortened to debug bri)**

**8** Which **show** command allows you to discover the true state of the ISDN BRI Layer 2?

**show isdn status**

**9** Which **show** command displays information about all BRI and Dialer interfaces (if there are any) of a router?

**show dialer**

**10** If you are troubleshooting an ISDN call, which **debug** command allows you to observe the cause of the call (dialing cause), the interface used for the call, and the string (number) that was used to make the call?

**debug dialer**

**11** Which **debug** command provides detail information on ISDN Layer 3 activities such as call setup?

**debug isdn q931**

**12** Provide one **show** and one **debug** command that are useful for ISDN Service Profile Identifier (SPID) troubleshooting.

**show isdn status**

**debug isdn q931**

**13** Which **debug** command allows you to observe PPP's LCP, authentication, and NCP process?

**debug ppp negotiation**

**14** Which **debug** command displays information on the ppp authentication process?

**debug ppp authentication or debug ppp chap**

**15** Which command displays the status of both of the B channels of the BRI0 interface of a Cisco router?

**show interface bri 0 1 2**

**16** Which command allows you to examine the status of your Cisco router's active Multilink PPP sessions?

**show ppp multilink**

# Q&A

**1** List at least two generic types of devices that are classified as ISDN customer premises equipment in North America.

**The customer equipment may include terminal equipment (types 1 and 2), terminal adapters, and network termination equipment (types 1 and 2).**

**2** What kind of wiring facility is used for ISDN local access loop?

**A common two-wire facility forms the local access loop for ISDN.**

**3** Are the line termination (LT) and exchange termination (ET) part of CPE or are they components of the service provider's (telco's) equipment?

**The LT and ET equipment are components of the service provider's network.**

**4** How are TE1 and TE2 different?

**The ISDN terminal equipment (TE) is classified into two types: TE2 and TE1. TE2 devices are non-ISDN terminals such as a standard telephone, a personal computer, or a router with no ISDN interface. TE1s are ISDN devices such as an ISDN telephone or a router with a BRI interface.**

**5** Which one of TE1 and TE2 needs to be connected to a TA?

**A TE2 needs (to be connected to) an ISDN TA to get connected to an ISDN network.**

**6** If the TA is an external device, how is the TE connected to it?

**If the TA is an external device, the TE2 connects to it with a standard serial cable/connection such as EIA/TIA-232-C (formerly RS-232-C), V.24, or V.35.**

**7** What kind of wiring is used between the TE and the NT1 device?

**The TE1 (and TA) connects to NT1 using a four-wire cable (RJ48). You can also use a straight-through RJ45 cable for this purpose.**

**8** In North America, is NT1 considered part of CPE or is it considered part of the service provider's equipment?

**In North America, the NT1 device is considered part of CPE.**

**9**   Name the ISDN reference point for the interface between TE2 and TA.

**R.**

**10**   Name the ISDN reference point for the interface between the NT2 and the NT1 device.

**T.**

**11**   Name the ISDN reference point for the interface between the NT1 and the service provider's (carrier's) LT device.

**U.**

**12**   Name the ISDN reference point for the interface between TE1 or TA and the NT2 device.

**S.**

**13**   What does the label U mean on a BRI interface?

**If the BRI interface of a router has NT1 built in, then the interface is marked with the U label.**

**14**   Name the ISDN BRI channels and specify each channel's bandwidth.

**The ISDN BRI interface offers two B channels (B1 and B2) and a D channel (2B+D). The B channels are 64 kbps and the D channel is 16 kbps.**

**15**   What is the difference between ISDN BRI B channels and the ISDN D channel?

**The D channel is used for carrying control and signaling information. The B channels are meant to carry user data. (Note: If the service provider permits, the D channel can also be used to carry data. This is not a common implementation, certainly not one that is discussed in this book.)**

**16**   What is the protocol that runs over ISDN D channel?

**The protocol used for this purpose is called Link Access Procedure on the D channel (LAPD).**

**17**   Which two ISDN **show** commands allow you to discover the status of ISDN Layer 1?

**show controller bri *bri-number* or show isdn status**

**18**   Which **show** command displays the ISDN switch type you have configured your router for?

**The first line of the show isdn status command displays the ISDN switch type you have configured the router for.**

**19**  Which **debug** command allows you to observe the activation process of ISDN BRI Layer 1?

**debug bri-interface (this command can be shortened to debug bri)**

**20**  Which **show** command allows you to discover the true state of the ISDN BRI Layer 2?

**show isdn status**

**21**  Which **show** command displays information about all BRI and Dialer interfaces (if there are any) of a router?

**show dialer**

**22**  Which **show** command displays all of the map statements configured on your router's BRI interfaces?

**show dialer maps**

**23**  If you are troubleshooting an ISDN call, which **debug** command allows you to observe the cause of the call (dialing cause), the interface used for the call, and the string (number) that was used to make the call?

**debug dialer**

**24**  Name at least three ISDN Q.931 messages.

**ISDN Q.931 messages include SETUP, CALL PROCEEDING, CONNECT, CONNECT ACK, DISCONNECT, RELEASE, RELEASE COMPLETE, INFORMATION, CANCEL, STATUS.**

**25**  Provide an example of the failure cause of an ISDN Q.931 SETUP failure.

**The ISDN switch type is not configured, or it is configured incorrectly in either the caller's or the called party's side (or both!).**

**The called party has no B channel free to accept an incoming call (i.e., the called party is busy).**

**Due to some form of call screening (based on called number or the calling party's number), the called party rejects the call.**

**26**  Name at least two ISDN BRI switch types that are supported by Cisco router IOS?

**Basic-5ess, basic-ni1, basic-dms100, basic-net3.**

**27**  Which command configures a Cisco router (IOS-based) for the ISDN switch type ntt?

**isdn switch-type ntt**

**28**  Which **debug** command provides detail information on ISDN Layer 3 activities such as call setup?

**debug isdn q931**

29  Provide one **show** and one **debug** command that are useful for ISDN SPID troubleshooting.

**show isdn status or debug isdn q931**

30  Name at least two ISDN B channel protocols (on Cisco routers).

**The supported ISDN BRI B channel protocols on Cisco routers are frame-relay, HDLC (Cisco's Serial HDLC synchronous), LAPB (X.25 Level 2), PPP (Point-to-Point protocol), and X25 (X.25).**

31  Name at least two of the link options that PPP's LCP negotiates.

**LCP negotiates link options such as Authentication, Multilinking, Callback, Compression, and Line Quality Protocol.**

32  Which **debug** command allows you to observe PPP's LCP, authentication, and NCP process?

**debug ppp negotiation**

33  Which **debug** command displays information on the ppp authentication process?

**debug ppp authentication or debug ppp chap**

34  Which command displays the status of both of the B channels of the BRI0 interface of a Cisco router?

**show interface bri 0 1 2**

35  Which command allows you to examine the status of your Cisco router's active Multilink PPP sessions?

**show ppp multilink**

36  Using the following figure, for each of the segments identified by the letters A through E, provide the appropriate ISDN troubleshooting command(s) requested as follows:

For Segment A, Provide 1 **debug** command

For Segment B, Provide 1 **show** command

For Segment C, Provide 3 **debug** commands

For Segment D, Provide 1 **show** command

For Segment E, Provide 3 **debug** commands

Review of ISDN Troubleshooting Commands

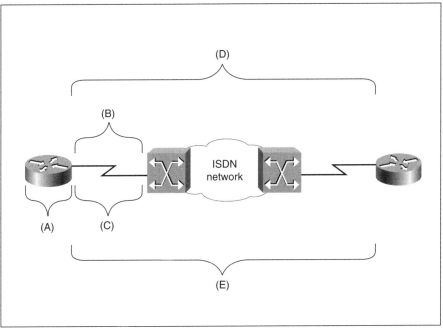

A. debug dialer

B. show interface

C. debug serial interface, debug bri, debug isdn q921

D. show isdn status

E. debug isdn q931, debug ppp negotiation, debug ppp chap

# INDEX

# H-K

# Q-R

# S

# U

# CCIE Professional Development

### Cisco LAN Switching

Kennedy Clark, CCIE; Kevin Hamilton, CCIE

**1-57870-094-9 • AVAILABLE NOW**

This volume provides an in-depth analysis of Cisco LAN switching technologies, architectures, and deployments, including unique coverage of Catalyst network design essentials. Network designs and configuration examples are incorporated throughout to demonstrate the principles and enable easy translation of the material into practice in production networks.

### Advanced IP Network Design

Alvaro Retana, CCIE; Don Slice, CCIE; and Russ White, CCIE

**1-57870-097-3 • AVAILABLE NOW**

Network engineers and managers can use these case studies, which highlight various network design goals, to explore issues including protocol choice, network stability, and growth. This book also includes theoretical discussion on advanced design topics.

### Large-Scale IP Network Solutions

Khalid Raza, CCIE; and Mark Turner

**1-57870-084-1 • AVAILABLE NOW**

Network engineers can find solutions as their IP networks grow in size and complexity. Examine all the major IP protocols in-depth and learn about scalability, migration planning, network management, and security for large-scale networks.

### Routing TCP/IP, Volume I

Jeff Doyle, CCIE

**1-57870-041-8 • AVAILABLE NOW**

This book takes the reader from a basic understanding of routers and routing protocols through a detailed examination of each of the IP interior routing protocols. Learn techniques for designing networks that maximize the efficiency of the protocol being used. Exercises and review questions provide core study for the CCIE Routing and Switching exam.

**www.ciscopress.com**

# Cisco Press Solutions

### Enhanced IP Services for Cisco Networks
Donald C. Lee, CCIE

**1-57870-106-6 • AVAILABLE NOW**

This is a guide to improving your network's capabilities by understanding the new enabling and advanced Cisco IOS services that build more scalable, intelligent, and secure networks. Learn the technical details necessary to deploy Quality of Service, VPN technologies, IPsec, the IOS firewall and IOS Intrusion Detection. These services will allow you to extend the network to new frontiers securely, protect your network from attacks, and increase the sophistication of network services.

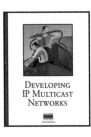

### Developing IP Multicast Networks, Volume I
Beau Williamson, CCIE

**1-57870-077-9 • AVAILABLE NOW**

This book provides a solid foundation of IP multicast concepts and explains how to design and deploy the networks that will support appplications such as audio and video conferencing, distance-learning, and data replication. Includes an in-depth discussion of the PIM protocol used in Cisco routers and detailed coverage of the rules that control the creation and maintenance of Cisco mroute state entries.

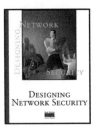

### Designing Network Security
Merike Kaeo

**1-57870-043-4 • AVAILABLE NOW**

*Designing Network Security* is a practical guide designed to help you understand the fundamentals of securing your corporate infrastructure. This book takes a comprehensive look at underlying security technologies, the process of creating a security policy, and the practical requirements necessary to implement a corporate security policy.

CISCO SYSTEMS

CISCO PRESS

**www.ciscopress.com**

# Cisco Press Solutions

### EIGRP Network Design Solutions
Ivan Pepelnjak, CCIE

**1-57870-165-1 • AVAILABLE NOW**

*EIGRP Network Design Solutions* uses case studies and real-world configuration examples to help you gain an in-depth understanding of the issues involved in designing, deploying, and managing EIGRP-based networks. This book details proper designs that can be used to build large and scalable EIGRP-based networks and documents possible ways each EIGRP feature can be used in network design, implmentation, troubleshooting, and monitoring.

### Top-Down Network Design
Priscilla Oppenheimer

**1-57870-069-8 • AVAILABLE NOW**

Building reliable, secure, and manageable networks is every network professional's goal. This practical guide teaches you a systematic method for network design that can be applied to campus LANs, remote-access networks, WAN links, and large-scale internetworks. Learn how to analyze business and technical requirements, examine traffic flow and Quality of Service requirements, and select protocols and technologies based on performance goals.

### Cisco IOS Releases: The Complete Reference
Mack M. Coulibaly

**1-57870-179-1 • AVAILABLE NOW**

*Cisco IOS Releases: The Complete Reference* is the first comprehensive guide to the more than three dozen types of Cisco IOS releases being used today on enterprise and service provider networks. It details the release process and its numbering and naming conventions, as well as when, where, and how to use the various releases. A complete map of Cisco IOS software releases and their relationships to one another, in addition to insights into decoding information contained within the software, make this book an indispensable resource for any network professional.

**www.ciscopress.com**

# Cisco Press Solutions

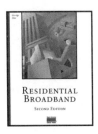

### Residential Broadband, Second Edition
George Abe

1-57870-177-5 • **AVAILABLE NOW**

This book will answer basic questions of residential broadband networks such as: Why do we need high speed networks at home? How will high speed residential services be delivered to the home? How do regulatory or commercial factors affect this technology? Explore such networking topics as xDSL, cable, and wireless.

### Internetworking Technologies Handbook, Second Edition
Kevin Downes, CCIE, Merilee Ford, H. Kim Lew, Steve Spanier, Tim Stevenson

1-57870-102-3 • **AVAILABLE NOW**

This comprehensive reference provides a foundation for understanding and implementing contemporary internetworking technologies, providing you with the necessary information needed to make rational networking decisions. Master terms, concepts, technologies, and devices that are used in the internetworking industry today. You also learn how to incorporate networking technologies into a LAN/WAN environment, as well as how to apply the OSI reference model to categorize protocols, technologies, and devices.

### OpenCable Architecture
Michael Adams

1-57870-135-X • **AVAILABLE NOW**

Whether you're a television, data communications, or telecommunications professional, or simply an interested business person, this book will help you understand the technical and business issues surrounding interactive television services. It will also provide you with an inside look at the combined efforts of the cable, data, and consumer electronics industries' efforts to develop those new services.

### Performance and Fault Management
Paul Della Maggiora, Christopher Elliott, Robert Pavone, Kent Phelps, James Thompson

1-57870-180-5 • **AVAILABLE NOW**

This book is a comprehensive guide to designing and implementing effective strategies for monitoring performance levels and correctng problems in Cisco networks. It provides an overview of router and LAN switch operations to help you understand how to manage such devices, as well as guidance on the essential MIBs, traps, syslog messages, and show commands for managing Cisco routers and switches.

**www.ciscopress.com**

# Cisco Press Fundamentals

### IP Routing Primer

Robert Wright, CCIE

1-57870-108-2 • **AVAILABLE NOW**

Learn how IP routing behaves in a Cisco router environment. In addition to teaching the core fundamentals, this book enhances your ability to troubleshoot IP routing problems yourself, often eliminating the need to call for additional technical support. The information is presented in an approachable, workbook-type format with dozens of detailed illustrations and real-life scenarios integrated throughout.

### Cisco Router Configuration

Allan Leinwand, Bruce Pinsky, Mark Culpepper

1-57870-022-1 • **AVAILABLE NOW**

An example-oriented and chronological approach helps you implement and administer your internetworking devices. Starting with the configuration devices "out of the box;" this book moves to configuring Cisco IOS for the three most popular networking protocols today: TCP/IP, AppleTalk, and Novell Interwork Packet Exchange (IPX). You also learn basic administrative and management configuration, including access control with TACACS+ and RADIUS, network management with SNMP, logging of messages, and time control with NTP.

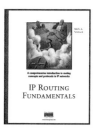

### IP Routing Fundamentals

Mark A. Sportack

1-57870-071-x • **AVAILABLE NOW**

This comprehensive guide provides essential background information on routing in IP networks for network professionals who are deploying and maintaining LANs and WANs daily. Explore the mechanics of routers, routing protocols, network interfaces, and operating systems.

**www.ciscopress.com**

# Cisco Press Fundamentals

## Internet Routing Architectures, Second Edition

Sam Halabi with Danny McPherson

**1-57870-233-x • AVAILABLE NOW**

This book explores the ins and outs of interdomain routing network design with emphasis on BGP-4 (Border Gateway Protocol Version 4)--the de facto interdomain routing protocol. You will have all the information you need to make knowledgeable routing decisions for Internet connectivity in your environment.

## Voice over IP Fundamentals

Jonathan Davidson and James Peters

**1-57870-168-6 • AVAILABLE NOW**

Voice over IP (VoIP), which integrates voice and data transmission, is quickly becoming an important factor in network communications. It promises lower operational costs, greater flexibility, and a variety of enhanced applications. This book provides a thorough introduction to this new technology to help experts in both the data and telephone industries plan for the new networks.

For the latest on Cisco Press resources and Certification and

Training guides, or for information on publishing opportunities, visit

**www.ciscopress.com**

**Cisco Press books are available at your local bookstore, computer store, and online booksellers.**

# Cisco Press

## ciscopress.com

## Committed to being your long-term resource as you grow as a Cisco Networking professional

Help Cisco Press **stay connected** to the issues and challenges you face on a daily basis by registering your product and filling out our brief survey. Complete and mail this form, or better yet ...

## Register online and enter to win a FREE book!

Jump to **www.ciscopress.com/register** and register your product online. Each complete entry will be eligible for our monthly drawing to win a FREE book of the winner's choice from the Cisco Press library.

May we contact you via e-mail with information about **new releases, special promotions** and customer benefits?

❐ Yes                    ❐ No

E-mail address _____

Name _____

Address _____

City _____ State/Province _____

Country _____ Zip/Post code _____

### Where did you buy this product?

❐ Bookstore                          ❐ Computer store/electronics store
❐ Online retailer                    ❐ Direct from Cisco Press
❐ Mail order                         ❐ Class/Seminar
❐ Other_____

### When did you buy this product? _____ Month _____ Year

### What price did you pay for this product?

❐ Full retail price          ❐ Discounted price              ❐ Gift

### How did you learn about this product?

❐ Friend                        ❐ Store personnel              ❐ In-store ad
❐ Cisco Press Catalog           ❐ Postcard in the mail         ❐ Saw it on the shelf
❐ Other Catalog                 ❐ Magazine ad                  ❐ Article or review
❐ School                        ❐ Professional Organization    ❐ Used other products
❐ Other_____

### What will this product be used for?

❐ Business use              ❐ School/Education
❐ Other_____

Cisco Press
201 West 103rd Street
Indianapolis, IN 46290
**ciscopress.com**

Cisco Press
Customer Registration—CP0500227
P.O. Box #781046
Indianapolis, IN 46278-8046

# Cisco Press

**c i s c o p r e s s . c o m**

**How many years have you been employed in a computer-related industry?**
☐ 2 years or less   ☐ 3-5 years   ☐ 5+ years

**Which best describes your job function?**
☐ Corporate Management   ☐ Systems Engineering   ☐ IS Management
☐ Network Design   ☐ Network Support   ☐ Webmaster
☐ Marketing/Sales   ☐ Consultant   ☐ Student
☐ Professor/Teacher   ☐ Other

**What is your formal education background?**
☐ High school   ☐ Vocational/Technical degree   ☐ Some college
☐ College degree   ☐ Masters degree   ☐ Professional or Doctoral degree

**Have you purchased a Cisco Press product before?**
☐ Yes   ☐ No

**On what topics would you like to see more coverage?**

**Do you have any additional comments or suggestions?**

**Thank you for completing this survey and registration. Please fold here, seal, and mail to Cisco Press.**
CCNP Support Exam Certification Guide (0-7357-0995-5)

CISCO SYSTEMS

BUSINESS REPLY MAIL
FIRST-CLASS MAIL     PERMIT NO. 25788     SAN FRANCISCO CA

POSTAGE WILL BE PAID BY ADDRESSEE

CISCO SYSTEMS / PACKET MAGAZINE
PO BOX 60939
SUNNYVALE  CA  94088-9741

NO POSTAGE
NECESSARY
IF MAILED
IN THE
UNITED STATES

# PACKET

*Packet* magazine serves as the premier publication linking customers to Cisco Systems, Inc. Delivering complete coverage of cutting-edge networking trends and innovations, *Packet* is a magazine for technical, hands-on users. It delivers industry-specific information for enterprise, service provider, and small and midsized business market segments. A toolchest for planners and decision makers, *Packet* contains a vast array of practical information, boasting sample configurations, real-life customer examples, and tips on getting the most from your Cisco Systems' investments. Simply put, *Packet* magazine is straight talk straight from the worldwide leader in networking for the Internet, Cisco Systems, Inc.

We hope you'll take advantage of this useful resource. I look forward to hearing from you!

Jennifer Biondi
*Packet* Circulation Manager
packet@cisco.com
www.cisco.com/go/packet

---

☐ **YES!** I'm requesting a **free** subscription to *Packet* magazine.

☐ No. I'm not interested at this time.

☐ Mr.
☐ Ms.

First Name (Please Print) _____ Last Name _____

Title/Position (Required) _____

Company (Required) _____

Address _____

City _____ State/Province _____

Zip/Postal Code _____ Country _____

Telephone (Include country and area codes) _____ Fax _____

E-mail _____

Signature (Required) _____ Date _____

☐ I would like to receive additional information on Cisco's services and products by e-mail.

**1.0 Do you or your company:**
- A ☐ Use Cisco products
- B ☐ Resell Cisco products
- C ☐ Both
- D ☐ Neither

**1. Your organization's relationship to Cisco Systems:**
- A ☐ Customer/End User
- B ☐ Prospective Customer
- C ☐ Cisco Reseller
- D ☐ Cisco Distributor
- DI ☐ Non-Authorized Reseller
- E ☐ Integrator
- G ☐ Cisco Training Partner
- I ☐ Cisco OEM
- J ☐ Consultant
- K ☐ Other (specify): _____

**2. How would you classify your business?**
- A ☐ Small/Medium-Sized
- B ☐ Enterprise
- C ☐ Service Provider

**3. Your involvement in network equipment purchases:**
- A ☐ Recommend
- B ☐ Approve
- C ☐ Neither

**4. Your personal involvement in networking:**
- A ☐ Entire enterprise at all sites
- B ☐ Departments or network segments at more than one site
- C ☐ Single department or network segment
- F ☐ Public network
- D ☐ No involvement
- E ☐ Other (specify): _____

**5. Your Industry:**
- A ☐ Aerospace
- B ☐ Agriculture/Mining/Construction
- C ☐ Banking/Finance
- D ☐ Chemical/Pharmaceutical
- E ☐ Consultant
- F ☐ Computer/Systems/Electronics
- G ☐ a. Education (K–12)
- ☐ b. Education (College/Univ.)
- H ☐ Government—Federal
- I ☐ Government—State
- J ☐ Government—Local
- K ☐ Health Care
- L ☐ Telecommunications
- M ☐ Utilities/Transportation
- N ☐ Other (specify): _____

# PACKET